The Young Child in the Family and the Community

Fourth Edition

Janet Gonzalez-Mena
Professor Emerita,
Napa Valley College

PEARSON

Merrill
Prentice Hall

Upper Saddle River, New Jersey
Columbus, Ohio

Library of Congress Cataloging-in-Publication Data

Gonzalez-Mena, Janet.
  The young child in the family and the community / Janet Gonzalez-Mena.— 4th ed.
    p. cm.
  Rev. ed. of: The child in the family. 3rd ed. c2002.
  Includes bibliographical references and index.
  ISBN 0-13-118921-2 (pbk. : alk. paper)
  1. Socialization. 2. Child rearing. 3. Family. I. Gonzalez-Mena, Janet. Child in the family. II. Title.
HQ783.G59 2006
649'.1—dc22   2004026836

Vice President and Executive Publisher: Jeffery W. Johnston
Publisher: Kevin M. Davis
Editor: Julie Peters
Editorial Assistant: Michelle Girgis
Production Editor: Sheryl Glicker Langner
Production Coordination: Thistle Hill Publishing Services, LLC
Design Coordinator: Diane C. Lorenzo
Photo Coordinator: Monica Merkel
Cover Design: Terry Rohrbach
Cover Image: Getty One
Production Manager: Laura Messerly
Director of Marketing: Ann Castel Davis
Marketing Manager: Autumn Purdy
Marketing Coordinator: Tyra Poole

This book was set in Novarese Bk Bt by Integra. It was printed and bound by Courier/Stoughton, Inc. The cover was printed by Courier/Stoughton, Inc.

Photo Credits: Scott Cunningham/Merrill, pp. 4, 118; Frank Gonzalez-Mena, pp. 9, 39, 108, 128, 136, 144, 150, 155, 162, 170, 188, 195, 213, 217, 222, 244, 257, 273, 288, 321; Doris Pfalmer, pp. 10, 50, 62, 63, 85, 130, 142, 168, 187, 188, 199, 226, 231, 253, 274, 276; National Institute on Aging, p. 12; National Institutes of Health, p. 13; Laura Vitale, pp. 15, 36, 332, 343; Jim Darter, pp. 23, 48, 176, 236, 239, 260; Anne Vega/Merrill, pp. 26, 54, 72, 139, 238, 315; Tim Gonzalez-Mena, p. 30; Lauren Zahner, pp. 41, 61, 71, 75, 97, 123, 182, 204, 330; Pearson Education Corporate Digital Archive, p. 74; PH College, pp. 80, 291; Barbara Schwartz/Merrill, pp. 88, 126, 175; Ken Karp/PH College, p. 90; Dan Floss/Merrill, p. 95; Shirley Zeiberg/PH College, p. 111; Anthony Magnacca/Merrill, p. 152; Lloyd Lemmerman/Merrill, p. 189; Michael Newman/PhotoEdit, p. 194; Laima Druskis/PH College, p. 300; Pearson Learning Photo Studio, p. 306; Susan Woog Wagner/PH College, p. 323; Rebecca N. Gilbert, p. 340.

Pearson Education Ltd.
Pearson Education Singapore Pte. Ltd.
Pearson Education Canada, Ltd.
Pearson Education—Japan

Pearson Education Australia Pty. Limited
Pearson Education North Asia Ltd.
Pearson Educación de Mexico, S.A. de C.V.
Pearson Education Malaysia Pte. Ltd.

10 9 8 7 6 5 4 3 2 1
ISBN: 0-13-118921-2

*To Mo, who always gave me such
a lot to think about!*

EDUCATOR LEARNING CENTER: AN INVALUABLE ONLINE RESOURCE

Merrill Education and the Association for Supervision and Curriculum Development (ASCD) invite you to take advantage of a new online resource, one that provides access to the top research and proven strategies associated with ASCD and Merrill—the Educator Learning Center. At www.educatorlearningcenter.com, you will find resources that will enhance your students' understanding of course topics and of current educational issues, in addition to being invaluable for further research.

How the Educator Learning Center Will Help Your Students Become Better Teachers

With the combined resources of Merrill Education and ASCD, you and your students will find a wealth of tools and materials to better prepare them for the classroom.

Research

- More than 600 articles from the ASCD journal *Educational Leadership* discuss everyday issues faced by practicing teachers.
- A direct link on the site to Research Navigator™ gives students access to many of the leading education journals, as well as extensive content detailing the research process.
- Excerpts from Merrill Education texts give your students insights on important topics of instructional methods, diverse populations, assessment, classroom management, technology, and refining classroom practice.

Classroom Practice

- Hundreds of lesson plans and teaching strategies are categorized by content area and age range.
- Case studies and classroom video footage provide virtual field experience for student reflection.
- Computer simulations and other electronic tools keep your students abreast of today's classrooms and current technologies.

Look into the Value of Educator Learning Center Yourself

A four-month subscription to Educator Learning Center is $25 but is **FREE** when packaged with any Merrill Education text. In order for your students to have access to this site, you must use this special value-pack ISBN number **WHEN** placing your textbook order with the bookstore: 0-13-154957-X. Your students will then receive a copy of the text packaged with a free ASCD pincode. To preview the value of this website to you and your students, please go to **www.educatorlearningcenter.com** and click on "Demo."

Preface

The fourth edition of *The Young Child in the Family and the Community* continues in the same personal style as the first three editions. Written to the reader directly from the author, the text focuses on the socialization of young children in child rearing, caring, and educational contexts. The book examines developmental theory and adds diverse perspectives from a base of solid academics, constructivist theory, and the author's experience. Readers will find the text full of real-life examples and personal insight. They are also asked to bring their own ideas, experiences, and insights to their reading, in accordance with Jean Piaget's ideas about learners attaching new knowledge to existing knowledge. In other words, readers are encouraged to reach into their own experience to make sense of new information in terms of what they already know.

Because whatever we read is always filtered through our own subjective experience, this text acknowledges that fact and capitalizes on it. Thus, students can feel at home and find their own voices. The author, too, lets her voice come through as she tells personal stories and shares insights. All students are asked regularly to look at the issues, information, and examples in light of their own ideas, feelings, and experience. Examples are designed to appeal to both traditional and nontraditional students, reflecting the changing demographics of the United States today.

This book comes from 28 years of experience teaching a course on socialization—"Child, Family, and Community"—in early childhood departments in several community colleges and in the Child and Family Studies Program at Napa Valley College in northern California. It provides information that students need to work with and rear young children. It is written for early childhood students who plan to be preschool, kindergarten, and primary teachers, infant care teachers, caregivers, child care workers, family child care providers, or parents. General education students will also benefit. Trainers in the field will find the book valuable for use in in-service training, and parent educators will find it useful as well.

A slight change of title, adding the word *young*, makes clear the audience for this text. Although much of what is laid out here applies through adolescence, that age range is not the focus of this book.

WHAT'S NEW IN THE FOURTH EDITION

1. *Emphasis on the importance of caring relationships.* Brand new to this edition is information about the Pikler Institute in Budapest, Hungary. This residential nursery uses a particular method to socialize very young children—a method that combines caring and education. The institute was started by a pediatrician researcher, Emmi Pikler,

after World War II. Using a combination of ongoing research and intensive training, Pikler created an exemplary approach to group care. According to a study by the World Health Organization, the Pikler approach avoids the problems that often occur in later life when very young children are raised in group homes. Instead of showing the effects of institutionalization, the children turn out to be healthy, well functioning adults. The implications of the Pikler model for early care and education programs in the United States and beyond are enormous! Coupled with the information about Pikler is the work of Nel Noddings at Stanford University, whose theories about the ethics of care is receiving attention at all levels of education. Both of these researchers put an emphasis on caring as an essential ingredient in education. Both see the importance of carers and educators creating an authentically caring relationship. The work of these two remarkable women adds important insights and directions for the readers of this text.

2. *Expansion of coverage of children with special needs.* In this latest edition, information about children with additional needs—including disabilities and other challenges— has been expanded. In light of the current trend for increased inclusion of children with special needs in programs with their typically developing peers, this edition focuses on practical information about how to ensure that children with disabilities gain access to programs and what those programs have to offer. Special attention is given to helping children with disabilities so that they will:

   - Gain a feeling of belonging when placed in programs with their typically developing peers
   - Reach higher levels of achievement
   - Develop a broader range of social skills
   - Learn about the larger world that they will live in as adults

3. *More on partnering with parents and families.* Parents have always been an important feature of this book. This edition adds more coverage and practical suggestions for how to partner with parents in early care and education programs. Partnering with parents goes beyond simply educating them or requiring that they be involved in the program. Partnerships imply collaboration, shared power, and a working relationship. Communication skills are the key to partnerships.

4. *More on child abuse and neglect.* Another aspect of partnering involves the support that some parents need to avoid the isolation that so often lies behind abuse and neglect. The early childhood professional has a mandate to connect those families who need more support than the professional or the program can give with community resources that can help them. This edition provides even more coverage of this subject than earlier editions.

5. *Expansion of diversity.* This topic has always been a focus of this text, and each edition expands and updates the coverage. An addition to this text includes an explanation about how preserving diversity is not merely a politically correct approach to take, but is a survival issue for all of us. Using arguments from Barbara Rogoff and others, the point is made that valuing diversity and providing culturally

responsive early care and education make a difference in whether children move away from their roots or honor them. When children grow up as part of their own culture, they then pass it on to their children. The resulting diversity in future generations preserves expanded worldviews and the possibility of increased approaches to problem solving. With an uncertain future facing humanity, we need all the resources we can get for figuring out the issues and meeting the challenges to come. Some of those issues and challenges we know about, and others awaiting us are bound to be ones that we haven't even conceived of yet.

6. *Expanded coverage of family structures.* Part of the theme of respecting and responding to differences is the message about honoring diversity in family structures rather than looking at them as deficits. The new edition expands the coverage of family structures and makes the point more than once that *different* isn't the same as deficient.

7. *Updated research.* Currency is vital, so updated research is a feature of this and every edition. The References and the section titled Further Reading reflect the latest scholarship as well as classic studies. Examples of increased coverage of classic theorists include expansion of Ainsworth's research on attachment and Vygotsky's work on socio-cultural theory and its application, including the integration of children with special needs into groups of typically developing children.

8. A *balanced perspective on "readiness."* A good deal of attention lately is directed at "leaving no child behind" and getting children "ready to learn." Those phrases have a particular meaning for the politicians and general public who want a major emphasis on schooling in early academics. Others, who understand the complexity of providing for the needs of families and their young children see a bigger picture. This edition explains that bigger picture in terms of trusting relationships, security, optimum brain development, health, nutrition, housing, financial stability, and other important factors in the early years. This edition discusses the many misconceptions that some well-meaning policy makers have about what it takes to prepare a child to have a successful educational experience.

SUMMARY OF CHAPTERS

Part 1, The Child: Socialization in a Developmental Context, examines the developmental context of socialization, providing information about the foundations of socialization and examining four major issues of the first 8 years. The reader is led to examine brief overviews of three perspectives of child development theory and then is introduced to the dynamic theory on which this book is based. An inclusive theory, it regards behavior as a result of the interplay of the biological organism (and his or her individual genetic makeup) with developmental stage theory, behaviorism, and social learning theory.

Chapter 1, Attachment, looks at Erik Erikson's stage of trust versus mistrust and examines how attachment relates to this stage. Building relationships and meeting needs are important themes of this first chapter, which looks at early care and education outside the home, as well as parenting. Issues of attachment in group care are examined and the Pikler approach in Budapest, Hungary, is explored. Inclusion and the related issues of feelings of belonging are discussed, including the implications of Vygotsky's work to inclusion programs. The attachment of a baby who was prenatally exposed to drugs is a sidelight of this chapter.

Chapter 2, Autonomy, explores the toddler behaviors that indicate the push toward becoming a separate independent individual—behaviors such as rebellion and negativity, exploration, self-help skills, and a sense of possession. Loss and separation and helping toddlers develop the skills needed to cope are also features of this chapter. Partnering with parents is discussed. A story about a teen parent is a sidelight of the chapter.

Chapter 3, Initiative, explores the development of a conscience by explaining the second and third of Erik Erikson's conflict stages: autonomy versus shame, and doubt and initiative versus guilt. Also featured are the role of imagination and fantasy, a look at shy children and aggressive children, and how to empower *all* children, including those with special needs. Discussion of considerations to make play more accessible for children with special needs is part of this chapter, as well as how Vygotsky's ideas about peer relationships contribute to learning through play. Sidelights of the chapter include a look at a child with attention deficit/hyperactivity disorder (ADHD), differing perspectives on child rearing, and addressing the roots of violence by teaching problem-solving skills.

Chapter 4, Self-Esteem, discusses what self-esteem is and how to influence it. Dimensions of self-esteem are laid out and suggestions of how to promote self-esteem are given. The chapter also includes an examination of the relationship of cultural differences to self-esteem and how an antibias approach can promote self-esteem. A sidelight of the chapter is a peek into a preschool staff meeting where teachers discuss the self-esteem of 4-year-old Travis.

Part 2, The Family: Socialization for High Self-Esteem in Healthy Families, looks at the socialization of the child in a family context and is designed to present a view of the array of components essential for high self-esteem and mental health.

Chapter 5, Goals, Values, and Culture, starts with a look at cultural differences in goals and values plus the relationship of those goals and values to child rearing. It explores contrasting cultural patterns and the cultural conflicts that sometimes occur. Another major theme of this chapter is teaching morals and values to children, which includes Nel Noddings's and Emmi Pikler's approaches related to creating caring relationships as a method of enhancing moral development. A sidelight of this chapter is a comparison of the values of independence and interdependence and how they show up in child-rearing practices.

Chapter 6, Child Care: An Extension of the Family, looks at child care as a child-rearing environment that supplements the home. It examines the state of child care in America today as well as the issues of affordability and availability. Quality is considered, as well as what goes into the making of quality child care settings. The concept of the gap between home and school is discussed, and there is an exploration of the relations between parents and early childhood professionals. The ideal is to create a parent-professional partnership, keeping in mind that such a step is especially important when the family has a child who has special needs. Sidelights of this chapter are the stories of Debbie, Walt, and Sean, who are looking for child care for their children.

Chapter 7, Disciplining for High Self-Esteem, starts by defining the word *discipline*. It looks at seven ways to *prevent* the need for controlling children's behavior and then examines seven ways to respond to unacceptable behavior. Sidelights of this chapter are the story of one mother who stopped using punishment and started using consequences to guide the behavior of her son, the story of a mother who has abused her child, and the story of what one town did to work toward preventing physical abuse of its children.

Chapter 8, Accepting Feelings, starts with the proposition that all feelings are positive and need to be accepted, and then it discusses how we learn feelings, including cultural scripts. Ways to teach children to express and cope with feelings are explored. Sidelights of this chapter show how Marcie, a stepmother, learns to cope with her anger in healthy ways, and how Julie, another mother, learns to let go of responsibility for her child's feelings.

Chapter 9, Problem Solving, is about conflicting needs and what to do about them. For instance, what to do when the child has the problem is different from what to do when the parent has the problem or when both have problems. The chapter also explains the problem-solving process and gives a structure to follow. How problem solving relates to cognitive development is also explored. When parents don't know how to use problem-solving approaches, emotional abuse can occur. A sidelight of this chapter is the story of a stepfather named Brian who was emotionally abused as a child; Brian refuses to do the same to his stepchildren.

Chapter 10, Strokes and Affirmations: A Path to Self-Esteem, looks closely at promoting self-esteem in specific ways. The chapter advocates using strokes to change behavior and affirmations to create self-fulfilling prophecies. Nel Noddings's concept of a special relationship—which she calls "engrossment"—is a way to help ensure that the strokes are honest rather than manipulative. Adult self-esteem relates to child self-esteem, so suggestions for how adults can work on their own self-esteem are included. A sidelight of this chapter tells how Mary and her daughter Susan disagree over the need for stroking Susan's baby. Another sidelight is the story of how Jennifer, a single parent, discovers that she is inadvertently sexist in the ways she strokes her children.

Chapter 11, Modeling and Teaching Gender Roles, starts with a quick history of the struggle for women's equality and goes on to look at sex equity and child rearing. It explores the relationship of choice of toys to broadening or narrowing children's options. Language issues and differential socialization are examined, and guidelines for parents and teachers are laid out. A sidelight of this chapter is a discussion about cultural differences in sex roles, and where traditional roles end and oppression begins.

Chapter 12, Stress and Success in Family Life, looks at what it takes to be a healthy family and examines the lives of six families who, in spite of many stresses, are struggling to be successful. This chapter touches on the issues of substance abuse, divorce, child custody, and poverty. It examines the influence of family structure and makeup and defines the family broadly so there is room for all kinds of families in the definition: nuclear families as well as single-parent families, stepfamilies, blended families, extended families, families with teen parents, and families with children who have special needs. A sidelight of this chapter looks at what families do in early childhood that helps ensure later school success.

Part 3, The Community: Socialization in the Community Context, looks at the broader issues of socialization. The child, with developmental issues unfolding within the family, is now viewed in a community context. Part 3 includes society's goals and values from diverse perspectives and discusses the effects of racism, classism, and sexism on the socialization of children.

Chapter 13, Community Resources, looks at the way the community serves and supports families through social networks and institutions. The chapter shows how the six families of Chapter 12 connect to the resources in their community. The subject of child abuse is also explored. A sidelight of the chapter is a description of various ways that families find and connect to community resources.

Chapter 14, Socializing Agents, looks at a number of agents, including the family, schools, peer groups, and the media. The chapter also examines factors in socialization—such as inequity and diversity, classism, and racism. It also explores some stories of what can happen when parents and teachers are adversaries instead of partners. Sidelights of the chapter include a look into what "ready to learn" really means, and recommendations regarding television and young children.

Chapter 15, Social Policy Issues, considers what the community can do to ensure that all children get an equal chance to develop high self-esteem and fulfill themselves in our society. This chapter examines social policy issues and addresses the question: Who is responsible for America's children? A feature of the chapter is a discussion of the movement toward inclusion of children with special needs in programs with their typically developing peers. The chapter ends with a discussion of child advocacy. Sidelights of the chapter include culturally responsive care, and statistics responding to the question: Does every child get an equal start?

ACKNOWLEDGMENTS

So many people have helped me get to where I am today as I write this fourth edition of *The Young Child in the Family and the Community*! The number is large and the space too small for me to name them all! I am deeply indebted to my many friends, colleagues, students, and associates—who have helped me grow in my understanding of early childhood care and education, diverse perspectives on development, cultural responsiveness, antibias, and the communication skills that lead to healthy and close relationships.

I want to give special recognition to a few people who have involved me in what they were doing so that I was pushed to learn, not only about them but more about myself as a white person. These people have supported me through the ups and downs that occur when the learning is emotional and some of the lessons hard, as I continue to discover what it means to be me in a racist society. Many thanks to Intisar Shareef, Susan Lee, Marion Cowee, Lynne Doherty Lyle, Douglas Quiett, Yolanda Torres, Norma Alicia Pino, Dora Pulido-Tobiassen, Equoya Thomas, Alice Nakahata, Jean Monroe, Cheryl Williams Jackson, Ruth Major, Judith K. Bernhard, Hedy Chang, Lisa Lee, Marcela Clark, and Christina Lopez Morgan.

I appreciate the time and care Julie Peters, Editor, Early Childhood Education, Merrill/Prentice Hall, took to help me get this revision into shape. I also want to thank the following reviewers for their insights and comments: Jane Christine Catalani, San Antonio College; Patricia Clark, University of Maine at Augusta; Holly Hoffman, Central Michigan University; and Alycia Maurer, University of Texas, San Antonio.

Last but not least, I thank my family and especially my husband, Frank Gonzalez-Mena, who has given me firsthand experience of what it is like to live in a multicultural family!

ANCILLARIES TO ACCOMPANY THIS TEXT

Instructor's Manual and Test Bank

The Instructor's Manual and Test Bank accompanying this text contains a lengthy Introduction and orientation to teaching a course using this book; chapter sections containing a Summary, In-Class Activities, Outside-of-Class Activities, possible artifacts to include in a professional portfolio, Personal Reflection questions, and assessment items requiring written responses.

Companion Website

A Web site at **www.prenhall.com/gonzalez-mena** provides several self-assessments for students to check their understanding of each chapter. See the Multiple Choice, Fill in the Blank, and True/False modules on this site. In addition, students and instructors can browse selected annotated Internet site links in Web Destinations. Each chapter on the site also provides a list of learning objectives, a summary of the chapter, and summary of topics discussed.

Syllabus Manager™

The Syllabus Manager™ provides the instructor with an easy, step-by-step process to create and revise syllabi, with direct links into the Companion Website and other online content.

Brief Contents

Contents

Note: Every effort has been made to provide accurate and current Internet information in this book. However, the Internet and information posted on it are constantly changing, so it is inevitable that some of the Internet addresses listed in this textbook will change.

PART 1

The Child

Socialization in a Developmental Context

I ask my students to examine their assumptions about child development by doing the following exercise. I indicate a line on the floor with an X at each end. I designate one end the "flower" and the other the "tree." Then I explain that I want each participant to decide where he or she stands.

I start at the flower end and explain how a child is like a flower. I paint a word picture of a seed planted in good soil and carefully nurtured as it grows. I explain that all the potential of the flower is already in the seed and that all that is necessary for it to be fulfilled is that its needs be met. One must water, feed, and protect the plant but need not direct its growth, because it has in it the capacity to know its own direction. Given a nurturing environment, one can count on the plant's sense of self-direction to be the right one.

Then I ask the participants to consider the tree on the other end of the continuum. The tree also has potential contained in its seed, and it also must have its needs met to grow. However, to have a tall, straight, shade-giving tree, it is necessary to clip and prune. The tree will be very different if left to grow wild. One must direct its growth if it is to be the very best tree it can be. Left to chance, it may grow crooked or too bushy, or its many limbs may crowd each other and be unattractive. Therefore, besides the nurturing that must be done, one must also watch the direction of the growth—guiding and controlling it.

When I finish my speech, most students dutifully pick their spots on the continuum—a few going to stand at either end, and the bulk of the rest clustering around the middle—either dead center or off toward one end or the other. I then ask the students farthest out on either end to discuss with each other why they chose the position they did.

What ensues is a discussion about the basic nature of the child. The flower-end person paints a picture of a little being that is placed on earth to grow and develop according to some internal process that is preprogrammed into the package. Sometimes the student relates this process to a divine plan of some sort; at other times divinity is not included in the picture. No matter how it's stated, it becomes clear that within the organism is a benevolent driving force guiding it toward health and wholeness, supplying it with behaviors that meet its needs. The child (or the flower) who isn't stunted or warped by neglect, abuse, or other negative factors *unfolds* in the way he or she was designed to unfold. It's a natural process and a beautiful one. You can almost see a rosebud opening before your very eyes as this process is being described. It's awe-inspiring.

Child development textbooks are written from an academic perspective that brings out the many complexities of the developmental process. Although not one is written purely from the "flower" view of the basic nature of the child, most show leanings in that direction. The very word *develop* means to "unfold."

The person at the other end of the spectrum has a different view and is usually cynical about the rosy picture painted at the opposite end. This person also sees a driving force from within, but one that puts temptations and obstacles in the way of positive growth. It too is a natural process—but one that needs constant monitoring and intervention if it is to result in a desirable end product. Children are not naturally born pure and good; they cannot be allowed just to unfold according to their human nature. The words vary with the person's philosophical stance or religious background, but what is clear is that the child's sense of direction is not always toward the good. Some people feel that the natural inclination of human nature is *never* toward the good. Others see progress through life as a crooked path; if the final destination is to be desirable, a good firm adult hand is needed to control the stroll through childhood. Some say that it's more natural to be bad than it is to be good. *Sin* is a word that comes up in this discussion. If the child is to turn out all right, it's vital that adults take a strong hand in guiding the direction of the development.

I have never seen a child development text written from the view at this end of the continuum, but I have read parenting books that were. Also many parents I have known have felt strongly that when children are left to grow as in the "flower" theory, they will turn out "spoiled."

The students in the middle make a case for how both ends are true and that it's impossible to exclude either.

Once in a while there's a student who refuses to stand on the continuum at all. That student says that the child has no basic nature and that there is no driving force. What determines the kind of adult that the child becomes is how the environment shapes him or her. This student subscribes to the principle that the person is the sum total of all of his or her behavior and that behavior is set by what happens, not by any built-in sort of unfolding mechanism, divine plan, invisible force, or natural motivation toward either good or bad. This person has the same idea of the importance—indeed, the *necessity*—of controlling the behaviors the child exhibits, through careful attention to and manipulation of the rewards and punishments the child receives. This person usually stresses rewards over punishments because the positive approach is more effective and predictable than the negative one. This is a "behaviorist" view, and it seems to go along with the tree image. However, there is a basic difference between the "tree" end of the continuum and behaviorism, which is scientific and quite detached from such concepts as "bad" and "good." Behaviors are more likely to be seen as acceptable or unacceptable rather than branded with moral judgments.

All of these views are simplistic. In reality, development is more dynamic and involves a much more complex picture. Children grow and change through a complicated process composed of many interacting elements, some that can be controlled and others that cannot. A *dynamic theory* is more in keeping with the information and experience on which this book is based. According to this view of growth and development, behavior is the result of the interplay of the biological organism (and his or her individual genetic makeup) with culture, developmental stage, environmental input, and the natural inclination to imitate or model after others.

We each carry within ourselves a personal view of how growth and development works, whether or not we are aware of the existence of our own viewpoint. This personal view influences what we actually see when we are around children, how we interpret their behavior, and what we perceive their needs to be. Most of all, our viewpoint determines our own behavior and our approaches to socialization. Keep that fact in mind as you read this text. Your view of the basic nature of the child and how development comes about will influence what you learn from your reading.

CHAPTER 1

Attachment

In this chapter you'll discover . . .

- How "getting in sync" with a baby relates to attachment
- What helps babies develop trust
- How parents show they are attached to their baby
- How babies show they are attached to their parents
- What factors affect attachment patterns
- How child care affects attachment
- Whether all behaviors of good parents and good caregivers should be similar

What is attachment, and why is it important? Attachment is a lasting emotional relationship that begins to develop in infancy and serves to tie the infant to one or more people in his or her life. It is a two-way process—adults (usually parents or other family members) attach to infants, and infants attach to adults. This two-way process results in a significant relationship. Although attachment is an emotional process that we associate with "the heart," other processes engaging the brain are also involved. Healthy attachment provides the foundation for later intellectual development, according to the latest brain research. The positive nurturing experiences associated with attachment produce hormones called *neurotransmitters* that give the infant a sense of well-being. This sense of well-being reinforces certain pathways in the brain, which leads to mental growth. Children who have no attachment and therefore lack a sense of security experience stress, which has a detrimental effect on the brain's development.

ATTACHMENT AND TRUST

The basis of socialization is attachment, and the basis of attachment is a synchronous relationship, which grows from a number of synchronous interactions. Here's what a synchronous interaction looks like:

> *A caregiver is bent over a 3-month-old baby lying on her back. The caregiver is expressionless. The baby rounds her mouth and lets out a breathy sound while reaching out her arms. The caregiver responds by widening her eyes, rounding her own mouth, and imitating the sound. She reaches for the baby's hands and holds them in her own. The baby pulls her hands away, kicks her feet, and widens her own eyes in imitation of the caregiver. The caregiver smiles. The baby smiles back. The caregiver keeps smiling, makes clucking noises, and claps her hands. The baby turns away. "Oh, that was too much for you," responds the caregiver, quieting her activity. The baby looks back. The caregiver smiles. The baby smiles, then arches and reaches. "You want up?" the caregiver asks, reaching out her arms to the child.*

These two are "in sync" with each other. The caregiver is sensitive to the baby's signals and reads the turning away as a need to tune out, not a personal rejection of her. The baby knows how to "light up" the caregiver's face. The caregiver knows how to "turn on" the baby. The two are good together. If they are not already attached, they are becoming attached.

Babies become attached when people in their lives are sensitive and responsive. That means that they pay attention to the baby's signals and read them accurately, responding readily and appropriately. Adults practice being responsive when they play with babies, as in this scene. They also meet needs by reading babies' cues and responding in a timely fashion. Both play and meeting needs contribute to the development of attachment.

> *Imagine yourself a very young baby, lying asleep in a crib. You open your eyes—suddenly you're wide awake. You see nothing except a blur of light—there are no objects, no movement within your visual range. You feel a very uncomfortable sensation in your midsection.*

You squirm around. Changing position doesn't help. Suddenly you feel desperate. The sensation in your midsection takes over your whole body. You squeeze your eyes shut tight and open your mouth wide. Into your ears comes a piercing sound. You don't know that it's your own cry. You only know that something is terribly wrong, and your whole being reacts to it. Your heart pounds, your face burns, and you scream in agony, then gasp for breath, only to start screaming again once you get your lungs full. You're like this for what seems an eternity but is actually less than 2 minutes. You feel something touch you. You open your eyes and find something very distinctive and vaguely familiar in front of the blur of light that was all that was there before. The something moves in a way that makes you feel comfortable. As you pause for breath, you hear another sound—not the high, agonized one of before, but a soft, soothing one. You feel a blanket of pleasure surround you, providing immeasurable relief, and, true to your most cherished hope, you find yourself lifted in the air out of the loneliness—the isolation—and snuggled into a pair of warm arms. You're basking in the glow of the feelings of this, when—wonder of wonders—something familiar touches your cheek. You jerk toward the something, manage to get your mouth around it, and begin sucking. A warm, sweet sensation floods your mouth and you're in heaven.

That's one scenario—here's another:

You wake up in heaven, surrounded by human warmth, touch, sound, and smells. You open your eyes drowsily, look at the familiar sight of your favorite human, close them again, and snuggle deeper into the comfort around you. But that comfort quickly dissolves as a midsection pain swells out over your whole body. You scream in agony, but only once. Immediately you find in your mouth something to suck on and suck you do, letting the warm sweetness take you back to heaven.

These two scenes illustrate how needs, attachment, and trust all come in a bundle in the beginning of life. The scenes are slightly different. In the first one, the infant wakes up alone and must signal the caregiver to meet hunger and comfort needs. In the second scene, the infant wakes up already in the arms of the caregiver, who may even anticipate the needs before the infant signals them.

You may prefer one scene over the other—you may actually feel critical of the nonpreferred one. However, both of these patterns of relating to the needs of the very young infant lead to healthy attachment of a type that serves the individual and the culture. It's important to remember that attachment patterns are related to parental values and goals (Chang, 1993; Gonzalez-Mena, 1997). Parents rear their children to fit the world as they perceive it. (See Chapter 5 for more on this subject.)

Attachment is vital. It is a means of ensuring survival of the child and also of the species (Bowlby, 2000). It creates the caring (the feeling) that motivates the *action* of giving care. It ensures that nurturing and protection will be provided to the relatively helpless infant. But beyond physical survival, the first attachment(s) provide(s) the basis for all future relationships.

If the infant finds that when needs arise they are met with reasonable promptness, as in the two prior scenes, he or she comes to see the world as a welcoming place. A sense of trust grows from fulfillment and satisfaction in the 1st year of life.

Infants who are left screaming for long periods, gripped in the agony of hunger pangs, come to see the world as an unfriendly place. They find that they can't trust anyone to take care of them. If they give signals and no one responds, they see themselves as powerless and the world as cold and hostile. When these children grow out of infancy, they continue to view the world with distrust.

This early issue of developing trust versus mistrust was originally defined and described by Erik Erikson (1963), who sees life as a series of what he calls *psychosocial dilemmas* to be resolved (see Figure 1.1).

Trust is a lifelong issue for all of us. However, children who develop a sense of distrust in infancy grapple with the issue more intensely than others. Some of these children are left with unresolved trust issues; others successfully deal with the problem if the situation changes and those around them become more responsive and meet their needs more promptly. Children with unresolved trust issues often reach adulthood still seeking the early caregiver who left their needs unmet. Because it is never too late to resolve trust issues, some adults seem continually to choose to connect to people who treat them much as their early caregiver(s) did. They put themselves back into their infant situation, to perhaps give themselves another chance to relive the situation and manage a different outcome. The human being is very resilient!

Attachment is a powerful process—and it seems that even a little goes a long way. Look at studies of survivor types—children who manage to cope and live a productive life in spite of factors in their early years that work against that. The one thing that all these survivor children have in common is a person they could attach to sometime in their 1st year—even though it might not have been an ideal attachment or a long-lasting one. Emmy Werner, a developmental psychologist, did the classic research on resiliency over the last 40 years. Her findings show that attachment in the early years with a caregiver who had predominantly positive interactions with the child acts as a protective factor (Werner, 1984, 1995, 2000; Werner & Smith, 1992).

Child's Stage	Approximate Age	Task		
Infancy	0 – 1	Basic trust	versus	Basic mistrust
Toddlerhood	1 – 3	Autonomy	versus	Shame and doubt
The preschool years	3 – 6	Initiative	versus	Guilt
School age	6 – 10	Industry	versus	Inferiority

Figure 1.1
Erikson's psychosocial stages of development
Source: From Erikson (1963).

HOW ATTACHMENT OCCURS

In a model situation in European American middle-class society, attachment begins prenatally, as two parents begin to relate to their visions of the growing fetus. This is a two-way process, as the fetus becomes familiar with the outside happenings that come into the womb. For instance, babies are born recognizing the sound of their mothers' voices.

Many parents cannot relate to the reality of a baby until it is actually born. They may feel more attached to the pregnancy than to the product—the growing fetus. However, parental attachment can begin at birth—or thereafter—even if there has been no prenatal attachment.

Back to the ideal. If all goes well during the birth, and if hospital procedures allow, the parents may spend an hour or so "bonding" with their baby right after birth. This get-acquainted period can be a great bonus to future attachment. Imagine a peaceful hour in which the new family member is alert and responsive and the parents are completely available and attentive. They're not distracted by any medical or health procedures; they're not feeling some kind of obligation to be elsewhere, doing something more important. They are fully present and receptive. They see the value of establishing this new relationship. Sometimes this is a love-at-first-sight experience, full of emotion and wonder. Tears may flow. When all goes well, the family "bonds"—that is, establishes the beginning of an emotional tie to one another. Though not exactly the same as attachment, bonding is a means of facilitating the later process, which grows over a period of time.

Attachment may begin prenatally, as parents begin to relate to their visions of the growing fetus.

Providing for bonding at birth is an excellent idea and is encouraged for many reasons, one of which is the supposition that child abuse and/or neglect is more likely in families without attachment. In a good number of cases in modern American society, caregiving may depend on feeling some attachment to the baby rather than on a deep sense of obligation that compels one to fulfill a caregiving role from which attachment grows. The American mainstream cultural tradition demands that emotion precede commitment. Love comes first, then marriage. Attachment (love for a baby) produces commitment to the baby, which ensures that he or she will be taken care of. All cultures don't work that way. In some, marriage comes first (arranged for the couple) and love follows. The baby is born and then cared for because with the role of parent comes commitment, whether attachment comes early on or not. Attachment grows from the commitment.

It is important to realize that, wonderful though immediate bonding at birth may be, not all relationships grow from a love-at-first-sight beginning. And not all love-at-first-sight relationships last. Relationships take work; no instant cementing can take the place of the long period of sensitive interaction that eventually grows into a lasting attachment (Brazelton & Cramer, 1990).

Let's continue with the ideal. The baby comes home from the hospital (unless he or she was born at home), and life as a member of the family begins. At first baby and caregiver parent(s) experience what seems to be an unending cycle of very basic functions. Time is spent signaling and fulfilling needs—sleeping, eating, eliminating. Each of these needs is communicated by baby to caregiver parent(s) in a variety of individual ways, which the caregiver(s) must learn to read in order to respond appropriately.

As caregiver parent(s) and baby become more and more in tune with each other, the attachment grows (Stern, 1985). The vision that the parents carried while the baby was in the womb may be transferred onto the person before them. However, some

The two are "in sync" with each other.

parents recognize early on the difference between their own vision and the real live individual who has come into their lives. The baby helps them do that differentiation task by not quite fitting the expectations. Sensitive parents recognize when their vision is getting in the way of the baby's growing into the unique individual he or she is.

ATTACHMENT BEHAVIORS

Attachment can be observed in adults and babies alike. There are certain sets of behaviors that indicate attachment is forming or is already fully established.

Signs of Attachment in Parents

Some parents show signs of attachment right away. They're smitten. They feel close to their offspring. They find parenting pleasurable—even the hard and frustrating parts. One mother recalls how her whole life changed when her first baby was born. Suddenly she became important to someone. She had been casual about using her seat belt in the car until the birth. On the way home from the hospital she fastened her seat belt consciously, because it was vital that nothing happened to her. Her baby depended on her. She was never casual about the seat belt again. Becoming a parent changed her perceptions of herself and even the world she lived in. She had taken little notice of the peace movement until the birth of her baby. Suddenly it seemed important to make the world a safe place for her baby to grow up in. Not all parents go through such a transformative process, but some do.

Some cultural rituals are related to attachment. Giving a name to the baby and calling him or her by that name is a way of acknowledging the child as an individual. Buying possessions for the new baby is also a way of recognizing individuality and personhood. These are so expected that they don't seem to relate to attachment, but when they don't occur, it can be a sign that something is wrong with the attachment.

Signs of Attachment in Infants

Babies take longer to show signs of attachment, although careful research shows that signs exist from birth. Babies just a few hours old can distinguish their mother's smell and her voice, for example (Cernoch & Porter, 1985; DeCasper & Fifer, 1980). Before long, babies begin to act differently around their primary caregiver (who may or may not be the mother). They may be more animated, less fussy, more interested and alert.

Eventually some babies begin to show distress when someone they don't know arrives in their field of vision. The distress may accelerate if the stranger approaches. This stranger anxiety shows that the baby can distinguish between the person(s) he or she is attached to and others.

However, some babies never show stranger anxiety, not because they are not attached but because they have had a secure and trusting life with multiple caregivers (either at home or in child care). If babies skip this milestone, some parents and even some experts become distressed because they think it shows lack of attachment. That's not necessarily true.

For some babies, the next milestone is *separation anxiety*, as the baby protests at being away from the caregiver. (More about this subject appears in the next chapter.)

Attachment behaviors can be seen in both of the preceding situations—as the baby looks or moves toward the primary caregiver for comfort and reassurance. Clinging, crying, fussing, whining, and following are all attachment behaviors that can show the emotional bond between the child and someone else. Although they are indicators of attachment, an absence of these behaviors does not necessarily signal a lack of attachment in children with multiple caregivers.

OBSTACLES TO ATTACHMENT

Sometimes the attachment process doesn't start with prenatal attachment, continue with bonding at birth, and follow a continuous progression from there (Lieberman & Zeanah, 1995). For many reasons, parents may not feel an emotional connection to their unborn baby. They may be unhappy about the pregnancy or with each other, and those feelings may influence their feelings for the baby. The father may not be in a relationship with the mother—so any feeling for the baby on his part will necessarily be "long-distance." Even for the mother, the reality of the baby may be fuzzy. It's hard to love someone you can't see or touch or interact with.

Attachment patterns can vary depending on the makeup of the family.

Then, at birth, the time may still not be right. The birth itself may not be a pleasant experience, and that unpleasantness can carry over into the period after. Or the birth may be complicated. If the baby or the mother is in any kind of physical distress, medical procedures may take precedence over time alone together. For one reason or another, baby and parents often miss out on the initial bonding period. Even if it is arranged so that parents and baby can spend the first hour or so together, there may be worries or disappointments that cast an emotional overlay over the bonding process and prevent the magical happy moment from occurring.

Adoption presents another obstacle to bonding at birth and attachment following. The new parents may not have been a part of the birth or had a period together immediately afterward.

Attachment can proceed very well in spite of all these obstacles to early bonding, as long as the relationship grows and flourishes, preferably in the 1st year—the earlier the better. If you think back to what you know about your own birth, the chances are that you didn't experience "bonding" immediately there in the delivery room (if you had a hospital birth). Allowing parents and babies time together right after delivery is a relatively new procedure in standard medical practice in this country. Perhaps your life might have been different if your parent(s) had been given a chance to fall in love with you at first sight immediately after your birth. Or perhaps it wouldn't have made a difference.

Attachment, the process of creating a close and lasting relationship, may be delayed for many reasons. If the infant is very sick, parents may unconsciously protect themselves from getting attached by putting an emotional distance between themselves and the baby. Sometimes the difficulty is that, for whatever reason, the baby remains unresponsive to the caregiver's initiations. Some infants are born with disabilities, a circumstance that cuts down on their ability to respond. Others simply don't have the kinds of behaviors that draw adults to them. They're not cute, or cuddly, or smiley. They

If a baby is very sick and separated from family, attachment may be delayed.

don't make eye contact. These infants, who don't reward the adults around them, need adults who make a conscious effort to attach. Even mismatches of temperament can delay attachment as the quiet, placid parent gets used to a highly active baby, or the reverse.

If babies experience early lengthy separation, the attachment process can be disrupted. Babies in foster care may be moved around; changing caregivers can disrupt attachment. These delays or disruptions in attachment can influence future life in drastic ways if a sense of basic trust is not established. The child may put up barriers so that no one can get close. The hurt from loss is too great to chance again.

Temperament and Attachment

Temperament can affect attachment in either a negative or positive way, depending on the temperamental match between the infant and parent. Temperament is built in and can be detected early in a child's life. Genetically determined, temperament becomes obvious as infants show differing levels of activity, emotionality, and sociability that tend to remain the same over time. Thomas, Chess, and Birch (1963), the pioneers in temperament research, categorized babies as "easy," "slow to warm," and "difficult." Their work helps today's parents and caregivers understand how temperament affects behavior and shapes personality. J. Ronald Lally and his colleagues in the WestEd Program for Infant-Toddler Caregivers renamed the categories "fearful," "flexible," and "feisty," which puts them in a more objective light. A good match between parent temperament and child temperament promotes attachment; a mismatch may hinder it. If the two aren't a natural fit, the parent must adjust to the baby rather than expecting the reverse.

What would a mismatch look like? If an active and intense mother with a high energy level finds herself with a slow, calm, mild baby, she may be disappointed. She may even wonder whether something is wrong with her baby, even though the baby is perfectly normal. If this high-energy mother is not aware of what she is doing, she may overstimulate her baby. She has to learn to read the signs that the baby has had enough. Some parents keep on after the baby turns away or closes her eyes. A serious mismatch occurs when the mother interprets this behavior as bored and continues to try to "wake the baby up and make her more lively."

Or imagine a calm, relaxed father who loves things done on schedule and appreciates predictability in his life. He'll find a mismatch with a highly active, intense baby who never seems able to regulate his rhythms or body needs. Some babies don't keep any sort of routine, even eating at a different time every day. Napping is as unpredictable as appetite and never follows a schedule. If the father of such a baby doesn't accept that his son is different from himself, he may have trouble being sensitive to the child's needs.

Parents who have children whose temperaments don't match their own have to adjust their expectations, accept their babies as is, and learn to understand them. They have to be flexible about how and when they respond. They have to be supersensitive so that they can meet their baby's needs. All that may be hard for a parent whose temperament isn't flexible or sensitive.

Developmental Differences

Babies who are born with developmental differences may not have the attachment behaviors that draw adults to them. For example, neurological issues can cause babies not to be cuddly. Some stiffen when held. Some even cry out in pain when held or touched. Others who can't control their facial muscles may not smile or look interested in the same way typically developing babies do. Or eye contact may be missing. A child with a visual impairment, for example, may not use eye contact to establish a relationship. A child with a hearing impairment may not respond to soft talking. In these cases it is important for adults to look for the attachment behaviors the children do exhibit. Adults must be constantly aware of the importance of establishing connections even if the baby's behaviors tend to get in the way. Sometimes outside help is needed to support parents, caregivers, teachers, or family child care providers when attachment isn't occurring in spite of efforts to encourage a close connection.

LEARNING TO COPE WITH FEELINGS OF LOSS

Babies who are attached experience feelings when separation occurs. Separation is the other side of the coin of attachment. Each human has the lifelong task of coming to grips with separations and coping with the feelings that occur as people come into and go out of one's life. Each broken relationship, physical departure, or death brings into play all the coping skills learned earlier. The skills for dealing with separation begin to develop in infancy.

You can perhaps get in touch with the power of the feelings surrounding separation by thinking back to a time in your own life when you were apart from someone

Learning to cope with feelings of loss: Children who are attached experience feelings when separation occurs.

you cared about. Perhaps it was the first day of school, or a trip to the hospital, or even the first time you were left with a babysitter. It may be a less significant event—but one that sticks in your memory—like the time you took the wrong turn in the grocery store and were "lost" for a minute or two. It might be an even more significant event like the day your father walked out, never to return, or the day your mother died. All of us have experience with separation, and those experiences start earlier for some than for others.

If you can remember your feelings surrounding these experiences, you can probably get in touch with one or more of the following: panic, fear, anxiety, misgivings, apprehension, qualms, terror, horror, bewilderment, confusion, annoyance, irritation, anger, outrage, fury, wrath, frenzy, desperation, indignity, sadness, loneliness, desertion, and abandonment. The feelings come from the need for security as well as a sense of loss of control over the situation.

The memory of your pain may be intense, or it may have muted over time. Or perhaps you have a fuzziness around the feelings or even an absence of feeling. You may even dredge up a sense of depression when you get in touch with this early separation experience.

There are all kinds of separation experiences in infancy—some that help the child grow to independence, others that leave scars and long-lasting aftereffects. One common separation infants experience comes when they are put into cribs to sleep by themselves. In cultures that place a high priority on independence, this physical separation from the beginning is regarded as important. Learning to sleep alone as an infant is a skill that is valued by many in this country. It's an important step for children coming to see themselves as separate individuals. Some parenting experts are adamant about babies sleeping alone. Some experts, including Ferber (1985), who wrote *Solve Your Child's Sleep Problems*, say that babies can't get a good night's sleep if they have to "interact" all night with someone else.

Ironically, information on sudden infant death syndrome (SIDS, or crib death) indicates that an undisturbed night's sleep may put infants at risk. In cultures where infants are held, jostled, and put to bed with an adult or another child, the rate of SIDS is dramatically lower than in cultures where infants sleep apart from the hustle and bustle of family life in cribs in their own rooms (Grether, Shulman, & Croen, 1990; McKenna, 1992). Of course, that doesn't mean babies should be in bed with someone. The "back-to-sleep" campaign is designed to lower the risk factor of sleeping alone, and it has worked! Statistics show that placing babies on their backs to sleep makes sleeping alone in a crib safer.

Where babies sleep is a cultural issue. Some cultures value sleeping alone and others don't, even if they have the space and means to do so. They aren't as interested in their children becoming independent individuals as they are in creating a spirit of interdependence and connectedness to others. In many families both in the United States and around the world, infants and toddlers sleep with the mother or both parents until the next baby comes, then move into the bed of siblings or grandparents. Some European Americans have made an attempt to change the way they were raised by instituting what is called the "family bed" (Thevenin, 1987).

A number of articles and books have been written about getting babies to sleep by themselves, because it isn't as easy to accomplish as it might seem. Many babies comfort themselves while alone in the crib by developing an attachment to a particular object. This process fits right in with being part of an object-oriented culture. Most parents and caregivers are delighted when a child attaches to a favorite blanket or a stuffed animal. Experts see this particular way of self-comforting as a sign that the child has coping skills.

Learning to put oneself to sleep and stay by oneself is a step toward independence and is a valued behavior in many families. It's a healthy sign that infants are able to handle separation.

Trent

Trent's mother took drugs when she was pregnant. No one was aware of this problem until the day Trent was born. He arrived in the world full of the harmful substances his mother had ingested, and his first days of life were spent in withdrawal. He suffered and so did the hospital staff who tended him.

"Poor little guy!" said a nurse, as she tried to make him more comfortable.

Getting the drugs out of his system didn't end his problems. Trent was a difficult baby from the beginning. He cried incessantly—it seemed sometimes as if he would never stop. He'd scream and scream until he finally wore himself out; he'd sleep restlessly for a period and then start again. It was hard to be around Trent.

His foster mother, a patient woman, understood how hard life was for Trent just now. Although she had other babies to care for, she spent special time with him, trying to give him the message that he was cared about—that he was loved. It wasn't easy. When an adoptive family came along that knew Trent's history and his problems, she was relieved because she felt he deserved a permanent home and parents—a family of his own who could give him a good deal of time and energy—the time and energy she had were stretched so thin!

Trent's new parents were special people. They didn't go into the adoption expecting to rescue a child and have him be forever grateful to them. They knew something about the kinds of problems that Trent had at the time and the kinds he was likely to have in the future. They were prepared to deal with these problems.

They started out right away to establish an attachment with Trent. It wasn't easy—he wasn't an appealing baby. When his new parents picked him up, he stiffened and shook. He didn't cuddle like lots of babies. He seldom seemed relaxed; in fact, his movements were jerky and uncontrolled. He twitched, jiggled, and shook as he lay in his crib.

Trent didn't like to be touched; often he screamed louder when he was touched than when he wasn't. It was tempting to leave him alone, since picking him up seemed agonizing to him. But his parents knew that leaving him in his crib wasn't the answer, so they did some observing and brainstorming to discover what ways they could pick him up that would cause him the least discomfort. They felt proud when they were able to discover some. It became more rewarding to pick him up.

Trent didn't look at anyone very often. Even when his parents tried to get his attention, he tended to look away. It's hard to develop a relationship with someone who doesn't make eye contact, but they managed. They just kept on trying until the day came that Trent looked his mother right in the eye. What a moment that was for her—worth waiting for. That was the beginning of the development of a series of positive behaviors that made Trent easy to love. On the big day when Trent smiled for the first time, his father grinned back as if his face would split in two. "You're going to be okay, Trent," he said, patting his son.

Since happily-ever-after stories only occur as fairy tales, I have to tell you that Trent did continue to feel the influence of his early drug exposure into his preschool years. But with the help of his parents and their love for him, he was able to cope with the cards that life had dealt him.

VARYING ATTACHMENT PATTERNS

Although the classic research has been done on attachment between mothers and babies, attachment patterns can vary significantly from that one pattern. The early research is still worth understanding because many look at attachment from the view of the research designed to assess it.

Bowlby and Ainsworth's Research

John Bowlby was the first to apply to humans the idea that attachment behaviors evolved because they promote survival. He took a psychoanalytic view that attachment of infant to caregiver affects an infant's sense of security and ability to trust.

Mary Ainsworth was a student of John Bowlby and her research is used widely in assessing attachment of infants and toddlers. She set out to study how securely attached babies are to their mothers (Ainsworth & Bell, 1977; Ainsworth, Blehar, Waters, & Wall, 1978). She used something she called "the Strange Situation," in which a baby is observed in an experimental room with toys designed to entice. The situation involves the mother and a stranger in a series of comings and goings. How the baby reacts to the separation, the stranger, and the reunion is used to judge the type of attachment.

From her research, Ainsworth came up with different types of attachment. If the baby is what Ainsworth called securely attached, he or she uses the mother as a base to move out from and explore the interesting toys in the room. You can see this happening in any setting where there are toys and a baby with enough mobility to get to them. Babies move away from their mothers, checking back periodically to see where they are, and crawling back to get a snuggle, hug, or a bit of comfort when needed. If the mother leaves, securely attached babies usually show some distress, but not always. They show they are delighted to see her when she returns.

Not so with insecurely attached infants. They may show what's called avoidant attachment, resistant attachment, or disorganized/disoriented attachment. Avoidant attachment shows when babies act the same around the stranger as they do around the mother. They seem not to care when the mother leaves the room. When reunited, they are slow to greet the mother and either ignore or avoid her.

Babies who show resistant attachment stay close to the mother before she leaves and do little exploration in a strange place. They get upset when she leaves, but when she comes back they show anger and sometimes behave in a push-pull fashion—for example, alternating between clinging and pushing her away. Sometimes even picking them up fails to comfort them.

Disorganized/disoriented attachment was the product of more recent research (Main & Solomon, 1990; Solomon & George, 1999). This type of insecure attachment shows up as a pattern of confused, contradictory behaviors when reunited with the mother. Sometimes infants look frozen, dazed, and disoriented. Some rock or engage in other repetitive behaviors. Some cry after the mother has managed to get them settled down.

One criticism of this way of judging attachment is the unnatural setting. Do babies and mothers behave the same in a laboratory as they do at home or somewhere else?

Another criticism of the Strange Situation as a way of assessing attachment is that it is based on a particular model of mother-child attachment. There are a lot of variations on that model. What if the baby has been in child care and is used to multiple caregivers? Is he really showing insecure attachment if he avoids the mother when she returns, or is he accustomed to having an interesting environment and being separated from his mother? Or what if the baby comes from a large family in which the mother isn't the only caregiver? What if the mother isn't the person the baby is most attached to?

Questions About Classic Attachment Research

Ainsworth and other researchers focused on attachment as it relates to the insular or nuclear family. Today we know better. We can see with our own eyes that, even in the nuclear or insular family, caregiving may be shared between mother and father or between one parent and another relative or child care provider. Under these circumstances, attachment is not just between mother and baby, although often the mother remains the primary attachment.

As mentioned earlier, much of the focus on attachment has been related to the insular or nuclear family with mother, father, and child. This, of course, isn't the only kind of family. Another type of family is the single-parent family. Sometimes the parent(s) and baby are not a unit by themselves but are part of a larger extended family. Stack (1991) describes *kinship networks* as clusters of people who are related through children, marriage, and friendship who come together to provide domestic functions. This domestic network may spread over several households, and changes in individual household composition do not significantly affect cooperative arrangements. The single-parent family that finds itself in this type of network may be thought of as "embedded" rather than alone.

A woman once told me a story about how she had changed her perspective on her family. This person was a single parent with two children, who lived with her parents in their house. She thought of her situation as two families living in one house, until she decided to have a family portrait taken. She included all five family members, deciding for herself that this was one family, rather than two. This story of her family portrait started me thinking about my own family situation as I grew up. My mother, my sister, and I lived most of my childhood in the house of my grandparents. We never had a family portrait taken. We didn't see ourselves as a unit; rather, we were two families—an intact one (my grandparents) and a "broken" one (my mother and her two children). Nowadays, of course, we would call ourselves a single-parent family rather than a broken one, but many would still see us as deprived without a father in the household, rather than enriched because of grandparents and the uncles who lived there for periods during my growing up. I now prefer to think of myself as growing up embedded in my extended family.

The concept of an embedded family is a more positive and realistic one. In an embedded family the attachment might be quite different because of shared caregiving. Certainly that was my experience. My attachment to my grandmothers was as strong as my attachment to my mother. Although we may think of the mother-child dyad as the way "it should be," that's not necessarily so. The child can become attached to several caregivers or to a group rather than to just one or two individuals. When you are used to looking at attachment as an exclusive relationship, you may be concerned about the infant who is attached to multiple caregivers (Zimmerman & McDonald, 1995). However, cultures all over the world raise their children this way. Shared care has advantages over one or even two parents carrying total responsibility for a child's well-being. What a burden that much responsibility can be, especially for a new parent who may have had little previous experience with babies!

Some child care programs function as an extended family, a kinship network, or a family support system, rather than as just a place to leave children during the day. These programs are able to provide families with the kind of connections they would find in embedded families if they had them. One such family support system is the Parent Services Project, which a visionary child care director, Ethel Seiderman, started in California, and which has now spread nationwide in the United States. The purpose of this project is to help programs recognize that the well-being and sense of significance of parents are of central importance to the child's development. Furthermore, support is important to all families, and social support networks reduce isolation and promote the well-being of the child, the family, and the community.

ATTACHMENT AND INFANT MORTALITY

Sometimes attachment patterns are influenced by infant mortality rates. When families have the expectation that the infant may die before the 1st year is up, they treat babies differently from families who don't consider their babies at risk for survival.

Adults with fears about survival concentrate on ways to save the baby, rather than worrying about attachment or emotional development (LeVine, 1977). The goal of saving the baby is so ingrained into the child-rearing practices that it isn't thought of in those terms. In fact, even a generation or more after the danger is past—say, the family climbs up the economic ladder and/or moves to a location where the infant mortality rate is vastly improved—the child care practices continue. Here are examples of caregiving behaviors when survival is the priority, according to the research of Robert LeVine (1977) at Harvard University:

1. The infant is on or near a caretaker's body at all times day and night, so he or she can be monitored. It is important to determine whether the baby is getting sick. It is also important to keep the baby out of danger when families live in conditions where babies have no safe place to be free to move about.

2. Crying is quickly attended to and becomes relatively rare. Caregivers know that it is important to eliminate other causes if they are to determine whether crying is a sign that the baby is getting sick.

3. Feeding is a frequent response to crying. The constant feeding helps prevent dehydration, which is the most common cause of death in infants throughout the world. Infants easily get diarrhea, which by itself isn't necessarily a killer—but the diarrhea causes the dehydration, which is.

4. There is relatively little treatment of the infant as an emotionally responsive individual (as in eye contact, smile elicitation, or chatting). The concern is to save the child's life. It may even be that attachment in the sense that we are discussing it in this chapter is delayed until the child gets through the difficult period when so many children are lost.

These are adaptive responses, and they influence attachment. Behavioral patterns such as those in the preceding list become customs that are ingrained in the cultural approach to infant care. It is hard to separate these survival practices from cultural values and attachment patterns.

JUDGING ATTACHMENT IN A CROSS-CULTURAL SITUATION

When a mother doesn't seem sensitive to the baby's emotional signals, seldom speaks to the baby, and/or never holds the baby in a face-to-face position so adult and baby can make eye contact, it is not clear whether these are functional or dysfunctional behaviors. Do they fit customs and expectations and make sense if viewed in cultural context? Or are they left over from a time when survival was the main issue? Or do they have another explanation? For example, in a situation in which the baby is never called by the given name, it is not immediately evident what is going on, unless you are of the same culture and social class as the family you're wondering about. If you don't thoroughly understand the culture and perhaps even the individual family, you can't make judgments about the way people are raising their children and whether they have a healthy attachment.

Language is another area in which an outsider may misjudge what is happening. European American middle-class families are very vocal, and all this vocalization is part of the attachment process. Watch most middle-class European American parents and you'll see that they talk face-to-face with their babies—chattering away as if the baby understands. They even wait for a response, creating a turn-taking situation that imitates real conversations in which both participants talk. Research (done by European Americans on European Americans for European Americans) shows the value of this kind of behavior, not only for attachment but also for future development. For example, this early emphasis on verbalization makes a difference later in school performance; children with good verbal skills do better academically.

In contrast, some families rarely speak to their infants. What is not clear to the outsider is how much the family is using *nonverbal* communication that the observer isn't aware of. Because a family doesn't behave the same as a European American middle-class family toward babies doesn't necessarily mean that there is an attachment problem—it may be more a matter of cultural difference.

CHILD CARE AND ATTACHMENT

A major concern of many who come from the tradition of mother-child attachment as an exclusive relationship is the question: What does child care do to attachment? The term *maternal deprivation* rings in the ears and sends chills down the spine. Horror stories of old-time orphanages come to mind—babies left to themselves in rows of cribs along sterile walls. The picture is heartbreaking. Those babies had no attachment, few interactions, little power to influence anyone in their lives, a feeling that no one cared about them, and a great lack of any kind of sensory stimulation. No wonder many died and the rest were left impaired. More recent orphanage pictures come to us from Rumania and China. Not pretty pictures!

From Budapest in Hungary comes a different picture. The children thrive in the Pikler Institute, founded after World War II by Dr. Emmi Pikler, a pediatrician and researcher. There attachment has been carefully thought through and fits into a comprehensive approach that has been studied by the World Health Organization. According to their results, children who spent their first 3 years in this residential care nursery end up as adults who show none of the signs of impairment that children from deprived orphanages show. A key factor is the approach taken to attachment described in a book called *Loczy: An Unusual Approach to Mothering* (David & Appell, 2001).

Effects of Child Care on Attachment

Child care is not an orphanage; the children have families who are raising them. Child care is supplemental to these families, not a replacement for them.

Children in child care have not just one person who cares about them—a parent—but often two or more. They usually arrive in child care already firmly attached to their own family and may well acquire a secondary attachment or two in child care. As far as sensory deprivation goes, child care usually has more than enough stimulation—not too little—especially for babies. The problem is cutting down to appropriate limits rather than raising stimulation to make up for other lacks.

A look to Israel reassures us that parents and children can remain attached even if the parents never live with their children or are never responsible for their day-to-day care. In some of the kibbutzim in Israel, where communal living was a norm and a value, children were raised from infancy separate from their parents. They visited their parents, but they didn't live with them. Full-time caregivers/teachers, rather than the parents, were in charge of child rearing and education.

Children can acquire secondary attachments in child care in addition to those at home.

There was no lack of attachment between parents and children in the kibbutzim. Attachment looked different because children split their attachment between parents and peer group. However, each child was well aware of his or her identity as a member of his or her own family—and each felt a sense of belonging.

When looking at the question of how attachment might be affected by child care, one has to ask: What kind of care? One huge problem in infant-toddler care is the lack of continuity. When babies have multiple caregivers in large group settings, they may never feel at home and secure. Further, in the name of developmental appropriateness, babies are placed in "classes" and "graduate" to the next level as they develop. For some that means being in one environment with one set of caregivers for a few months and then moving to another environment for another few months, and so forth, for the first 3 years. They may never get attached to anyone and if they do, the feelings of loss from being separated and leaving the object of their attachment behind can make them resist getting attached again.

Another question to ask when looking at the effects of child care on attachment to family is: What kind of family? Obviously if a family is overwhelmed by stress and the members are not functioning well, and a baby is born into the family at this point, the baby is at risk.

Let's say that a single mother, living by herself in a one-room apartment, doesn't have money to make ends meet, so she drinks herself into a stupor and the baby cries from hunger constantly. How will putting this child into child care influence his attachment? It's hard to tell, because it depends on what kind of child care. If the baby goes into a program where he gets consistent loving care, finds attachments, and gets the food he needs, and if his mother gets connected to the community resources she needs to get back on her feet, obviously the baby will do far better in child care than if he is left crying in that one room 24 hours a day. *In this situation child care is a lifesaver.*

Such programs exist. Some child care and early education programs in the United States today not only give quality care to children but also give families the support they need to get on their feet so they, themselves, can provide for their children's needs. These kinds of programs are cost-effective because they deal with attachment and other needs at the beginning rather than trying to fix problems that arise later (which is much more expensive) (Pawl, 1995; Raikes, 1996). We could use many more of these kinds of programs! *Prevention* is a key word when looking at early deprivation and attachment problems.

Unfortunately, these kinds of comprehensive programs are too few in number. If the baby in the example is placed in a child care program in which he never gets to know any of his caregivers and his mother gets little or no support, it's a different story. Attachment may be delayed because caregivers come and go too fast. Not one of the adults gets to know him well enough to read his signals, understand his uniqueness, become fond of him. Child care may save his life yet still not provide for his attachment and trust needs. Because of underfunding, that's the tragedy of the state of many child care programs in the United States today. The turnover rate of caregivers and teachers in underfunded programs is shocking.

You can't know exactly how child care affects attachment without considering countless variables that have to do with the quality of the care and the way the family works. One important aspect of quality care is the partnership between the parents and the program. When child care staff and providers develop a collaborative relationship with the parents that includes more than just parent education and involvement, everybody stands to gain—including the child!

What about the question of when to put a child into child care? Is there an optimum period? We can look at this question in more than one way. If you are to avoid the period of stranger anxiety and separation distress, putting a baby into child care before the age of 6 months or after a year or so may help the adjustment. In other words, *avoid* choosing 9 months as the age to start out-of-home care. However, at the same time, consider the establishment of attachment. Some parents worry that if they don't have enough time with the new baby—if they go back to work right away—they won't really become attached as firmly as they might. According to Caldwell (1987, p. 106), "If a baby has an insecure attachment to the mother, being placed in childcare at an early age may cause this already shaky relationship to become more so."

Some parents don't have much choice and won't until parental leave becomes a societal policy. It may reassure them to know that most studies have shown that babies become attached to their own parents even when child care is begun quite early.

How Caregiver and Parent Roles Differ

Good caregivers have many of the qualities of good parents, and those qualities promote attachment (Katz, 1980). One vital quality is sensitivity. When a caregiver learns to read each infant's signals, he or she can respond appropriately and in a timely fashion (if the staff-child ratio is good). Infants learn that they can give messages. They can influence the people in their world. They have personal power. They become attached.

The attachment not only grows out of the sensitivity and the ability of the caregiver to communicate but also promotes further communication. The infant becomes better at sending signals when someone is trying to read them. The caregiver gets better and better at reading them as he or she grows to know the baby as an individual. A synchronous relationship results.

Good caregivers and good parents have many similar behaviors and goals, but they also have some differences, which Lilian Katz, professor at the University of Illinois and a longtime leader in the field of early childhood education, wrote about. Katz (1980) says that the caregiver's attachment is necessarily short-term, and it's important for him or her to remember that fact. This child care arrangement isn't forever; the caregiver has little control over the future. It's the parents' job to have a vision for the child's future, just as they have the knowledge of the past. It's the parents—the family—who connect the child in time, giving a sense of continuity. The child has a life beyond child care; that's a fact that the caregiver must keep in mind.

Parents and caregivers differ in the degree of closeness that's appropriate. The goal of *parental* attachment is to establish *optimum closeness* with the child; the *caregiver's* goal is *optimum distance*. The child benefits from attachment to both, but it's a different kind of attachment. The caregiver must put limits on the degree of attachment; after all, the family may move out of town tomorrow. In addition, caregivers usually have other children to consider; they can't allow themselves to get completely wrapped up in just one to the neglect of the others.

Fairness is another category in which parents and caregivers differ. Parents can be advocates for their own children. They don't have to be fair and consider all the children in the program. It's appropriate for parents to focus on their own children. Caregivers can't afford to favor one child over another, but that doesn't mean that they must treat all the children in their care alike. Similar treatment in the face of differing needs doesn't create fairness.

Attachment in Full-Inclusion Programs

Full-inclusion programs are those where children with developmental differences, disabilities, and particular challenges are placed in child care with their typically developing peers rather than being separated into special programs. Every adult involved in such programs must aim to help all children feel they belong. That means that the children with exceptional needs must be integrated into the group. Unless the adults in the program have time and skill to facilitate this integration, some children may feel left out. Although this attention to integration is slightly different from the kind of attachment this chapter has focused on so far, it brings up the issue of attachment not just to an adult or two, but also to the group.

The work of Lev Vygotsky has implications for integration. Vygotsky worked at the Institute of Psychology in Moscow where he created what's called sociocultural theory, which emphasizes social interaction as an influence on development and learning. His *zone of proximal development*, or moving children forward from where they are to where they can be, involves peer interaction (Berk, 2001).

The goal is to help every child feel he or she belongs.

SUMMARY

Trust and attachment are lifelong issues. When conditions are right, parents and babies get "hooked" on each other right from the beginning. The relationship that results serves both well. It not only ensures the baby the nurturing and protecting he or she needs at the beginning, but also sets the stage for later relationships. Being attached feels good. It offers security.

This security is just what the baby needs to move out from the parent and become a fully functioning individual. That subject is the focus of the next chapter.

FOR DISCUSSION

1. Have you been aware of attachment occurring? Describe the kinds of interactions that encourage attachment that were part of this experience. Was synchrony involved? How did the attachment serve the people who were becoming attached? Tell about that experience.

2. What are your experiences with obstacles to the bonding or attachment process? Did the people involved get over or around these obstacles? How?

3. Discuss separation anxiety. What behaviors indicate the child is trying to keep the attached person from leaving? What emotions might a child display? How can an adult help the child to separate from the person he or she is attached to?

4. Have you had any experience with how child care might affect attachment? What are your ideas or thoughts about this subject?

REFERENCES

Ainsworth, M. D. S., & Bell, S. (1977). Infant crying and maternal responsiveness. *Child Development*, 48, 1208–1216.

Ainsworth, M. D. S., Blehar, M. C., Waters, E., & Wall, S. (1978). *Patterns of attachment: A psychological study of the Strange Situation.* Hillside, NJ: Erlbaum.

Berk, L. (2001). *Dialogues with children: Creating learning-environments at home and school.* New York: Oxford University Press.

Bower, B. (2000). Attachment disorder draws a closer look. *Science News*, 1157(22): 343.

Bowlby, J. (2000 [1969]). *Attachment and loss: Vol. 1. Attachment.* New York: Basic Books.

Braungart-Rieker, J. M., Garwood, M. M., Power, B. P., & Wang, B. (2001). Parental sensitivity, infant affect, and affect regulation: Predictors of later attachment. *Child Development*, 72(1), 252–270.

Brazelton, T. B., & Cramer, B. G. (1990). *The earliest relationship: Parents, infants, and the drama of early attachment.* New York: Addison-Wesley.

Bronfenbrenner, U. (2000). Ecological system theory. In A. Kazdin (Ed.), *Encyclopedia of Psychology.* Washington, DC: American Psychological Association & Oxford Press.

Butterfield, P. M., Martin, C. A., & Prairie, A. P. (2004). *Emotional connections: How relationships guide early learning.* Washington, DC: Zero to Three.

Caldwell, B. M. (1987, April). The tie that binds. *Working Mother*, 105–107.

Carlebach, D., & B. Tate. (2002). *Creating caring children: The first three years.* Miami: Peace Education Foundation.

Cernoch, J. M., & Porter, R. H. (1985). Recognition of maternal axillary odors by infants. *Child Development*, 56, 1593–1598.

Chang, H. (1993). *Affirming children's roots: Cultural and linguistic diversity in early care and education.* San Francisco: California Tomorrow.

David, M., & Appell, G. (2001 [1973, 1996]). *Loczy: An unusual approach to mothering.* Translated from *Loczy ou le maternage insolite*, by Jean Marie Clark; revised translation by Judit Falk. Budapest: Association Pikler-Loczy for Young Children.

DeCasper, A. J., & Fifer, W. P. (1980). Of human bonding: Newborns prefer their mothers' voices. *Science*, 208, 1174–1175.

Elliot, E. (2003, July). Challenging our assumptions: Helping a baby adjust to center care. *Young Children*, 58(4), 22–28.

Erikson, E. (1963). *Childhood and society.* New York: Norton.

Ferber, R. (1985). *Solve your child's sleep problems.* New York: Simon & Schuster.

Gandini, L., & Edwards, C. P. (Eds.). (2000). *Bambini: The Italian approach to infant-toddler care.* New York: Teachers College Press.

Gerber, M., & Johnson, A. (1998). *Your self-confident baby.* New York: Wiley.

Gonzalez-Mena, J. (1997, September). Understanding the parent's perspective: Independence or interdependence? *Exchange* (117), 61–63.

Gray, H. (2004, September). You go away and you come back: Supporting separations and reunions in an infant/toddler classroom. *Young Children*, 100–107.

Greenfield, P. M., Quiroz, B., Rothstein-Fisch, C., & Trumbull, E. (2001). *Bridging cultures between home and school.* Mahwah, NJ: Erlbaum.

Greenough, W., Emde, R. N., Gunnar, M., Massinga, R., & Shonkoff, J. P. (2001, April-May). The impact of the caregiving environment on young children's development: Different ways of knowing. *Zero to Three*, 21(5), 16–24.

Grether, J. K., Shulman, J., & Croen, L. A. (1990). Sudden infant death syndrome among Asians in California. *Journal of Pediatrics*, 116, 525–528.

Hesse, E., & Main, M. (2000). Disorganized infant, child, and adult attachment: Collapse in behavior and attachment strategies. *Journal of the Psychoanalytic Association*, 48(4), 1–5.

Honig, A. S. (2002). *Secure relationships: Nurturing infant/toddler attachment in early care settings.* Washington, DC: National Association for the Education of Young Children.

Howes, C., Ritchie, S. (2002). *A matter of trust.* New York: Teachers College Press.

Katz, L. G. (1980). Mothering and teaching: Some significant distinctions. In L. G. Katz (Ed.), *Current topics in early childhood education* (Vol. 3, pp. 47–63). Norwood, NJ: Ablex.

Lee, L. (2002). *Serving families: A handbook on the principles and strategies of the parent services project approach.* San Rafael, CA: Parent Services Project.

LeVine, R. A. (1977). Child rearing as cultural adaptation. In P. H. Leiderman, S. R. Tulkin, & A. Rosenfeld (Eds.), *Culture and infancy: Variations in the human experience* (pp. 15–27). New York: Academic Press.

Lieberman, A. F., & Zeanah, C. H. (1995, July). Disorders of attachment in infancy. *Infant Psychiatry*, 4(3), 571–585.

Main, M., & Solomon, J. (1990). Procedures for identifying infants as disorganized/disoriented during the Ainsworth Strange Situation. In M. Greenberg, D. Cicchetti, & E. M. Cummings (Eds.), *Attachment in the preschool years: Theory, research and intervention* (pp. 121–160). Chicago: University of Chicago Press.

McKenna, J. J. (1992, Winter). SIDS research. *Mothering* (62), 45–51.

O'Brien, M. (1997). *Inclusive child care for infants and toddlers: Meeting individual and special needs.* Baltimore: Brookes.

Pawl, J. H. (1995, February–March). The therapeutic relationship as human connectedness: Being held in another's mind. *Zero to Three*, 15(4), 48–49.

Pinto, C. (2001, Spring). Supporting competence in a child with special needs: One child's story. *Educaring*, 22(2), 1–6.

Raikes, H. (1996, July). A secure base for babies: Applying attachment concepts to the infant care setting. *Young Children*, 51(5) 59–67.

Rofrano, F. (2002, January). "I care for you": A reflection on caring as infant curriculum, *Young Children*, 57(1), 49–51.

Schneider, B. H., Atkinson, L., & Tardif, C. (2001). Child-parent attachment and children's peer relations: A quantitative review. *Developmental Psychology*, 37, 86–100.

Shonkoff, J. P., & Phillips, D. (2001, April-May). From neurons to neighborhoods: The science of early childhood development—An introduction. *Zero to Three*, 21(5), 4–7.

Solomon, J., & George, C. (1999). The measurement of attachment security in infancy and childhood. In J. Cassidy & P. Shaver (Eds.), *Handbook of attachment* (pp. 287–318). New York: Guilford.

Stack, C. B. (1991). Sex roles and survival strategies in an urban black community. In R. Staples (Ed.), *The black family: Essays and studies* (4th ed.). Belmont, CA: Wadsworth.

Stern, D. N. (1985). *The interpersonal world of the infant.* New York: Basic Books.

Thevenin, T. (1987). *The family bed.* Garden City, NY: Avery.

Thomas, A., Chess, S., & Birch, H. G. (1963). *Behavioral individuality in early childhood.* New York: New York University Press.

Vinson, B. M. (2001, January). Fishing and Vygotsky's concept of effective education. *Young Children*, 56(1), 88–89.

Vygotsky, L. S. (1978). *Mind in society: The development of higher psychological process.* Cambridge, MA: Harvard University Press. (Original works published 1930, 1933, and 1935)

Werner, E. E. (1984, November). Research in review: Resilient children. *Young Children*, 40(1), 68–72.

Werner, E. E. (1995, June). Resilience in development. *Current Directions in Psychological Science*, 4(3), 81–85.

Werner, E. E. (2000, February-March). The power of protective factors in the early years. *Zero to Three*, 20(4), 3–5.

Werner, E. E., & Smith, R. S. (1992). *Overcoming the odds: High risk children from birth to adulthood.* Ithaca, NY: Cornell University Press.

Zimmerman, L., & McDonald, L. (1995). Emotional availability in infants' relationships with multiple caregivers. *American Journal of Orthopsychiatry*, 65(1), 147–152.

FURTHER READING

Barnard, K., & Brazelton, T. B. (Eds.). (1990). *Touch: The foundation of experience.* New York: Bantam.

Bernhard, J. K., & Gonzalez-Mena, J. (2000). The cultural context of infant-toddler care. In D. Cryer & T. Harms (Eds.), *Research to practice in infant-toddler care* (pp. 237–267). Baltimore: Brookes.

Bhavnagri, N., & Gonzalez-Mena, J. (1997, Fall). The cultural context of caregiving. *Childhood Education*, 74(1), 2–8.

Chang, H. N. L., Muckelroy, A., & Pulido-Tobiassen, D. (1996). *Looking in, looking out: Redefining child and early education in a diverse society.* San Francisco: California Tomorrow.

David, M., & Appell, G. (2001 [1973, 1996]). *Loczy: An unusual approach to mothering*. Translated from *Loczy ou le maternage insolite*, by Jean Marie Clark; revised translation by Judit Falk. Budapest: Association Pikler-Loczy for Young Children.

Derman-Sparks, L. (1995). The process of culturally sensitive care. In P. Mangione (Ed.), *Infant/toddler caregiving: A guide to culturally sensitive care* (pp. 40–73). Sacramento: Far West Laboratory and California Department of Education.

Egeland, B., & Farrell Erickson, M. (1999, October-November). Findings from the parent-child project and implications for early intervention. *Zero to Three*, 20(2), 3–9.

Gonzalez-Mena, J. (2001). *Multicultural issues in child care* (2nd ed.). Mountain View, CA: Mayfield.

Gonzalez-Mena, J. (2004, September). What can an orphanage teach us? Lessons from Budapest. *Young Children*, 58(5), 26–30.

Gonzalez-Mena, J., & Bernhard, J. K. (1998, Summer). Out-of-home care of infants and toddlers: A call for cultural and linguistic continuity. *Interaction*, 12(2), 14–15.

Honig, A. S. (2002). *Secure relationships: Nurturing infant/toddler attachment in early care settings*. Washington, DC: National Association for the Education of Young Children.

Phillips, C. B., & Cooper, R. M. (1992, June). Cultural dimensions of feeding relationships. *Zero to Three*, 12(6), 10–13.

Schneider, B. H., Atkinson, L., & Tardif, C. (2001). Child-parent attachment and children's peer relations: A quantitative review. *Developmental Psychology*, 37, 86–100.

Stern, D. N. (1990). *Diary of a baby*. New York: Basic Books.

Weissbourd, B., & Powell, D. (1990). For children's sake: Family-centered childcare. *Family Resource Coalition*, 9(1), 2–3, 18.

CHAPTER 2

Autonomy

In this chapter you'll discover . . .

- ◆ Why toddlers poke, prod, and bang everything they can get their hands on
- ◆ Why some adults teach children interdependence instead of independence
- ◆ What has to happen before children can learn to share, in the true sense of the word
- ◆ What toddler behaviors have to do with power issues
- ◆ What to do about biting
- ◆ How setting limits gives toddlers a sense of power
- ◆ How to handle separation problems
- ◆ Why those who work with toddlers should partner with parents

TODDLERS AND AUTONOMY

Sometime around the 1st birthday, most babies pull themselves to their feet and stagger forward. That first shaky baby step represents a huge developmental leap. The baby is now a toddler, and the central task of his or her life is to become a separate independent being. Erik Erikson (1963) calls this the *stage of autonomy* (see Figure 2.1). Of course, not all babies get up and take steps. Some children with disabilities go through the stage of autonomy without becoming mobile. The term *toddler* doesn't apply to all children, but most of the material in this chapter applies to both typically and atypically developing children sometime before the 4th year of life.

Many adults find the way that toddlers carry out this thrust for autonomy to be a headache. They see the behaviors that come along with this push for independence as difficult to manage. The theorists (who generally see things from a perspective that rates independence as a higher priority than interdependence) explain the meaning behind the behaviors and expect adults to understand and put up with the difficulties. The labels put on this stage by some parents (*the terrible twos*) and by some experts (*the terrific twos*) reflect the various ways to look at the behaviors of this stage. The words the theorists use to label the process are *seeking autonomy*, *separating*, and *individuating*. Experts are willing to concede that the behaviors associated with this stage are sometimes "difficult." The words parents commonly use are *stubborn*, *obstinate*, and sometimes even such loaded terms as *willful*, *contrary*, and *spoiled*.

SIGNS OF DEVELOPING AUTONOMY

What are the behaviors that indicate a child is becoming an autonomous individual who will one day be self-sufficient and self-reliant? The most notable are negativity, exploration, self-help skills, and a sense of possession.

Child's Stage	Approximate Age	Task		
Infancy	0 – 1	Basic trust	versus	Basic mistrust
Toddlerhood	1 – 3	Autonomy	versus	Shame and doubt
The preschool years	3 – 6	Initiative	versus	Guilt
School age	6 – 10	Industry	versus	Inferiority

Figure 2.1
Erikson's psychosocial stages of development
Source: From Erikson (1963).

Negativity

The first sign of the coming of one of these behaviors that signal developing autonomy is when the darling baby who happily opened his mouth for each bite of cereal or strained vegetables suddenly one day clamps his lips shut and turns aside. His meaning is clear. Without a word spoken, this is the beginning of "No!"

The theory says that the child can now begin to see himself as an individual separate from his mother or other object of attachment. He finds power in his difference— he's not the same person as this adult in his life. He finds power, and he uses it.

This is only the beginning. By 2 years of age, this child is likely to be contrary about everything. If his mother likes peas, he hates them. If his father wants to take him for a ride, he balks. He refuses to get into the bathtub, and when he is finally coaxed in, he refuses to get out again. Life becomes a struggle because he is so busy asserting his individuality.

Sometimes toddlers say no so much because they hear the word all the time. If parents or caregivers use the word *no* as the primary means of managing behavior, the first *no*'s of their children may be imitations of adults.

However, even if adults use a variety of means of guiding behavior and minimize the number of *no*'s in their child's life, toddlers still learn to say that magic word.

It's important to realize that learning to say no is a vital skill. What would your life be like if you never said no to anything? Do you remember the temptations of your teen years? Do you wish you had learned to say a good strong "No!" earlier? What are your temptations now? Do you find saying no a useful skill in your life today? How much do you remember about your own toddler years? Did the adults who were in your life regard your *no*'s as skill building, or as defiance of their authority? Their perception of you then may influence *your* perception of children in the toddler stage now.

Exploration

Exploration starts in infancy and grows out of attachment and increases as children move toward autonomy. It may seem ironic that a child who is firmly attached explores more than one who is not. But it makes sense if you think of the attachment as providing a secure base to move out from. In fact, you can even see this phenomenon in action by watching a parent and a young child who are in a strange environment. The child will move out from the parent but will check back regularly. Sometimes it's just a glance; other times she runs back to the parent and clings for a moment before venturing out again.

The other factor in exploration is the freedom to move that the child is given in infancy. The research of Dr. Emmi Pikler indicates that babies who develop their movement skills independent of adults learn that they are capable individuals. Their trust in their own skills make them remarkable explorers (Gonzalez-Mena, 2004; Pikler, 1971, 1973; Pikler & Tardos, 1968). Babies in the Pikler Institute, a residential nursery in Budapest, are put on their backs where they have the most freedom to use their bodies. They are free of restrictive devices like infant seats, swings, even high chairs. No one puts the babies into positions they can't get into by themselves. Adults don't sit them up, stand them up, or walk them around. As they grow, these babies show an amazing sense of physical security. This same approach is also used by the staff at the Resources for Infant Educarers in Los Angeles, California. Founded by Magda Gerber and known as RIE, the program follows the teachings of Emmi Pikler, who was the teacher of Gerber (Gerber, 1979).

Infants who learn to use their bodies well and experience adult appeciation of their exploration urges become toddlers who move around a lot when they feel secure. Toddlers, without urging, spontaneously explore the space around them. In my classes I've asked students to observe a toddler in child care and to map the territory the child moves through. The maps that come out of these observations are amazing. A toddler can cover miles in a single day just by trotting back and forth across a room or a play yard.

Toddlers explore with their hands—and use their other senses as well. Given something new, they'll bang it, smell it, try to pull it apart, maybe throw it, and quite often taste it. They are little scientists. They want to know what everything can do—how it works.

Toddlers are "doers" but not "producers." They explore, experiment, and try things out to see what will happen. That means if you give them a toy or an activity that is designed to be used in a certain way, they're sure to try a dozen other ways to use it. They are not interested in outcomes or products. They enjoy the process of exploring and experimenting for its own sake, and they don't need anything to show for it.

Independence and Interdependence

Newborn babies are faced with two major tasks: (1) to become independent individuals, and (2) to establish connections with others. The parents' job is to help their children with these tasks. Most parents focus more on one task than the other. Some even ignore the other and leave its accomplishment to chance.

European American parents and researchers focus on *independence* and individuality, which is also the focus of this chapter. Parents from other cultures are more concerned about their children's ability to create and maintain connections. These parents have a different view of practically everything because of their focus on *interdependence,* or mutual dependence, instead of independence.

Parents whose primary goal is to establish and keep connections may have little concern about teaching their children self-help skills. For example, self-feeding may be postponed because feeding is a time in which connections are nourished. They may continue spoon-feeding long past infancy, into toddlerhood and beyond. This practice can get them in trouble if their child enters child care. Teachers may be shocked when a 3-year-old sits down at breakfast the first day and waits to be fed. Parents can be quite surprised and disappointed when they learn of a program's policy on self-help skills.

Although parents who stress independence look down on the idea of "coddling" children, to the parent focused on making connections there's nothing negative about doing things for children. These parents see no reason to keep from prolonging babyhood and continuing the closeness. Their attitude makes sense if you understand their goal. They worry about too much independence, so they try to discourage it. Independent-minded parents have the opposite worry. They fear that if they don't encourage independence, their children will remain dependent on them, maybe forever!

Parents who stress connectedness expect their children to be independent as well, but they believe it will happen naturally. In fact, they worry that the drive for independence is too strong; that's why they have to work so hard to maintain connections.

Self-Help Skills

Another behavior that indicates growing autonomy is the push for self-help skills. How the adults respond to this and to the exploring behavior will determine to some extent the child's adult behavior. Children who aren't allowed to touch or to try things on their own get a message about their own capabilities. When restricted to an extreme, they can lose their curiosity, their willingness to take risks, and their drive to be independent of others and do things for themselves.

Consider the difference between these two scenes:

Little Hannah has unbuckled herself from her car seat and is demanding that she be allowed to climb out of the car by herself. "Hannah do it!" she proclaims loudly.

She has never done this before and nobody knows if she can do it safely or not. Her father, annoyed by her demands, steps back out of reach and says in a sarcastic tone, "Go ahead, little girl, show me how grown up you are!" True to her father's expectations, she falls out the door and onto the ground. Crying, she reaches for her father. He picks her up and comforts her. Brushing away her tears, he tells her that she's too little to do things by herself. He makes it clear that she needs him. Later he tells the story, and the whole family laughs at the little girl who is "too big for her britches." It becomes a family joke—the "Let Hannah do it" joke.

Now let's replay that scene:

Here's Hannah, unbuckled from her car seat, demanding, "Hannah do it!" Her father, instead of trying to prove to her that she is too young, decides to help her find out what she can do, but he will protect her while she's making the discovery. Instead of being sarcastic and stepping back, he says, "I'm here if you need my help." He stands far enough away that Hannah can maneuver but close enough to help her if she needs it. She does fine until the slick sole of her shoe slips on the door frame. She starts to fall and reaches out a hand. Her father grabs it and restores her balance. She lets go of his hand, holds on to the armrest, and climbs the rest of the way out safely. They both rejoice at her accomplishment. Later her father tells the family proudly, "Hannah climbed out of the car by herself today!"

Consider the difference in the messages of the two scenes. Scene 1: "You're too uppity and you need a good lesson. When you learn it, you'll know that you're too young to try things on your own." In scene 2, the father encouraged self-help but

"Look, I can do it all by myself!"

provided the protection needed for Hannah to be successful. The Hannah of scene 2 sees her father as a facilitator of her independence; the Hannah of scene 1 does not.

When independence is a strong cultural priority, the first stirrings of it prompt adults to begin to encourage and facilitate it. However, in some cultures *interdependence* is the priority, and signs of independence may trigger a push on the part of the adult to work harder to promote the cultural goal. For example, in Japan some parents find their children too independent from the start, so they begin right away giving lessons in dependence. The goal is to help children see themselves as connected, not separate. When at about 9 months of age children begin to assert themselves—pushing away the adult hand trying to feed them, for example—the lessons in interdependence intensify. The specific objective is to teach children to accept help graciously, even if they can do it for themselves.

Sometimes adults share responsibility for the same child, and one pushes independence while the other struggles against the same behaviors. These two adults may be parents in a cross-cultural marriage or teacher and parent. If they are in disagreement about their goals and priorities for the child, they need to sit down and talk about their differences. It's hard on a child to have two conflicting approaches to deal with.

Self-Feeding.   Take, for example, self-feeding. The caregiver who values independence encourages self-feeding as soon as the baby grabs for the spoon or can pick up a teething biscuit and get it to her mouth. This caregiver gives the baby her own spoon and lets her help, and before long lets her feed herself—as soon as she can get enough in her mouth to count. Also, she cuts up small bits of appropriate finger foods and makes them available for the child to self-feed. Because what this caregiver does is considered developmentally appropriate practice among early childhood practitioners, she won't feel a conflict until she runs into a parent who see things differently.

Some parents have different priorities for toddlers. Self-feeding is not one of them. Their goal for their children is learning to help others rather than helping oneself. Therefore, they model helping skills by spoon-feeding children into the preschool years. They may justify their actions in a number of ways, including their desire to keep things neat and clean and not waste food, for example. When a caregiver and a parent see something like self-feeding from very different perspectives, arguments and angry feelings can result.

Toilet Training and Learning.   Toileting toddlers is another area where values of independence and interdependence can collide. Just as no culture produces adults who are unable to feed themselves, no matter how late they start, no culture produces adults unable to toilet themselves. But the approach and the timing are different depending on whether you believe in *toilet training* or *toilet learning*, which can be related to whether your stress is independence or interdependence.

Most experts discuss toilet learning, and they consider it from the independence perspective. Their advice is to watch for signs of readiness, which fall into three general categories: physical, intellectual, and emotional. *Physical readiness* means the ability to hold on and let go. A first sign is when children go for longer and longer periods with a dry diaper. Physical readiness also is determined by children's ability to handle their own clothing—pulling down pants, for example. A sign of *intellectual readiness* is when children tell the adult *after* eliminating or in other ways indicate that they are aware and can communicate what is happening with their own body. *Emotional readiness* comes when children show a willingness to use a potty or a toilet instead of diapers. The timing for these signs varies with each individual, but in general they seldom appear before the 2nd birthday.

An adult with a priority of interdependence may look at toileting from an entirely different point of view. This person won't wait for a couple of years to start but may start as early as a few months or even at birth to try to "catch" the baby and hold him or her over a potty. Readiness takes on a whole different meaning when the goal is interdependence. This approach emphasizes the training aspect rather than the learning aspect of toileting. It involves a conditioned reflex.

The experts in the United States frown on training children in the 1st year, partly because in the past this approach has sometimes been associated with using harsh methods. It is important to recognize that toilet training differences can be cultural and that harshness is not necessarily a part of the process. When a difference becomes apparent, it is important for one to set aside assumptions and judgments and talk about the differences until each party understands the other.

Here's how toilet training using a conditioning method works. Timing is crucial. Sometimes the caregiver can predict based on the baby's regularity. "Time to hold her over the potty," says the caregiver periodically. Also, the caregiver learns to read subtle body messages that indicate the baby is about to wet or defecate. The baby learns to let the caregiver know, and the caregiver trains the baby to let go at a signal—usually a shoosh or a whistling sound. It's truly amazing to a caregiver whose only experience is from the independence perspective how young babies and their caregivers can manage dry, clean diapers most of the time.

"It's the adult who's trained, not the baby!" is a common reaction to this interdependence approach. Caregivers who use the learning approach rather than the training approach are sometimes critical of those who train—and vice versa—yet each method works well for the adults and children who are using it. Both approaches eventually result in fully trained children who are able to handle all of their own toileting.

Toilet training or learning can become difficult when the child perceives that his or her autonomy is being usurped and fights back. Some children even feel that the adult is depriving them of something that is rightfully theirs—their body products! The resulting power struggle can be ugly and its effects long-lasting. Some children with an unfortunate toileting history may be left with big control issues that pop up in a variety of arenas. Whatever method you use, it is important to tread gently and avoid the use of harshness or force.

A Sense of Possession

It is important to note that not all cultures are object-oriented to the same extent and that not all regard personal possessions as important. In a culture that does prize possessions, a sense of ownership and its counterpart—a willingness to share—become important developmental steps. What many adults of this culture don't realize is that the one must come before the other. Without a firm sense of possession, children can't understand the concept of sharing.

There's quite a difference between the infant who doesn't have a sense of possession and the toddler who does. Most of us have seen babies receiving gifts that they have no feeling for or interest in. The adults have the concept of ownership—the baby doesn't. That picture is a contrast to the toddler holding a toy as far out of reach as possible and screaming "Me! Mine!" at an advancing playmate.

The immediate adult inclination is to rush in with a lesson on sharing. However, it's a little too soon for the lesson to be truly effective. This toddler is just beginning to get the concept of ownership. She is starting to see herself as a person with possessions. She needs to grasp that idea fully before she can understand the idea of sharing. She'll just harbor a grudge if you take the toy away and insist that she share it. Anger and grudges are not involved in the true spirit of sharing, which is the lesson most adults want to get across when they teach the behavior.

At this point the conflict between the two children over a toy is more a momentary power issue than anything else, and there are feelings on both sides. An effective way to intervene in this situation is to reflect the feelings of both parties rather than to

An effective way to intervene in this situation is to protect both children from getting hurt and to reflect their feelings by saying what you see in a nonjudgmental way.

discuss issues of sharing or fairness. For example, here's a scene between Olivia and Jacob, both 2-year-olds:

> *Olivia is triumphantly holding a rag doll in her arms. Jacob is standing near her, crying his eyes out. An adult is squatting beside them.*
>
> *"You both want that same doll, and Olivia has it," says the adult.*
>
> *Jacob sits down on the floor and screams in response to the adult intervention.*
>
> *"I see how unhappy you are, Jacob," says the adult.*
>
> *Olivia flaunts the doll in front of Jacob's face, saying again, firmly, "Mine!"*
>
> *Jacob grabs for the doll, connects, and jerks it away. Olivia is the one screaming now.*
>
> *"Jacob has the doll now," says the adult, announcing the action rather than making any judgment about it. Then the adult reflects the feelings. "You don't like it when he grabs things from you. You can tell him 'No!'"*
>
> *Olivia screams "No!" at Jacob's departing back. A moment later Jacob drops the doll to pick up a cloth book that is lying at his feet. Olivia starts for the dropped doll, then changes her mind and grabs a page of the book, yelling, "Mine!" Jacob starts to cry.*
>
> *The adult says, "You don't like that, Jacob! You don't like it when she grabs things. Tell her 'No!'"*

And so it goes. Now look at these two a couple of years later:

> *They are painting side by side at an easel. Olivia reaches for the brush that Jacob has in his hand—the one that goes in the green paint. "That's mine," says Jacob firmly.*
>
> *"No, it's not, it's the school's," says Olivia, "and I need it."*
>
> *"I'm using it," says Jacob.*
>
> *Olivia continues to reach for the brush and grabs hold of it so Jacob can't paint.*
>
> *"Stop that!" says Jacob.*
>
> *"I need the brush!" insists Olivia.*

"Can't you wait until I'm through?" asks Jacob.

"No," says Olivia.

"I have an idea," says Jacob. "There's another green brush on the other side of the easel. Let's get that one."

Olivia lets go long enough for him to reach to the other side and retrieve the brush and the paint container. "Here," he says, handing it to her.

"Thanks," she replies.

Later in the same year, at the same easel, Olivia asks Jacob for the brush he is using. He says to her, "I'm almost finished. You can have it in a minute." She waits until he is finished, uses it, and then gives it back to him.

These two have learned the behaviors of sharing and also the spirit. They have experienced the benefits. They understand the concept of possession and ownership. In cultures where private ownership is not an issue and personal possessions do not play a large part in people's lives, this sequence might be very different.

DEALING WITH ISSUES OF POWER AND CONTROL

The behaviors discussed—saying no, exploring the world, learning self-help skills, and gaining a sense of possession—all have to do with issues of power and control. Just as the *infant* came to experience a sense of power through signaling his needs and satisfying them by means of the adults around him, so does the *toddler* need to experience a sense of power through these typical toddler behaviors.

An adult can do much to facilitate this empowerment and the controls that need to go with it to keep the toddler and others safe and secure.

Set Up a Developmentally Appropriate Environment

A developmentally appropriate environment will provide freedom for exploration with few prohibitions. Think of the difference between a toddler in a playroom set up for her, versus spending an hour in Grandma's living room, trying to keep her hands off all the precious and fragile treasures sitting around on display. Yes, toddlers need to learn that there are some things they can't touch, but you can limit this lesson to a few times when it's important and spend the rest of the time teaching them that there are many things in the world that they *can* touch.

When toddlers spend their time in an environment that is appropriate for their age, they are freer to explore. They won't be faced with so many *no*'s. If they don't have to hear the word *no*, they may decrease their own usage of the word. It is worth thinking about what kind of environment says "Yes!" to toddlers, and then arranging things so that where they spend their time affirms their developmental needs. At this stage they touch, explore, try things out, and use their bodies to learn about the world. Their natural inclination is to climb, push, poke, prod, and perform a huge variety of other movements. They need a safe place to do all this—a place where they feel empowered rather than prohibited.

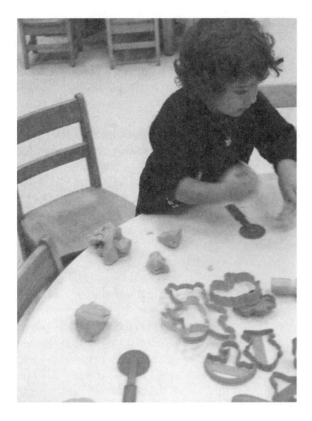

Provide a developmentally appropriate environment for youngsters.

Appreciate Play

Children gain power through playing. They play with themselves, other people, and objects. A baby who discovers her hand in the 1st year of life (called *hand regard*) is playing with herself. She stares at her hand, wiggles her fingers, and turns the hand around to get a different perspective on it. Some children find their own bodies endlessly fascinating. Later this same child will take a crayon in her hand and enjoy the feeling of circling her arm round and round. She doesn't care if the marks are on paper or on the wall, which is where they'll be if no one is monitoring her. The marks aren't the point of interest—the body movement is. Eventually the marks themselves become fascinating as she watches herself create them.

Children also play with people. They play with adults and with each other. Although the classic research by Parten (1932) labeled toddlers as mainly playing *parallel* to each other rather than *with* each other, a short period of observation in a child care program shows this isn't always so. An example of parallel play as described and named by Parten is in the sandbox when two 2-year-olds sit side by side, each shoveling sand and talking, but not paying obvious attention to each other. It may seem as though each is living in his own world, but when you listen you see that they are influenced by each other's play. They may not interact, but one picks up on what the other is saying or doing and incorporates it into his own play. Children today who are in child care or in other situations where they have peers in their lives daily go beyond parallel play into true interaction. They talk to each other, carrying on a back-and-forth conversation.

Children play with things. Anything within reach becomes a toy, as children reach out to learn about their world and the objects in it. They use all their senses. It may not seem important to adults to know how things taste and discover textures with their tongues. For babies, however, mouthing is a natural way to learn about any object they can get their lips around. That's why it is so important that young children be in a safe environment where they won't get hurt in their explorations. As they grow, their exploration of objects becomes more sophisticated, and they learn how things work and what they can do. In a consumer-oriented culture many adults place a high priority on toys and see them as educational. Even newborns are given toys and encouraged to touch, look, and hold them.

The typical child care program today relies on toys and other objects as part of their curriculum, and many programs have an abundance of things in their environment. These things may be recognizable commercially manufactured toys, or they may be "found objects" such as margarine tubs, egg cartons, and lids from frozen orange juice containers. Art supplies and materials include such items as wood scraps from a carpenter shop and homemade play dough consisting of flour, water, and salt. Construction materials made for children are also usually present in early childhood programs ranging from wooden blocks to small plastic pieces that link together. Although not literally objects, sand and water are considered educational materials in most programs.

Play has roots in imitation. From birth babies imitate what they see. If someone sticks his tongue out, even a newborn baby is likely to do the same. The adult is usually delighted at the baby's response to almost anything he does, and so begins a give-and-take sequence of playful interaction. The socialization aspects of this kind of play are obvious. The child is learning to take turns, which will become useful later when the baby has enough language to take part in real conversations. At the beginning the conversations are nonverbal and playful.

At first babies only imitate when they can see what they are imitating. By about 2, the typically developing child has moved from imitating only things he sees to playing pretend in creative and imaginative ways. Jean Piaget (1954, 1962), a pioneer in explaining cognitive development, had an explanation for the growing ability to pretend. The Swiss researcher explained that the shift occurs when children are able to make "internal representations" of things, actions, behaviors, and patterns. Piaget's stages of cognitive development have guided several generations of early childhood educators to understand more about how the intellect unfolds. The term *internal representations* means the child can hold images in her mind, and it is this ability that allows her to pretend. Using imagination, a block becomes a telephone and the child calls Daddy at work. Imaginary coffee comes out of toy coffee pots, and play dough rolled and molded becomes food. Although none of this may look *intellectual*, it is indeed an aspect of cognitive development. It is also vitally connected to self-development and socialization.

Encourage Self-Help Skills

Encourage children to do for themselves what they are capable of; don't do for them what they can do for themselves. This bit of advice comes from an author with a cultural priority on independence and may not apply to those from cultures who see early independence as a threat to interdependence. When independence is a priority, teaching self-help skills as a way of empowerment starts in infancy as the adult includes the child as a full partner in caregiving routines. For instance, diapering is a teamwork affair, and the baby is treated as a whole person worthy of respect, not just as a bottom that must be tended to while the top half is being entertained with something else.

This attitude of teamwork makes the toddler feel a little less rebellious because the adult is sometimes seen as a partner rather than as an adversary. It isn't a cure-all for rebellion, of course, because the struggle to defy the adult is a mark of the toddler stage.

When children are old enough to eat solid foods, giving finger food allows them to practice getting food to their mouths, even if they still need to be spoon fed. And before long they will want to take over completely. That means the adults have to put up with messy eating for awhile until children develop the skills to eat neatly. Children can learn to dress themselves at an early age if encouraged to do so. The learning process starts with undressing. Even a baby can pull off a sock that is sticking out from her toe. Setting it up so it is easy for her is encouraging self-help skills. Putting up with a less than perfect performance is also encouraging. Perfectionism on the part of the adult tends to discourage young children's self-help skills.

Give Choices

Help toddlers feel powerful by laying out options instead of giving a single directive. Instead of saying, "Get in that bathtub now!" offer an alternative such as, "Do you want to take a bath before supper or after?" When after supper comes and the child still balks, you can say, "After you get in, you can choose between the boats or the blocks to play with." And if the child still balks and it's time for a showdown, you can still give a choice: "Do you want to climb in by yourself, or should I put you in?" This way the child still feels empowered, and you are able to do what you perceive he needs to do. You're not being wishy-washy. The child *will* take a bath, but he has some choices about when, with what, and how he will enter the bathtub.

This is a culturally specific approach based on the concept of life as a series of choices. When you regard learning to make choices as important, you give children practice when they are young so that as they grow up they have had experience with making choices and living with the consequences. In cultures that don't see life in this same way and don't regard learning to make choices as important, giving toddlers choices doesn't make as much sense.

Provide Control

Provide the control toddlers need. Here are two scenes to illustrate that principle. Let's go back to Olivia and Jacob as 2-year-olds:

> They are playing happily and the phone rings. The adult turns her back to answer it, and Jacob grabs the toy Olivia has in her hand. Olivia, who hasn't learned to express her feelings in words yet (though the adults have been working on that) expresses her anger and frustration by sinking her sharp little baby teeth into Jacob's arm. Jacob lets out a yell, and the adult comes running. She scolds Olivia, telling her it isn't nice to bite, then puts her in a time-out chair. Olivia keeps getting up, so the adult continually puts her back, scolding her each time. Finally she hugs her, lets her up, and warns her not to bite again.
>
> Later that afternoon, when Olivia is tired and a little lonely for her mother and the adult is busy with another child, Olivia walks up to Jacob and bites his arm again. She remembers the stir it caused this morning, and she enjoys a repeat performance this afternoon. However, she feels vaguely uncomfortable because she knows that she should control that urge.

Contrast that scene with this one:

> Olivia and Jacob are playing together when the doorbell rings. The adult knows that Olivia has the urge to bite when she gets frustrated, so rather than taking the chance of leaving her alone with Jacob for even a minute, she takes Olivia with her to open the door.
>
> Later that morning, when Olivia and Jacob are playing together, Olivia gets frustrated. She makes a move toward Jacob's arm; before she can connect, the adult's hand covers her mouth gently. "I know you are unhappy, but I won't let you bite Jacob," she says in a clear tone that doesn't imply judgment—just fact. "You can bite this teething ring," she adds, "or this plastic toy." She offers the choice. Olivia grabs the teething ring and bites down hard. "You really are upset," affirms the adult.

This adult wisely provides the control that Olivia lacks at this age. She prevents the biting from occurring instead of dealing with it afterward in a way that rewards Olivia with extra attention.

Of course, it isn't realistic to assume that the adult will be there 100% of the time. Even with careful vigilance, Olivia might get her teeth into Jacob sometime. If that were to happen, the adult would then deal with the situation as a failure to control on her part—not as badness on Olivia's part. After all, Olivia is using her mouth to express her feelings in the only way she knows how. She lacks control—the control that it's up to the adult to provide.

If the bite occurs, the adult responds in much the same way she responded over the toy-grabbing incident earlier in this chapter. She approaches both children, modeling gentleness by touching them both lightly and lovingly. She says, "That really hurts, Jacob." To Olivia she says, "Jacob is unhappy because you hurt him." As she says the words, she touches gently the red place on Jacob's arm. Then she touches the same place on Olivia's arm. After the demonstration of gentleness and the words indicating the feelings, she deals with any first aid needed. She is careful not to give either child a great deal of the kind of extra attention that hooks children on either the victim or the aggressor role. She doesn't turn her back on Olivia and say, "Oh, poor little Jacob, let's put some ice on that bite—poor baby," because she knows that ignoring Olivia may make Jacob feel it's worth it to get bitten in order to enjoy this lavish sympathy. And Olivia is not left with the uncomfortable feeling of being ignored while realizing that she doesn't have the control she needs to keep from hurting someone. Being out of control is as scary for the person experiencing it as it is for the victim.

Set Limits

Setting limits and enforcing them also empower children by giving them freedom within those limits. You can think of limits as a fence around a pasture. The horse is free to graze within the fence. Without the fence his freedom would have to be limited by a rope, by vigilance, or by training—none of which gives the freedom of the fence.

Limits for toddlers work the same way. The limits may be environmental boundaries, such as a barricade across the stairs, a lock on the toilet lid, or a gate on the driveway. Or they may be human boundaries, such as consistently taking a child off a counter he insists on climbing up on, stopping a child from throwing toys, or holding a kicking child who threatens to hurt others.

Children will test limits until they find that they hold. The child locked out of the bathroom pounds on the door, jiggles the doorknob, and tries to poke something into the keyhole. He gives up when the physical barrier holds. Human boundaries are the same way. The child may continue to climb on the counter, and if the adult gives up and quits stopping him, he gets the message that this isn't a real limit—it doesn't hold if he's persistent enough. If the child is allowed to throw toys sometimes, he doesn't know there's a limit. His test shows that it doesn't hold up.

So to empower a child and provide security at the same time, it is necessary to set limits and hold to them. Because toddlers are persistent and are still discovering things about the world, you can also expect those limits to be tested until the toddler is satisfied that they're firm. The testing makes sense if you understand what's going on. If you don't, it seems as if the child is just trying to make you unhappy with his persistently unacceptable behavior. Don't get unhappy—just outpersist him!

Janice and Emily

Janice is 17 and has an 18-month-old, Emily, who is driving her crazy. Janice has just started in a teen parent program that allows her to continue her high school education. Emily is taken care of at the school in a portable building that has been set up for infants and toddlers. Although Emily protests at being left in the morning, which really bothers Janice, she quickly becomes contented while playing with the other babies. Janice misses her, so she pops in briefly between her classes—which almost always results in another crying spell when she has to leave again. That annoys Janice. Why can't she just come and go without all this fuss!

Whenever she is around Emily, the child clings to her, making it impossible for her to even walk from one place to another. Janice doesn't like this.

Janice also doesn't like it when the child care teachers assure her that Emily was fine all day and didn't miss her at all. That doesn't feel good. And she doesn't like the way Emily is beginning to hang around one of the teachers and even hugs her good-bye when they leave at the end of the day. Janice wonders whether Emily still loves her when she shows affection toward the teacher.

Some of Emily's other behaviors bother Janice as well. She doesn't like the defiant look Emily gets in her eye when Janice tells her to do something. That makes Janice feel angry, and she gets just as stubborn as Emily has become.

Sometimes she feels like hitting Emily, but she talks about that feeling in her parenting class, where she is learning a variety of ways to guide Emily's behavior. Somehow talking about hitting helps her control herself, so she doesn't do it. She's seen another child in the center whose mother got carried away with spanking and ended up abusing her daughter. It was pretty awful, both how the child looked and what happened to her mother. She ended up losing her baby. Janice couldn't stand to lose Emily, and she cries at the thought that she might ever hurt her. So she is careful to never spank her, no matter what.

Another thing that bothers Janice is how dirty Emily gets. She insists on doing things for herself—like feeding herself. She isn't very neat! And the child care staff doesn't seem to understand how important it is to Janice that Emily look like a sweet little doll. They let her feed herself, which means that often her clothes get messed up. Sometimes Janice comes in and finds Emily in the center's old beat-up clothes, because they ran out of changes for her. Janice doesn't like seeing her like this.

And the sand! Can't they understand how hard it is for Janice when Emily gets sand in her hair? It seems that whenever they go out in the yard, Emily ends up with her head full of sand. It's a lot of trouble to wash that out and redo her hair. Besides, Emily *hates* to have her hair washed and puts up quite a fight.

This is all so different from when Emily was younger and she used to just lie around and laugh and look cute. It was a lot easier then. But this is a different stage, and it isn't so easy!

Janice knew that none of this would be easy when she decided to keep Emily. She had lots of warnings about the life of a teen mother. But with her family's support and the help of the center staff, she's making it. And Emily is an important part of her life!

COPING WITH LOSS AND SEPARATION

Separation issues start in infancy and continue into toddlerhood and beyond; they are never handled once and for all. The infant who has learned to sleep alone may well become the toddler who, because new fears arise, balks at going to bed and staying there. Even though a toddler copes very well with separation and independence during waking periods, she may resist sleep because she must give up the control she has. Lack of control can be very scary because it means that coping mechanisms don't work in the same way they do during waking periods. In addition, dreams, which can also create fear, enter in. Parents and child care teachers who recognize this fact will be more understanding when children develop sleeping problems at home or react badly to sleeping away from home.

Taking Separation in Small Steps

It is easier for children if they first experience separation in small steps. Sleeping alone is one of these steps. Having a babysitter or being away from the person(s) they are attached to for short periods are other examples of steps of separation.

With a succession of periods away from the parent(s), either at home or away from home, children come to trust that the attachment holds and that they will be reunited.

Be aware of the dangers of giving children more to cope with than they can handle. If parents feel a need to take an extended vacation away from their child, they should realize the possible effects of a prolonged separation during the toddler period. Obviously, if the child has someone else he or she is attached to, the effects of such a separation won't be as serious as if the only person or two people in the world the child feels close to suddenly disappear for a few weeks. Such an interruption in attachment can be devastating to the child's sense of trust.

Some sudden and prolonged separations can't be helped, of course. If the child must undergo an extensive hospitalization, he or she will get through it better if parents stay at the hospital with the child or at least visit frequently. Visiting isn't the perfect solution because of the continual anguish of painful good-byes; it's better if a parent can stay with the child. When this isn't possible, visiting is preferable to nothing, even though parents may be tempted to cut down on their visits because of the pain their departures cause the child. But children who feel deserted can experience depression, according to the research of John Bowlby (2000a, 2000b), who studied the effects of long-term separations in childhood.

When both parents work, sometimes separation problems can be minimized by hiring a nanny if the family can afford it. With a nanny, the child can stay in a familiar setting with one familiar person. The problem is that the child may get overly attached to someone who is an employee rather than a friend or a relative. Employees come and go, in most cases without causing too many disruptions. However, when a nanny quits, the child can experience untold grief.

Entering Child Care

When a separation such as going into child care is on the horizon, it's best to prepare the child (McCracken, 1986). Imagine being the child of a mother who has been with you day and night for the first 2 years. Your mother suddenly decides to go back to work, and one day she drives you to a strange place and leaves you there for the entire day. How would you feel?

It's far gentler to visit beforehand and to keep the first experiences short, so the child gets to know the place and the people. Being left for only an hour or so in the beginning, the child learns that the parent will return after a time. If the day is gradually lengthened, the child gets used to it and it's not such a shock.

Helping Children Adjust.   Some children walk right into child care without batting an eye. They're so intrigued with the new setting that they forget their fears. Other children cling and suffer greatly. In this case it helps to let the child make the decision to separate rather than peeling him off and walking out the door, leaving him screaming.

One program has a room for the use of parents whose children hesitate to leave them. The doorway just beyond the separation room is open and is filled with the sounds and sights of children playing, which serve to entice the child to leave the parent's side. Parents are asked to be patient about the separation process, and they're given some help and support to make it a healthy coping experience for both parent

Some children walk right into child care without any fear. Other children are less brave about the new situation.

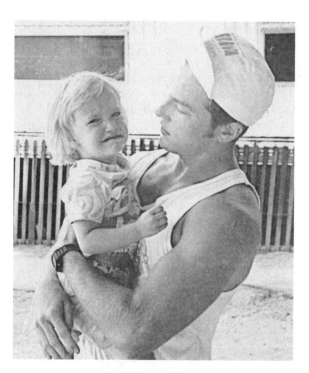

and child. Of course, everyone doesn't have the option of a slow departure. However, if more people understood the value, they might find ways to open up their options.

When the good-byes come, it helps to make things predictable. When parents sneak out and leave the child playing without saying good-bye, trust issues arise. Instead of feeling secure, the child is left with the feeling he or she never knows when the parent is there or gone. How can the child feel any power in the world if there's no way to predict what will happen? Saying good-bye may bring tears and protests, but it's the open, honest way of helping the child understand what's happening.

Accepting Feelings. When strong feelings are a part of the good-byes, it's important to acknowledge and accept the feelings rather than distracting the child from them. If the adult has leftover issues of separation and loss from childhood, it may be very hard for him or her to deal with the child's feelings. It's just too painful. If that's your problem, it's important to recognize how your own unresolved issues may be influencing your ability to deal with a child in the throes of a separation. Separation experiences remain with us—especially the unexpressed and unresolved feelings. Bringing these to awareness can help us cope with them in ways that are healthy for us and allow us to be available to the child who needs us.

Many adults who find separation painful because of their own experiences do whatever they can to distract the child and not acknowledge what he or she is feeling. Far better to put the child's feelings into words: "You're upset that your mother left you." It's also important to emit a sense of confidence that the child will be all right and that she will be reunited with the loved one. Don't go overboard, however. If you constantly reassure the child, she'll begin to wonder whether you're reassuring yourself because what you're saying is not true. Better to be empathetic about the feelings and reassuring without discounting them.

It's also important to recognize that parents may have strong feelings about separation. It may hurt to leave their child with someone else. They may feel guilty. Some parents prolong good-byes because of their own feelings of ambiguity. These slow departures can be torture to everyone, especially if the child has shown willingness to be left but has second thoughts because of the way the parent is dragging his or her feet. In these situations, caregivers sometimes have to help parents see how the child's feelings are affected by their reluctance to leave. Caregivers need to support parents and accept their feelings in the same way they do with children, without supporting detrimental actions such as agonizing, lingering departures.

Helping Children Cope. Some children are comforted and reassured by what's called a *transition object*—some kind of comfort device, such as a stuffed animal or a favorite blanket. Having something from home that they're attached to provides a link between home and child care. Leaving something of the parents at child care can help, too. One child was comforted when his mother left her purse (she carried her wallet with her) because he figured if she forgot to come back for him, she'd at least remember her purse. He knew how important it was to her.

Providing something to do that's compelling and interesting is a good technique for helping the child cope with feelings of loss. Often the child will migrate to an

Some children are comforted and reassured by what's called a "transition object" such as this boy's blanket.

interesting activity or a friendly person after the pain of arrival is beginning to pass. Don't hurry this process of moving to an activity or other person, however. Give time for the feelings. There's a fine line between helping children cope with feelings and distracting them from those feelings. It is important that the feelings be accepted and acknowledged.

In addition, allow the child to play out the feelings. Often you can see children over among the dolls or out in the sandbox, working through what's on their minds. This is a healthy way to deal with feelings that may be hard to express directly in words.

PARTNERING WITH PARENTS OF TODDLERS

Throughout this chapter, mention was made of partnering with toddlers. This section focuses on parents as partners. Some teachers and child care providers consider the child their client. They'd just as soon leave the parents out of the picture. This book takes the opposite view. Parents are the client and the child comes embedded in a family context. Teachers and providers always have to think of child and family together.

There is no way to separate the child from the family. I remember the impression I got from taking my first child development course. The textbook was called something like *The Child*. I know now that there's no way to study children out of context. It's like disembodying the child. You can't study children without taking into consideration that they come with a body. You can't understand a child without taking into consideration that he or she comes with a family.

Partnering with parents goes beyond just educating them or requiring that they be involved in the program. Partnerships have to do sharing, collaboration, participation. Partners do not necessarily bring the same things to the partnership, but two partners often complement each other. If one feels superior and regards the other as inferior, those complementary strengths may never be acknowledged.

It's hard to be an educated early childhood professional in a profession that lacks status and not put yourself above parents who don't have your training and background. Obviously you have a lot to offer them. But they have a lot to offer you too. Nobody knows their child the way they do. Nobody has the history or the vision of the future for this child. If information is shared in a give-and-take way, it's a lot better than if one person just hands it down to the other. Everybody stands to gain when parents and professionals are partners—not least of all the child!

For example, say a child is displaying a good deal of defiance and other kinds of negative behavior, and the parent is thinking that the child's personality is somehow warped. You can offer up the information that you have about the stage of autonomy and that may help the parent see the behaviors in a slightly different light. If this is a first-time parent, he or she may not realize that children aren't 2 forever. You can lend perspective the parent may not have. On the other hand, you may wonder why this child crawled under the table and refused to come out when the nurse came to give eye exams. The parent might tell you something you didn't know about the child's medical history and the painful procedures he had to go through for a long time. Maybe you didn't know that he had been hospitalized periodically. With this knowledge the extreme reaction makes more sense.

SUMMARY

This chapter explored the variety of behaviors that accompany the task of developing autonomy. It looked at exploration and self-help skills, as well as examining ways of handling behavior that is difficult, ways of empowering children, and helping children cope with separation and loss. It took a quick look at the value of play, which is carried on as an important theme in the next chapter.

FOR DISCUSSION

1. Do you agree that negativity, exploration, self-help skills, and a sense of possession are indeed signs of developing autonomy? What are some examples? Can you think of other signs?

2. Have you ever known a family that valued interdependence over independence? Which parts of this chapter would not pertain to them? Which parts would?

3. How much do you help a child who is struggling to do something on his or her own? What experience do you have in teaching self-help skills? Do you agree that children should be given opportunities to do things on their own, or do you feel better about helping children, especially when they are struggling? Which was stressed more when you were growing up—independence or interdependence?

4. How does typical toddler behavior relate to power issues? Can you give an example of how an adult can empower a toddler? Does everyone agree that toddlers need to feel powerful? How are power and autonomy related?

5. Saying good-bye can be hard for some children. What experience do you have with helping children cope with separation issues? What advice would you have for a parent who is leaving his or her child in child care for the first time? What advice would you have for the teacher/caregiver or family child care provider of that child?

REFERENCES

Bowlby, J. (1969). *Attachment and loss: Vol. 1. Attachment.* London: Hogarth.

Bowlby, J. (2000a [1972]). *Attachment and loss: Vol. 2. Separation: Anxiety and anger.* New York: Basic Books.

Bowlby, J. (2000b [1980]). *Attachment and loss: Vol. 3. Loss: Sadness and depression.* New York: Basic Books.

Carlebach, D., & Tate, B. (2002). *Creating caring children: The first three years.* Miami: The Peace Education Foundation.

Erikson, E. (1963). *Childhood and society.* New York: Norton.

Gerber, M. (1979). *The RIE manual.* Los Angeles: Resources for Infant Educarers.

Gonzalez-Mena, J. (2001, September). Making meaning of separation: Contrasting pictures of the first good-bye. *The First Years, Nga TauTuatahi* (New Zealand Journal of Infant and Toddler Education), 3(2), 4–5.

Gonzalez-Mena, J. (2004, September). What can an orphanage teach us? Lessons from Budapest. *Young Children,* 59(5), 26–30.

Gray, H. (2004, September). "You go away and you come back": Supporting separations and reunions in an infant/toddler classroom. *Young Children,* 59(5), 100–107.

Greenfield, P. M., Quiroz, B., Rothstein-Fisch, C., & Trumbull, E. (2001). *Bridging cultures between home and school.* Mahwah, NJ: Erlbaum.

Greenough, W., Emde, R. N., Gunnar, M., Massinga, R., & Shonkoff, J. P. (2001, April-May). The impact of the caregiving environment on young children's development: Different ways of knowing, *Zero to Three,* 21(5), 16–24.

McCracken, J. B. (1986). *So many good-byes: Ways to ease the transition between home and groups for young children.* Washington, DC: National Association for the Education of Young Children.

National Association for the Education of Young Children (1996, January). Linguistic and cultural diversity position paper. *Young Children,* 51(2), 4–12.

Parten, M. B. (1932). Social participation among preschool children. *Journal of Abnormal Psychology,* 27, 756–759.

Piaget, J. (1954). *The construction of reality in the child.* New York: Ballantine.

Piaget, J. (1962). *Play, dreams and imitation in childhood.* New York: Norton.

Pikler, E. (1971). Learning of motor skills on the basis of self-induced movements. In J. Hellmuth (Ed.). *Exceptional infant* (vol. 2, pp. 54–89). New York: Brunner/Mazel.

Pikler, E. (1973). Some contributions to the study of gross motor development of children. In A. Sandovsky (Ed.), *Child and adolescent development* (pp. 52–64). New York: Free Press.

Pikler, E, & Tardos, A. (1968). Some contributions to the study of infants' gross motor activities. Proceedings of the 15th International Congress of Applied Psychology, Amsterdam.

Szanton, E. S. (2001, January). For America's infants and toddlers, are important values threatened by our zeal to "teach"? *Young Children,* 56(1), 15–21.

Van Hoorn, J., Nourot, P., Scales, B., & Alward, K. (2003). *Play at the center of the curriculum* (3rd ed.). Upper Saddle River, NJ: Merrill/Prentice Hall.

Vinson, B. M. (2001, January). Fishing and Vygotsky's concept of effective education. *Young Children,* 56(1), 88–89.

FURTHER READING

Bernhard, J. K., & Gonzalez-Mena, J. (2000). The cultural context of infant-toddler care. In D. Cryer & T. Harms (Eds.), *Research to practice in infant-toddler care* (pp. 237–267). Baltimore: Brookes.

Gerber, M. (1979). *The RIE manual.* Los Angeles: Resources for Infant Educarers.

Gonzalez-Mena, J. (1995). Cultural sensitivity in routine caregiving tasks. In P. Mangione (Ed.), *Infant/toddler caregiving: A guide to culturally sensitive care* (pp. 12–19). Sacramento: Far West Laboratory and California Department of Education.

Gonzalez-Mena, J. (2000, July). In the spirit of partnership: High maintenance parent or cultural difference? *Exchange,* 134, 40–42.

Gonzalez-Mena, J. (2001). *Multicultural issues in child care* (3rd ed.). Mountain View, CA: Mayfield.

Gonzalez-Mena, J. (2004, September). What can an orphanage teach us? Lessons from Budapest. *Young Children,* 59(5), 26–30.

Gonzalez-Mena, J., & Bernhard, J. K. (1998, Summer). Out-of-home care of infants and toddlers: A call for cultural and linguistic continuity. *Interaction,* 12(2), 14–15.

Gray, H. (2004, September). "You go away and you come back": Supporting separations and reunions in an infant/toddler classroom. *Young Children,* 59(5), 100–107.

Harmon, C. (1996, May). In the beginning: Helping parents and children separate. *Young Children,* 51(4), 72.

Lieberman, A. F. (1993). *The emotional life of the toddler.* New York: Free Press.

Szanton, E. S. (2001, January). For America's infants and toddlers, are important values threatened by our zeal to "teach"? *Young Children,* 56(1), 15–21.

CHAPTER 3

Initiative

In *this chapter you'll discover* . . .

- ◆ How guilt helps or harms children and what determines which it does
- ◆ What children get out of playing
- ◆ The difference between a child with high energy and one who is hyperactive
- ◆ Whether all shy children are shy for the same reason
- ◆ How some children learn to be aggressive
- ◆ What can be done about aggression in young children
- ◆ Some considerations for supporting play in children with special needs

The United States is built on individual initiative, which has a high value for many in this country. When does initiative begin to develop? What factors facilitate its development? How do adults socialize children to have initiative?

According to Erik Erikson (1963), initiative is the developmental task of the 3- to 6-year-old. The child of preschool or kindergarten age, whether in a program or at home, is usually bursting with initiative. Sometimes the behavior behind these urges gets the child into trouble, especially around adults who don't understand developmental ages and stages. Take a look at Briana, a 4-year-old who shows initiative.

WHAT INITIATIVE LOOKS LIKE IN A 4-YEAR-OLD

Briana runs in the door of her child care center, leaving behind her mother, who is still coming up the steps. She flings a hasty "Hi" at the teacher seated by the door, glances at the interesting "science" display set out to capture the interest of the arriving children, tosses her coat at a hook on the rack by the door, and runs into the classroom with her teacher on her heels.

"Whoa," says her teacher good-naturedly. "Let's go back and do that again." She gently guides Briana back toward her coat on the floor, where her mother waits. Briana kisses her mother good-bye and then starts to take off again. Her teacher grabs her as she goes by. She patiently reminds her again to hang up her coat, which Briana does hastily. Then, released from the teacher's grasp, the lively girl takes off again into the classroom at a fast clip. She heads straight for the art table, which is set up with wood scraps and glue. She elbows her way into a spot at the table, finds an interesting assortment of wood within reach, and begins applying glue to various pieces, which she stacks one on another. She works busily for quite a while, absorbed in what she is doing. After her flighty entrance, the focused attention is quite a contrast. At last she looks up from her project. Turning to a boy sitting next to her, she remarks, "I'm making a house."

He answers, "I'm making a spaceship. See how it launches?" He waves his creation in the air several times. Briana ducks and then turns to the boy on the other side of her. "My mommy's gonna have a baby, and I'm making her a bed," says Briana. The boy ignores her, concentrating on his gluing. Briana goes back to work on her project, concentrating her whole attention on the wood in front of her.

"I need scissors," says Briana to the teacher, who is seated at the end of the table. "I need to put something here," she says, indicating a spot on her wood project. The teacher looks interested and says, "You know where the scissors are."

Briana gets up with her creation in her hand and dances to a nearby table set up with scissors, crayons, various kinds of paper, hole punches, and tape. She sits down at the table and carefully chooses a piece of yellow paper. She painstakingly cuts the paper into an irregular shape, folds it in half, and glues it on a piece of wood sticking out at right angles from the central core of her work. It takes her about 10 minutes to complete this task. She gets up to leave and then turns back to the table, picks up the paper scraps she left there, and hurriedly glues them on too. Then she grabs a pencil, writes a B on the paper, then another B, and then a third. She then "flies" her sculpture over to the art table and passes it under the nose of her teacher, saying, "I wrote my name on my art."

She gives her teacher a hug. The teacher hugs her back. "I see," is the response. Then, "If you're finished, put your art in your cubby."

Briana flies her sculpture to a row of lockers by the coat rack, pokes it inside one of them, and takes off running to the dramatic play area. She ignores the children already there and pulls out a frilly smock from a box of clothes, puts it on, pats it down the front, looks in the mirror, and turns away satisfied. She flounces over to the little table, sits down, picks up a small empty teacup, and pretends to drink.

"You can't play," announces a girl already seated at the table. Briana ignores her and continues slurping noisily into the cup. Then she gets up and takes the cup and the pot with her to the sink, where she swishes them around in the soapy water she finds there. She stands there for a long time, relishing the sensory experience. "Let's play house," suggests a boy, thrusting his hands into the soapy water.

"OK," agrees Briana. "I'll be the mom," she says.

"I'm the mom," says the girl who told her she couldn't play.

"Then I'll be the *other* mom," says Briana, squeezing a sponge out and carrying it over to wipe off the table. "You're my baby," she announces to the boy, who immediately falls to the ground and clings to her foot, clawing at her legs and making a whimpering sound.

"Stop being bad!" Briana scolds him in a harsh voice. "Bad baby, bad, bad, bad!" she screams angrily. The boy cries louder. A teacher passing by smiles at them and continues on her way.

"Pretend I have to spank you," Briana tells the boy. He responds by crying even louder.

She gives him a couple of dramatic whacks, which only connect lightly. He screams in agony. Then she gives him a third whack, which accidentally lands hard.

"Hey, stop that! You hurt me." The boy jumps to his feet and his voice becomes his own. He looks mad.

A quick look of surprise, a touch of fear, then remorse comes across Briana's face. She hastily retreats to where four children are lying on cushions looking at books. She flings herself to the ground and takes a book out of the hand of the only child within reach.

"Don't!" protests the child, reaching to grab it back. Briana holds up a hand as if to slap her, then slowly lowers it. She turns two pages of the book carefully and deliberately, then tosses it back toward the waiting child, gets up, and leaves.

Seeing the door open, she runs toward it, snatching off the smock and dropping it on the floor as she runs. She stops, looking around to see whether a teacher has spotted the smock on the floor. No teacher is around. Briana hesitates. Then she goes back, picks up the smock, and takes it over to the box where she found it. She dumps it in and hurries back to the open door. She pauses in the doorway for a moment, glancing around. Then she shouts "Sarah!" joyfully and runs down the ramp into the play yard.

ANALYZING INITIATIVE IN A 4-YEAR-OLD

Let's examine that scene in terms of initiative. Because Briana is now 4 years old, she is able to use her fertile imagination quite effectively, and she can solve problems. She is also becoming increasingly more competent in her physical abilities and communication skills.

Her attention span has lengthened, and she can spend long periods in concentrated focus. She's active, curious, and energetic. A phrase that describes Briana is *get-up-and-go*. She's got it!

What does she do with all this energy and newly developed ability? She uses it to make decisions about what she wants to do. She is so interested in everything that you could almost describe her as in an "attack mode." It's not a negative kind of attacking but a thrusting kind of energy that propels her toward activities and materials that seem to draw her. Briana needs no motivation from her teachers to get involved. She has her own inner motivation.

Much of what Briana undertakes is spontaneous, but that doesn't mean that she is incapable of planning and executing a plan. For example, she had something definite in mind when she asked the teacher for scissors at the wood-gluing table. The teacher, understanding the value of encouraging initiative, responded in a positive way instead of restricting Briana to what was available on the table for that particular project. Briana also had something definite in mind when she scanned the play yard, found Sarah, and headed over to play with her.

It's important to note that some children are as active as Briana but lack her ability to focus attention and concentrate on any one thing. They don't plan out what they want to do but impulsively rush from one thing to another, perhaps destroying things in their path. These children may not yet have learned to channel their energy. Or perhaps they are overstimulated by too many choices or too much going on around them. Just because they are not displaying the same kind of high energy that goes with the stage of initiative, some adults may think of them as hyperactive. Indeed the word *hyper* is now commonly used for children who move a good deal and have trouble being still. Although there is a condition known as an *attention deficit/hyperactivity disorder* (ADHD) (Barkley, 1997) there is some controversy over diagnosing and treating children as young as 3 or 4.

Julie and ADHD

Julie is a 7-year-old who has just been diagnosed as having an attention deficit/hyperactivity disorder (ADHD). In a way, her mother, Shannon, is glad to get the diagnosis because it confirms her idea that Julie is not "bad." She has been worried about her for a long time. It seems as though Julie was born kicking. She was an irritable baby who cried a lot. She seemed to sleep very little. She was in constant motion and she hasn't slowed down yet. Once she got on her feet, life got even harder, if that was possible. Julie was into everything. She never sat still for a minute. Shannon compared her with a neighbor child, Hannah, and saw that Julie was very different. By age 4, Hannah would sit for periods of time looking at books or drawing with crayons. Julie never did that. When she looked at a book, she flipped through at a rapid rate, threw the book down, grabbed another one, threw it down, and was off to something else in the space of less than a minute. In fact, none of Julie's activities lasted more than a minute. What was wrong?

Shannon decided to send Julie to preschool, but that didn't help much. Although it gave Shannon a few hours of peace each day, the reports from school kept her in a constant state of tension. Every week it was something new. "What can we do about Julie's behavior?" the teachers kept asking. "She's so impulsive that she constantly makes decisions that result in unfortunate consequences. But she doesn't seem to learn from her mistakes. She just keeps jumping into things and making rash decisions." Shannon felt discouraged that they called her in for her ideas and opinions. Why didn't they know how to handle Julie? They were the trained experts!

When the school called a meeting and the teachers and Shannon sat down and did some brainstorming, things improved. They all shared ideas and information about what worked best at home and what worked best at school for Julie. One of the problems was that preschool was so stimulating. There was just so much to do that Julie was overwhelmed with the number of choices. She ended up constantly running around and not doing anything. Also, the room tended to be noisy and sometimes a little chaotic when all the children were inside. Julie reacted to the high energy level of the classroom by losing what little control she had.

At home two things captured her attention: television, sometimes, and video games, almost always.

Things didn't improve by kindergarten, and 1st grade was a nightmare. When the school finally suggested that testing Julie might be in order, Shannon felt relieved. When she got the results, she felt even more relieved. However, then she was faced with the question of whether to medicate Julie. That's where she is right now. She has joined a parent support group and is discussing the decision of whether to go for medication.

DEVELOPMENTAL CONFLICTS

With all the energy and activity that this stage of initiative brings with it, Briana is bound to run into trouble—at least occasionally. How she handles adult guidance and corrections has to do with her stage of development.

Autonomy Versus Shame and Doubt

As a toddler, Briana learned about getting into trouble. In her constant search for autonomy, 2-year-old Briana got into trouble all the time. She learned to look for one of her parents or a caregiver when she did something she knew was wrong. She reacted to their reactions by showing shame for what she had done. If they weren't watching, however, and she didn't get caught, she didn't show signs of remorse.

Erikson defines the major task for toddlerhood as working out the conflict between autonomy and shame or *doubt*. Briana has done that and come out with a sense of what she can do that is not greatly overshadowed by a sense of shame. She has managed a positive resolution for this dilemma.

Initiative Versus Guilt

Briana has now moved into Erikson's next stage, which signifies a new dilemma—that of initiative versus guilt (see Figure 3.1). She's a big girl with a beginning sense of responsibility *and* a budding conscience. She has taken the watchful eye of her parents and teachers inside herself and can now begin to judge her own behavior. She can feel the kind of guilt whose nagging warns her when she's about to violate some behavior standard and gives her a sense of remorse when she carries out the action anyway. Her guilt is useful because it helps keep her in control sometimes. It guides her toward positive and acceptable behavior.

Briana now has an internal government that dictates the ideals and standards of behavior that are requirements of society. Her government is a benevolent one. Her guilt serves as a little warning sign when her parents or teachers aren't present. She needed reminding to hang up her coat, but she knew not to leave the smock lying on the floor. She stopped herself from hitting the child who was trying to grab the book back.

Briana's guilt is not expected to always control her actions. She still needs adults close by to help her control herself when she can't manage. They do this without making too big a fuss, knowing that Briana has the beginning of control within her.

Briana's guilt is only a small sign—a signaling device. It's not a battering ram hitting her over the head or an acid eating away her insides.

Not all children are as fortunate as Briana. Some are governed by an inner tyranny. They judge themselves so harshly to enforce the standards of those around them that they lose their initiative. They're afraid to act. Their energy is sapped by the overkill methods of their inner government.

This situation happens when adults go overboard and use heavy-handed punishment, accusations, threats, or torments on young children. Children who grow up in this atmosphere develop an exaggerated sense of guilt, and they torture themselves even for trivial offenses.

Child's Stage	Approximate Age	Task		
Infancy	0–1	Basic trust	versus	Basic mistrust
Toddlerhood	1–3	Autonomy	versus	Shame and doubt
The preschool years	3–6	Initiative	versus	Guilt
School age	6–10	Industry	versus	Inferiority

Figure 3.1
Erikson's psychosocial stages of development
Source: Erikson (1963).

IMAGINATION AND FANTASY

What's perhaps most notable about the stage of initiative is the way children work their imaginations and how they use fantasy. By the preschool years, pretend play has become far more complex than the simple imitation of infancy (Berk, 1994; Jones & Reynolds, 1992; Van Hoorn, Nourot, Scales, & Alward, 2003). The toddler shows the beginnings of the complexity by using objects to stand for other objects (a plastic banana or block for a telephone). By age 4, the imagination soars! What was Briana doing when she was playing house? She was doing just what adults do with dreams and daydreams. She was experiencing hopes and fears by dealing with the past symbolically and rehearsing for the future. She tried on roles and feelings in the same way she tried on dress-up clothes. Fantasy play gives Briana practice in interacting with others while in these roles. She also uses fantasy play to express fears and anger and to discover ways to adjust to painful situations.

THE VALUE OF PLAY OF ALL SORTS

Play is an arena where children learn new skills and practice old ones, both physical and social. Through play they challenge themselves to new levels of mastery. They gain competence in all areas of development, increasing language, social skills, and physical

What's perhaps most notable about the stage of initiative is the way children work their imaginations and use fantasy.

skills, for example. Briana not only practices such important skills as eye-hand coordination but also at times uses her whole body to improve balance and coordination.

Play also provides for cognitive development, which is tied in with physical and social interactions in the preschool years as children are constructing a view of the world and discovering concepts. There's nothing passive about play—even if the body is passive for a time, the mind is busy working. Children at play are active explorers of the environment as they create their own experience and grow to understand it. In this way they participate in their own development.

Through play, children work at problem-solving, which involves mental, physical, and social skills. While playing, they can try on pretend solutions and experience how those solutions work. If they make mistakes, those mistakes don't hurt them as they would in real life. They can reverse power roles and be the adult for a change, telling other children what to do. They can even tell adults what to do, if the adults are willing to play along.

Play enables children to sort through conflicts and deal with anxieties, fears, and disturbing feelings in an active, powerful way (Frost, Wortham, & Reifel, 2001). Play provides a safety valve for feelings. When they pretend, children can say or do things that they can't do in reality.

Play makes children feel powerful and gives them a sense of control as they create worlds and manipulate them. Watch children playing with blocks, or dolls and action

Play provides for cognitive development, which is tied in with physical and social interactions.

figures, or even in the sandbox. Think about how they create the worlds they play in. What power!

Children also get a sense of power by facing something difficult and conquering it—like finding a place for a puzzle piece that just won't fit anywhere or climbing higher on the jungle gym than they've ever climbed before. Think back to your own childhood. Think of a time when you were challenged in play. What was your feeling as you overcame obstacles (including perhaps your own fear) and met the challenge?

HOW THE ENVIRONMENT CONTRIBUTES TO A SENSE OF INITIATIVE

The environment reflects whether the adults in charge of it regard developing a sense of initiative to be of value. Individual initiative, like independence, is not a universal priority. In some cultures, individual initiative is less important than going along with the group spirit. So as you read along about how the environment setup relates to the value of initiative, realize that what you are reading reflects the value behind it.

Suppose that initiative is a value; then the environment in which children spend most of their time will be set up to give them a range of options so they can choose

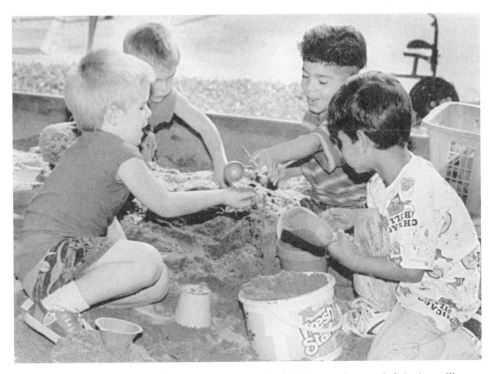

If initiative is a value, then the environment in which children spend most of their time will be set up to give them a range of options so that they can choose how to spend their time.

how to spend that time. Not only will there be choices of developmentally appropriate activities, toys, and materials, but they will be enticingly arranged to attract attention and draw children to them. Not all adults see giving children choices as valuable. Some people expect children to adapt to what is and to entertain themselves in the environment of adults, rather than selecting from a number of options that have been provided for them. They disagree with the notion of a child-oriented environment isolated from the real world of adults (Mistry, 1995; Rogoff, 2003). Some adults do not believe in creating learning situations to teach their children; they put their children in adult-oriented environments and expect them to learn by observation, not from playing in an environment specially set up for them. For an example of this different view of what children need and are capable of, see the following "Perspectives on Child Rearing."

Perspectives on Child Rearing

A preschool teacher enjoying a sunny afternoon in San Francisco sat on a bench watching two street musicians playing music from the Andes for a crowd in Ghiradelli Square. She noticed their daughter, who appeared to be about 4 years old, sitting on a bench next to where the parents were playing. The child sat quietly on the bench until her parents took a break. She had no toys and nothing to do. She seemed to be able to content herself with people watching and listening to the music. When her parents took a break, she moved over to be with them. She hung around listening to what they were saying and periodically taking short excursions to look in shop windows around the perimeters of the plaza. She was never gone too long but kept coming back to where her parents were. She never demanded their attention while they were talking. When they went back to playing music, she went back to sitting. She never left or distracted them in any way while they were working. She was obviously well trained.

The little girl was a contrast to two little boys about 2 and 4 who were also entertaining themselves as their parents stood watching the performance. They had toys with them that they played with. When they got tired of the toys, they started running around the plaza, with one parent trailing after them. To the preschool teacher the boys' behavior was more to be expected than the little girl's behavior, not because of gender but because of age. She marveled at the ability of the little girl to sit on the bench. She wondered what would happen if this child went off to child care or to a preschool where active play was considered vital to development. Would the philosophy of the preschool upset the situation the parents had created so they could earn their living? Would the little girl get bored with sitting (she never looked bored that afternoon)?

Dimensions of Play Environments

Elizabeth Jones and Elizabeth Prescott (1978) at Pacific Oaks College in Pasadena, California, looked at children's play environments in terms of what they call *dimensions*.

To create an optimum environment for the kind of play that enhances initiative, Jones and Prescott advocate a balance of these dimensions: soft/hard, open/closed, intrusion/exclusion, high mobility/low mobility, and simple/complex.

Balancing the *soft/hard* dimension means that the environment is both responsive and resistant. Softness in play environments comes from things like rugs, stuffed animals, cozy furniture, grass, sand, play dough, water, soft balls, pads, and laps, to name a few. Hardness comes in the form of vinyl floors, plastic and wooden toys and furniture, and concrete.

The *open/closed* dimension has to do with choices. Low open shelves displaying toys to choose from are an example of openness. Some closed storage is also appropriate, so that the number of choices are manageable. Closed storage also gives a sense of order and avoids a cluttered feeling. Balance between open and closed is important.

The open/closed dimension also has to do with whether there is one right way to use a toy or material (e.g., a puzzle, a form board, or graduated stacking rings) or whether it encourages all kinds of exploration. A doll, finger paint, and play dough are open; so is water play. Children need both open and closed toys, materials, and equipment.

The environment should provide for both optimum *intrusion* and optimum *exclusion* or *seclusion*. Desirable intrusion comes as the children have access to the greater world beyond their play space—for example, through windows that allow them to see what is happening outside but protect them from dangers and noise. Desirable intrusion also occurs as visitors come into the play environment.

Seclusion should be provided so children can get away by themselves. Think of the hideaways you had as a young child. Given a little freedom, children will find these kinds of places for themselves; however, in a child care center or home, they sometimes need to be provided. Lofts, large cardboard boxes, and tables covered with sheets provide semienclosed private spaces in which children can make "nests" to hide from the world.

A balanced play environment provides for both *high-* and *low-mobility* activities. Children need quiet and still occupations as well as opportunities to move around freely and engage in vigorous movement.

We all know that young children can be satisfied with the simplest things. A baby can be fascinated with something that an adult wouldn't give more than a glance. This fact relates to the *simple/complex* dimension. As children grow older, they need complexity, which they often provide for themselves by combining simple toys with other materials. Watch a child who finds sand, water, and utensils conveniently close to each other. The park designers may never have thought of how that drinking fountain close to the sandbox would be used, but the 4-year-old who finds an empty soda can is almost certain to think of using it to carry water to the sand. Complexity presents increased possibilities for action. Preschool teachers know this, so they put a dripping hose in the sandbox on warm days and give the children scoops, buckets, cups, spoons, and a variety of other implements to use. They know that attention span lengthens when children find or create complexity in the environment. The more complex a material or toy (or combination of materials and toys), the more interesting it is. Blocks are fun. Blocks with small figures and wheel toys are even more fun!

HOW ADULTS CONTRIBUTE TO CHILDREN'S INITIATIVE

Adults contribute to the development of children's sense of initiative in several ways. They are responsible for setting up the environments for children's play. As just stated, the kind of environment they set up determines to some extent whether initiative is a value. Adults are the ones who must guide and control children's behavior in these environments. How they do that also contributes to a sense of initiative. Discipline methods that encourage children to continue to explore, try things out, and solve problems contribute to their growing initiative. Methods that squelch children's interest, inhibit their behavior, and make them afraid to try things because they might make a mistake take away their confidence in themselves and work against bringing out each child's own initiative. In addition, adults encourage initiative in children by modeling it themselves. (Chapter 7 examines this subject at length.)

SPECIAL CONSIDERATIONS FOR CHILDREN WITH DISABILITIES

Some children arrive in a play environment with less initiative and motivation to play than others. It may be that they have not been encouraged to play and explore. Or children who are medically fragile may have parents who concentrate more on keeping them safe than on encouraging them to play. Or it may be that the child is interested, but has little or no access to the toys, materials, and activities. It's up to the adult to ensure that all children have access, including those with disabilities and other challenges.

Sometimes providing access is as simple as restructuring the environment so that a child in a wheelchair, for example, can move around. Putting toys within reach of a non-ambulatory child is another practical strategy. Or positioning a child so he feels secure enough to use his hands and arms to explore and manipulate will enable a child who has a disability to more fully experience his environment. Close attention to what interests each child can guide the teacher when selecting toys and materials to make available. Also being aware of what playthings will build on a child's strengths is important when setting up the environment. Toys and materials that are responsive—that the child can have an effect on—are usually winners. Some toys that are already available can be adapted so they are easier to use. One teacher glued tongue depressors to the pages of a cardboard book to make them less difficult for a child with cerebral palsy to turn. One way to figure out how to modify the environment is for teachers to put themselves at the level of the child in question and look around. For example, a child lying on his back may be looking directly into a bright ceiling light.

Children who have attention deficit disorders may be distracted in a play space where there is too much going on. The way their brains are wired seems to give them the urge to seek novelty and everything attracts their attention (Jensen, 1998). The early childhood educator can simplify the environment, but it isn't enough just to create an appropriate play environment and then expect children with certain challenges to automatically start playing with their typically developing peers. Special strategies are necessary to support interactions with other children and promote skill development

(Chandler, 1998). One such strategy is to slow down the pace for those who need it and allow plenty of time to react. Some children need the slow pace to help them focus. Others need help to refocus. For example, giving plenty of time for a reaction can be a help to those with Down syndrome who need the extra time to change the focus of their attention. Asking a question and expecting an immediate response, for example, doesn't work as well as pausing after the question and just waiting quietly for the child to absorb it before expecting a response.

A child with language delays can benefit when the other children see the teacher responding to communication attempts and building on the skills the child has. Modeling has a strong effect and other children pick up on what the teacher is doing and do it also.

Children with autism benefit from playing with their peers who are more accomplished players. Their ability to play increases with the support of the teacher in an integrated setting where the environment and the learning plan focus on play. Their imagination increases as well (Wolfberg, 1999).

Vygotsky's sociocultural theory has implications for including children with special needs in programs with their typically developing peers. As mentioned in Chapter 1, Vygotsky used the term *zone of proximal development* to describe how social interactions increase understanding. Certainly in a play environment there are lots of opportunities for children to help one another move forward in their understanding and skill building (Vygotsky, 1967).

THE SHY CHILD

Some children seem to lack get-up-and-go. Even though they have no developmental differences, challenges, or disabilities, they seem to lack initiative. They may be labeled *shy*, or perhaps they are looked at as withdrawn.

Let's look at one of these children:

> *Dakota has always been the quietest child in the preschool she attends. She hangs out on the fringes of things and seldom talks or even smiles. When someone talks to her, she lowers her eyes and stares at her shoes. She follows the routine of the program but never really joins in with anything that is going on. She's so quiet that sometimes she's almost invisible.*

What could be going on with Dakota?

Some children are born extra cautious. This trait may even be in their genes. They don't enjoy putting themselves out in the world, taking risks, trying new things. Sometimes this trait doesn't really hinder them, because it's more a matter of timing than a deficiency. Some children are observers; they learn a good deal by watching for long periods before they try something themselves. When they do try something, they make rapid progress because of their careful observations. They may be thought of as being slow to warm up. Other children jump in with both feet without giving a thought to the consequences. If these more impulsive children are successful in their endeavors, they may be valued for their speed and compared with children like Dakota.

(Bright and quick are sometimes thought to be synonymous with intelligent.) Thus, Dakota's slow, cautious way of doing things may be undervalued, both in the family and in the school setting. It may look as though she lacks initiative when indeed it's more a matter of timing than initiative. And maybe it's even an unfamiliar environment that slows her down. Dakota at home with a sibling or a playmate may be much more secure and outgoing, and not look so shy and cautious. Shyness and caution are sometimes situational.

The teachers at Dakota's school have discovered that pushing her doesn't do any good. She's very resistant to joining an activity until she decides on her own to do so. She has the ability to absorb by watching—far more ability than any of her teachers, who think she must be bored, because they are projecting their own needs onto her. She isn't bored. In fact, she is getting much more out of preschool than anyone realizes; but she's doing it in her own way. The teachers have decided to be patient with her and to respect her style. They also, when they can, arrange for her to be in smaller groups and play alone with one or two children rather than always urging her to join into large-group activities.

The teachers have been rewarded to discover that this quiet, cautious child has grown into something of a leader in the class. The other children are drawn to Dakota and are influenced by her. In fact, the day doesn't truly begin until Dakota arrives. The teachers were really surprised when they discovered that Dakota's quiet presence now influences the activities in the classroom.

Factors other than those that influence Dakota may be at work on another child who exhibits the same behavior. Take Brandi, for example:

Brandi is shy and cautious for entirely different reasons—she has a history of abuse and attachment issues. As a result, she has a great deal of trouble separating from her foster mother, who delivers her to school. She cries loudly and must be peeled off, so that the foster mother, who has other children to deliver to another school, can leave. Once Brandi quits crying, she goes into mourning. She stands by the art table with one finger in her mouth and her eyes staring vacantly. The teachers have decided that she isn't even really "there" most of the time. She stares into space. She sits in circle time silently. She doesn't seem to have learned a single song (compared with Dakota, who never sings at school but at home can go through every word of every verse, complete with hand movements). Brandi is withdrawn, and it isn't just that she has a slower pace than most children. She has a problem. In fact, this child might well have been born quick, lively, and a willing risk taker, but her life circumstances have beaten her into the child she is now—one who needs more help than her teachers alone can give her. Under ideal circumstances, Brandi's teachers, foster parents, and biological family are working with social workers and therapists to help her family get back together, help her resolve her attachment issues, and heal the raw scars of her abuse. If all goes well and everyone cooperates, Brandi will get her life back together and her spark will come back. She'll be the child she really is rather than the child she has become.

The vital difference between Dakota and Brandi is that Dakota is the child she is and Brandi is not—she's been damaged.

A LOOK AT AGGRESSION

Let's examine the subject of aggression in the preschool-age child—where it comes from and what to do about it.

We'll start with Cory. He's a 4-year-old who attends an all-day preschool in which he is one of a group of 30 children. He gives his teachers a lot of trouble because he seems always to be hurting someone. Someone is constantly having to deal with the aftermath of his aggressive behavior. What's going on with Cory?

Causes of Aggression

It's not easy to say what's going on with Cory. There are many possible reasons for his aggressive behavior—some simple and fairly easy to solve, and some much more complex. It could be simple—Cory has just not learned any other way to behave. In that case, he needs to be taught. Or it could be that Cory was rewarded for this behavior in the past and is continuing to be rewarded for it, so he continues his aggressive behavior. It could also be that Cory's behavior is the result of bottled-up emotions. Maybe something is going on at home, and he's feeling very upset by it. He's letting off steam at school. His behavior might even stem from a physical source—either his own body chemistry or influences of the environment interacting with his physical makeup. Or his aggression can come from an extreme defensiveness. The following sections explore these sources of aggression more closely.

Learned Aggression.   Children can learn aggression from watching others get what they want through aggressive means. They may see this on television or in their own homes or neighborhoods. They can even learn it at preschool from watching classmates. They can, of course, also learn it from firsthand experience.

For example, a child wants a toy. She grabs it from another child, and pushes him when he fights back. She has the toy—she gets her reward. Or, if adult attention is the reward she's looking for, she gets that attention when the adult marches across the room, grabs the toy out of her hand, and holds her arm tight while squatting down to look her in the eye and give her a good long scolding. She gets even more when she is marched over to apologize. Her final rewards come when placed in a time-out chair and brought back every time she gets up. She has the adult's full attention—including eye contact, touch, and a long stream of words. She can get the adult to notice her even from clear across the room simply by her behavior. If she still wants more reward, all she has to do is push one of the adult's buttons. Spitting at her will probably do it. A "bad word" will usually do it too.

If this child has learned this way of getting attention, the solution is to give her the attention she needs in other ways, and to make her "unlearn" the ingrained behaviors. Behavior modification is the answer. The adult must unlink the behavior and the reward by withdrawing attention rather than pouring it on. This is not easy to do while keeping everyone safe. Sometimes it is a matter of providing physical control while giving the least attention possible. Other times just ignoring the behavior will eventually make it go away. However, if this is a longtime pattern, it will probably get worse before it gets better, until the child learns that the attention she so desperately needs will come, but linked to a different kind of behavior.

The problem is that most adults who have to deal with this kind of aggression in a child are sorely tempted to turn to punishment; they want to hurt the child either physically or emotionally. What they may not realize is that hurting children doesn't work. You don't make a child less aggressive by hurting her—you make her more aggressive. Way back in 1975, Barclay Martin reviewed 27 studies on the effects of harsh punishment and concluded that children were likely to store up frustration from being punished and vent it later, using the violence that was used on them. The message regarding avoiding using aggression to deal with aggression is still valid today.

Power may be behind the child's need for aggression. Power issues are never solved by being overpowered, which is the message behind punishment.

Aggression as the Result of Bottled-Up Feelings.   Some children react to tension with aggression. Their feelings are bottled up inside them, and even a little incident can "uncork" them. What "pours out" is more than the provoking incident calls for. That's a clue to tension as a cause of aggression. Any little frustration can cause "the top to blow off the bottle." When tension is behind the aggression, it is best to work on the source of the tension. However, that may be a job for a social worker and a therapist. If you're Cory's teacher, for example, you don't have the opportunity to work on his home tensions, and you're not a trained therapist. What you *can* do is reduce frustration for him at school. You can also give him outlets for his angry feelings. Some examples of outlets are as follows:

1. Vigorous physical activity can serve as an outlet—for example, running, jumping, and climbing.

2. Aggressive activities are also beneficial—for example, pounding punching bags, digging in the dirt, hammering nails, and even tearing paper.

3. Soothing sensory activities can help calm the aggressive child—activities like water play, clay work, and finger paint. Cornstarch and water available as a paste to play in is a wonderfully soothing sensory activity.

4. Art and music activities also serve as outlets for emotional expression. Many children paint picture after picture, covering every inch of the easel paper with paint. From the looks on their faces, you can tell that they are finding the activity soothing.

Physical Influences on Aggression.   Teachers *can* work on the problem of physical influences on aggression. For example, Cory's diet may be terrible. Perhaps some parent education is in order. Careful observation can determine whether low blood sugar is influencing his behavior. Is he particularly aggressive when he's hungry? Steps can be taken to remedy that situation, both with a change of diet and with increased high-protein snacks. If physical problems are suspected, a visit to the doctor is in order.

It's easy to see how environment can influence behavior. If Cory is part of a group of 30 children and they spend much time together in one classroom, he may well be overstimulated, which can easily result in a lack of control on his part. Crowding is

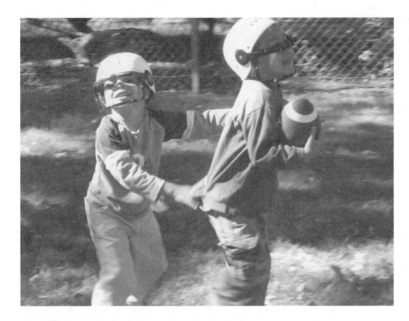

Vigorous physical activity can serve as an outlet for strong feelings.

a clear cause of aggression in animals. I think we, as a society, try to ignore this problem in people because crowding is a part of our daily lives and we just expect children to adjust to it.

Other environmental influences can be heat, lighting, and environmental pollution. Even weather can make a difference. If you've ever been with a group of children on a windy day, you know how it can affect their behavior.

Extreme Defensiveness.   According to Selma Fraiberg (1959) in her classic book, *The Magic Years*, some children imagine danger everywhere and interpret every little action of playmates as threatening to themselves. They are defensive to an extreme. Out of their fear, they attack first, rather than waiting to be attacked and then striking back. They need help to change their perspective and come to see the world as a nonthreatening place. Their worldview may be due to attachment or abuse issues, in which case those are the areas in which they need help. That help may need to come from a trained therapist rather than a layperson, though teachers may carry out whatever program the therapist suggests. All by themselves, the teachers probably can't solve the problem of Cory's aggression if that problem comes from damage inflicted on him.

TEACHING YOUNG CHILDREN PROBLEM-SOLVING SKILLS

The roots of violence start in the first years of life as children who don't know how to solve problems turn to aggression. You can spot children in preschool who are at risk for becoming violent teens. They are the 4-year-olds who solve all their social problems physically. If they want a truck, they grab it and then sock the little kid who had it first. If accidentally bumped, they shove the offender back harder.

Of course, all children who grab, hit, and shove won't become violent teens. After all, this is normal behavior for young children. Some will outgrow it, but others won't. Instead they will develop deeply ingrained ways of approaching problems, which can lead directly from preschool aggression to teenage violence.

Four weaknesses in problem-solving skills are exhibited by teenage offenders:

1. They make assumptions about a situation and neglect to get further information.
2. They seldom give anyone the benefit of the doubt, but see everyone as a potential adversary. They think people are "out to get them."
3. They have a narrow vision of alternative solutions and rely mainly on violence.
4. They fail to consider consequences when they lash out.

Adults can help young children develop problem-solving skills before the weakness becomes ingrained. They can help children clarify situations, consider consequences, and explore alternatives to aggression.

To help, the adult must be on the spot when difficulties arise between children. It's important to intervene before the action gets physical. For example, as the 4-year-old grabs for the truck in the other child's hands, the adult can stop him and say, "You really want the truck. I wonder what you can do besides grabbing it." If the child's response shows he can't think of anything but grabbing, the adult can list some other ideas.

Teach young children problem-solving skills so they learn to work things out verbally instead of physically.

It's important that adults not be critical or judgmental when they intervene. This approach is about talking it through, not giving lectures on being nice. Tone of voice and attitude are all-important as the adult guides the talking. The goal is for the children to begin to see the other's perspective and consider alternative solutions.

Four qualities are important when helping children talk to each other in a conflict situation:

1. Firmness should come through—"I won't let you grab or hurt."
2. Empathy also should come through—"I know how much you want that truck."
3. A problem-solving attitude rather than a power play must be part of the exchange—"He might give it to you if you ask him."
4. Persistence is critical—"Well, asking didn't work. I wonder what else you could try."

The objective is not to solve the problem in a particular way for the child but to help him discover his own alternatives to violence.

Adults often short-circuit this kind of learning by putting children in time-out. Or they solve the problem themselves: "He had it first; give it back to him." "If you're going to fight over that toy, you can't play with it." Those adult actions don't teach the problem-solving skills so necessary for the future.

Skillful intervention makes a difference. We can teach children nonviolence in the preschool years. Of course, teaching alone won't eliminate violence. Other factors come into play. If the child sees violence at home, on the streets, or on TV, the modeling effect comes in. Or if the child is a victim of abuse, the likelihood of his becoming a perpetrator is increased.

Safe Start is a nationwide program designed to deal with the roots of violence through prevention and intervention. Supported by the Ounce of Prevention Fund, a public/private partnership based in Chicago and built on decades of research on child development, this program is a most promising approach to reducing violence through focusing on children ages birth to 5. Brain research points to the impact of early emotional experiences on brain development, altering both structure and brain chemistry. Early experiences set up patterns of response that can last a lifetime. The program stresses prevention approaches that include helping adults understand how to teach children self-control. Adults in the program learn how to set limits, discourage unacceptable behavior, model appropriate behavior, and reduce the risk factors for violence. Early intervention includes quality early childhood education programs for children, including specialized teacher training in violence prevention. Safe Start approaches are making a lasting difference.[1]

There is no single simple solution to violence. If we are to create a peaceful world to live in, we must take a many-pronged approach. A good prong to start with is to help children learn effective nonviolent problem-solving in the early years.

---

[1]Safe Start puts out a 6-page brochure called "Safe Start: How Early Experiences Can Help Reduce Violence," an Ounce of Prevention Fund paper by Theresa Hawley (2000). It can be obtained from the Ounce of Prevention Fund, 122 S. Michigan Ave., Suite 2050, Chicago, IL 60603–6198; (312) 922–3863.

EMPOWERING THE PRESCHOOL-AGE CHILD

Adults often believe that to manage children's behavior and set them on the right path, they must dominate them by overpowering them. Trying to *overpower* children often leads straight to power struggles, which are the antithesis of *empowering* children. Children miss out whether they win or lose the power struggle. If they win, they discover that they can dominate an adult, which is frightening. Young children know that they need adults and they want someone to look up to, to protect and support them. It shakes their confidence in the adult to learn that they are stronger than the larger, more experienced adult. If children lose the power struggle, it takes them down a notch or two rather than convincing them of their own power. Power struggles are to be avoided rather than encouraged if you are working on empowerment.

To explore empowerment further, think of a time you felt powerful as a child. Avoid focusing on those times when you were overpowering someone; concentrate instead on personal power that gave you the feeling of being able to be yourself and of having some effect on the world or the people in it. Focus on this feeling. Isn't this a feeling you would like children to have?

When I ask students to give examples of times they felt powerful as a child, they come up with a variety of situations in which they demonstrated effectiveness. Sometimes the situation has to do with carrying out some responsibility; some remember a time when they were particularly competent at something; others remember a moment of strength or courage—particularly in relationship to being challenged and conquering their fear. Some felt powerful because of their affiliations—the support people in their

Empowered children feel as if they can be themselves and have an effect on the world.

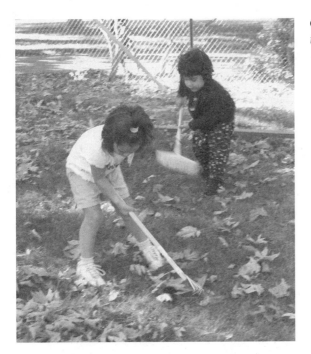

Children gain feelings of power by trying on powerful roles.

lives. Some people got a sense of their own power simply from being able to make choices—even when the consequences weren't what they expected.

One way that children gain a feeling of power is by "dressing up" and trying on powerful roles. They do this by itself or in conjunction with creating their own world and then playing. That puts them in the role of creator—a very powerful position indeed.

Even something as simple as physically changing perspective makes children feel powerful. One young woman remembered spending time as a child squatting on the top of the refrigerator, looking down from her vantage point at the world and the people beneath her. Another had a secret hideout on the garage roof, under the shelter of a tall spreading tree.

One less than desirable way that children gain power is by misbehaving and making adults angry. Only when you watch a scene of a little child sending an adult into a frenzy do you realize what a feeling of power the child must get from this reaction. It's a little like being the person who pushes the button that sends a rocket into space. Wow! It's also a bit frightening to feel so powerful.

Sometimes a child in a preschool situation will cause a good deal of trouble. This child manages to affect everyone around him. It gets so that everyone breathes a sigh of relief on the days he is absent because things are so different. Children who behave like this are often so needy for power that they get it in the only way they know how—by making a big impact on the environment, including the people in it.

If you recognize power as a legitimate need, it seems reasonable to find ways to empower children so that they won't need to manipulate or disrupt to feel a sense of their own power. The following are some ways that adults can empower children:

- *Teach children effective language and how to use it.*   Even very young children can learn to hold up a hand and firmly say "Stop!" to someone threatening them. They won't need to hit or shove once they learn to use the power of words. They can learn to express feelings. They can learn to argue their point. They can become effective language users. (More information on this subject is given in Chapter 8.) Remember, though, that some cultures have a different view of teaching children to express their feelings. The goal is group peace and harmony over individual expression of feelings. It is important to recognize this difference when working with children who come from these cultures.
- *Give children the support they need while they are coming to feel their personal power.*   Don't let them continually be victimized until their personal power becomes so trampled that it threatens to disappear from sight altogether. Use your personal power *for* them so they can come to use their own eventually. Don't rescue them. Instead, teach them ways to protect themselves—with your support at first; later they can do it without your support.
- *Teach them problem-solving skills*   (see Chapter 9).
- *Help children tune in on their uniqueness and appreciate their differences.*   Help each child become more fully who he or she really is rather than trying to cast him or her into some preset mold. Do remember, however, that not all cultures see uniqueness and individuality as a value. Some emphasize downplaying any characteristics that make one stand apart from the group.

We can't leave the preschool-age child without a discussion of early learning. The scene with Briana showed a developmentally appropriate preschool setting with activities and approaches that encouraged initiative. Unfortunately, everyone doesn't understand the value of such a program. Many well-meaning adults take the position that academics rather than play should be the focus of the preschool curriculum. They base their view on the facts that the early years are important ones and that most young children are equipped with a good memory and a willingness to please. A response to this view is: Just because children *can* do something doesn't mean that they *ought* to.[2]

When children are pushed to engage in rote learning or to perform for adults, their initiative can be squashed. Their need to please the powerful others in their lives conflicts with their own inner motivation. The need to please often wins out, and children take to heart the message that adult-directed learning is more valuable than child-directed activity. Polly Greenberg (1990), editor of the journal *Young Children*, has written an article about this subject, titled "Why Not Academic Preschool?"

---

[2]I've heard Lilian Katz, early childhood education professor at the University of Illinois, make this statement a number of times.

SUMMARY

This chapter focused on the preschool-age child, who, according to Erik Erikson, has the task of developing a sense of initiative and grappling with feelings of guilt when faced with social restrictions. We examined how adults provide for initiative in children by setting up an appropriate environment and by their own actions. We also looked at shy and aggressive children and explored the roots of these behaviors, as well as ways to respond to them. We ended with an examination of personal power and how to encourage it in children.

The next chapter continues with the subject of personal power and looks at it from a slightly different vantage point, under the label of self-esteem.

FOR DISCUSSION

1. The chapter gives the perspective of a culture that values independence, initiative, and individuality. What might be the perspective of a culture that instead puts a priority on interdependence, obedience, and putting the group before one's own needs, urges, wishes, and desires?

2. Consider Briana. Remember how she pretends to spank a boy. If you were the teacher, how would you know that it was just "pretend"? Would you stop that behavior? How would you describe a child who had a high level of initiative but was different from Briana?

3. How do you react to the idea of an "internal government"? Do you believe it is better for children to always have someone in authority watching them and taking charge of their behavior?

4. Analyze the environment you're in right now in terms of the five dimensions named by Elizabeth Jones and Elizabeth Prescott. Is it an appropriate environment for 3- to 6-year-old children to play in? Why or why not?

5. What is your opinion of the expectations that the street musicians ("Perspectives on Child Rearing," p. 64) have of their daughter? Are the parents' expectations hampering her development? How much play time do children need? Does it harm them to put the good of the parents over their own urges to play and run around all the time? Remember, these are cultural questions. Different perspectives give different answers. If you talk with someone about this subject who disagrees with you, try to create a dialogue instead of a debate or argument.

REFERENCES

Barkley, R. A. (1997). ADHD *and the nature of self-control*. New York: Guilford.

Berk, L. E. (1994, November). Vygotsky's theory: The importance of make-believe play. *Young Children*, 50(1), 30–39.

Chandler, L. (1998). Promoting positive interaction between preschool-age children during free play: The Pals Center. *Young Exceptional Children*, 2(2), 13–19.

Duckworth, E. (2001). *"Tell me more": Listening to learners*. New York: Teachers College Press.

Edmiaston, R., Dolezal, V., Doolittle, S., Erickson, C., & Merritt, S. (2000). Developing individualized education programs for children in inclusive settings: A developmental framework. *Young Children, 55*(4), 36–41.

Erikson, E. (1963). *Childhood and society.* New York: Norton.

Fraiberg, S. H. (1959). *The magic years.* New York: Scribner's.

Fromberg, D. P. (2002). *Play and meaning in early childhood education.* Boston: Allyn & Bacon.

Frost, J., Wortham, S., & Reifel, S. (2001). *Play and child development.* Upper Saddle River, NJ: Merrill/Prentice Hall.

Greenberg, P. (1990, January). Why not academic preschool? *Young Children, 45*(2), 70–80.

Hyson, M. (2004). *The emotional development of young children,* (2nd ed.). New York: Teachers College Press.

Jensen, E. (1998). *Teaching with the brain in mind.* Alexandria, VA: Association for Supervision and Curriculum Development.

Jones, E. (2003, May). Playing to get smart. *Young Children 58*(3), 32–33.

Jones, E., & Prescott, E. (1978). *Dimensions of teaching-learning environments: Vol. 2. Focus on day care.* Pasadena, CA: Pacific Oaks.

Jones, E., & Reynolds, G. (1992). *The play's the thing: Teachers' roles in children's play.* New York: Teachers College Press.

Kamii, C. (With L. B. Housman). (2000). *Young children reinvent arithmetic: Implications of Piaget's theory* (2nd ed.). New York: Teachers College Press.

Katch, J. (2001). *Under deadman's skin: Discovering the meaning of children's violent play.* Boston: Beacon.

Katz, L. G., & Chard, S. (2000). *Engaging children's minds: The project approach* (2nd ed.). Stamford, CT: Ablex.

Kelly, J. F., & Booth, C. L. (1999). Child care for children with special needs: Issues and applications. *Infants and Young Children, 12*(1), 26–33.

Kemple, K. M. (2004). *Let's be friends: Peer competence and social inclusion in early childhood programs.* New York: Teachers College Press.

Klein, M. D., & Chen, D. (2001). *Working with children from culturally diverse backgrounds.* New York: Delmar.

Kostelnik, M., Onaga, E., Rohde, B., & Whiren, A. (2002). *Children with special needs: Lessons for early childhood professionals.* New York: Teachers College Press.

Levin, D. E. (2002). *Teaching young children in violent times: Building a peaceable classroom* (2nd ed.). Cambridge, MA: Educators for Social Responsibility; Washington, DC: NAEYC.

Martin, B. (1975). Parent-child relations. In F. D. Horowitz (Ed.), *Review of child development research* (Vol. 4). Chicago: University of Chicago Press.

McCathren, R. B. (2000). Teacher-implemented prelinguistic communication intervention. *Focus on Autism and Other Developmental Disabilities, 15*(1), 21–29.

Mistry, J. (1995). Culture and learning in infancy: Implications for caregiving. In P. L. Mangione (Ed.), *Infant/toddler caregiving: A guide to culturally sensitive care.* Sacramento: California Department of Education and the Far West Laboratory for Educational Research.

Odom, S. (Ed.). (2002). *Widening the circle: Including children with disabilities in preschool programs.* New York: Teachers College Press.

Okagaki, L., & Diamond, K. E. (2000). Responding to cultural and linguistic differences in the beliefs and practices of families with young children. *Young Children, 55*(3), 74–78.

Olds, A. R. (1998). Places of beauty. In D. Bergen (Ed.), *Play as a medium for learning and development* (pp. 123–127). Olney, MD: Association for Childhood Education International.

Paley, V. G. (1986). *Bad guys don't have birthdays: Fantasy play at four.* Chicago: University of Chicago Press.

Paley, V. G. (1992). *You can't say you can't play.* Cambridge, MA: Harvard University Press.

Paley, V. G. (1999). *The kindness of children.* Cambridge, MA: Harvard University Press.

Perry, J. (2001). *Outdoor play: Teaching strategies with young children.* New York: Teachers College Press.

Rogoff, B. (2003). *The cultural nature of human development.* New York: Oxford University Press.

Sandall, S. R. (2003, May). Play modifications for children with disabilities. *Young Children, 58*(3), 54–55.

Shonkoff, J. P., & Phillips, D. (2001, April-May). From neurons to neighborhoods: The science of early childhood development—An introduction. *Zero to Three, 21*(5), 4–7.

Shore, R. (1997). *Rethinking the brain: New insights in early development.* New York: Families and Work Institute.

Trawick-Smith, J. (2001). Play and the curriculum. In J. Frost, S. Wortham, & S. Reifel (Eds.), *Play and child development.* Upper Saddle River, NJ: Merrill/Prentice Hall.

Van Hoorn, J., Nourot, P., Scales, B., & Alward, K. (2003). *Play at the center of the curriculum* (3rd ed.). Upper Saddle River, NJ: Merrill/Prentice Hall.

Vygotsky, L. S. (1967). Play and its role in the mental development of the child. *Soviet Psychology, 12,* 62–76.

Wasserman, S. (2000). Serious players in the primary classroom: Empowering children through active learning experiences (2nd ed.). New York: Teachers College Press.

Wellhousen, K., & Kieff, J. (2001). A *constructivist approach to block play in early childhood.* Albany, NY: Delmar.

Wolfberg, P. L. (1999). *Play and imagination in children with autism.* New York: Teachers College Press.

FURTHER READING

Bergen, D. (Ed.). (1998). *Play as a medium for learning and development.* Portsmouth, NH: Heinemann.

Berk, L. E. (1994, November). Vygotsky's theory: The importance of make-believe play. *Young Children, 50*(1), 30–39.

Bronson, M. B. (2000, March). Research in review: Recognizing and supporting the development of self-regulation in young children. *Young Children, 55*(2), 32–36.

Cajete, G. (1994). *Look to the mountain: An ecology of indigenous education.* Durango, CO: Kivaki.

Cartwright, S. (1999, July). What makes good early childhood teachers? *Young Children, 54*(4), 4–7.

Duckworth, E. (2001). *"Tell me more": Listening to learners.* New York: Teachers College Press.

Edmiaston, R., Dolezal, V., Doolittle, S., Erickson, C., & Merritt, S. (2000). Developing individualized education programs for children in inclusive settings: A developmental framework. *Young Children, 55*(4), 36–41.

Frost, J., Wortham, S., & Reifel, S. (2001). *Play and child development.* Upper Saddle River, NJ: Merrill/ Prentice Hall.

Holland, P. (2003). *We don't play with guns here: War, weapon, and superhero play in the early years.* Philadelphia: Open University Press.

Hyson, M. (2004). *The emotional development of young children* (2nd ed.). New York: Teachers College Press.

Jones, E. (2003, May). Playing to get smart. *Young Children 58*(3), 32–33.

Jones, E., & Reynolds, G. (1992). *The play's the thing: Teachers' roles in children's play.* New York: Teachers College Press.

Katz, L. G., & McClellan, D. E. (1997). *Fostering children's social competence: The teacher's role.* Washington, DC: National Association for the Education of Young Children.

Kostelnik, M., Onaga, E., Rohde, B., & Whiren, A. (2002). *Children with special needs: Lessons for early childhood professionals.* New York: Teachers College Press.

Lillard, A., & Curenton, S. (1999, September). Research in review: Do young children understand what others feel, want, and know? *Young Children, 54*(4), 52–57.

Sandall, S. R. (2003, May). Play modifications for children with disabilities. *Young Children, 58*(3), 54–55.

Slaby, R. G., Roedell, W. C., Arezzo, D., & Hendrix, K. (1995). *Early violence prevention: Tools for teachers of young children.* Washington, DC: National Association for the Education of Young Children.

Van Hoorn, J., Nourot, P., Scales, B., & Alward, K. (2003). *Play at the center of the curriculum* (3rd ed.). Upper Saddle River, NJ: Merrill/Prentice Hall.

Wolfson-Steinberg, L. (2000, May). "Teacher! He hit me!" "She pushed me!" Where does it start? How can it stop? *Young Children, 55*(3), 38–42.

CHAPTER 4

Self-Esteem

In *this chapter you'll discover . . .*

- ◆ Some ways to promote self-esteem
- ◆ What criticism, labels, and name calling do to self-esteem
- ◆ What happens when the media stereotype in negative ways
- ◆ Why always being positive is not a way to raise children's self-esteem
- ◆ How "scaffolding" a child's learning works toward the development of self-esteem
- ◆ How rescuing children from their problems works against the development of self-esteem
- ◆ How cultural differences affect the way parents perceive self-esteem

Who am I? That's a question asked over and over throughout each person's lifetime. The first "askings" start nonverbally in infancy as the child begins to define the boundaries between herself and the rest of the world. She learns where she ends and the world begins. She learns about her separateness. She also learns about her personal power by discovering that her actions have consequences—she cries and someone responds, for example. Self-esteem development continues in toddlerhood and in the preschool years as children learn to observe themselves, which gradually helps them become more and more aware of themselves as separate, individual people.

The answer to the question "Who am I?" reflects our *self-concept*, which is our self-definition. How we *feel* about how we define ourselves reflects *self-esteem*. Much attention is being given nowadays to promoting high self-esteem in children because a link is seen among achievement, behavior, positive growth patterns, and high self-esteem. This chapter looks at the development of self-esteem.

PORTRAIT OF A PERSON WITH HIGH SELF-ESTEEM

What does a person with high self-esteem look like? On the surface, this seems like a fairly simple question to answer. Without much thought it's easy to come up with a portrait that's something like this:

> *People with high self-esteem have self-confidence that shows in the way they dress, groom themselves, walk, and talk. People with high self-esteem are secure and happy. They're outgoing, energetic, brave, strong, and proud. They're also motivated, successful, independent, and assertive.*

That description is a typical one produced by students of mainstream cultural backgrounds. But in a class where the students are diverse, and comfortable enough to speak up, the items on the list come into question. This way the students discover that the traits listed are not particularly indicative of high self-esteem, but rather reflect a cultural ideal.

If you think of a specific person who seems to have high self-esteem, the picture changes, even if that person is of the mainstream culture. The person is not likely to be a walking example of this list of culturally specific ideal traits. Rather, the person is more likely to be herself. And if you compare that person with another who also has high self-esteem, they may be very different from each other because the second person is also likely to be herself.

High-self-esteem people aren't necessarily happy, though we would like to think that happiness comes from boosting self-esteem. Often people who are themselves and feel good about it run into problems when they are in circumstances that challenge their ability to express who they are and have their needs met. A person in a refugee camp may have high self-esteem but probably won't be too happy. More is said about this later in the chapter, but here let me just point out that part of being who you are has to do with feeling your feelings, which means that you'll have a wide range—not just constant sunshiny happiness.

High-self-esteem people also aren't necessarily talented, good-looking, strong, or financially successful. If they were, ordinary people wouldn't have much of a chance, and people with disabilities would have even less of a chance. Just look around you and you'll discover that a person's looks, abilities, possessions, or wealth aren't necessarily related to self-esteem. Some of the best-looking people in the world feel inferior. They either think they're not *really* good-looking, or they worry that all they have is their looks, which are destined to fade. If they feel significant or powerful based on looks alone, they're in trouble.

Actually, if you scratch the surface of people who seem to have high self-esteem, you'll find that some are covering up perceived inadequacies. People are often the opposite of what they seem. The extremely assertive person may be hiding a shy, scared child underneath. The paragon of virtue may have a core of hidden vices. Judging self-esteem in others isn't easy! There's lots of room for error. People just aren't always what they seem.

So instead of trying to judge the degree of self-esteem in adults, let's look at where it comes from in childhood. Let's start with some definitions.

DEFINITION OF SELF-ESTEEM

What is self-esteem, anyway? Self-esteem is a valuing process and results from an ongoing self-appraisal in which traits and abilities are acknowledged and evaluated. Self-esteem is made up of *self-image*—the pictures we carry of ourselves—and *self-concept*—the ideas we have about ourselves.

High self-esteem comes when, after a realistic appraisal of pluses and minuses, a person decides that she has more positive attributes than negative ones. High self-esteem means that a person feels good about herself—she holds herself in esteem. Overall, she likes herself, warts and all. Low self-esteem means that a person lacks a global sense of self-worth.

This concept of self-esteem or self-worth is entirely tied to culture. For example, in a culture that values independence and individuality, the perception is that infants are born unable to differentiate themselves from the rest of the world. It is the family's job to help the infant learn to draw boundaries and discover her separateness. She must come to see herself as an individual, independent human being. When she does, she feels successful. Another family from a different culture sees the infant as separate and independent to start with. That family wants to blur the boundaries and deemphasize the independence. Jerome Kagan, in his book *The Nature of the Child* (1984), says, "The Japanese, who prize close interdependence between child and adult . . . believe they must tempt the infant into a dependent role . . . in order to encourage the mutual bonding necessary for adult life" (p. 29). Self-esteem in a family that emphasizes separateness will look different from a family that deemphasizes separateness.

When a family promotes self-assurance, self-help, competence, and being "special," self-esteem rises if the individual is proud to perceive herself as being in possession of those traits. However, in some cultures the proud, independent, self-assured individual who stands out in a crowd will be given strong messages about the importance of fitting in, belonging, and putting others first. Culture makes a difference in one's view of what comprises self-esteem. In some cultures the very notion of holding oneself in esteem is abhorrent, and pride is a no-no. Instead, humility and humbleness are valued (Greenfield, Quiroz, Rothstein-Fisch, 2001; Rogoff, 2003). People in those cultures find other ways of feeling worthy. Conflicting cultural messages can tear down self-esteem. Although some people can rise above cultural messages and continue to feel good about themselves, others can't. Self-esteem isn't simply deciding that you're great just as you are and giving that message to the world.

Children from any culture can sometimes have an exaggerated sense of their own power that doesn't reflect self-esteem at all but rather their stage of cognitive development. Take, for example, the 3-year-old who feels angry about having been dethroned by a baby sister. He makes ugly wishes concerning the baby. Then the baby gets sick—or worse, *dies*—and the 3-year-old thinks he caused the tragedy by willing it. The child's misconceptions aren't caused by the degree of his self-esteem but rather by thinking himself capable of willing things to happen. He lacks logic at this age.

Self-perception must relate to reality to create true self-esteem. Exaggerated misperceptions that aren't stage-related, as in this example, are delusions. A picture that appeared on the cover of *Newsweek* on February 17, 1992, depicts this problem: An ugly, skinny, weak, flabby, sickly looking man stands in front of the mirror, and the reflection he sees is the opposite of what he is. The mirror shows a strong, well built, handsome, self-assured man, whom we can assume to be talented and intelligent as well. Nothing in the reflection is the same as the man creating it—nothing relates to reality. That's not self-esteem!

If, in the name of promoting self-esteem, you try to fool a child by painting her a false picture of herself, it won't work. (If it did, it wouldn't be healthy, anyway.) Take a child who is miserably aware of her lack of ability, feels unloved, has little power to control anything in her life, and is behaving in unacceptable ways. You can't raise her self-esteem by telling her none of what she is experiencing is true. She simply won't believe you. If there is no reality to back up what you're saying, you're wasting your breath. Even if you point out her good traits, if she's focused on what she perceives to be her bad ones, she won't pay attention.

It's harder to change someone's self-esteem than it seems. In fact, only when the person herself decides to change her perceptions will she allow someone else to be effective in helping her. *Building self-esteem involves a collaboration, not a deception.* The goal is to help the child build a sense of self that is both valued and true.

DIMENSIONS OF SELF-ESTEEM

According to Stanley Coopersmith (1967), pioneer researcher in the subject, self-esteem has at least four dimensions: significance, competence, power, and virtue. Other researchers use similar ideas but employ different words. Susan Harter (1983), for example, uses the words *acceptance, power and control, moral virtue,* and *competence*. Your self-esteem depends on what you value, which is likely to be influenced by what your family and culture values for you (which may depend on gender) and where you perceive that you fall in each category. Let's take a look at each of these dimensions in turn.

Significance

Significance has to do with a feeling of being loved and cared about, the feeling that you matter to someone. You can't instill this feeling in a child. You can try to influence it with words and deeds, with nurturing and protection, with caring, and with meeting needs, but you can't ensure that the messages you send are the ones the child will receive. A feeling of significance, the feeling that you are important because you are cared about, is a choice the individual makes.

It is vital to understand that children are active participants in the development of their sense of self. No matter what hand fate deals, it's not the events themselves that determine self-esteem—it's how the child reacts to those events. Obviously some children are born into more fortunate circumstances than others, yet there are children who have everything going for them who don't feel good about themselves. Other children are just the opposite. They manage to emerge from a series of traumas with self-esteem intact and, indeed, growing. These children seem to be able to use adverse circumstances to their own advantage. They grow and learn from their experiences and come out stronger than ever. They seem to take the negative and twist it around to have a positive effect.

Significance has to do with a feeling of being loved and cared about.

Competence

You can influence *competence* in a child by helping him become increasingly skilled in a number of areas. But whether the child *feels* competent depends on whether he compares himself with someone who is more competent than he is. It's a decision the child makes, not one that you make, though you can push him toward this decision by making comparisons yourself or demanding perfection. If competence is particularly important to him, he may experience lower self-esteem, even though he is highly competent, simply because he doesn't see himself as competent *enough*. There's a discrepancy between where he thinks he should be (or wants to be) and where he is. He doesn't meet his own standards (which may or may not have come from his family or his culture).

Power

Let's look at *power*, the third dimension of self-esteem. Feeling that you have some control over being who you are, making things happen in the world, having an effect on the people and events in your life, and living your life satisfactorily give a sense of power. If power is of major importance to you, having a feeling of it can raise your self-esteem. Notice that power is not defined here as having control over other people—it's not a matter of *overpowering*, but power in the pure sense of the word: personal power, which reflects the root meaning of the word—"to be able." Power has to do with effectiveness.

Virtue

Virtue is the fourth dimension of self-esteem. Being good is important to some people. Their self-esteem relates to how much of a gap there is between how good they perceive themselves to be and how good they want or need to be. Virtue is not a supreme value to everyone.

THE ROLE OF BELIEFS AND EXPECTATIONS IN SELF-ESTEEM

So suppose that self-esteem depends on two things: the dimensions that are of utmost importance to the individual, and the gap between where this person perceives herself to be and where she wants to (or feels she should) be. Take the housewife who sees herself as good and loved (excels on the scales of virtue and significance) yet values only power and competence, where she sees herself sadly lacking. In this case her self-esteem may be quite low.

The housewife is a contrast to, for example, a monk who values virtue above all and derives his self-esteem from being obedient to his faith. He doesn't care about power, competence, or significance. These are extreme examples, granted, but they make the point. A discrepancy between where you are and where you want to be on the scale(s) most valuable to you is what counts in self-esteem.

Although self-esteem eventually becomes established and relatively stable over time, it's not forever fixed and static. For one thing, it changes as children develop. If we look at Erikson's (1963) stages in view of the dimensions described here, we see that different periods of development have different emphases. For example, power is a particularly strong issue for 2-year-olds, who are in Erikson's stage of autonomy. Competence comes into focus in the school-age years when children enter Erikson's stage of industry versus inferiority (see Figure 4.1). Industry as Erikson uses the term is about developing areas of competence.

Self-esteem also changes when circumstances change. It can even change instantly. The child who is competent at many things, active, and talkative at home may become quiet and hide his competence when he enters school for the first time. A severe trauma can also make a difference in the child's feelings about himself. Creating and maintaining self-esteem is a lifelong process—it gets shaped and reshaped.

Self-esteem brings with it self-confidence, which is a vital trait for development. What a child *believes* he can or cannot do sometimes influences what he *can* or *cannot* do. Children who perceive that they lack competence, for instance, may not try something because they've had bad experiences in the past, or simply because they have no confidence in themselves. What we *believe* influences our behavior greatly. Our beliefs create a self-fulfilling prophecy. What we expect is what we get, for no other reason than that we expect it.

Past experience can play a big part in raising or lowering expectations. The research on learned helplessness is eye-opening. Dogs who were shocked when they tried to get out of their cages learned to stay in even after the shocks stopped and the cages were left open. They were free to leave, but they didn't perceive it that way. They continued to act on past experience even though the circumstances of the present were different. Their perceptions didn't relate to reality (Seligman, 1975).

Picture this cartoon: A man stands in a cage, gripping bars in both hands with his face pressed up against them. But those two bars are the only ones holding him in the cage—there are no other bars. His perceptions are what are trapping him, not the reality of the situation. Perceptions make up self-esteem. They may be wrong perceptions.

Child's Stage	Approximate Age	Task		
Infancy	0 – 1	Basic trust	versus	Basic mistrust
Toddlerhood	1 – 3	Autonomy	versus	Shame and doubt
The preschool years	3 – 6	Initiative	versus	Guilt
School age	6 – 10	Industry	versus	Inferiority

Figure 4.1

Erikson's psychosocial stages of development

Source: Erikson (1963).

WHERE DOES SELF-ESTEEM COME FROM?

Self-esteem comes along with self-identity from early experiences and continues up through the school years into adolescence and adulthood. Children define them-selves partly by looking at the images that they see reflected in the people around them (Briggs, 1975; Lally, 1995). If they develop close attachments with people who love and value them, the reflection they see is positive, and they're likely to have pos-itive feelings about themselves. They decide that they are lovable. If they create an impact on the world—starting as babies when they cry and are responded to in ways that meet their needs—they develop a sense of self-efficacy, which they then include in their self-definition. If they develop a wide variety of competencies that are well received by those around them, they are likely to decide that they are competent. If they learn acceptable ways to behave and are given recognition for their good behav-ior, they are likely to decide that they are virtuous. Put all together, the child who sees more positive reflections of himself is likely to develop a global sense of self-worth: self-esteem.

So it seems as though a child who has someone who cares about him and meets his needs and creates positive reflections will likely develop a healthy sense of self-worth. But what if the outside world gives you a different set of messages because of your color, your gender, your ethnicity, or your physical/mental abilities? What if the reflections you see in the eyes of those outside your home depict you as somehow inferior? What if you go to the movies or watch TV and you see people like you either not pictured at all or pictured in negative ways? What will all that do to your self-esteem?

What if the people and/or institutions you encounter outside your home give you differential treatment and act as if you are inferior? Furthermore, what if those people

Children define themselves partly by looking at the images they see reflected in the people around them.

or institutions create insensitive or even assaultive environments and you find yourself in those environments?

Under these circumstances, can the positive messages you get from home counteract the negative ones you get from outside? Maybe. Some parents provide their children with lessons on how to survive and stand up to racism, sexism, or ablism. Their children go out into the world with something like a protective shield that can help them maintain their self-esteem in the face of bombardment of negative messages. Surely what children get at home from these aware parents will make them stronger and probably more able to withstand the negative images thrust on them. But what about children who go out into the world with self-esteem already a bit damaged? What happens to them when they enter an insensitive or assaultive environment outside the home? The results can be devastating.

PROMOTING SELF-ESTEEM

This section examines some general ways to promote self-esteem. It also examines some that are specific to changing those negative messages just mentioned to positive ones.

One way to promote self-esteem in children is to work on closing the gap on the four scales representing the dimensions of self-esteem. Be careful about putting expectations on children that are beyond their reach. Help them examine their own expectations and where they came from. Above all, help children to feel lovable, capable, powerful, and good.

Start by getting rid of critical attitudes, labeling, and name calling. Even in the name of socializing a child, *you can't make him feel better about himself by making him feel bad about himself.* That doesn't mean to move right to "La-La Land," where everything is sweetness and light and nothing connects to reality. Of course children misbehave, make adults angry, and act in less than loving ways. They need guidance and protection. They need honest feedback. But the form in which you guide, protect, and give honest feedback matters.

Just consider for a moment whether your methods *overpower* children or *empower* them. Do correction methods help children see themselves as good people or bad ones? Are they given confidence in their abilities, or is it torn down by the correction methods? Do they come to see themselves as unloved? Chapter 7 gives many ways of guiding behavior that build self-esteem rather than tearing it down.

Give More Honest Feedback and Encouragement Than Praise

Some adults, in the name of building self-esteem, vow always to be positive and to praise children at every possible opportunity. They replace honest feedback with constant overblown praise. Praise is no cure for low self-esteem. All it does is create a need for the child to look to the adult for a judgment of everything he does. Children need coaches rather than cheerleaders (Curry & Johnson, 1990). If you overdo praise, your words become meaningless. For example, if you say "Great job!" about every little thing, it becomes an empty phrase. It's more effective and less damaging to use encouragement instead of praise. Call attention to children's legitimate successes, but

Give honest feedback and encouragement.

don't butter them up with heavy judgments. Compare past performances with present ones, but not with those of other children—"You picked up more blocks this time than last time," rather than "You're the best block-picker-upper I've ever seen." Better yet, explain why this behavior is valuable (Hitz & Driscoll, 1988).

Give Children Opportunities to Experience Success

Even more important than just talking is to give children many chances to experience success of all sorts. Challenge them so that when success comes they've worked for it—it didn't just arrive on a platter. Do this by creating a manageable, yet challenging, environment that is appropriate to their age and stage of development. The book *Developmentally Appropriate Practice in Early Childhood Programs Serving Children from Birth Through Age 8*, by Sue Bredekamp and Carol Copple (1997), gives many ideas about how to respond to children appropriately.

When adults give children a helping hand, they also help them experience success. Lev Vygotsky (1978) came up with the term *assisted performance* to describe this helping hand. He suggested that other children can be the ones who provide the helping hand, not just adults. Others now use the term *scaffolding*. Scaffolding is a process that can be viewed as similar to the temporary structure one puts up to paint a building. In other words, the adult provides the support the child needs, allowing him to problem-solve at new levels. The scaffolding helps the child experience success, which encourages the child to challenge himself further, thereby meeting with the possibility of new success. Scaffolding, because it is temporary, can be built for a specific need on each occasion and can easily be remodeled to serve changing needs.

Travis

Travis is 4 years old, and he's big for his age. His size alone commands attention, but what he does with it commands even more. He pushes kids around every chance he gets. He walks with a swagger and with a challenge on his face. "Just try to get the better of me," his expression seems to say. He's also loud and sometimes unruly. What he wants, he wants *now*—and he lets everybody know it.

One day at staff meeting, one of his teachers confessed her discomfort about Travis and his attitude. "I don't like him very much," she said in a quiet voice. "I try, but his behavior just gets in the way of the warm feelings I *want* to have for him. It seems like self-esteem is just oozing out all over him, and I don't like that."

The rest of the staff was silent for a moment, amazed at her confession. Then her coteacher spoke up. "I don't see Travis as a high-self-esteem child," he said cautiously. "Sure, he acts like he's got all the confidence in the world, but I think he's just making up for what he thinks he lacks."

"What do you mean?" asked the first teacher.

"Well, his bullying, for instance. When kids bully, it's not a mark of high self-esteem. Rather, it's a mark of low self-esteem. Kids who feel good about themselves—who they are and their capabilities—don't have to push other kids around."

"What else makes you think that Travis doesn't feel good about himself?" asked the first teacher. "I always thought that he felt *too* good about himself."

"The way he avoids doing anything that would show he's not as capable as the other kids. I think that because of his size people always expect more out of him than he can manage. It must be hard for him. I know I keep forgetting that he's not as old as he looks. So, if it's a problem for me, it's probably a problem for other people too."

"I've noticed that," acknowledged another teacher. "He puts a lot of energy into avoiding things. But he's so loud about his demands that we pay attention to those and not to the fact that he rarely gets involved in much of anything."

"I wonder if he has picked up my negative feelings," worried the first teacher. "It won't help him much to be around someone who admits she doesn't like him."

"I like him," said her coteacher. "But he probably doesn't know it because I'm always dealing with his negative behavior. That's when he gets attention from me. I think I'll work on changing that situation."

"I wonder how we can help him have more positive experiences in our program," mused the first teacher out loud. "Maybe we can gently move him toward activities that particularly interest him. I saw him trying to fold a paper airplane yesterday. Maybe I can get him to help me set up a project of paper airplanes for all the kids. That might give him some recognition."

"We could focus more on giving him some social skills, so he can quit bullying," was another suggestion.

"I wonder what would happen if we used the video camera and showed him what he looks like when he bullies," another colleague offered. "Or maybe that would be too threatening at this point."

"I think what he needs is a friend," said another. "I've noticed he seems drawn to Paul. Maybe we could encourage that relationship."

"Well," said the first teacher, "I'm glad I brought the subject up. I see Travis differently now, and I'm already beginning to like him better!"

Optimum challenge and risk taking is the secret to development, to learning, and to skill building. Scaffolding supports children so they have experiences with positive results when challenged to take a risk. When children encounter a problem or an obstacle and are about to get stuck in the problem-solving process, instead of rescuing them, adults can provide help—not heaps of help, but the smallest amount necessary. In this way they facilitate the continuation of the problem-solving process. They provide the missing link in the chain that allows children to move forward toward solutions. Thus, children's success is eventually their own, not the adult's. Experiencing personal success in the face of obstacles gives children messages about their abilities, about their self-worth.

Look at the following scenario, which illustrates scaffolding:

Dashinique wants to try out for the school play but has to choose a scene, and she can't make up her mind. An adult helps her sort out the possible contenders and then offers to listen to her try the part in each scene to see which works best. The answer becomes obvious to both of them as Dashinique acts out each scene. But then comes the second problem. Dashinique is scared of the tryout. She can speak her lines fine, but the thought of standing up in front of people makes her nervous. Again the adult helps by gathering some people to listen to her say her lines so she can practice in front of them and get used to being watched. It works. By the day of the tryouts, Dashinique has gained self-confidence and does well in spite of a few leftover nerves. Dashinique gets the part, and her success is her own. She only had a small bit of help (but lots of support and encouragement).

The next situation shows the difference between scaffolding and rescuing by providing too much help:

Brandon and Shelby are having an argument over who gets to use the glue gun to finish the craft projects they are both working on. Brandon had it first, but Shelby grabbed it and is holding it out of Brandon's reach when an adult comes up to the table. He could rescue Brandon by taking the glue gun from Shelby, but instead he helps the two sort out the situation. He starts by merely saying what he sees: "Brandon wants the glue gun." He waits to see what happens. Shelby answers, "Yeah, but I need it." Brandon cuts in, "I had it first." Shelby responds, "But you were just holding it—you weren't using it." Brandon turns to the adult, "Make her give it to me—I had it first! It isn't fair!" Shelby responds, "I really need it. If I don't hold down this piece the whole thing is going to fall apart." "Well . . . ," says Brandon, "I could let you use it for a minute if that's all you want to do. But next time don't grab!" he says emphatically. No longer needed, the adult walks off, and the two continue to work on their projects. Think about what the children learn and how they feel when they solve a problem themselves rather than depending on adults to fix it.

Most of us are tempted to take care of problems quickly when the solution is something we can deliver. When an adult sees a toddler fall, the urge is to pick him up and set him back on his feet. If the same person saw an adult fall, he would be more likely to come over and ask some questions and see what was needed at the moment. Maybe getting back on his feet isn't the best solution. Even without medical training, most of us know that it is better if the person can get back on his own feet after a fall. It's a test to see whether there is an injury. But with a child we tend to think differently. Why? Does it make us feel powerful? Does it feel good to help someone less capable than we are? Why are we more likely to use a scaffolding approach in a situation involving an adult and just fix the problem for a child? Scaffolding is appropriate for both children and adults. Rescuing doesn't promote self-esteem. It's more important to build real skills and remark about them than it is to try to boost self-esteem through empty words and pretending to be excited about nonexistent successes.

While you're thinking about skill building, consider all skills. Social skills are as important as physical and intellectual ones. When a child doesn't have a clue as to the effect of his or her behaviors on others, help that child come to see what is effective and what is not. Teach the skills the child may lack.

CHILDREN LEARN FROM FAILURE

One of the best feedback devices we have is failure. When we try something and it doesn't work, that's clear feedback. Of course, children need an array of positive experiences every day of their lives. However, in the name of success we sometimes go overboard in protecting children from failure, thus cutting them off from valuable learning experiences.

The problem with failure is that it often comes accompanied with heavy value judgments, spoken or unspoken. For example, many of us were called "dummy," or something comparable, as children when we made a mistake. It's hard not to pass on that kind of response to children when they make mistakes if that is the way we were treated. However, if children are to learn from mistakes as well as emerge from failure with an intact sense of self-worth, it is important that adults be supportive rather than critical. After all, a mistake is just that. We all make them, and we all stand to learn from them.

CELEBRATING DIFFERENCES: AN ANTIBIAS APPROACH

How adults react to differences in people affects how children react to differences, which influences self-esteem. Louise Derman-Sparks (1989) and her antibias curriculum task force have brought awareness of issues of bias that were hidden from many until recently.

The tendency in early childhood education and mainstream cultural child rearing has been to be blind to both privilege and injustice. The motto of many is that "Children are children," by which they mean differences such as skin color and gender don't matter (although the expression "Boys will be boys" dispels the gender-blindness myth). Many people who are "blind" to differences are those who don't carry a number of bruises and scars left by unfortunate remarks and by the biased behavior of those who promote stereotypes and practice unfair treatment. Conscious and unconscious racism, classism, sexism, and ablism are areas of bias still with us in spite of the fact that many assume that the way to equity is to ignore differences.

Instead of disregarding differences, we should celebrate them. "Celebrate differences"—what does that mean? A loving attempt to do just that occurs regularly, as well meaning adults bring "culture" into children's lives in order to teach them about people who are different from themselves. I remember a Japanese "tea party" put on in the classroom of one of my children. I attended as a parent guest and happened to sit next to a Japanese parent, who was also a guest. She was aghast at what she saw. "There's nothing Japanese about this!" she whispered to me, insulted by the whole proceeding. What had happened was that the teacher, based on what she had read and on her own ideas, had created a strange conglomeration of stereotypes and fantasy, which she believed was promoting cultural knowledge in the children.

Michael Dorris, in an article titled "Why I'm Not Thankful for Thanksgiving" (1978), writes about this phenomenon as it occurs with Native American children who may know nothing about their own heritage other than the mistaken stereotypes they encounter everywhere. Stereotypes of fighting savages come televised year-round from sports arenas across the country. Thanksgiving arrives every year, and cute little savages come out of the woodwork and get pinned on the bulletin boards, complete with feathers and tomahawks. Throughout the rest of the year, children are told not to act like "wild Indians" (a stereotype) but to sit quietly "Indian-style" (another stereotype) and sing songs that are deeply insulting to Native Americans, such as "Ten Little Indians" (dehumanizing). How can Native American children get a sense of who they are and of their worth if their culture is so stereotyped, devalued, and misrepresented?

Many mistakes and insults occur in the name of "celebrating differences." What is largely unrecognized or at least little discussed is that differences are connected with privilege and power. Differences carry values. It shouldn't be that way, but it is; and until that fact is recognized, there is little hope for change. That's where the antibias

Teach children to respond positively and appropriately to differences.

approach comes in. Adults must begin to recognize that value messages, both spoken and unspoken, are constantly sent and received about color, language, gender, and differences in physical abilities. Once adults become aware of the messages, they can begin to intercept them and change things. They can stop teaching children to ignore differences and instead teach them to respond positively and appropriately to differences.

Bias Can Hurt

Bias is natural, but it can be bad for children, and bad for adults. It's bad for those who are the target of bias. It not only harms self-esteem but sucks energy from the developmental process. It hurts to feel inferior. To be disempowered influences your life course.

Bias is also bad for those who are regarded as superior. When you see others as beneath you, you're out of touch with reality. It's dehumanizing to act superior and to enjoy unearned privilege, even when you are not aware of what's happening (Derman-Sparks, 1989; Howard, 1999).

It may seem easier to just pretend we're all alike in the name of equality. It may be easier to say to someone who is a different color than you are, "I don't think of you as different from me." But we're not all alike, and to pretend we are is to ignore the truth.

That kind of ignorance can be very insulting. If you are a woman, how would you like it if a man said to you, "I never think of you as female," meaning that remark as a compliment. Personally, I would be shocked if someone looked at me and didn't see me as a female. If you are a man, reverse the situation. Can you imagine yourself without your maleness? What if someone thought it was a compliment to you to remain ignorant of the fact that you are a male? How would you feel?

People want others to respond to who they are—not some blind, misguided version of who they should be. They want to be valued for who they are. For example, we would all be very uncomfortable around those who pretend to be "gender-blind," if, indeed, such a thing were possible. But adults pretend to be "color-blind" all the time in the name of equity. *Discriminating* on the basis of skin color is immoral. *Recognizing differences* in skin color is not, as long as you don't present one color as better than another.

People with disabilities also face these same problems, and any antibias approach should include them as well. Children need to learn to appreciate people for who they are and respond respectfully. With the push now for including children with disabilities into early care and education programs with their typically developing peers, children have opportunities to get to know people who don't have the same abilities that they have. And it also means that adults have to ensure that all children are treated fairly and with respect. They have to teach all children to get along with each other in the face of what may be big differences in ability. It's good learning for citizenship in a diverse society.

So, how can you teach children to respond positively in the face of differences if they've been taught to be blind to them? How can they respond positively if they've been exposed to biased attitudes and behaviors?

Start by modeling *antibias* behaviors. Become aware that the white able-bodied male is the norm in the society, and then try to get beyond that. Acknowledge the existence and experience of others by creating an antibias environment; expose children to pictures, books, and experiences of adults and children both like themselves and unlike themselves.

Point out stereotypes in the media when they occur. For example, when a book or a TV program shows weak, helpless women in limited roles, remark about the fact that women can be strong, intelligent people capable of doing many things.

Make it clear that bias is unacceptable. Children understand the concept of fair and unfair. Bias is definitely not fair. It is only fair that people of all races, religions, cultures, and physical abilities be treated with equal respect. It is only fair that both genders be allowed and indeed encouraged to expand beyond the limits of narrow gender roles. It is not fair to exclude someone from playing because of skin color, gender, or ability. Children need to understand that biased behavior is unacceptable.

Cultural Differences and Self-Esteem

Who am I? Each of us continues to explore that question throughout our lifetime. The answer we come up with and the value judgment we make about that answer make up our self-esteem.

Who am I? Each of us continues to explore that question throughout our lifetime. The answer we come up with, and the value judgment we make about that answer, make up our self-esteem.

As children grow, they develop an idea of themselves. This idea influences the behavior of the actual self—the one that operates in the world. The actual self in turn influences the self-concept, which continues to influence behavior. Thus, the actual self and the self-concept are forever tied together, and self-esteem grows from the interaction of the two.

Self-esteem is culturally based and depends on the basic concept of what makes up a person. As stated earlier, one culture looks at each person as a unique, potentially self-sufficient individual; another deemphasizes individuality and regards each person as an inseparable part of a greater whole. How parents focus their socialization efforts depends on which view they take.

An example that illustrates this point is how two people answer the question "Who are you?" As one talks about herself, she points out her personal characteristics and lists her roles and her accomplishments. She is emphasizing her individuality. The other one answers it by explaining her family lineage. She explains herself by pointing out relationships and ignoring individual accomplishments. A native Hawaiian person explained to me how hard it was to fill out an application for the university that asked her to list her achievements. "That's not who I am," she said. Instead she wanted to explain all the people she was related to in her family, including her ancestors.

Parents whose goal is individualism see their baby arriving in the world connected and dependent. The responsibility of the parent then is to help the baby learn that he or she is separate and apart. So those parents concentrate their efforts on autonomy, stressing self-help skills as the baby is ready. "I can do it all by myself" is music to their ears.

Parents who are more concerned about their children's ability to maintain connections have a different goal. They perceive an independent streak in their baby and see that independence as getting in the way of the close lifelong relationship to family that is their goal. So they focus on showing the baby in every way that dependence is a value and relates to connections—the greatest value. They know that some independence is inevitable, but they want to be sure that the baby is forever connected before he discovers autonomy. These parents focus on interdependence instead of independence. They are more likely to help the baby and young child than to teach self-help skills. They are not eager for the young child to brag, "I can do it all by myself."

How you build self-esteem in the early years is influenced by your view of the individual. However, realize that both views are valid, and they are not mutually exclusive. It isn't an either-or situation. When two people disagree about which is most important—individuality or group embeddedness—it's a matter of *where* they are placing the emphasis and *when* they see independence as an issue. It isn't independence versus interdependence. We all need both to survive. It is a matter of timing. One person may see the importance of *early* independence and its relationship to later getting along in a group. Another may perceive that only through subduing early independent urges can the child be truly part of the group, which will *later* lead to his or her developing or finding the *individual* skills, feelings, dreams, and desires that contribute to furthering group goals.

A valid goal of self-esteem is to enable children to stand on their own 2 feet as well as to stand together—indeed, lean on each other. It is important to get and give support and to feel good about it.

A True Story from the Author

When I was a new teacher faced with the job of educating parents, I had great enthusiasm for sharing all that I had learned in my teacher training, plus what I knew from experience. My energy was boundless, matched only by my zeal.

I will never forget trying to explain the concept of self-esteem to Teresa, a Mexican immigrant mother. Teresa kept insisting that there was no such concept in Spanish. I didn't give up. I kept trying to explain it to her. She stood there the whole time with a blank look on her face. She wasn't getting it. Finally she said in complete bewilderment, "*Self-esteem* doesn't make any sense at all. You can't esteem yourself; you can only esteem others."

I've been thinking about that exchange for 25 years. She didn't get what I was saying, but I didn't get what she was saying, either.

I've become less zealous in my parent education efforts as I've gotten older. I am much more willing to accept parents as they are; and if they want to "get better," I'll help—but only when I know what they perceive their weaknesses to be. Mainly I just support them in the good things they are doing. I don't decide where they need to improve; that's their decision. I help parents sort out what isn't working for them rather than tell them what I think and give advice. My motto is: The less advice the better.

But I still try to teach concepts. Self-esteem is one I haven't given up on; however, I've broadened my view of what I mean when I define self-esteem. I include the fact that though the concept fits European American culture, it probably doesn't fit everybody in the same way.

That's why I am not surprised when my students and I don't agree on what the term *self-esteem* means. For example, a student described a child who thought only of himself, never of others. He had a fierce temper and got out of control when he didn't get his way. He even hit his parents. His parents' efforts to guide his behavior didn't work. This little boy didn't get along with anybody and didn't have any friends either.

The student concluded that the child's problem was his self-esteem; he had too much of it. That isn't the way I see self-esteem. You can't get too much. When you have a good strong sense of self-worth, you are more able to see others as being worthy too. That's the point. Esteem breeds esteem.

Maybe it was just a translation problem with this student. Like Teresa, this student was a Spanish-speaker. However, I suspect that it wasn't a simple language difference. I believe our mismatch went deeper than that.

I decided to start with language as the path to understanding. I looked in my husband's huge Spanish-English dictionary. It had 196 entries under *self* in English and only 13 entries in Spanish. The concept of "self" is different in Spanish, and that difference influences the way people feel about the term *self-esteem*.

My experience with some parents, especially those from cultures where interdependence is more important than independence, is that focusing on "self" is a negative thing to do. To them, any word that has *self* connected to it is suspicious. They don't want to raise "self-ish" children. They want to raise children who put others first and think of themselves last.

I didn't understand that when I was trying to teach Teresa about self-esteem. I did understand it when I read my student's self-esteem paper. This latest time I put less effort into trying to teach her my way of looking at self-esteem and more into trying to understand her way.

Values show through misunderstandings. Every day I live I discover new ways of conceiving reality. The older I get the less I try to change people in general and parents in particular, and the more I try to tune in on their realities.

SUMMARY

We all ask ourselves the question "Who am I?" periodically, beginning in infancy when we must learn to distinguish ourselves from the environment around us. As we answer that question, we become more and more aware of ourselves as individuals. We learn about our personal power.

The answer to "Who am I?" reflects our *idea* of ourselves—our *self-concept*. How we *see* ourselves reflects our *self-image*, which is related to *self-concept*. How we *feel* about our self-concept and self-image reflects our *self-esteem*. Children are in a malleable state; and their self-esteem is, to some extent, in the hands of the adults in their lives. Those adults need to see the importance of keeping self-esteem intact so that children can grow to their fullest potential.

FOR DISCUSSION

1. How much does self-esteem show? Is it easy to tell who has high self-esteem and who doesn't? The text says that people aren't always what they seem. Do you believe that statement? Has that been your experience? Do you have some examples to back up your opinion?

2. Building self-esteem in a child involves a collaboration, not a deception. What does that sentence mean? What are some ways to collaborate with a child to help build self-esteem? What are some ways to help a child change a bad feeling about herself to a good feeling?

3. No matter what hand fate deals, it's not the events themselves that determine self-esteem; it's how the individual reacts to those events. Explain. Do you agree? If that is the case, how can adults help children who consistently have reactions that indicate low self-esteem?

4. What effect do bias and stereotyping have on self-esteem? Do you think that children in target groups for bias automatically have low self-esteem? Why or why not?

REFERENCES

Bredekamp, S., & Copple, C. (Eds.). (1997). *Developmentally appropriate practice in early childhood programs serving children from birth through age* 8. Washington, DC: National Association for the Education of Young Children.

Briggs, D. C. (1975). *Your child's self-esteem.* New York: Dolphin.

Bronson, M. (2000). Research in Review: Recognizing and supporting the development of self-regulation in young children. *Young Children,* 55(2), 32–27.

Butterfield, P. M., Martin, C. A., & Prairie, A. P. (2004). *Emotional connections: How relationships guide early learning.* Washington, DC: Zero to Three.

Coopersmith, S. (1967). *The antecedents of self-esteem.* San Francisco: Freeman.

Curry, N. E., & Johnson, C. N. (1990). *Beyond self-esteem: Developing a genuine sense of human value.* Washington, DC: National Association for the Education of Young Children.

Delpit, L., & Dowdy, J. K. (2002). *The skin that we speak: Thoughts on language and culture in the classroom.* New York: New Press.

Derman-Sparks, L. (1989). *Anti-bias curriculum: Tools for empowering young children.* Washington, DC: National Association for the Education of Young Children.

Dorris, M. (1978). Why I'm *not* thankful for Thanksgiving. *Interracial Books for Children Bulletin,* 9(7), 6–9.

Erikson, E. (1963). *Childhood and society.* New York: Norton.

Gonzalez-Mena, J. (2004). *Diversity in early care and education.* New York: McGraw-Hill.

Greenfield, P. M., Quiroz, B., Rothstein-Fisch, C., & Trumbull, E. (2001). *Bridging cultures between home and school.* Mahwah, NJ: Erlbaum.

Grieshaber, S., & Cannella, G. S. (2001). *Embracing identities in early childhood education: Diversity and possibilities.* New York: Teachers College Press.

Harter, S. (1983). Developmental perspectives on the self-system. In E. M. Heatherton (Ed.) &

P. H. Mussen (Series Ed.), *Handbook of child psychology: Vol. 4. Socialization, personality, and social development* (4th ed., pp. 275–386). New York: Wiley.

Hitz, R., & Driscoll, A. (1988). Praise or encouragement? New insights into praise: Implications for early childhood teachers. *Young Children, 43*(5), 6–13.

hooks, b. (2003). *Rock my soul: Black people and self-esteem.* New York: Atria.

Howard, G. (1999). *We can't teach what we don't know: White teachers, multiracial schools.* New York: Teachers College Press.

Kagan, J. (1984). *The nature of the child.* New York: Basic Books.

Kranowitz, C. S. (1998). *The out of sync child: Recognizing and coping with sensory integration dysfunction.* (1998). New York: Paragee.

Lally, J. R. (1995, November). The impact of child care policies and practices on infant/toddler identity formation. *Young Children, 51*(1), 58–67.

Landy, S. (2002). *Pathways to competence: Encouraging healthy social and emotional development in young children.* Baltimore: Brookes.

Markus, H. R., Mullally, P. R., & Kitayama, S. (1997). Selfways: Diversity in modes of cultural participation. In U. Neisser & D. Jopling (Eds.),

The conceptual self in context (pp. 12–61). New York: Cambridge University Press.

Marshall, H. H. (2000, November). Cultural influences on the development of self-concept. *Young Children, 56*(6), 19–22.

Morrison, J. W. (2001, Spring). Supporting biracial children's identity development. *Childhood Education, 77*(3), 134–138.

Noddings, N. (2002). *Educating moral people: A caring alternative to character education.* New York: Teachers College Press.

Paley, V. G. (1992). *You can't say you can't play.* Cambridge, MA: Harvard University Press.

Rogoff, B. (2003). *The cultural nature of human development.* New York: Oxford University Press.

Seligman, M. E. P. (1975). *Helplessness: On depression, development and death.* San Francisco: Freeman.

Teaching Tolerance Project. (1997). *Starting small: Teaching tolerance in preschool and the early grades.* Montgomery, AL: Southern Poverty Law Center.

Vygotsky, L. S. (1978). *Mind and society: The development of higher psychological process.* Cambridge, MA: Harvard University Press.

Wardel, F. (1993, March). How young children build images of themselves. *Exchange, 90.*

FURTHER READING

Akbar, N. (1985). *The community of self.* Tallahassee: Mind Productions.

Allen, P. G. (1998). *Off the reservation.* Boston: Beacon.

Billman, J. (1992, September). The Native American curriculum: Attempting alternatives to tepees and headbands. *Young Children, 47*(6), 22–25.

Butterfield, P. M., Martin, C. A., & Prairie, A. P. (2004). *Emotional connections: How relationships guide early learning.* Washington DC: Zero to Three.

Cajete, G. (1994). *Look to the mountain: An ecology of indigenous education.* Durango, CO: Kivaki.

Chang, H. N. L., Muckelroy, A., & Pulido-Tobiassen, D. (1996). *Looking in, looking out: Redefining child and early education in a diverse society.* San Francisco: California Tomorrow.

Chu, G. (1985). The changing concept of self in contemporary China. In A. J. Marsella, G. GeVos, &

F L. K. Hsu (Eds.), *Culture and self: Asian and Western perspectives* (pp. 252–277). New York: Tavistock.

Coll, C. G., Lamberty, G., Jenkins, R., McAdoo, H. P., Crnic, K., Wasik, B., Garcia, H., & Vazquez, H. (1996). An integrative model for the study of developmental competencies in minority children. *Child Development, 67,* 1891–1914.

Delpit, L., & Dowdy, J. K. (2002). *The skin that we speak: Thoughts on language and culture in the classroom.* New York: New Press.

Fadiman, A. (1997). *The spirit catches you and you fall down: A Hmong child, her American doctors, and the collision of two cultures.* New York: Noonday.

Fernea, E. W. (1995). *Children in the Muslim Middle East.* Austin: University of Texas Press.

Greenfield, P. M., Quiroz, B., Rothstein-Fisch, C., & Trumbull, E. (2001). *Bridging cultures between home and school.* Mahwah, NJ: Erlbaum.

Grieshaber, S., & Cannella, G. S. (2001). *Embracing identities in early childhood education: Diversity and possibilities*. New York: Teachers College Press.

Harwood, R. L., Miller, J. G., & Irizarry, N. L. (1995). *Culture and attachment: Perceptions of the child in context*. New York: Guilford.

hooks, b. (2003). *Rock my soul: Black people and self-esteem*. New York: Atria.

Hopson, D. P., & Hopson, D. S. (1990). *Different and wonderful: Raising black children in a race-conscious society*. Upper Saddle River, NJ: Merrill/Prentice Hall.

Kawagley, A. O. (1995). *A Yupiaz worldview: A pathway to ecology and spirit*. Prospect Heights, IL: Waveland.

Kendall, F. E. (1996). *Diversity in the classroom: A multicultural approach to the education of young children*. New York: Teachers College Press.

Kitayama, S., Markus, H. R., & Matsumoto, H. (1995). Culture, self, and emotion: A cultural perspective on "self-conscious" emotions. In J. Tangney & K. Fisher (Eds.), *Self-conscious emotions: The psychology of shame, guilt, embarrassment, and pride* (pp. 439–463). New York: Guilford.

Knight, P., Bernal, M. E., & Carlo, G. (1995). Socialization and the development of cooperative, competitive, and individualistic behaviors among Mexican American children. In E. E. Garcia & B. McLaughlin (Eds.), *Meeting the challenge of linguistic and cultural diversity in early childhood education* (pp. 85–102). New York: Teachers College Press.

Landy, S. (2002). *Pathways to competence: Encouraging healthy social and emotional development in young children*. Baltimore: Brookes.

Marshall, H. H. (2000, November). Cultural influences on the development of self-concept. *Young Children*, 56(6), pp. 19–22.

Mintzer, D., Als, H., Tronic, E. Z., & Brazelton, T. B. (1984). Parenting an infant with a birth defect: The regulation of self-esteem. *Psychoanalytic Study of the Child*, 39, 561–589.

Morrison, J. W. (2001, Spring). Supporting biracial children's identity development. *Childhood Education*, 77(3), 134–138.

Noddings, N. (2002). *Educating moral people: A caring alternative to character education*. New York: Teachers College Press.

Phillips, C. B. (1995). Culture: A process that empowers. In P. Mangione (Ed.), *Infant/toddler caregiving: A guide to culturally sensitive care*. Sacramento: Far West Laboratory and California Department of Education.

Pulido-Tobiassen, D., & Gonzalez-Mena, J. (1998). *A place to begin: Working with parents on issues of diversity*. Oakland: California Tomorrow.

Rael, J. (1993). *Being and vibration*. Tulsa: Council Oak Books.

Rashid, H. M. (1984, January). Promoting biculturalism in young African-American children. *Young Children*, 39(2) 13–23.

Rogoff, B. (2003). *The cultural nature of human development*. New York: Oxford University Press.

Ross, A. C. (Ehanamani). (1989). *Mitakuye oyasin: We are all related*. Denver: Wichoni Waste.

Stipek, D. (1998). Differences between Americans and Chinese in the circumstances evoking pride, shame, and guilt. *Journal of Cross-Cultural Psychology*, 29(5), 616–629.

Tedla, E. (1995). *Sankofa: African thought and education*. New York: Lang.

Ten quick ways to analyze children's books for racism and sexism (1986). New York: Council on Interracial Books for Children.

Valdes, G. (1996). *Con respeto: Bridging the distances between culturally diverse families and schools*. New York: Teachers College Press.

Wardle, F. (1987). Are you sensitive to interracial children's special identity needs? *Young Children*, 42(2), 53–59.

Werner, E. E. (1995, June). Resilience in development. *Current Directions in Psychological Science*, 4(3), 81–85.

PART 2

The Family

Socialization for High Self-Esteem in Healthy Families

Part 1 looked at the child in a developmental context. Part 2 examines the child in a family context. The next eight chapters explore specifics on families and socialization.

TOWARD A DEFINITION OF FAMILY

What is meant by the word *family*? Close your eyes and imagine a family. Does this family fit your *concept* of a family? Look around at symbols of families. Think of logos of agencies that serve families. What is the image conveyed by most? The images I usually see are a male, a female, and one or two children. Perhaps the balance and symmetry cause this type of family to be chosen as a logo—it's visually attractive. Or perhaps we're still living in the aftermath of the *Leave It to Beaver* tradition. Whatever the reason, many of us carry in our heads an image that doesn't apply to a large number of families in the United States today.

What are some of the many different ways a family can vary from the mother-father-child model? It can have more children or fewer. It can involve a marriage or not. The members can be all the same gender. Its members can vary greatly in age—by more than just two generations. It can include a number of people who are not related but are living under the same roof. It can include people who are related by blood or marriage along with those who are not related and who do not live under the same roof. (This kind of family is called a *kinship network*.) Its members can share the same bloodlines or name, or both, or neither. Its members can share the same history or not. The family can be *blended*—that is, composed of individuals coming together as a couple who each have children of their own. The blended family can live all together or not. The family can be composed of people who have traditional relationships to each other but were not born into them. Children may come into the family from outside—through adoption, fostering, or less formal arrangements.

There are numerous traditional names for these varying kinds of families. They include nuclear, insular, extended, embedded, single-parent, step, blended, adoptive, foster, communal, kinship networks, gay, and lesbian.

Families can vary infinitely in their makeup. Each variation has an effect on the socialization of any children in them. Families may originate through interracial or inter-religious unions. Families may have members who are differently abled. Families may come about through marriages or affiliations that cross generational lines.

FAMILY CORE FUNCTIONS: PROTECTION, COMMUNICATION, AND SELF-ESTEEM

The family's job is to turn any children in it into well functioning citizens for tomorrow's world. To do this job, families must provide for protection, communication, and the promotion of self-esteem. Self-esteem has a chapter all to itself; communication and protection are not set apart in separate chapters but are discussed throughout the book. A few additional words here may shed further light on the subject of protection when it needs to come from the society because the family no longer functions as protection from the outside or because harm to the children is coming from inside the family itself.

It used to be that wives and children belonged to men as possessions. A man could own property, a herd of cattle, a horse and buggy, and a house and furnishings. His family fell in the same category with the rest of his belongings. The law supported such a notion. No one interfered with what a man did to his property. If he destroyed what he owned, it was his business, until around the turn of the last century, when the Society for the Prevention of Cruelty to Animals (SPCA) stepped in to protect his pets, work animals, and livestock. In those days, wives and children still had no legal recourse if they were abused by the man who "owned" them. A man's home was his castle, and no one could penetrate it. Eventually the SPCA took on the task of protecting children too. Ironically, it was originally the only agency available to respond to child abuse!

Times have changed. Women managed to gain status as citizens in their own right; however, protection under the law has been slow in coming. Many battered women through the second half of the 20th century appealed to the law for help but were reprimanded for their part in their own victimization and sent back to their abusing husbands.

It has also taken a long time for children to gain rights as human beings entitled to protection under the law. It has been hard for society to decide that intervention was necessary to provide protection to children from their own parents. The idea that a family "owns" their children is still with us, though the law is now clear that abuse is illegal.

Of course, when a family is functioning well, they don't abuse their children, and the children don't need outside protection. But when things break down, intervention is necessary. The Child Abuse Prevention Act passed in 1974 made such intervention possible. The law becomes clearer and clearer, and now legal sanctions exist for those who are considered "mandated reporters" (e.g., child care workers, teachers, and counselors) and fail to report suspected abuse.

As a society, we are still new at intervening when families fail to function properly. Sensitivity is sometimes missing, and legal red tape can cause more problems than it solves. But we must step in. Far too many children have been permanently damaged, physically and emotionally, and sometimes killed by abuse. It's time to stop that kind of treatment and help families and children to heal.

One big problem concerns the questions: Where does society stop when it comes to intervention? How much and under what circumstances should the authorities step in and interfere? The newspapers every day carry accounts of families resisting governmental attention to what they consider their business. For example, differing views of medical treatment can end with a court case. If the parents' views and the medical establishment's views of what a child needs differ, the issue goes to a judge to decide whether the parents are withholding medical treatment or just looking at the child's condition from a different point of view.

Another issue is: To what extent can parents protect their children by making demands of the society's institutions? For example, do parents have the right to demand that certain books—some considered classics—be banned from school libraries because they don't want their children to read them? Should censorship be instituted in the media at the insistence of parents who want to ensure children won't watch certain programs on television or visit Web sites on the computer? We, as a society, are dealing with these issues every day and haven't come to a clear understanding about where parents' rights end and society's rights begin in certain matters, such as censorship.

OTHER FAMILY FUNCTIONS

Besides providing for protection, communication, and self-esteem, families perform a variety of other functions. Those functions may include financial support, emotional support, concepts of authority, housing, elderly care, child care and child rearing, education and intellectual stimulation, carrying on of traditions, religious education, and training in matters of the spirit.

Not all families perform all of these functions directly. Some use sources outside the family; others provide all of these roles and more.

One of the most important family functions is teaching about intimate and personal relationships. Through the early experiences described in Chapters 1 through 4, children develop the capacity to establish relationships with others. They learn what it means to get along in a family setting. They learn to share space, possessions, time, attention, and any available resources. From their family life, children learn ways of cooperating and competing and how those ways either fit or don't fit in their family's value system. They learn what to do when what they want or need conflicts with what other family members want or need. They learn about feelings and authority, and about being protected or not being protected.

Patterns of interactions among family members become a model for children. They learn about closeness and distance (between parents and children and between males and females). Each child experiences the patterns of his or her own home life and, as a result, is socialized in certain ways. Children learn what to expect from an alcoholic parent, for example. Perhaps what they learn is that there is no predictability. Children of alcoholics are socialized differently from those who do not have to deal with alcoholism. Loving or indifferent parents affect socialization; so do domineering or submissive siblings. Socialization is different if a child lives in a relaxed household where interactions tend to be good-natured instead of where tension prevails.

THE SHIFTING SHAPES OF TODAY'S FAMILIES

Today's family may come in a variety of changing forms and shapes. Living patterns are shifting, and those shifts change family structure. The changes aren't necessarily good or bad—they just are.

We are in a period of change regarding the family—its definition, its functions, and its structure. The family in some ways is in transition from an older system in which members played specific roles based on their position in the family to a newer one in which division of labor is agreed on rather than dependent on roles and in which decision making is not the realm of a single authority. Some families today are tied together more by companionship, mutual affection, and communication than by legal ties and traditional mandates. In some cases, commitment lasts only as long as the arrangement is working. When it breaks down, the configuration of the family may change as well.

The reality is that many children (more in some cultures than in others) will live in a single-parent family for some period of their childhood. And of those, many will live in blended families, as stepchildren or half-brothers and half-sisters.

This reality means that not only will they have to learn to be flexible, but also many will live in poverty for at least part of their childhood. When couples split up, the children usually go with the mother (though that tendency has changed slightly in recent years). A woman's standard of living drops drastically when she is supporting herself and her children without other sources of income.

Some of the patterns may seem new but aren't. For example, the divorce rate among today's parents isn't much different from the death rate of parents a century ago. Many children in those days were raised in single-parent families, by grandparents, in step and blended families, just as today's children are. We often put a glow on the past that makes it seem much kinder, healthier, and happier than the present—a glow that doesn't relate to reality.

Although parts of the next eight chapters have the slant of a white middle-class perspective, please read them with an eye to cultural sensitivity. Child rearing is not the same in all cultures, and what works for one culture may not be right for another. We need to know more about all the varieties of socialization in a multicultural society. We need to know more than will fit into one book. Some day, perhaps, we will have a multitude of books describing the many different cultural processes of socialization for high self-esteem in healthy families.

I must hasten to add that even though Part 2 is written from a white middle-class perspective, it is not the traditional white middle-class view of socialization. Rather, it is written from a developmental, research-oriented perspective (done mostly by white middle-class researchers). Raising your children traditionally—that is, as you were raised— is not necessarily better or worse than what is advocated here, but it may well be different.

FURTHER READING

Akbar, N. (2003). *Akbar papers in African psychology*. Tallahassee: Mind Productions.
Ballenger, C. (1999). *Teaching other people's children*. New York: Teachers College Press.

Brody, H. (2001). *The other side of Eden: Hunters, farmers, and the shaping of the world*. New York: North Point Press.

Bruno, H. E. (2003, September-October). Hearing parents in every language: An invitation to ECE professionals. *Child Care Information Exchange*, 153, pp. 58–60.

Cicchetti, D., & Toth, S. L. (Eds.). (1993). *Child abuse, child development and social policy: Advances in applied developmental psychology* (Vol. 8). Norwood, NJ: Ablex.

Copple, C., (Ed.). (2003). *A world of difference: Readings on teaching young children in a diverse society*. Washington, DC: National Association for the Education of Young Children.

Eggers-Pierola, C. (2002). *Connections and commitments: A Latino-based framework for early childhood educators*. Newton, MA: Educational Development Center.

Flaherty, M. J., Facteau, L., & Garver, P. (1991). Grandmother functions in multigenerational families: An exploratory study of black adolescent mothers and their infants. In R. Staples (Ed.), *The black family: Essays and studies* (pp. 192–199). Belmont, CA: Wadsworth.

Golden, O. (2000). The federal response to child abuse and neglect. *American Psychologist*, 55, 1050–1053.

Goldenberg, C., Gallimore, R., & Reese, L. (2003). Cause or effect? A longitudinal study of immigrant Latino parents' aspirations and expectations, and their children's school performance. *American Educational Research Journal*, 38, 547–582.

Gonzalez-Mena, J. (2004). *Diversity in early care and education*. New York: McGraw-Hill.

Kaiser, B., & Rasminsky, J. S. (2003, July). Opening the cultural door. *Young Children*, 58(4), 53–56.

Kozol, J. (1991). *Savage inequalities: Children in America's schools*. New York: Crown.

Lee, L. (2002). *Serving families: A handbook on the principles and strategies of the parent services project approach*. San Rafael, CA: Parent Services Project.

McLoyd, V. (1990). The impact of economic hardship on black families and children: Psychological distress, parenting, and socioemotional development. *Child Development*, 61, 311–346.

Payne, R. K. (2003). *A framework for understanding poverty*. Highlands, TX: Aha Process.

Raeff, C., Greenfield, P. M., & Quiroz, B. (2000, Spring). Conceptualizing interpersonal relationships in the cultural contexts of individualism and collectivism. *New Directions for Child and Adolescent Development*, 87, 59–74.

Reese, L. (2002). Parental strategies in contrasting cultural settings: Families in Mexico and El Norte. *Anthropology & Education Quarterly*, 33, 30–59.

Rogoff, B. (2003). *The cultural nature of human development*. New York: Oxford University Press.

Sammons, W. A. H., & Lewis, J. M. (2000, September). What schools are doing to help the children of divorce. *Young Children*, 55(5), 64–65.

Scott, J. W., & Black, A. (1991). Deep structures of African-American family life: Female and male kin networks. In R. Staples (Ed.), *The black family: Essays and studies* (pp. 201–209). Belmont, CA: Wadsworth.

Skeen, P., Robinson, B. E., & Flake-Hobson, C. (1984, January). Blended families: Overcoming the Cinderella myth. *Young Children*, 39(2), 64–74.

Staples, R. (Ed.). (1991). *The black family: Essays and studies*. Belmont, CA: Wadsworth.

Tan, A. L. (2004). *Chinese American children and families: A guide for educators and service providers*. Onley, MD: Association for Childhood Education International.

Thaxton, S. M. (2003). Grandparents as parents: Understanding the issues. In B. & R. Neugebauer, (Eds.), *The art of leadership*. Redmond, WA. Child Care Information Exchange.

Valdes, G. (1996). *Con respeto: Bridging the distances between culturally diverse families and schools*. New York: Teachers College Press.

White, E. (Qoyawayma, P.). (1992). *No turning back: A Hopi woman's struggle to live in two worlds*. Albuquerque, NM: University of New Mexico Press.

CHAPTER 5

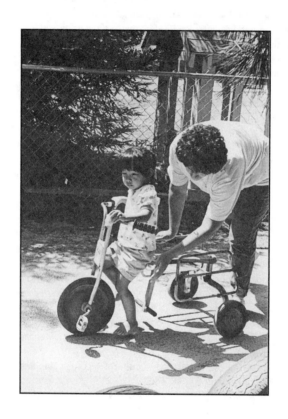

Goals, Values, and Culture

In *this chapter you'll discover* . . .

- ◆ Why a salad bowl is pluralistic and a melting pot is not
- ◆ The goals for a pluralistic society
- ◆ How unconscious culture is
- ◆ Two contrasting cultural patterns that affect child rearing
- ◆ Why one parent teaches her child pride while another criticizes her child for being proud
- ◆ A particular way of approaching problems, called "RERUN"
- ◆ How children learn morals and values
- ◆ Prosocial behaviors and how adults teach them to children

RELATIONSHIP OF GOALS AND VALUES TO CHILD-REARING PRACTICES

A worthwhile exercise for all parents, caregivers, and teachers is to examine their values, see how they relate to their goals, and decide whether what they are doing with their children is in tune with what they believe in. Take, for example, a family who highly values peace. Their goal is that each child be raised to always pursue nonviolent solutions to problems. If a parent in this family spanks as a means of controlling behavior, the child-rearing practice is out of tune with the value and the goal.

Anyone who works with other people's children—for instance, as a teacher, child care provider, or social worker—should understand the values and goals of the parents of those children. They should examine their own behaviors to see whether what they are doing with the children, or with the families, is in harmony with what the families want for themselves and their children.

Recognizing that cultural learning starts at birth and is mostly nonverbal, it is imperative that those who work with families familiarize themselves with cultural differences. The ideal is that families and the agencies that work with them are involved in a joint process to ensure that each child will become and remain a member of his or her own culture through a steady developmental progress toward cultural competence. Children may become bicultural in the process, but taking on another culture should be adding to what they already have—not replacing the original culture of the family.

Preserving diversity is a vital issue for all of us in the United States and the world beyond. It's not just that it's nice to be nice or even that it's good to be fair. Kindness is important and so is equity, especially when one group dominates another. It's not just because of the shifting demographics. Preserving diversity is a way to save us all!

Look at the biological argument. The rain forest that disappears today may well contain a plant that holds the cure for a disease that doesn't yet exist or that we haven't discovered (Rogoff, 2003). As variety in the grain supply is more and more determined by the profit in selling certain seeds and not in others, globalization occurs and diversity disappears. When a devastating disease comes along that wipes out the world's grain supply, there's nothing to replace it. Native grasses with immunities no longer exist and the world goes hungry.

Look at the cultural argument. In the name of unity through uniformity, making everyone in America "American" by acculturating them in the dominant culture of the United States moves them away from their culture of origin. Whether intended by the society at large, the common pattern of acculturation is the loss of the original culture. In other words, the process tends to be a subtractive one—one culture replacing another rather than an additive one resulting in a bicultural person. Cultures disappear every day in this country as the last person of that culture who speaks the language dies. When that happens, the survival of all of us becomes riskier. We face an uncertain future, one in which we can't even conceive of the problems that will arise. As cultural diversity diminishes, the solutions to those problems may disappear. For example, Native wisdom has allowed some cultures to continue countless thousands of years and should not be looked down on as primitive, but should be held in high regard as containing potential solutions we need now and in the future (Brody, 2001). We have a lot to learn about preserving the environment and alternative approaches to medicine and healing.

We find better, more effective solutions when we have a diverse team working on a problem. Differing worldviews and life experiences bring more opportunities for new and creative ways of looking at things in a new light, which offers a wider range of solutions.

This view of preserving diversity is based on cultural pluralism as a value. *Cultural pluralism* is the label for the idea that groups should be allowed, even encouraged, to hold on to what gives them their unique identities while maintaining their membership in the larger social framework. The old concept of the United States was of a melting pot, where all cultures blended into one. The new image, for those who believe in cultural pluralism, is of the United States as a salad bowl, where each of the many ingredients retains its own unique identity, but the parts combine into a "delicious" whole.

CULTURAL DIFFERENCES IN GOALS AND VALUES

Our culture affects everything we do, from determining the precise way we move our arms and legs when we walk to deciding the objectives we're moving toward. Culture rules how we position our bodies, how we touch each other, what we regard as mannerly, how we look at the world, how we think, what we see as art, how we sense time and perceive space, what we think is important, and how we set immediate and lifelong goals.

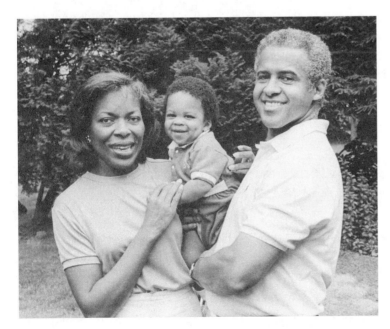

Cultural learning starts at birth and is mostly nonverbal.

Because culture is 90% unconscious, most people find it hard to talk about their own culture until it bumps up against one that's different. Culture is so much a part of our lives that we don't see it or pay attention to it. Yet it determines our values, which are also so much a part of our lives that they, too, remain invisible most of the time. Values are behind everything we do and every decision we make. They guide us in child rearing.

Everybody is influenced by his or her culture. Sometimes people describe themselves as a mixture or "a mutt" because their ancestors came to the United States from a number of different countries. They explain that they don't have a culture. What they mean is that they don't have particular heritage that they can put their finger on—but they do have a culture. It may be influenced by several ethnicities in their background, but nonetheless cultural rules of behavior are behind their behavior—whether they keep them or break them. Most of those people who think they don't have a culture are part of the dominant culture of the United States, which is uniquely American but highly influenced by its European roots. It's not that the dominant culture has a blandness about it. There are lots of different flavors within the culture, which can be influenced by the part of town or the area of the country where one grew up. Someone from California has only to spend a short time in New England, the South, or the Midwest to begin to taste those flavor differences, even when they only remain among people of the dominant culture. Some people didn't grow up in just one place. Take the case of military families; the military life adds its own special flavor.

Most people recognize when they meet up with people of their culture because they find they have things in common and feel comfortable with each other, unless class differences get in the way of the comfortable feeling. Culture, race, ethnicity, class, gender, religion, sexual orientation, and ability all mix together to make the study of culture difficult and confusing. For this reason instead of continuing to focus on culture alone, I'm going to examine a set of patterns that influence how parents raise their children. This set of patterns has come up in each of the chapters preceding this one, but here the pattern is named and explicitly explained. The pattern has to do with independence and interdependence. Most parents put more emphasis on one or the other and they set goals for their children based on their own pattern which is their top priority (Greenfield, Quiroz, & Raeff, 2000; Greenfield, Quiroz, Rothstein-Fisch, & Trumbull, 2001).

How Do Independence and Interdependence Goals Show?

What do parents who focus on independence actually do that shows their focus? They encourage early self-help skills, for one thing. They expect toddlers to feed themselves and soon after to dress themselves. They teach their children to sleep alone in their own beds. They may take them into their bed for short periods, but their goal is to get the child back to bed. If they "baby" their children, they feel guilty.

Parents who focus on interdependent relationships are less adamant about babies learning to sleep through the night alone. The idea of "babying" children is viewed in a positive light, not a negative one. Babies and parents tend to have strong connections, so prolonging baby-hood makes sense if your goal is *inter*dependence. These parents are more worried about maintaining relationships than creating an independent individual, so they see nothing wrong with coddling children.

It's a completely different way of looking at getting needs met. Children who grow up in an individualistic home learn that it's each person's job to take care of his or her own needs. But children who grow up in "other-centered" homes learn that the needs of the others are their problem. They still get their needs met, because while they are taking care of others, they are being taken care of. In both kinds of homes, basic needs get met, but the process is different in each.

Of course, most people, no matter how they were raised, do become *both* independent individuals and people who create and maintain relationships. Children accomplish both the major tasks even if their parents only focus on one. Parents expect their children to be both independent and connected, but they work harder on what they believe to be most impor-tant. They leave to chance what they are less concerned about or work toward it in random bits and pieces.

CONTRASTING CULTURAL PATTERNS

What are some cultural differences? Because one culture is best seen in contrast to another, I've taken the approach of pointing out cultural patterns that are quite different from each other, rather than listing characteristics of various cultures. These patterns have been intro-duced earlier but will be expanded on here. It is important to point out that to make a con-trast I've exaggerated differences. Although some families may fit neatly into one category or the other, many defy categorization. As you read about pattern 1 and pattern 2 families, you'll probably find that your family fits somewhere between the two. The point is not to fit families into categories but to show contrasts and differences by highlighting them.

Pattern 1 values people as unique individuals, starting at birth. Stress is on inde-pendence of both thought and action. Members of this culture regard the individual's feelings highly and encourage expression of those feelings. Individuals in this culture are perceived to have personal power, and they are taught assertiveness from an early age. If you're not a pattern 1 person yourself, you probably know some people who are. You probably also realize that there is diversity even among people who all belong to pattern 1. They aren't all alike.

Pattern 2 sees the group as more important than the individual. Individual unique-ness is valued only as it serves the group. Children are taught to blend in, to fit. They learn to see the group as the basic unit and themselves as a part of it, rather than see-ing the individual as the basic unit. In other words, the individual is nothing by him- or herself—the individual counts only as a part of the group.

This pattern stresses interdependence (mutual dependence) and obedience. Obedi-ence has to do with the group will, which is often expressed by a hierarchy of authority.

The sense of identity of a pattern 2 person comes from membership in the group rather than from personal competence, power, significance, lovability, or virtue. The behavior of an individual is never just a reflection of him- or herself; instead it reflects on the group and either adds to or detracts from the group identity. Remember, all pattern 2 people are not alike. There is always diversity in any group.

The two patterns differ in their view of the attachment process, which was mentioned in Chapter 1. The pattern 2 person sees early attachment as important—something that must happen to ensure that the baby will be properly cared for. Attachment and separation cannot be divided and are viewed as two parts of a single process that follows a progression leading to later independence from the family of origin. Indeed, the separation part of the process is as important as the attachment part and occurs in stages throughout childhood and then finally culminates in "leaving home" at some point after adolescence. After he or she leaves home, the individual is expected to take full charge of his or her own life and no longer look for parental advice or support more than just occasionally.

The pattern 2 person sees attachment differently. The focus is on keeping the child in the family/group rather than on teaching separation skills. Attachment is not such an issue at the beginning because group expectations ensure that each baby will be taken care of properly—if not by the mother, then by another member of the group. It's not up to the individual to be drawn to the baby and therefore give it the care it needs; instead, it's up to the group member to fulfill an expected role that is unquestioned.

Attachment in the pattern 2 culture is a lifetime process; the child is expected to remain unto death a viable member of the family into which he or she is born. Each person in the group is connected to and interdependent on the other members of the group.

How might these themes of individual versus group, attachment versus separation, and independence versus interdependence show up in child-rearing practices? Where might the conflicts lie if a pattern 1 person married into a pattern 2 family, or if a pattern 1 person were the teacher or child care provider of a pattern 2 person?

WHEN PARENTS AND/OR CAREGIVERS OR TEACHERS HAVE CONFLICTING GOALS AND VALUES

Pattern 1 parents might put their baby daughter to sleep in a crib in a room separate from their bedroom. In fact, if they can afford it, they might give her a room of her own from the beginning. A goal would be to get her to put herself to sleep in her own bed and stay there asleep all night long. Families might vary about when they would expect this to occur—and some would "baby" the child longer than others—but eventually the child is expected to show her ability to manage on her own by sleeping alone.

Pattern 2 parents might sleep with their daughter from birth on, never buying her a crib or planning to provide her with a room of her own. They might move her out of the parental bed when another baby came along, but most likely would move her into a sibling's bed or perhaps in with her grandmother. Being alone, even when asleep, is not sought after by most members of a pattern 2 culture.

A pattern 1 caregiver or teacher may expect to raise each child's self-esteem by emphasizing individuality. He or she may purposely set out to praise accomplishments—drawing attention to individual behavior. Comments like "You did that all by yourself!"

illustrate this emphasis on the individual. Along the same lines, the caregiver or teacher may provide for each child a storage cubby that is decorated with the child's name in bold print and a picture of him or her. The idea is for the child to gain a sense of his or her own personal identity while experiencing private ownership, even in the group situation.

A pattern 2 caregiver or teacher may put energy into being sure no one child is singled out but that all remain firmly fixed in the group. He or she will point out group accomplishments rather than individual achievements. He or she will focus on rewarding cooperative efforts instead of individual efforts. This caregiver or teacher will downplay individual achievement by refusing personal credit when given a compliment. He or she will teach "modesty" to those children who "brag" about themselves.

Several examples common to preschool and some homes serve to show the difference between a group emphasis and an emphasis on individuals. In one program children use clay to create objects to fire and take home. Another program uses clay to explore and experiment with, and when it is time to clean up, all the clay goes back into the common pot. One parent bought each of his four children a small box of crayons so each would have a full set. Another parent bought a big box of crayons for his six children to share. A similar example in a preschool shows the same two mind-sets. One teacher sorted the crayons and gave each child a paper cup with a variety of colors of crayons in it. Another teacher sorted them by colors and put a cup of each color in the middle of the table. One program has a finger paint table where children work together experiencing the qualities of the material and then wash off the finger paint when they are finished. Another program has separate pieces of paper, and each child does a finger painting, which, when dried, is hung up on the wall and eventually taken home. One mother made play dough and colored each of the wads a different color so the children could tell which one was theirs, while another mother made one big batch all of one color. These examples are designed to show not right or wrong but differences in perceptions of what children need to learn. They also aren't intended to show pure pattern 1 or 2 programs, only in little ways how diversity works. Many programs and parents combine the two styles.

Other differences show up in ordinary daily routine activities. In a pattern 1 culture, the emphasis is on helping oneself; in a pattern 2 culture, the emphasis is on helping others. This difference shows up in the attitude about training for self-help skills. A pattern 1 parent, teacher, or caregiver is in a hurry for the child to learn to feed himself, for example. When the baby first grabs the spoon, many pattern 1 people will get another spoon and let the baby begin to help. If the baby isn't yet capable of using a spoon, finger food is given so the child gets the idea that he or she can feed independently.

A pattern 2 parent, teacher, or caregiver is too busy modeling "helping," in keeping with the goal of interdependence, to worry about teaching the baby to "do it himself." Needless to say, pattern 1 children are able to do things for themselves at a surprisingly young age, and pattern 2 children are able to do things for other children at a surprisingly young age. In some cultures around the world with pattern 2 tendencies, preschool-age children take charge of their younger siblings, doing for the baby what was done for them only a short time before.

Toilet training is another area where the two patterns may conflict. The pattern 1 caregiver, teacher, or parent puts the emphasis on self-help, so he or she doesn't see signs of readiness for toilet training until the child is somewhere around 2 years of age. To this adult, toilet training starts when children are able to control bladder and bowels, handle clothing, and get to the toilet or potty on their own.

A pattern 2 caregiver, teacher, or parent has a very different view. With the deemphasis on self-help and the emphasis on interdependence, the adult is part of the child's elimination processes from the beginning. The adult watches from the early months on for signals preceding bowel and bladder activity. When the signals appear, the adult responds immediately. Eventually the two set up a system of signals that allow the adult to get the child bare-bottomed and to the proper place, and then trigger the elimination response. If you've never seen this, I can assure you, it's impressive!

A pattern 2 caregiver, teacher, or parent may view manners as much more important than self-expression. Learning manners reflects the goal of becoming a good group member. Pattern 2 caregivers, teachers, or parents may be horrified as they watch a pattern 1 adult encourage children to speak out, express anger, and eat in any way they want.

To illustrate the difference in the early months, contrast these two approaches. One adult touches a screaming baby lightly on the shoulder and says, "I know you're mad. It's OK to cry!" After reviewing the situation—he's not tired, hungry, or in need of a change—she leaves him alone to express himself, checking in periodically to let him know that he hasn't been deserted. She doesn't try to distract him or lull him with words or touch because she thinks that his expression of emotion is healthy.

Another adult, rocking and lulling, holding the baby tight, says, "There, there, quiet down, it's OK! You're upsetting everyone else. Please don't cry!" She tries to stop the crying, using all the verbal and nonverbal techniques she has. She doesn't regard displays of anger as healthy. She doesn't feel that the baby has the individual right to destroy the peace of the household. She tries to teach him to consider others, even though she understands that he's too young to learn this lesson.

A pattern 1 caregiver, teacher, or parent is understanding when a 4-year-old cries when away from home or parents for the first time. But the expectation is that this child needs to learn to cope with separation and that this experience is good for him. The crying may go on for awhile, but the adult is confident that the child will gain coping skills and will eventually adjust. The adult sees this period as just one in a long series of separation experiences.

On the other hand, the crying of a pattern 2 child may be considered "bad behavior" because the goal is harmony and equanimity. In the book *Culture and Attachment*, Harwood, Miller, and Irizarry (1995) point out that many Puerto Rican mothers saw crying in this situation as showing a lack of manners. Crying in a pattern 2 child may be devastating to the adults in his life because they don't see that being away from family is in his best interests, even though circumstances have dictated the separation. They may be less willing to look at this situation as good for him. They may have less knowledge about teaching coping strategies or helping with separation because they don't value separation.

A pattern 1 caregiver, teacher, or parent says, "Call me by my first name," in her eagerness to be friendly. She values casualness. The pattern 2 adult who is more used to respecting titles and lives in a social hierarchy may be uncomfortable with such informality. She may insist on using the teacher's last name with *Mrs.*, *Ms.*, or *Miss* in front of it. She may even use the title *Teacher* instead of the name and teach her children to do the same. She doesn't see this first-name business as creating closeness but only showing a lack of respect.

WHAT TO DO WHEN CONFLICTS ARISE

Conflicts constantly arise—in families, between parents, and between parents and the professionals who serve them. In some cases these conflicts have cultural differences at their bases.

In the United States today, the professionals in most areas of expertise, regardless of their home culture, are trained from a white middle-class European American perspective. However, many of the families they deal with are not of this mainstream culture. Sensitivity to, understanding of, and respect for differences is vital if we are to fulfill the dream of a pluralistic society based on equity and justice.[1]

What do you do when you are having a cultural conflict? First, become aware that you are in a cultural conflict. Because we all tend to look at any situation from our own point of view, it may be very hard to understand another person's frame of reference, which, of course, is cultural. All of us are ethnocentric—that is, we look out of our own cultural eyes and measure others with our own cultural yardstick. It takes awareness and skill to move from our ethnocentric position.

Dialoguing is an approach to problem-solving a conflict that is effective at helping the disagreeing parties see each other's point of view. Rather than trying to convince another of one's own viewpoint, people engaged in dialogue try to understand the other perspective. The idea is not to win but to find the best solution for all concerned.

The following list summarizes the differences between an argument and a dialogue:

- The object of an argument is to win; the object of a dialogue is to gather information.
- The arguer tells; the dialoguer asks.
- The arguer tries to persuade; the dialoguer seeks to learn.
- The arguer tries to convince; the dialoguer wants to discover.
- The arguer sees two opposing views and considers hers the valid or best one; the dialoguer is willing to understand multiple viewpoints.

Most people are better at argument than they are at dialogue. When faced with a conflict or problem, almost nobody considers starting a dialogue. Especially when it is an emotional conflict, many people are likely to jump feet-first into an argument rather than begin a dialogue. When they argue, they are anxious to win, which makes them leap to conclusions.

---

[1]Stanley Sue and Thom Moore (1984) make a good case for why the United States should be a pluralistic society and do a good job of defining and describing such a society.

Dialoguing is an approach to problem-solving a conflict that is effective at helping the disagreeing parties see each other's point of view.

If you watch people arguing, you can see some types of body language that show each person is trying to convince the other of something. When arguing, many people tend to stand firm and tough when listening—assuming a defensive position. They are anything but open. They seem to be just waiting for their turn. When they talk, they lean forward and make aggressive gestures with their hands. Just by looking at them, even if you can't hear their words, you can tell that they are fighting about something. The body language of someone in a potentially win-lose situation is different from someone who is truly trying to understand another point of view, such as happens when people enter a dialogue. Gestures reflect their attitude—hands, especially. Instead of waving fists or making strong, tense movements, dialoguing people tend to let their hands remain open.

So how does one switch from an argument to a dialogue in the heat of the moment? Start by noticing your body language. Sometimes you can just change your body language, and an energy switch will follow. Then it's a matter of doing one simple thing: listening to the other person. To truly listen, one must suspend judgments and focus on what's being said rather than just gathering ammunition for the next attack. Really hearing someone is extremely simple, but it's not easy.

From then on it's a matter of working through a problem-solving procedure. To help remember the elements of this approach think of the word *rerun*. RERUN stands for reflect, explain, reason, understand, and negotiate. To explain further:

- *Reflect*. This is the action of acknowledging what you perceive the other person is thinking or feeling. If you understand where the person is coming from, say, "I think you're looking at it this way. . . ." Or if you perceive that the person is full of emotion, acknowledge your perception: "You really sound upset." Those two openers are invitations for the person to talk some more. People who know that their feelings and thoughts are received and accepted by you are likely to be more open to listening—if not right away, eventually.
- *Explain*. Remember, we have two ears and only one mouth; that's a reminder that we should listen twice as much as we talk. Only after you have listened, listened, and listened is it time to explain your point of view.
- *Reason*. Part of the explanation should include the reason you have for your perspective.
- *Understand*. Next comes the hardest part. Tune in to both thoughts and feelings and try to understand the situation from both points of view. You don't have to say anything out loud at this point, just be sure you have clarity. You may have to talk inwardly to yourself to get it. And while you're going inward, make sure you understand yourself as well as the other person. Self-reflection is an important part of the process. When you think you understand, you're ready for the next step.
- *Negotiate*. Now is the time for the finale. Try brainstorming together until you can find a mutually satisfying solution. Don't give up. Refuse to take an either-or attitude. ("It's either my way or your way, and it can't be both ways.") If you don't get stuck in a dualistic frame of mind, you can probably find a third or fourth solution that is different from or combines both your stances on the matter. Creative negotiators can open up new avenues of action that no one ever thought of before. Bredekamp and Copple (1997) point out that thinking in terms of either one solution or the other keeps us from communicating across cultures. We need to move into a "both-and" mode. Isaura Barrera, in *Skilled Dialogue* (Barrera & Corso, 2003), calls the move away from dualistic thinking "third space." She says that third space goes beyond compromise and includes both positions. It's not a meeting in the middle, but finding a different space altogether that is big enough to encompass more perspectives and a larger view of truth.

The finale is seldom final. In only the simplest situations do you negotiate an agreement without communication breaking down. When feelings arise, return to the beginning. Go back through the first four (R-E-R-U) parts. You may have to R-E-R-U-N many times before the problem is solved. Be patient.

Often, instead of taking time to really work through something, we get impatient and reach into the old hip holster and pull out a power play if we have one. It's unfortunate when that happens because one-upmanship destroys relationships rather than strengthening them. It may take a long time to solve a particular problem when the conflict is deep and serious, but a positive outcome in the form of a solution everyone is satisfied with is worth the time and effort it sometimes takes.

Though the RERUN device seems to consist of distinct steps or a sequence to follow, the elements are more holistic than that. They come as a package and may occur in a different order or all mixed up as one. The fact that the acronym spells *rerun* serves as a reminder that you can repeat the process as often as necessary until the problem is solved—you come to an agreement, or you agree to carry on while disagreeing.

The suggestions that follow for working on cross-cultural communication are inspired by Louise Derman-Sparks (1989) and her Antibias Task Force. These tips are designed to help facilitate communication when in a cultural conflict involving values, goals, and early childhood child-rearing and educational practices.

A Cultural Conflict

Helen is a vegetarian. When she put her daughter, Sissy, into child care, she had a talk with the director to explain her dietary beliefs. The director explained to her that the center's food was catered and that the protein was usually a meat dish. She suggested that Sissy be served everything but the meat and that Helen supplement with some kind of protein dish. Helen agreed, and everything went well for awhile.

Then the director moved on and a new director was hired. Sissy moved up from the younger group to the older group, and that meant a new teacher. Helen got busy one morning and forgot to send Sissy's protein dish. No one complained, including Sissy, so before long Helen was dropping her daughter off in the morning without the supplemental food. She assumed that her daughter was getting enough to eat without it.

Then one day Helen took the afternoon off and arrived at lunchtime to pick up her daughter. She was horrified to find Sissy sitting at the table with the other children, chewing happily on a chicken drumstick. She looked around to see who was responsible and found a substitute in charge. She complained to the substitute and then thought the matter was settled.

However, a few weeks later Sissy talked about the fish sticks she had had for lunch. Helen stormed into the center, demanding to see the director.

The director pushed herself back from her desk and its huge pile of paperwork and invited Helen to sit down. Angrily, Helen threw herself into a chair, launching into a bitter tirade. When she finally paused for breath, the director said, with concern in her voice and in her facial expression, "I see how upset you are about this!"

That got Helen going again. When she paused, the director said that she wanted Sissy's teacher in on the discussion and went to get her.

When the three of them sat down together, Helen was calmer. "Why did you feed Sissy meat?" she demanded of the teacher.

"I didn't—only fish. I know she doesn't eat red meat," answered the teacher.

"She doesn't eat any kind of meat," Helen shot back.

The teacher looked surprised. "I didn't realize you considered fish meat."

"And chicken!" added Helen.

"Oh!" responded the teacher, biting her lip. "I'm sorry," she went on. "It's just that Sissy always seems so hungry, like she can't really get full on the fruits and vegetables alone. I feel sorry for her."

The conversation went on—give and take—and slowly the facts and feelings on both sides began to emerge. The teacher's misunderstanding about what Helen considered meat gave way to her feelings about Sissy feeling hungry and left out as the other children enjoyed hamburgers and hot dogs and other foods forbidden to Sissy. She was obviously not committed to vegetarianism herself, and it was hard for her to see why Helen felt so strongly about it. She even questioned whether a vegetarian diet was a properly nutritious one for a child.

Helen in turn confessed that she had some resentment that children with food allergies were carefully monitored and given special consideration, yet no one seemed to care what Sissy ate. She felt the program should individualize more.

For awhile it looked as if these two might never see eye to eye, yet once the feelings got out in the open, the atmosphere began to change. It became obvious that both were concerned about Sissy, and once they realized that they had that in common, they found it wasn't so hard to sort out the problem and solve it. Respect and communication were the keys, they decided; and when the conversation ended, they both left with good feelings about each other.

Build Relationships

People who have good relationships are more likely to work on their conflicts in more healthy ways. Relationships sometimes just happen, but more often, they need to be initiated and then nurtured. Commit yourself to working constantly on the total relationship, not just the conflict.

Know Yourself

Be clear about what you believe in. Be aware of your own values and goals. Check to see whether your behavior reflects your values and goals. If you are in tune with yourself and are clear about what you believe in, you're less likely to present a strong defensive stance in the face of conflict. It is when we feel ambiguous that we come on the strongest.

Work to Bring Differences Out in the Open

Be sensitive to your own discomfort in response to the behavior of others. Tune in on something that bothers you, instead of just ignoring it and hoping it will go away. Work to identify what specific behaviors of others make you uncomfortable. Try to discover exactly what in yourself creates this discomfort.

You need to be honest with yourself and to do some soul-searching to get your prejudices out in the open. None of us likes to do that, but it's an important part of relationships and clear communication.

While you're looking at yourself, look for signs of discomfort in other people in response to your behavior. When you discover discomfort, talk about it!

Discuss Differences

Discussing differences isn't easy to do. Some people shy away from direct discussion of sensitive areas. Many want to cover up differences because they perceive that recognizing them will complicate the relationship. Others avoid discussion of differences in hopes of promoting equality and harmony. Some have never thought about values until they bump up against a set that is different from their own.

Become an Effective Cross-Cultural Communicator

Learn how to open up communication instead of shutting it down. Work to build a relationship with the person or the people with whom you're in conflict. You'll enhance your chances for conflict management or resolution if a relationship exists. Be patient. These things take time.

Learn about communication styles that are different from yours. Teach your own communication styles. Become aware of body language, voice tone, posture, and position. All of these carry cultural messages that are open to being misinterpreted across cultures. For example, if you're a parent, and a caregiver stands too close to you when carrying on a conversation, you may feel that she is pushy or at least strange, whereas she may think she is conveying warmth and friendliness. If you are a teacher, and a parent is very late to an appointment and then arrives and fails to apologize, you may make assumptions about his priorities or his manners. But he may have a very different time sense from yours and not consider himself late at all. He may have no idea that he has offended you.

If you tend to talk in a high-pitched voice when you are excited, and others interpret your tone of voice as anger, explain to them what you're really feeling. (Pitches and tones carry emotional messages that are culturally based and not the same across cultures.)

Problem Solve

Use a problem-solving approach to conflicts rather than a power approach (if you're the one with the power in the situation). Dialogue. Communicate. Be flexible when you can. Negotiate when possible. (See Chapter 9 for examples of how to use this approach with children.) Notice when you are getting defensive. Defensiveness gets in the way of problem solving.

Commit Yourself to Education

Learn about other cultures. Become a student of culture if you are in a cross-cultural situation. You don't have to become an anthropologist, but you can use some of the anthropologist's approaches to studying a culture. Read, but don't believe everything you read. Check it out. Observe and listen. Ask, but don't believe everything you are told. Check it out. You'll hear lots of generalizations about particular cultures. Don't get sucked into promoting more stereotypes! Discuss what you are seeing, hearing, reading, and being told with other people of the culture you are learning about. Be a critical thinker.

HELPING CHILDREN UNDERSTAND AND VALUE CULTURAL PLURALISM

Just as adults are ethnocentric, so are children. Ethnocentrism relates to the egocentrism that young children struggle with as they slowly learn to see the world from more than one point of view. Adults need to help children work through both their ethnocentrism and their egocentrism. They can do that only if they have grappled with their own ethnocentrism. It's a matter of getting children to communicate with each other, accept the reality of another as valid, and learn what it's like to walk in another's shoes.

Some children come from a multicultural background and have firsthand experience with cultural pluralism. This can be a great benefit for them and for those around them who can use them as models. When we see a person who is comfortable operating out of more than one culture, we gain an idea of how it works.

Here is an example of a bicultural child:

David was born in this country of a Mexican father and an Anglo American mother. The family traveled frequently to Mexico and enjoyed extended visits with the father's

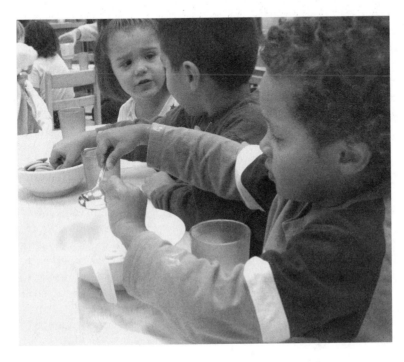

Sensitivity to, understanding of, and respect for differences are vital.

family. By the time David entered preschool at the age of 4, he was already bilingual and bicultural. He could perform amazing feats, such as making a judgment about which language to speak with someone he met for the first time. He was seldom wrong. He could also switch midstream from English to Spanish when the occasion demanded. For example, if he was playing in the sand with an Anglo child and a Spanish-speaking child approached, David would speak English with one and Spanish with the other, while playing with both. David fits very well in an all-Anglo group or an all-Mexican group or a Mexican American group. He has chameleon-like qualities. He is a truly bicultural person.

Children have the ability to compartmentalize—that is, to understand that one set of behaviors is appropriate at Grandmother's, another at child care, and still another at home. Although we, as adults, may try hard to make most of the environments children find themselves in consistent, that's not the way the world works. One set of behaviors is expected in the bank, another at the park. Part of socialization is learning how to behave in each of the many environments in which children find themselves. Learning culturally appropriate behavior is one aspect of this same skill.

TEACHING MORALS AND VALUES TO CHILDREN

How do children come to know what's important in life and set their goals accordingly? How do children come to know right from wrong? Although the two questions are in many ways the same, the answer to the first mostly concerns values; the answer to the second mostly concerns morals.

Our values begin to come to us in our cribs (or our parents' bed) when we are infants. They are absorbed along with the breast milk or the formula we drink. They come hand in hand with our culture. They are the *shoulds* and *shouldn'ts* that guide our footsteps through life and the beliefs we feel compelled to stand up for. They tell us what to respect and what to oppose.

Some values are simply absorbed in infancy; others come later in the form of little lessons. "Don't hurt the caterpillar" may reflect a value of life. "Be gentle with your brother" may reflect a value of peace and harmony. "Don't let people push you around" may reflect a value of self-assertion. "Work hard at school" may reflect a value of attaining individual success or of being an asset to your family. As children grow, they continually define, appraise, and, sometimes, modify their values. In a pattern 1 culture, children are expected to do some deep soul-searching at some point, usually in adolescence. They are expected to examine the set of values they've grown up with and come to their own conclusions about whether to embrace those values or to redefine them and come up with their own set. Upset as parents may be at the possibility that their children will reject their values, pattern 1 parents aren't entirely surprised, because the culture expects people to make up their own minds about values. After all, independence is a value—independence of thought as well as of action.

Pattern 2 parents may be far less tolerant if their children threaten to deviate from the set of values the family embraces. The younger generation is not supposed to question the older one. Deciding values is not an individual matter for children—or for adults either, for that matter.

TEACHING MORALS BY HELPING CHILDREN EXAMINE THEIR DECISION-MAKING PROCESS

We—children and grown-ups alike—deal with morals and values with every decision we make. Each time we are forced to choose an action (and each action is a choice, whether we realize it or not), we go through a process of determining whether we're making the right decision. The impulsive person puts less thought into decisions than the more considered one; however, unless the person is reacting from reflexes alone, there is a flash of thought behind each decision.

If you could tune in on the flash, you'd find some of the following questions:

- Will I be punished if I decide to do this (either by my own bad feelings or by someone else in a physical or emotional way)?
- Will I be rewarded? (Will I gain some benefit, including feeling good about doing this?)
- Will this action or decision make someone whom I care about happy—thus making *me* happy (another form of reward)?
- Is there a rule (or a law) that requires or forbids it? And if I break the law and get caught, what is the punishment? And if I break the law and don't get caught, how will I feel?
- Is this what I would want someone else to do? (This calls into play the Golden Rule: "Do unto others as you would have others do unto you.")
- What's the right thing to do? (Using my highest reasoning abilities—is this the best decision, most right, highest good, or least bad thing to do?)
- Who might be hurt by my decision or action?

We don't always ask these questions consciously, but on some level they govern each and every one of our decisions. We're more aware of that fact when the decision concerns a situation where there is a good deal at stake. The questions above came from the work of two researchers, Lawrence Kohlberg (1976) and Carol Gilligan (1982).Kohlberg, an early researcher on moral decision making, followed the work of Jean Piaget and saw a pattern of organization of moral thought, which he laid out in progressive stages that linked to Piaget's cognitive stages. Kohlberg described children in the early years determining what's right and what's wrong by whether they were rewarded or punished. Later they moved to being motivated to obey rules in order to uphold a social order. Kohlberg's final stages of development involved a personal commitment to an abstract hierarchy of principles. In Kohlberg's scheme, intellectual development—specifically the ability to reason—is vitally linked to moral development. It is, however, important to note that Kohlberg did his research on men and boys. Gilligan's work reflects the moral decision making of women and girls but not only females; she assures us that males also use this type of decision-making process.

Children don't worry about theory or stages. Their decision making is usually quick and unconscious. We can help children be more thoughtful about moral dilemmas they face by bringing the questions into the open and examining them. We can also be more thoughtful ourselves about what is motivating children to make the decisions they do. If you look at the questions listed earlier from Kohlberg's view, it is possible to determine which ones are most likely to be of importance to younger children. Most children under the age of 7 are able to think only in concrete terms, according to Piaget. Although they may feel emotions related to such abstract concepts as love, honesty, and justice, they don't think or reason about them. They do, however, have a sense of what's fair and what's unfair from their point of view. Instead of using sophisticated cognitive processes, young children are more likely to make judgments about right and wrong actions based on their past experience of the reactions of those around them. They consider the possibility of punishment or reward when trying to decide on the "right thing to do."

Carol Gilligan's work has focused most on the last of the questions posed in our list: "Who might be hurt by my decision or action?" From her work has come what is called an *ethic of caring*. Gilligan sees moral decision making as coming from a concern about acting so that the people one cares about will be hurt the least by one's decision.

Nel Noddings has written many books and articles about the ethic of caring. One takes the early childhood principles espoused in this book out of preschool and into the K-8 system. It's called *The Challenge to Care in Schools* (1992). One of her more recent books—*Educating Moral People: A Caring Alternative to Character Education* (2002a)—deals directly with how to develop morals in children using the ethic of caring. She says that moral development comes from creating conditions and relationships that support moral ways of life rather than teaching children to be virtuous, which is the approach

Caring relationships enhance moral development and involve a particular kind of attentiveness that Nell Noddings calls "engrossment."

taken by those who use character education. It's caring relationships that count. Caring relationships involve a particular kind of attention from the carer to the cared-for. Noddings calls this attentiveness *engrossment*, which she describes as acutely receptive. It also involves the carer directing motivational energy toward the needs of the cared-for. Another requirement of a caring relationship is that the caring must be detected and received. The response of the cared for is then received back by the carer in further moments of engrossment.

Caring must be genuine and not just a means of coercion or emotional manipulation to get the child to behave in ways the carer deems acceptable. Both Magda Gerber (1998) and Emmi Pikler (David & Appell, 2001; Gonzalez-Mena, 2004) have provided living examples of what Noddings calls *caring relationships*. At the Pikler Institute in Budapest, one can observe carers interacting with babies in genuinely caring ways. They are trained in a practical and effective approach to an ethic of caring, which makes a huge difference in outcomes of children who spend their first years in an institution. Magda Gerber's work based on an attitude of respect also demonstrates caring relationships. Her work can be seen in Los Angeles and wherever else her Resources for Infant Educarers (RIE) Associates are at work. Noddings notes how care and trust come together so that good behavior is more a result of the relationship than of the many manipulative techniques so often used by early educators. Following an ethic of care, according to Noddings, is more likely to produce caring, moral people than just teaching them to be good. Diane Carlebach and Beverly Tate (2002) assert that using an approach based on Gerber's work creates *peaceful* people, and leads to caring communities.

TEACHING MORALS BY PROMOTING PROSOCIAL DEVELOPMENT

How do caregivers, teachers, or parents promote prosocial development in the children they rear or care for? It helps to be clear about which prosocial behaviors are important to you. Start by making a list of some behaviors you want to encourage in children. Your list will probably include such items as sharing, nonviolent conflict resolution, consideration for others, sensitivity to feelings, cooperation, involvement with and responsibility to others, kindness, reverence for life, and respect for self, others, and the earth (nature). You will probably have these values on your list regardless of whether you are a pattern 1 or a pattern 2 person.

Here are some tips about how to encourage those behaviors:

1. *Model them yourself.* If you want children to share, they need to see you share. If respect is important, they need to see you being respectful. Modeling is the most powerful way to convey your messages. You'll see your own behaviors reflected in the children around you. If honesty is a value, be honest. If cooperation is important to you, show yourself to be cooperative—don't just expect it from children.

2. *Use the power of your attention.* A scene of a meal at a child care center comes to mind. One child said gruffly, "More toast!" Another child said, "May I please have more toast?" The teacher immediately responded to the second child, ignoring

the first, who quickly rephrased his question: "Please, may I have more toast?" Pay attention to children who exhibit the behaviors you're looking for. Notice how gently big sister is stroking the baby. Remark on how nicely Johnny is waiting for his turn.

3. *Explain why you are setting limits.* Say "I can't let you throw the blocks; you might hurt someone," rather than "The rule is no block throwing!" Children need to know the effects of their behaviors. They need to know the reasoning behind your prohibitions.

4. *Encourage cooperation by finding ways to get children to work and play together.* Every picture doesn't have to be individually drawn—how about painting a mural? Collage can be a group effort. A set of large wooden blocks that are too big for one child to transport encourages cooperation.

5. *Take a problem-solving approach when dealing with conflicts, rather than a power stance.* Help children talk to one another, explain their feelings, and brainstorm solutions. Don't rescue, but let them talk it through. If they don't have the words, provide the words for them. (Chapter 9 deals with this subject at length.)

6. *Avoid punishment as a way of disciplining.* Although punishment may suppress some behaviors, it doesn't eliminate them—they go underground. Besides, punishment doesn't teach prosocial behaviors—it models antisocial ones. (See Chapter 7 for ideas of ways to guide behavior without punishing.)

7. *Examine your power relations with children.* Do you *overpower* them rather than *empower* them? Don't rob them of opportunities to develop skills and experience their own

Encourage cooperation by finding ways to encourage children to work and play together.

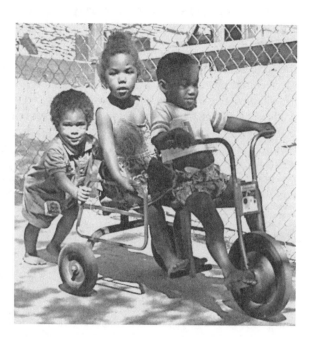

competence by doing things for them or to them. Use your power, your superior size and skills, to bring out their own sense of power—their sense of themselves—who they are and what they can do. Empowered people have less need to use force and violent means of solving problems than do people who feel powerless. When you find yourself in power struggles, take a close look at why the parties concerned need to feel power. Take steps to empower them (and yourself, if you are one of the parties).

8. *Avoid using competition to motivate.* If you value competition, you probably think that starting early to teach children to compete with each other won't hurt. But it does. Even though we live in a competitive society, we do a disservice to children if we start too young to teach them about competition. Young children are still figuring out who they are. Even though you may see competition as a motivation device, you may be setting up comparisons that damage self-esteem and relationships. Avoid questions such as "Who is the smartest?" "Who is the neatest eater?" or "Who is the fastest cleaner-upper?" Also avoid win-lose situations. When you play games with young children, you don't need a winner and losers. You don't have to make a big deal over who gets bingo first. You can continue playing until everyone gets bingo. No young child can afford to be stuck with the label "loser"! Losers have poor self-images, and they behave according to their labels.

9. *Help children appreciate the world they live in and the people they share it with by appreciating things with them more than using lecture or instruction to teach.* Adults can do this best by feeling the sense of wonder children feel and encouraging the awe they experience at the beauty and mystery of nature. It's vital to help children perceive their connection to the earth and to all the earth's creatures, including other humans.

10. *Give choices.* Only by experiencing the effects of their own actions on the world around them can children understand how things work. When they are faced with choosing from alternatives, they get practice in becoming good decision makers.

11. *Teach children to solve conflicts without violence.* Conflict is natural and is to be encouraged, but violence is never an appropriate response to conflict. Especially never use violence as a last resort, because the message then is that when all else fails, you can always fall back on violence. Do allow children their violent *feelings*—it's healthier to feel them than to deny them. Make it clear, however, that children won't be allowed to act on those feelings. Teach a number of ways to express those feelings in ways that do no harm. (See Chapter 8 for further explanation.)

12. *Teach children to be peacemakers.* Peacemaking is a vital part of moral education. Peace is not an absence of tension or conflict. Creating peace is an active process of balancing opposing forces and dealing with conflicts and tensions. True peace cannot be imposed. Peacemaking requires resourcefulness in using a number of skills, including confrontation, debate, dialogue, and negotiation. The goal of peacemakers is to bring conflicts to the surface and to respect differences while resolving or managing those conflicts in ways that preserve the self-esteem of everyone involved. Children learn both the philosophy and the skills of peacemaking from the adults around them who daily help them settle the numerous disputes that occur in the natural course of life, both at home and in early childhood programs.

Teach children to be peacemakers.

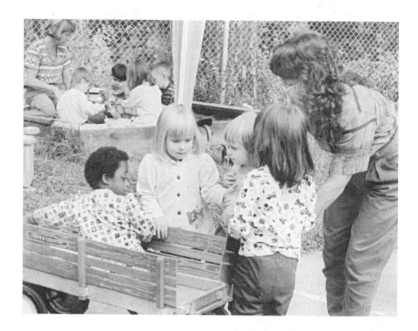

SUMMARY

This chapter looked at goals and values, including the differing ones reflected in cultural conflicts. The chapter also looked at how children learn morals and values from living day to day with adults who pass them on. Some priorities are specific to the family's culture, but universal values can also be found in most early childhood education settings. This chapter examined the relationship of goals and values to child rearing in both the home and the child care center. The next chapter focuses specifically on the child care setting.

FOR DISCUSSION

1. What did you think of the two contrasting patterns in this chapter? Do you or someone you know fit one or the other of these patterns? Which pattern do you think is more likely to emphasize modesty over pride? Why? Which pattern do you think is likely to emphasize manners over honest self-expression? Why?

2. Some people say that to talk about culture *conflicts* creates a different mind-set than if you think of them as cultural bumps or cultural dilemmas. How might different wording change the picture of what is happening when two people or two groups disagree? Can you think of other examples of when a change of vocabulary made a difference?

3. Although the title of one of this chapter's boxes, "A Cultural Conflict," indicates that the difference between the parent and the teacher is a cultural one, nothing in the story shows that the two are of different cultures. Does it matter? Is it important to

know whether diversity is related to culture, religion, family traditions, or just individual differences? If yes, how might a teacher respond differently after learning what was at the root of the issue?

4. The cultures in this chapter are not labeled. Does that frustrate you? Why do you think the author chose to deal with patterns rather than particular cultural differences? Why do you find no lists in this book of typical characteristics of the most common cultures in the United States and Canada today?

5. What are some of the factors in children's lives that work against their prosocial development?

REFERENCES

Ballenger, C. (1999). *Teaching other people's children.* New York: Teachers College Press.

Bandtec Network for Diversity Training. (2003). *Reaching for answers: A workbook on diversity in early childhood education.* Oakland, California: Bandtec Network for Diversity Training. Available at the Bandtec Web site (www.bandtec.org).

Barrera, I., & Corso, R. (2003). *Skilled dialog.* Baltimore: Brookes.

Bredekamp, S., & Copple, C. (Eds.). (1997). *Developmentally appropriate practice in early childhood programs serving children from birth through age eight.* Washington, DC: National Association for the Education of Young Children.

Brody, H. (2001). *The other side of Eden: Hunters, farmers, and the shaping of the world.* New York: North Point Press.

Bruno, H. E. (2003, September-October). Hearing parents in every language: An invitation to ECE professionals. *Child Care Information Exchange,* #153, 58–60.

Butterfield, P. M., Martin, C. A., & Prairie, A. P. (2004). *Emotional connections: How relationships guide early learning.* Washington, DC: Zero to Three.

Carlebach, D., & Tate, B. (2002). *Creating caring children: The first three years.* Miami: Peace Education Foundation.

Charney, R. S. (2002). *Teaching children to care: Classroom management for ethical and academic growth.* Greenfield, MA: Northeast Foundation for Children.

Copple, C. (Ed.). (2003). *A world of difference: Readings on teaching young children in a diverse society.* Washington, DC: National Association for the Education of Young Children.

David, M., & Appell, G. (2001[1973, 1996]). *Loczy: An unusual approach to mothering.* Translated from *Loczy ou le maternage insolite,* by Jean Marie Clark; revised translation by Judit Falk. Budapest: Association Pikler-Loczy for Young Children.

Delpit, L., & Dowdy, J. K. (2002). *The skin that we speak: Thoughts on language and culture in the classroom.* New York: New Press.

Derman-Sparks, L. (1989). *Antibias curriculum.* Washington, DC: National Association for the Education of Young Children.

Eggers-Pierola, C. (2002). *Connections and commitments: A Latino-based framework for early childhood educators.* Newton, MA: Educational Development Center.

Friend, M., & Cook, L. (2003). *Interactions: Collaboration skills for school professionals* (4th ed.). Boston: Allyn & Bacon.

Gandini, L., & Edwards, C. P. (Eds.). (2000). *Bambini: The Italian approach to infant-toddler care.* New York: Teachers College Press.

Gerber, M. (1998). *Dear parent: Caring for infants with respect.* Los Angeles: Resources for Infant Educarers.

Gilligan, C. (1982). *In a different voice.* Cambridge, MA: Harvard University Press.

Goldenberg, C., Gallimore, R., & Reese, L. (2003). Cause or effect? A longitudinal study of immigrant Latino parents' aspirations and expectations, and their children's school performance. *American Educational Research Journal, 38,* 547–582.

Goldstein, L. (2002). *Reclaiming caring in teaching and teacher education.* New York: Lang.

Gonzalez-Mena, J. (2002, September). Working with cultural differences: Individualism and collectivism. *The First Years: Nga Tautuatahi, 4*(2), 13–15.

Gonzalez-Mena, J. (2004) *Diversity in early care and education*. New York: McGraw-Hill.

Gonzalez-Mena, J., & Peshotan Bhavangri, N. (2001, March). Cultural differences in sleeping practices. *Exchange*, 138, 91–93.

Goodman, J. F., & Lesnick, H. (2001). *The moral stake in education*. New York: Longman.

Greenfield, P. M. (1994). Independence and interdependence as developmental scripts: Implications for theory, research, and practice. In P. M. Greenfield & R. R. Cocking (Eds.), *Cross-cultural roots of minority child development* (pp. 1–37). Mahwah, NJ: Erlbaum.

Greenfield, P. M., Quiroz, B., & Raeff, C. (2000). Cross-cultural conflict and harmony in the social construction of the child. *New Directions for Child and Adolescent Development*, 87, 93–108.

Greenfield, P.M., Quiroz, B., Rothstein-Fisch, C., & Trumbull, E. (2001). *Bridging cultures between home and school*. Mahwah, NJ: Erlbaum.

Guerra, P., & Garcia, S. (2000). *Understanding the cultural contexts of teaching and learning*. Austin, TX: Southwest Educational Development Laboratory.

Harwood, R. L., Miller, J. G., & Irizarry, N. L. (1995). *Culture and attachment: Perceptions of the child in context*. New York: Guilford.

Hoffman, M. L. (2000). *Empathy and moral development*. Cambridge: Cambridge University Press.

Hofstede, G. (2001). *Culture's consequences: Comparing values, behaviors, institutions, and organizations across nations* (2nd ed.). Thousand Oaks, CA: Sage.

Kaiser, B., & Rasminsky, J. S. (2003, July). Opening the cultural door. *Young Children*, 58(4), 53–56.

Kohlberg, L. (1976). Moral stages and moralization: The cognitive-developmental approach. In T. Lickona (Ed.), *Moral development and behavior*. New York: Holt, Rinehart & Winston.

Lee, L. (2002). *Serving families: A handbook on the principles and strategies of the parent services project approach*. San Rafael, CA: Parent Services Project.

Levin, D. E. (2002). *Teaching young children in violent times: Building a peaceable classroom*. (2nd ed.). Cambridge, MA: Educators for Social Responsibility; Washington, DC: National Association for the Education of Young Children.

Lustig, M. W., & Koester, J. (2003). *Interpersonal competence: Interpersonal communication across cultures* (4th ed.). New York: Addison Wesley Longman.

Martini, M. (2002, February-March). How mothers in four American cultural groups shape infant learning during mealtimes, *Zero to Three*, 22(4), 14–20.

Noddings, N. (1992). *The challenge to care in schools*. New York: Teachers College Press.

Noddings, N. (2002a). *Educating moral people: A caring alternative to character education*. New York: Teachers College Press.

Noddings, N. (2002b). *Starting at home: Care and social policy*. Berkeley: University of California Press.

Patterson, K., Grenny, J., McMillan, R., Switzer, A., & Covey, S. R. (2002). *Crucial conversations: Tools for talking when the stakes are high*. New York: McGraw-Hill.

Quintero, E. P. (2004, May). Will I lose a tooth? Will I learn to read? Problem posing with multicultural children's literature. *Young Children*, 59(3), 56–62.

Raeff, C., Greenfield, P. M. & Quiroz, B. (2000 Spring). Conceptualizing interpersonal relationships in the cultural contexts of individualism and collectivism. *New Directions for Child and Adolescent Development*, 87, 59–74.

Reese, L. (2002). Parental strategies in contrasting cultural settings: Families in Mexico and El Norte. *Anthropology & Education Quarterly*, 33, 30–59.

Rogoff, B. (2003). *The cultural nature of human development*. New York: Oxford University Press.

Rothstein-Fisch, C. (2003). *Readings for bridging cultures: Teacher education module*. Mahwah, NJ: Erlbaum.

Shweder, R. A., Goodnow, J., Hatano, G., LeVine, R. A., Markus, H., & Miller, P. (1998). The cultural psychology of development: One mind, many mentalities. In W. Damon & R. M. Lerner (Eds.), *Handbook of Child Psychology: Vol. 1. Theoretical models of human development* (5th ed., pp. 865–937). New York: Wiley.

Siraj-Blatchford, I., & Clarke, P. (2000). *Supporting identity, diversity and language in the early years*. Philadelphia: Open University Press.

Some, S. (2000). *The spirit of intimacy: Ancient African teachings in the ways of relationships*. New York: HarperCollins/Quill.

Sue, S., & Moore, T. (Eds.). (1984). *The pluralistic society*. New York: Human Sciences Press.

Trumbull, E., Greenfield, P. M., Rothstein-Fisch, C., & Quiroz, B. (2001). *Bridging cultures between home and school: A guide for teachers*. Mahwah, NJ: Erlbaum.

Trumbull, E., Rothstein-Fisch, C., & Greenfield, P. M. (2000). *Bridging cultures in our schools: New approaches that work*. Knowledge brief. San Francisco: WestEd.

Trumbull, E., Rothstein-Fisch, C., & Hernandez, E. (2003). Parent involvement—according to whose values? *School Community Journal*, 13(2), 45–72.

U.S. Department of Health and Human Services, Administration on Children, Youth and Families.

(2000). *Celebrating cultural and linguistic diversity in Head Start*. Washington, DC: Department of Health and Human Services.

Wong Fillmore, L. (2000). Loss of family languages: Should educators be concerned? *Theory Into Practice*, 39(4), 203–210.

FURTHER READING

Akbar, N. (2003). *Akbar papers in African psychology*. Tallahassee: Mind Productions.

Allen, P. G. (1998). *Off the reservation*. Boston: Beacon.

Bandtec Network for Diversity Training. (2003). *Reaching for answers: A workbook on diversity in early childhood education*. Oakland, California: Bandtec Network for Diversity Training. Available at the Bandtec Web site (www.bandtec.org).

Barrera, I. & Corso, R. (2003). *Skilled dialog*. Baltimore: Brookes.

Bhavnagri, N. P., & Gonzalez-Mena, J. (1997, Fall). The cultural context of caregiving. *Childhood Education*, 74(1), 2–8.

Brody, H. (2001). *The other side of Eden: Hunters, farmers, and the shaping of the world*. New York: North Point Press.

Bruno, H. E. (2003, September-October). Hearing parents in every language: An invitation to ECE professionals. *Child Care Information Exchange*, 153, 58–60.

Carlebach, D., & Tate, B. (2002). *Creating caring children: The first three years*. Miami: Peace Education Foundation.

Chang, H. N., & Sakai, L. (1993). *Affirming children's roots: Cultural and linguistic diversity in early care and education*. San Francisco: California Tomorrow.

Chao, R. (1994). Beyond parental control and authoritarian parenting style: Understanding Chinese parenting through the cultural notion of training. *Child Development*, 65, 1111–1119.

Chen, X., Rubin, K., Gen, G., Hastings, P., Chen, H., & Stewart, S. (1998). Child-rearing attitudes and behavioral inhibition in Chinese and Canadian toddlers: A cross-cultural study. *Developmental Psychology*, 34(4), 677–686.

Coll, C. G., Lamberty, G., Jenkins, R., McAdoo, H. P., Crnic, K., Wasik, B., Hanna, G., & Vazquez, H. (1996).

An integrative model for the study of developmental competencies in minority children. *Child Development*, 67, 1891–1914.

David, M., & Appell, G. (2001[1973, 1996]). *Loczy: An unusual approach to mothering*. Translated from *Loczy ou le maternage insolite*, by Jean Marie Clark; revised translation by Judit Falk. Budapest: Association Pikler-Loczy for Young Children.

Delpit, L. (1995). *Other people's children: Cultural conflict in the classroom*. New York: New Press.

Delpit, L., & Dowdy, J. K. (2002). *The skin that we speak: Thoughts on language and culture in the classroom*. New York: New Press.

Eggers-Pierola, C. (2002). *Connections and commitments: A Latino-based framework for early childhood educators*. Newton, MA: Educational Development Center.

Ellison, S. (1998). *Don't be so defensive!* Kansas City, MO: Andrews McMeel.

Fadiman, A. (1997). *The spirit catches you and you fall down: A Hmong child, her American doctors, and the collision of two cultures*. New York: Noonday.

Fernea, E. W. (1995). *Children in the Muslim Middle East*. Austin: University of Texas Press.

Friend, M., & Cook, L. (2003). *Interactions: Collaboration skills for school professionals* (4th ed.). Boston: Allyn & Bacon.

Garcia, E. E., & McLaughlin, B. (Eds.). (With B. Spokek & O. N. Saracho). (1995). *Meeting the challenge of linguistic and cultural diversity in early childhood education*. New York: Teachers College Press.

Gerber, M. (1998). *Dear parent: Caring for infants with respect*. Los Angeles: Resources for Infant Educarers.

Goldenberg, C., Gallimore, R., & Reese, L. (2003). Cause or effect? A longitudinal study of immigrant Latino parents' aspirations and expectations, and their children's school performance. *American Educational Research Journal*, 38, 547–582.

Gonzalez-Mena, J. (1994, May). Learning to see across a cultural gap. *Child Care Information Exchange, 97,* 65–68.

Gonzalez-Mena, J. (1997, July). Cross-cultural conferences. *Exchange, 116,* 55–57.

Gonzalez-Mena, J. (1999, July). Dialogue to understanding across cultures. *Exchange, 128,* 6–8.

Gonzalez-Mena, J (2004) *Diversity in early care and education.* New York: McGraw-Hill.

Hale, J. (1991, September). The transmission of cultural values to young African American children. *Young Children, 46*(6), 7–15.

Hale, J. E. (1992). An African-American early childhood education program: Visions for children. In S. A. Kessler & B. B. Swadener (Eds.), *Reconceptualizing the early childhood curriculum: Beginning the dialogue* (pp. 205–224). New York: Teachers College Press.

Hall, E. T. (1977). *Beyond culture.* Garden City, NY: Anchor.

Hall, E. T. (1984). *The dance of life.* Garden City, NY: Anchor/Doubleday.

Harkness, S., & Super, C. M. (Eds.). (1996). *Parents' cultural belief systems.* New York: Guilford.

Hyun, E. (1998). *Making sense of developmentally and culturally appropriate practice* (DCAP) *in early childhood education.* New York: Lang.

Kagiticibasi, C. (1996). *Family and human development across cultures.* Mahwah, NJ: Erlbaum.

Kendall, F. (1996). *Diversity in the classroom.* New York: Teachers College Press.

Knight, G. P., Bernal, M. E., & Carlo, G. (1995). Socialization and the development of cooperative, competitive, and individualistic behaviors among Mexican American children. In E. E. Garcia & B. McLaughlin (Eds.), *Meeting the challenge of linguistic and cultural diversity in early childhood education* (pp. 85–102). New York: Teachers College Press.

Kochman, T. (1981). *Black and white: Styles in conflict.* Chicago: University of Chicago Press.

Lee, K., Cameron, C., Xu, F., Fu, G., & Board, J. (1997). Chinese and Canadian children's evaluations of lying and truth telling: Similarities and differences in the context of pro- and antisocial behaviors. *Child Development, 68*(5), 924–934.

Lee, L. (1997, July). Working with non-English-speaking families. *Exchange, 116,* 57–58.

LeVine, R. A., LeVine, S., Leiderman, P. H., Brazelton, T. B., Dixon, S., Richan, A., & Keefer, C. H. (1994). *Child care and culture: Lessons from Africa.* Cambridge: Cambridge University Press.

Lewis, C. C. (1995). *Educating hearts and minds: Reflections on Japanese preschool and elementary education.* New York: Cambridge University Press.

Lubeck, S. (1996). Deconstructing "child development knowledge" and "teacher preparation." *Early Childhood Research Quarterly, 11*(2), 147–168.

Makin, L., Campbell, J., & Diaz, C. J. (1995). *One childhood, many languages.* Pymble, Australia: HarperEducational.

Mallory, B. L., & New, R. S. (Eds.). (1994). *Diversity and developmentally appropriate practices: Challenges for early childhood education.* New York: Teachers College Press.

Medicine, B. (1985, Fall). Child socialization among Native Americans: The Lakota (Sioux) in cultural context. *Wicazo Sa Review, 1*(2), 23–28.

Morelli, G., Rogoff, B., & Oppenheim, D. (1992, July). Cultural variation in infants' sleeping arrangements: Questions of independence. *Developmental Psychology, 28*(4), 604–619.

National Association for the Education of Young Children. (1996, January). Linguistic and cultural diversity position paper. *Young Children, 51*(2), 4–12.

Noddings, N. (2002). *Educating moral people: A caring alternative to character education.* New York: Teachers College Press.

Patterson, K., Grenny, J., McMillan, R., Switzer, A., & Covey, S. R. (2002). *Crucial conversations: Tools for talking when the stakes are high.* New York: McGraw-Hill.

Payne, R. K. (2003). *A framework for understanding poverty.* Highlands, TX: Aha Process.

Pence, A. R. (1998). Reconceptualizing ECCD in the majority world: One minority world perspective. *International Journal of Early Childhood, 30*(2), 19–30.

Phillips, C. B. (1995). Culture: A process that empowers. In P. Mangione (Ed.), *Infant/toddler caregiving: A guide to culturally sensitive care.* Sacramento: Far West Laboratory and California Department of Education.

Price, W. F., & Crapo, R. H. (1999). *Cross-cultural perspectives in introductory psychology.* Belmont, CA: Wadsworth.

Raeff, C., Greenfield, P. M., & Quiroz, B. (2000, Spring). Conceptualizing interpersonal relationships in the cultural contexts of individualism and collectivism. *New Directions for Child and Adolescent Development, 87,* 59–74.

Reese, L. (2002). Parental strategies in contrasting cultural settings: Families in Mexico and El Norte. *Anthropology & Education Quarterly, 33*, 30–59.

Rogoff, B. (1990). *Apprenticehip in thinking: Cognitive development in social context.* New York: Oxford University Press.

Rogoff, B. (2003). *The cultural nature of human development.* New York: Oxford University Press.

Rogoff, B., Stott, F., & Bowman, B. (1996). Child development knowledge: A slippery base for practice. *Early Childhood Research Quarterly, 11*(2), 1169–1184.

Rothstein-Fisch, C. (2003). *Readings for bridging cultures: Teacher education module.* Mahwah, NJ: Erlbaum.

Russell, J. A., & Yik, M. S. M. (1996). Emotion among the Chinese. In M. H. Bond (Ed.), *The handbook of Chinese psychology* (pp. 166–188). Hong Kong: Oxford University Press.

Small, M. (1998). *Our babies, ourselves: How biology and culture shape the way we parent.* New York: Anchor.

Some, S. (2000). *The spirit of intimacy: Ancient African teachings in the ways of relationships.* New York: HarperCollins/Quill.

Stipek, D. (1998). Differences between Americans and Chinese in the circumstances evoking pride, shame, and guilt. *Journal of Cross-Cultural Psychology, 29*(5), 616–629.

Tan, A. L. (2004). *Chinese American children and families: A guide for educators and service providers.* Onley, MD: Association for Childhood Education International.

Tobaissen, D. P., & Gonzalez-Mena, J. (1998). *A place to begin: Working with parents on issues of diversity.* Oakland: California Tomorrow.

Trumbull, E., Rothstein-Fisch, C., & Greenfield, P. M., (2000). *Bridging cultures in our schools: New approaches that work.* Knowledge Brief. San Francisco: WestEd.

White, E. (Qoyawayma, P.). (1992). *No turning back: A Hopi woman's struggle to live in two worlds.* Albuquerque, NM: University of New Mexico Press.

Wu, D. (1996). Chinese childhood socialization. In M. H. Bond (Ed.), *The handbook of Chinese psychology* (pp. 143–154). Hong Kong: Oxford University Press.

CHAPTER 6

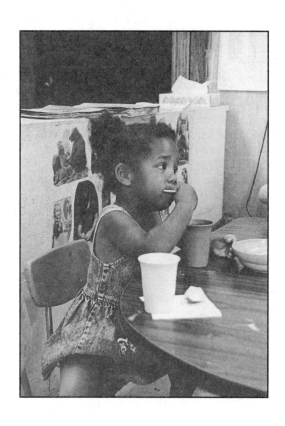

Child Care
An Extension
of the Family

In *this chapter you'll discover* . . .

- Why child care can be considered child rearing
- Three things that influence quality in child care
- Some arguments about breaking large centers into small groups
- Some ideas about bridging the gap between the child care program and the home
- Advantages and disadvantages of matching teachers to the children's language and culture
- Some roadblocks to respect between parents and teachers

Who is rearing America's children, and how are they being reared? That is an increasingly compelling question. It was a nonquestion just a generation or two ago, because America's children were mostly reared by their own parents, or by specific substitutes whom the parents designated. Child rearing belonged to the family. Business, education, and government mostly stayed out of the picture, except for a period during World War II and except for protective and remedial reasons.

Today the picture has changed. According to the Children's Defense Fund (2004), 64% of mothers with children under 6 and 78% of mothers with children ages 6 to 17 work outside the home. The number of single-parent families in which the parent trains or works outside the home steadily rises. In a majority of two-parent families, both parents work outside the home. Child rearing is now shared, as families use an array of child care services. Furthermore, business and government have become part of the picture.

The Child Care Center Licensing Study of the Children's Foundation in Washington, D.C., indicates that there were 117,284 regulated child care centers in the 50 states, District of Columbia, Puerto Rico, and Virgin Islands. This is an overall increase of 26% since their 1991 study (see www.childrensfoundation.net).

Who is raising America's children? Perhaps you are or will be—either as a parent or as a teacher/child care worker or family child care provider. As the need for child care expands and services struggle to keep up with the need, more and more child care workers, teachers, caregivers, family day care providers, in-home care providers, and nannies supplement parent care.

CHILD CARE AS A CHILD-REARING ENVIRONMENT

Why does this text keep equating child care with child rearing? After all, the United States doesn't have a communal child-rearing system in which children are taken out of the home and socialized into a model consisting of a single set of ideals. We don't believe in social or political indoctrination for our children. Child rearing is an individual matter of individual families and always has been. As a society, Americans agree to disagree. Diversity has always been a key theme as well as a strong point of America's people. Families want to rear their children in their own way. However, these days individuals and families must look outside themselves for supplementary care. They can no longer do all the child rearing themselves.

But is child care really child rearing? Yes. You can drive your car to work, park it in a garage, and come back and pick it up in the afternoon, and, except for a new layer of dust, it is almost always in the same condition you left it in. You can even leave your car at home in the garage, take the bus or the train to work, and come back and find it just as you left it.

But you can't park your children. Wherever your children are, they are growing and learning, being changed by their experiences. They are being reared. How they are being reared is a big question. They can be reared in accordance with parental expectations and values, or they can be reared in ways that are quite contradictory.

The challenge for our society in these times is to offer enough choices so that parents can find child care in tune with what they want and need for their children. The

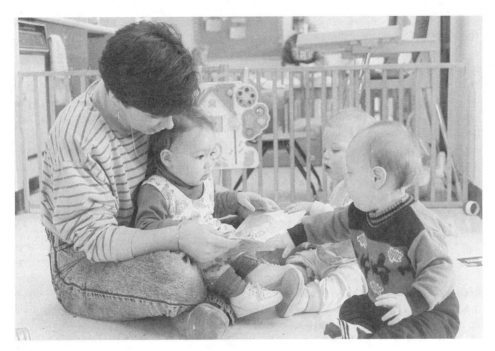

You can't park your children like your car. Children need to be in an environment where they can grow and learn.

choices could include both nonparental care solutions such as center care, family child care, and in-home care, as well as creative alternatives that allow working parents a greater role in caring for their own children. Flextime, one of these alternatives, allows parents to stagger their work schedules and manage to be with the child, doing the child rearing mostly themselves. Part-time work also allows more parental involvement in child rearing; job sharing is one way to become a part-time worker. In some countries, workers are subsidized to stay home with their children instead of working a full day or a full workweek. Flexible benefits plans and flexible leave and transfer policies can also be creative alternatives that allow parents to spend more time with their children.

Worthy Wages and Quality Care

Kayla is in a quality child care center with a stable staff who know her well and can provide just the kind of care and education she needs. It's a sensitive, well trained staff, with the time and energy to arrange the environment in appropriate ways and to set out a variety of interesting and worthwhile activities that promote growth and development. They are there to guide, protect, and teach her by relating to Kayla on an individual basis and supporting her development in numerous ways. Kayla is happy in her school, and her mother is happy that she is there. The whole picture is happy, but what about the teachers?

If the teachers are happy, it's because they love teaching and work in a well funded program in which they are paid what they deserve, have a good benefit package, and have adequate support through staff and other resources. Or perhaps they are happy because they have other sources of income and have figured out how to scrounge up the resources they need. Or they may get so many rewards from teaching that money isn't an issue with them. Many good teachers remain in the field despite the low pay.

However, in most child care programs, the staff is underpaid, and if any of them are the sole support for their families, they have a hard time managing on a child care teacher's wages. Child care teachers' wages reflect their status, which, according to the Bureau of Labor statistics, is equated with parking lot attendants. Some refuse to leave the field, even though they are being paid less than prison guards and animal tenders. These dedicated souls are helping to rear the nation's children—rearing them at the point of their lives when they are very impressionable.

What does it mean to children and families that child care teachers are underpaid and undervalued? It means a lot. It means that many people will never even consider going into the field—people who have a lot to offer children. It means that anyone who isn't totally dedicated to the profession and wants to make an adequate living will look elsewhere. It means that few men, especially those who don't have a partner who can supplement their income, will look to child care as a career option. This limits the field drastically.

The problem of low status and salary is reflected in the turnover rate (Whitebook & Sakai, 2004). Many people enter the field only to leave it in a short time, when they find the demands of the job too much and the pay too little. One-third to one-half of the people working in child care are new every year. That means that children see their teachers constantly changing—continually coming and going. As soon as they get to know and trust someone, that person leaves. Eventually children stop developing relationships with their child care teachers—it's just too painful to keep saying good-bye for good.

That's not good for children.

Quality is tied to status, salaries, and training. Who is going to spend the money for training if the status and salaries are so low?

We are in a crisis situation. We have a great need, as a nation, for child care, and it can be a very satisfying career. Yet the money for quality care just isn't there. Most parents couldn't possibly afford what quality care costs. They need subsidies. A few get them from the government; others get them from employers. But an enormous number receive their subsidies from the teachers who are willing to work for so little pay. That's not the ordinary way to look at subsidizing child care, but it is one way. Don't you think that it is time things changed?

AFFORDABILITY AND AVAILABILITY

Two A words loom up when we look at requirements for nonparental child care: *affordability* and *availability*. When we, as a society, work to create both cheap and widespread child care, quality often gets lost. We get into a double bind when we deal with both quality and cost: Most parents can't afford to pay what quality child care really costs, which can be

$10,000 a year. In 48 states, the cost of center-based child care for a 4-year-old is greater than tuition at a 4-year public college (Children's Defense Fund, 2004). If you consider that one-third of the families with young children earn less than $25,000 a year according to the Children's Defense Fund, you can see that child care costs are beyond them. Even when both parents are working, if they work at minimum-wage jobs, together they only make $21,000 a year. How can they pay half their salary?

Child care workers come out worse than that. They can't afford child care unless it is provided free where they work. Their average salary is far less than other educators and service workers, according to Whitebook and Sakai (2004). The families who need care most can't afford it, and as a society we can't afford not to pay it, especially for low-income families. Quality costs, but it saves in the long run. Studies show risk factors associated with cognitive delay and other developmental problems that can be lessened by early intervention in the form of quality child care (Illig, 1998; Karoly, 1998). Furthermore, quality early childhood education and care programs can cut the crime rate. A report prepared by an expert panel convened by Fight Crime: Invest in Kids shows that 989 children who had been enrolled in government-funded child-parent centers as 3- and 4-year-olds cut the risk of problems with the law in their teens. Half as many of the children in the program had arrests in their teens as a similar group not included in the program (Brazelton, Zigler, Sherman, Bratton, & Sanders, 1999).

The North Carolina Abecedarian Project showed that early childhood education can make a critical difference in the later success of poor children. This project was a carefully controlled research design project in which children had an individualized prescription of educational activities and games as a part of everyday activities, and they tested higher in cognitive test scores up to age 21, achieved higher levels in reading and math, completed more years of education, and were more likely to attend college than children not in the program (Campell, Pungello, Miller-Johnson, Burchinal, & Ramey, 2000).

A study of Head Start called FACES (U.S. Department of Health and Human Services, 2003) showed that the program narrowed the gap between the performances of children from poverty level families and their higher income peers. Low-income Head Start children showed significant improvement in social skills, emotional development, and behavior, which was linked to their cognitive development. Parent participation in educational activities with their children was positively correlated with children's behavior and early literacy skills. A different study found that Early Head Start, the program that serves infants and toddlers, also has significant benefits and impacts social-emotional development as well as children's cognitive and language development at age 3.

As a society we haven't yet learned the lesson that quality costs but pays off. We aren't willing to pay what child care really costs. We say we can't afford it. As a result, child care in the United States isn't as good as it could be.

Status and Salaries

Status and salaries of child care teachers are two problems related to quality and cost that haven't been solved yet. Child care teachers are still underpaid, and a majority receive no benefits. Their salaries put them at poverty level, and their status puts them in the same category as parking lot attendants. Not a pretty picture! The National Center for the Early Childhood Workforce in Washington, D.C., has been addressing this issue for a number of years. The pattern goes like this: The lower the salary, the higher the turnover rate. The greater the turnover, the lower the quality of services and the more likely the outcome for the children to have poor developmental outcomes. In a program with a high turnover rate, the less likely that children will experience responsive caregiving and sensitive interactions (Whitebook & Sakai, 2004).

Imagine the children in a program with a high turnover rate. They are constantly disrupted by changes in their routines. High turnover means that rules switch as teachers come and go. It means that just as the children get to know a teacher, he or she disappears suddenly and is replaced by a new person. Separation issues don't get resolved. The consistency of the stable environment that children need to flourish is a sought-after vision but seldom a reality.

We need to find ways to solve these problems. It isn't just up to the parents and the child care teachers to work toward solutions. Indeed, as mentioned earlier, many parents are paying more than they can afford now. A low-income family can pay as much as 26% of the family budget for child care. And teachers, by working for poverty wages, are subsidizing child care themselves. No, it's not up to parents and teachers to solve this problem alone. It is in the public interest to help in raising other people's children to the extent that they need it. Children are the future of America.

Child care has become a necessity for many families.

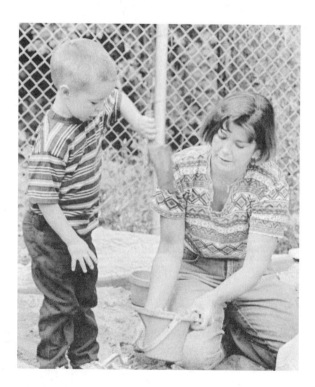

Even without platitudes, you can look at the situation from a very personal point of view. When you reach retirement age, you will be dependent on a strong, healthy, productive workforce to keep the society and the economy going. You won't be able to sit back and enjoy the fruits of your own labor if there is no one to carry on.

Even more personally, imagine yourself in a retirement home being cared for by men and women whose own upbringing left much to be desired. If today's society allows its future citizens to be neglected at home or warehoused in an institutional setting, how well will they treat you if and when you need their care in your old age?

THE STATE OF CHILD CARE IN AMERICA TODAY

The picture of child care is sad. We still have a long way to go. We aren't yet close to creating a system that fills the need and provides quality care. When President Bill Clinton signed away the traditional welfare system in 1996 and changed it to Temporary Aid to Needy Families (TANF), all of a sudden the need for child care increased dramatically, as former welfare recipients became trainees and their children, including babies, needed a place to go. Although infants had been trickling into child care for some time, all of a sudden they came pouring into the system at a rate programs couldn't keep up with. This situation meant that for TANF to work, child care had to expand, which called for more funding to keep up with the demand and more training dollars to increase the child care workforce. We still haven't met the current need, and a large number of children are in inadequate settings. Families of all income levels still have problems finding quality care, but the problems are worse for low-income families. These families have more at stake also because the consequences of inadequate care plus lack of effective educational approaches tend to be more severe for children of low-income families.

Our system of child care is notable for its diversity, which is both a strength and a challenge. Creating a seamless system that meets the needs of all children and all families is still a distant dream that we are only just beginning to realize. Unlike some smaller European countries, there is no single policy or program that can address the child care needs of all families and children. No single entity or organization can provide child care for the nation, but rather the responsibility for meeting the nation's child care needs has to be widely shared among individuals, families, voluntary organizations, employers, communities, and government at all levels.

LOOKING AT QUALITY

Defining, measuring, and monitoring the quality of child care are very hard tasks, because to some extent the definition of quality is highly subjective and personal. However, the classic study done in the 1970s—the National Day Care Study (Ruopp, Travers, Glantz, & Coelen, 1979)—came up with three variables that influence quality: *group size*, *caregiver-child ratio*, and *caregiver qualifications*. This study helped justify and substantiate the laws and regulations governing child care. It also helped back up the National Association for the Education of Young Children's (NAEYC) accreditation criteria, which are now contained in a major instrument to assess

Group size is a variable that influences quality.

quality across the nation. The 2004 program standards (found at www.naeyc.org) are 10 in number and organized into four focus groups. The first focus is on children and relates to what supports their development and learning. The others focus on what is needed to create and maintain excellence in programs and relate to teachers, family, and community partnerships (see Table 6.1).

Table 6.1
NAEYC accreditation standards

Focus Area:	Children
Program Standard 1:	Relationships
Program Standard 2:	Curriculum
Program Standard 3:	Teaching
Program Standard 4:	Assessment
Program Standard 5:	Health
Focus Area:	Teaching Staff
Program Standard 6:	Teachers
Focus Area:	Family and Community Partnerships
Program Standard 7:	Families
Program Standard 8:	Communities
Focus Area:	Leadership and Administration
Program Standard 9:	Physical Environment
Program Standard 10:	Leadership and Management

We continue to move forward as a profession, but still in many places in the United States child care remains unregulated—and even where it is regulated, laws and regulations provide only a bottom line (i.e., they define *minimum* standards). Various national and state professional organizations have provided more optimum guidelines, including a book of standards from NAEYC called *Developmentally Appropriate Practice* (Bredekamp & Copple, 1997).

Although it may be hard to define quality beyond health and safety issues, ratios, group size, and square feet per child, it's fairly easy to see what *isn't* quality child care, even if your personal tastes aren't quite like most people's. We all deplore mass-produced, institutionalized care. No one wants to see children warehoused in dehumanizing kinds of situations. Children should not be institutionalized. But then the question arises: Should programs be more like homes or schools? And: What is the best model for child care? There are no answers to those questions. Certainly children cared for in what are called family child care homes can get their needs met as well as those cared for in center-based programs, and vice versa. Parents may prefer one setting over the other depending on what they are looking for in a program. Both types of programs can exhibit high quality when group size, ratio, adult training, and consistency of care fit the standards.

ADULT-CHILD INTERACTIONS IN CHILD CARE AND EARLY EDUCATION SETTINGS

Perhaps a more important issue is: What is the quality of adult-child interactions, regardless of the program model? Taking into account that the first program standard of NAEYC's accreditation model relates to relationships, let's look at adult-child interactions with that in mind.

Most early childhood educators and many parents today would agree that children should spend their days actively involved in exploring and learning about the world and each other. A helpful adult close by is essential for providing resources, input, and guidance. Is that what happens in most child care programs? According to researchers Susan Kontos and Amanda Wilcox-Herzog, academics have only just begun to study how interactions take place and what kind are related to what outcomes in children. In an article titled "Teachers' Interactions With Children: Why Are They So Important?" (1997), Kontos and Wilcox-Herzog examine the research on interactions to see whether they could confirm that interactions foster relationships that promote development. They found that because children outnumber adults, the frequency of interactions is not high (31% of the children in one study received no individual attention) even though the adults studied spent 71% of their time interacting with children. Thus, because adults are necessarily spread thin—especially in center-based care—it is important that they become aware of how they distribute their attention. They must also be conscious of the quality of the interactions. Adult-child ratio and group size affects interactions. Smaller groups and good ratios allow adults to have more sensitive, responsive interactions with children. In programs with less than optimum ratios and group sizes, adults are much more likely to use pressure to seek compliance by issuing demands, giving orders, quoting rules, even ridiculing and making threats. In homes and in smaller centers or large centers where attention was paid to group size and ratios, adult input was more likely to be facilitative—encouraging, helping, and suggesting, rather than demanding. Kontos and Wilcox-Herzog conclude that it is possible to see a connection between sensitive, involved adult interactions with children and enhanced development. The effect of positive relationships shows in cognitive, socioemotional, and language development. From warm, sensitive interactions where adults are nurturing, accepting, and respectful, responsive relationships grow that encourage the development of autonomy and initiative, which, according to Erik Erikson (1963), is vital to healthy development in the early years.

A goal should be to break centers into smaller, self-contained groups. Group size is a vital factor to quality. Way back in 1979, the National Day Care Study (Ruopp et al., 1979) showed that group size has more effect than any other factor on teacher and child behavior and on intellectual development. Yet regulations about group size are still not universal.

To summarize: Quality care provides a safe, healthy, and nurturing learning environment designed to meet the needs—physical, emotional, intellectual—of the individual and the group. This environment can be in centers or in family child care homes. Good care, like good child rearing, enhances each child's development as a unique and powerful person who is capable of cooperating with others and living in a group situation. The goal is to establish a sense of being an individual while incorporating a growing sense of community. This happens most easily with a stable, consistent, trained staff, available at least some of the time to interact with children one-on-one and in small groups. Another contributing factor is plenty of play time during which the child is actively engaged with peers and practices decision making, problem-solving, and resolving conflict. Quality care can occur in a variety of environments, including home and center settings.

INCLUDING EVERYBODY: CHILDREN WITH SPECIAL NEEDS

In the past, children with special needs often ended up in special education programs rather than in child care programs designed for everybody's children. Since 1992, when the Americans with Disabilities Act (ADA) was passed, the mandate is to provide people who have disabilities access to all community services, including child care. Then, in 1997 came the Individuals with Disabilities Education Act (IDEA) amendments, which state: "To the maximum extent appropriate, children with disabilities . . . are educated with children who are not disabled." Children with disabilities are to be cared for and educated in a "natural environment," which means an environment where their typically developing peers are to be found. Furthermore, each child must have an individualized education program (IEP), which includes, among other things, a statement of the child's present levels of educational performance, measurable annual goals, short-term objectives, program modifications, or supports.

What is the definition of "a child with special needs"? A child with special needs is one who requires specialized care because of physical, emotional, or health reasons. The kinds of disabilities vary greatly, from physical challenges to developmental differences to illness. They may include communication disabilities, developmental disabilities and delays, emotional and/or behavioral disabilities, visual and hearing impairments, exceptional health needs, learning disabilities, and/or physical challenges. Some children have a combination of several conditions.

How do parents who have children with special needs approach putting their children into child care not designated special education? Some have great hesitation. What if the adults in the program don't pay close enough attention to their child? What if their child gets lost in the crowd? Most parents have this concern, but when the child has special needs the anxiety may be greatly heightened because of certain risk factors. What if the disability is severe allergic reactions and nobody is paying close enough attention to notice that the child is being served milk or is eating peanuts or is playing around the garden where bees are in abundance? Take the situation where a program has informed the family that increasing self-help skills are a major goal of their program, and the family worries that because the child is so physically challenged he will be neglected in the name of making him more independent? Of course, cultural differences enter in here, too. If a family sees dependence as a blessing, not a curse, it may not be as eager for its children to learn self-help skills as a family that wants to maximize independence.

Professional early childhood educators recognize that caring for a child with special needs does take extra watchfulness and thoughtfulness. It helps, though, when they remember that a child with special needs is more similar to than different from other children. These children need what all children need: a safe, nurturing environment with adults who respect them and know how to meet their needs. They need chances to explore, choices, and support when called for. They benefit from an individualized approach and also from being included in a group.

How could a caregiver, teacher, or family child care provider possibly know all about every condition of every child who might end up in a program designed primarily for typically developing children? That is a question often asked by early childhood educators who are faced with providing care and education for a child with a disability they know little about.

PARTNERING WITH PARENTS

One way to find out about a child is to observe that child. "The child is the teacher," is something that Magda Gerber, infant expert and founder of Resources for Infant Educarers, used to say all the time. Through observations and interactions the early childhood educator can learn a good deal, but not everything. He or she also needs resources. The first and most important resource is the family of the child. When programs take a parents-as-partners approach, they can learn more about all children in their care, including those with special needs. The family knows their child better than anyone else. If the child has been identified as having special needs, the family has already become part of the system of resources and support. The professional early childhood educator can find out from the family what they have been told, what agencies and individuals are working with the child, and who can help the child care program meet the child's special needs. Also, the early childhood educator can share observations with the family and other professionals and ask them what strategies and ideas work at home. Working closely with the family is essential. Connecting with the resources and supports they have is useful, too. Chapter 13 explores community resources, including those for families with a child with special needs. There are many ways to find help and support from agencies in the community.

Sometimes a child comes into a program without being identified as having special needs, but early childhood professionals have concerns about the child. Professionals with training and experience in development may notice that a particular child isn't following a typical pattern. It may be hard for that professional to put a finger on his or her concerns, but if there is a nagging feeling, it is important for the professional to begin to observe closely. That means writing down what is observed and keeping a record. Writing each observation as objectively as possible and recording the date can show progress or lack of progress as well as provide useful information about the child's developmental differences. Patterns may begin to emerge as the professional notices that the child often seems "stuck," can't remember things, or can't seem to get involved in anything. It may be that the child doesn't get along with other children, or has a low energy level, or seems confused often. Perhaps the difficulty has to do with the program, and a change or two makes all the difference. But maybe what the professional does fails to make a difference. After making specific observations and writing down the details, the professional may decide that this child needs more specialized help. Talking to the family about the professional's concern is the next step.

Suggesting to a family that something is going on with their child is a delicate matter and needs to be carefully thought out by the professional before setting up a meeting. Having a positive attitude and approach makes a difference. Having specific information with details about observed behavior gives a clearer, more objective picture than just pointing out problems the child may be having. Using neutral language is a key to keeping things positive, which means avoiding labels and negative judgments but discussing behavior and skills in terms of what has actually been observed. Sharing observations about strengths and areas of weakness to see how well the professional's observations match with the family's observations gives a more complete picture. When early childhood professionals use language families understand, they reduce any possible power differential and open up communication. When they speak in terms of developmental ranges rather than comparing the child to other children, they do the child and the family a service. The point of the meeting should be to share information, gain a clearer picture, and figure out together what has worked, what has not worked, and what is to be done to optimize development for the child. Perhaps further resources are needed. Pooling information about resources is useful.

How do family members feel when called to such a meeting? For some it may be a relief to know that what they have been noticing that has caused them concern is validated by a professional. Others feel a wide range of emotions. Typical reactions are tears, denial, guilt, fear, blame, and anger. Parents may feel they are failures or their child is a failure. If communication has occurred all along, the content of the meeting will be less of a surprise or shock than if this is the first conversation the early childhood educator has had with the parents. Having time to talk and sort things out, including feelings, gives parents the opportunity to cope with what may be painful news. Sometimes it just takes awhile to sink in and parents are unable to hear what is said at such a meeting. If the parents have heard and understood, having an idea what to do next can be helpful, too. Perhaps more observations are in order. Or they may want to contact their pediatrician or local school district about an evaluation and resources.

QUESTIONS CONCERNING CONTINUITY BETWEEN CHILD CARE AND HOME

How much should the child care program, whether in-home, home-based, or center-based, reflect the methods, approaches, and values of the parents? If special needs are involved, should there be continuity between what goes on at home and what happens in the child care program? It may be that home and program provide a balance, when what happens at home is different from what happens at the center. For example, if the family loves taking care of a child who can do very little for herself, the program can provide more opportunities for the child to try out self-help skills. This has to be done skillfully and sensitively if the child is to feel safe and secure away from those who constantly do everything for her.

What about value differences? The subject of values was discussed in the preceding chapter; however, following are two additional questions to consider:

♦ Is *continuity between home and program always valuable*?   A look at a cross-cultural example gives one view. In China today, couples are allowed to have only one child. Yet China is very family-oriented, so all the energy that went into the many children of the large families of the past is focused today on a single child. As a result, this child gets a good deal of attention—"spoiling," if you will—from two parents and four grandparents. Six adults are all vitally concerned with this one small child. So child care is set up to purposely counteract this effect. Child-adult ratios are large, so that adults cannot focus very much time on any one child. Group expectations are heavy—the child must learn to be a good group member, which happened easily at home in the old days of big families. It doesn't happen at home easily now. So the child is learning away from home what is very hard to teach at home. Child care is set up to create a gap between home and program—one is designed to counterbalance the other (Tobin, Wu, & Davidson, 1989).

♦ Is *the ideal to aim for racial and cultural similarities between caregivers and children or to aim for diversity*?   The advantage in similarity is that when children see adults of the same race as themselves, they identify with these people. When children of color see adults of their race in positions of authority and competence, they have models, which can be valuable for their self-esteem.

When consistency exists between family and program, cultural competence is more likely. All children, no matter what race, culture, or ethnicity, should be in settings that increase their cultural competence. An example of when continuity and consistency is important is when a child is in danger of losing home language and culture. For some children to keep their identity intact and continue to develop in their own language, being in a program where their language is spoken and they can continue to relate daily on a close basis with people of their culture can make a big difference. In infancy such continuity can be especially important because infants aren't born members of their culture but must learn to be culturally competent. If they don't get enough waking hours of exposure to their own people and language, the consequences can be negative.

That's not to say that cultural continuity is vital in every situation. For some children there are advantages of experiencing interracial, multicultural staff and children in their child care settings. They can learn early to respond in positive ways to diversity. Children in America today need to learn to adapt to people who are different from themselves.

Choosing Child Care: Debbie and Walt

Debbie is a physical therapist in her middle 30s. She and her husband Walt delayed having children, but now they have 18-month-old Evan. Debbie took a 6-month leave when Evan was born, but when it came time to go back to work, she had such strong feelings about leaving him that she and Walt worked out a time-share plan. She went back to work half-time, and he rearranged his work schedule so that he could be home when she wasn't. So far they haven't had to use child care. But now they've decided that their city apartment isn't the right place for Evan to grow up, so they're in the market for a house. In addition, Walt, who has two teenage children from his first marriage, is feeling some

Quality care provides a safe, healthy, nurturing learning environment designed to meet the needs—physical, emotional, intellectual—of the individual and the group.

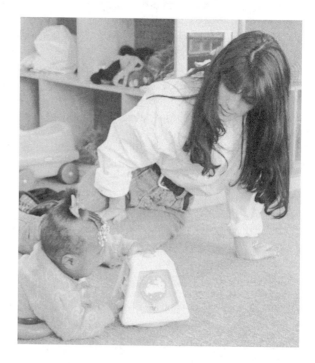

pressure because his oldest daughter is applying to expensive colleges. It's time for Debbie to go back to work full-time. She is looking for child care. Here's her story.

She started by calling a friend at work, who recommended the child care center that she uses. Debbie went over right away. She was appalled at what she saw. The place seemed like a madhouse—furniture overturned, paper on the floor, children everywhere yelling and screaming. Debbie couldn't imagine her precious little Evan here! A harried-looking teacher showed her around but was interrupted every 10 seconds by some squabble or a child demanding something. After 10 minutes the teacher handed Debbie a fistful of papers, told her that all the information she needed was on them, and left her standing wide-eyed by the door. She made a fast exit, depositing the papers in the trash can in the parking lot.

Next Debbie checked the phone book. At random, she picked another place, close to her work. She was astonished to find this center just the opposite of the first one. She arrived to find the children waiting in line to go outside. Although they were talking quietly and wiggling just a bit, they were not unruly. The room was immaculate, a little cold, and on the bare side. Debbie tried to imagine exuberant Evan in this setting. She couldn't. She left without talking to anyone.

The next place Debbie tried was down the street from her apartment. "At last!" she thought as she stepped inside a pleasant, well lighted room alive with healthy child activity. She liked what she saw—clusters of children playing busily, adults on the floor with them. "Good energy here," she concluded. But when she talked to the director, she discovered that this center took only low-income children, and even for them it had a waiting list with 100 names on it. She left disappointed.

"Your turn," she told Walt when she got home that night. "I'm just too discouraged."

By the end of a week she and Walt had learned a lot about child care. They found a local resource and referral agency that gave them information about centers as well as family child care providers—people who use their own homes for child care.

By the end of 2 weeks, they had visited a number of centers and family child care homes and found two that suited them that had openings. They sat down to make a decision.

First Walt brought up an earlier discussion about in-home care. "Are you sure you don't want to reconsider looking for someone to come here? If we could find someone it would be easier."

"Yes, it would be easier, but I want Evan to be with other children. I can't imagine him here all day every day by himself with someone who isn't me or you."

"So what will it be, Mrs. Watson's house or the River Street Center?" asked Walt, ready to settle this question. "They both have pros and cons. The center is more convenient and cheaper. It's warm and homelike. I like the way they plan curriculum around the children's interests. The staff seems stable—I asked each how long he or she had been there and was impressed at the low turnover rate. What do you think?"

"Well," Debbie said slowly, "I liked the center, too, but I wonder how Evan would fit in with those kids. They are so much older than he is."

"Mrs. Watson has a 5-year-old and a 4-year-old," said Walt.

"Yes, but the group is so small that the older kids are an asset rather than a liability. I don't worry that he will get lost in a crowd of big kids."

"But Mrs. Watson's is twice as far away."

"True, but I really like the fact that he'd be sort of part of a family. He has so many years to be in school, I'd rather he experience family life at this point. And when he's older he could go to the preschool down the block from Mrs. Watson, so he could have a larger group experience before he goes to kindergarten."

"I think you've made up your mind."

"I guess I have. What about you?"

"I think Mrs. Watson's house is great! Let's call her."

PARENT-PROFESSIONAL PARTNERSHIPS

An important aspect of child rearing is *care*—the feeling and the function. We can't legislate the feeling, only the function. But we can make it more likely that the feeling will follow if we have well trained, well paid, recognized staff and providers who are not overworked or burned out. This means that, as a society, we have to place a value on child care and on those who provide it.

Child care workers and parents—who together equal the full picture of child rearing—must be partners. A good many parents today can't do it alone. But a child care system can't do it alone, either, no matter how good it is. What parents give (most of them) is passionate feeling, highly personalized, that comes with a history and a future. Watch a power struggle between a parent and a child, and you'll see emotion seldom seen between two other people. Although providers and teachers are often critical of the passionate exchanges they witness from time to time, it is important to recognize that that's what parenting is about. It's about connectedness, which results in intense

Parents and early childhood professionals are partners; therefore, it is vital that they appreciate, respect, and support each other.

interactions. Parenting is passionate business—the anger as well as the love. Parenting is a long-term affair—much longer (excluding certain circumstances) than any child care arrangement. The parents provide the continuity through the child's life as he or she passes from program to program or from child care to school. Caregivers and teachers come and go, but children need continuity in their lives, and it's up to the parents to provide it.

Parent and caregiver are partners in child rearing. Therefore, it is vital that they appreciate, respect, and support each other.

Roadblocks to Mutual Appreciation, Respect, and Support

What gets in the way of this mutual appreciation, respect, and support? One roadblock on the part of some caregivers, teachers, and child care providers is the "savior complex." I remember my own period of being a savior. I was a beginner, and I thought I knew everything. And besides, I had a great desire to rescue children from their parents—especially the parents I didn't like much or understand very well. I went even further—I saw myself saving the world through the work I was doing with young children. Can you imagine how it must have felt to be a parent trying to communicate with me way up on my high horse?

Another roadblock I've encountered in others I've worked with is anger and resentment. Tune in on the following scene, which takes place in the living room of a modest home:

The sun is still just a hint in the eastern sky as the doorbell rings. A family child care provider in her bathrobe, who has barely managed to get her hair combed at this early hour, rushes to the door, followed by her fussing baby, who keeps raising his arms to be picked up. She is greeted by a mother who is dressed in a lovely print dress with jacket and jewelry to match. Hiding behind the woman is a sniffling toddler who is wiping her nose on the sleeve of her pajamas. After a rapid exchange of greetings, the mother explains briefly that she will be late tonight because she is taking an important client to dinner. She says a quick good-bye and then turns on her high heels and leaves.

The provider closes the door with a slight slam and leans up against it for a moment before she faces the two needy children who are both fussing at her. Although reminding herself that she made a conscious decision to stay home while her own child is a baby, she is nevertheless resentful of the nice clothes, jewelry, and makeup, as well as the freedom to attend power lunches and client dinners. All of that is totally unrelated to her own day of picking up messes, wiping noses, and changing diapers.

Meanwhile, in the car at the curb, the mother sits for a moment trying to rid herself of the distress she feels at leaving her daughter like this. She wonders whether the sniffles are the beginning of an illness. She wishes she could be there to watch her daughter closely and take care of her. She's resentful that the provider can be in her bathrobe at this hour and not have to worry about makeup or clothes. She starts up her car, thinking about how nice it would be to have all day to play with children instead of dealing with clients and coworkers in a dog-eat-dog world.

Neither woman in this scenario really wants to trade places with the other, but they both harbor resentments. Consider how these resentments might influence communication between the two. Imagine how the provider will feel tonight if the mother arrives later than she promised. Imagine how the mother will feel if the provider calls in the afternoon and says the child has a fever and must go home regardless of the important dinner scheduled. Will either one feel very understanding? Probably not, with all that resentment that was brewing earlier in the day.

A major issue between parents and child care workers is competition of all kinds, but especially competition for the child's affection. Because children are likely to be attached to both their parents and their providers, the competition is often intensified. Although in most cases child care workers remain only secondary attachments for children, parents can feel quite insecure about what they perceive as the threat of being replaced as number one in their child's eyes. It is up to both parents and providers to be aware of the feelings generated by this situation and to learn to respect and relate to each other in supportive ways. Acknowledging the feelings is a first step. Working on the relationship is also a positive approach to take. Setting out purposely to strengthen the relationships is accomplished most easily when all parties involved remind themselves that the child's welfare is at stake.

We have a model for sharing the care of a child: the extended family so prevalent in many cultures. In this model, the child experiences several simultaneous attachments instead of an exclusive one with the parent alone. There may be a single primary attachment, but the child who grows up in an extended family is likely to be parented by more than one person.

Choosing Child Care: Roberto

Roberto is a single parent and a physical therapist who works with Debbie, the mother in our earlier case study. Roberto has custody of his 4-year-old daughter, Mercedes. Now he is looking for child care, as Debbie had done previously.

When Mercedes was born, Roberto's mother, Barbara, offered to care for her on a daily basis. The arrangement worked out very well until just recently. Barbara inherited some money, and she's gotten the travel itch. This itch came at a convenient time, because Roberto was just thinking that Mercedes needed to expand her horizons a bit. Not that she didn't get what she needed in her grandmother's home, but Roberto wants her in a program with teachers and other children.

Roberto started his child care search about 6 months after Debbie did. He felt a good deal of pressure from Debbie to check out Mrs. Watson's, where Evan was so comfortably settled, so he did. He liked what he saw, but it wasn't what he wanted for Mercedes. Mrs. Watson was warm and kind, and obviously knew how to provide developmentally appropriate activities for the children in her care. She was also motherly to Roberto, but he bristled at that. "I don't need another mother," he told himself.

It was easy to decide against Mrs. Watson's family child care home. What Roberto wanted for Mercedes was a center.

He visited a number of places, including the ones that Debbie had gone to. Roberto wasn't as appalled as Debbie at the variety of programs he found.

Roberto knew what he wanted. It's just a matter of finding it, he told himself. He wanted a place where Mercedes could experience children and teachers of other cultures—one where teachers were trained to treat 4-year-olds as 4-year-olds and provide a rich variety of creative activities. It was hard for Barbara to open her house to easel painting, clay and play dough, carpentry, and other messy kinds of projects.

Barbara and Roberto have discussed this subject before. They are in agreement. "Those are the kinds of experiences a child care center should provide—ones it's hard to set up for at home," Roberto told Barbara.

Barbara agreed. "It will be nice for Mercedes to be with other children, too, instead of all by herself with just me."

Roberto found several programs that he liked. The one he liked best was in a church. He worried at first that they might teach religion there but was assured that the program was only renting the Sunday school rooms, and it wasn't affiliated with the church itself.

What Roberto particularly liked about this program was the racial mix of the staff and the atmosphere. He made a couple of visits and was pleased to see the variety of creative activities, including a sensory table and water play, available for the children. When he brought Mercedes to visit, some children were finger painting. Mercedes dived right in and was soon up to her elbows in oozing reds and yellows. She was having a

Children can grow and develop in a variety of settings, including their own homes, family child care homes, and child care centers.

glorious time smearing paint around. No one got upset that she went beyond the paper a couple of times.

Mercedes loved circle time and was the first to grab some streamers and start dancing to the music. She beamed as the teacher sang her name in a good-morning song. There wasn't anything that Mercedes didn't love.

"This is the place for us," Roberto told the teacher as he walked out the door, Mercedes in tow, protesting.

"Can't I just stay a few more minutes?" his daughter begged.

"You can come back tomorrow and spend all day!" Roberto answered.

SUMMARY

The United States has a long way to go as a society to solving the many problems of raising children, but we are at least becoming aware of the problems. A key term in child rearing today is *shared care*. We'll make great strides when parents and child care workers, teachers, and caregivers become true partners and when all the adults concerned with any one child come to respect, appreciate, and support each other. We know now that children can grow and develop in a variety of settings, including their own homes, family child care homes, and child care centers. The key word in any setting is *quality*.

We know, too, that early childhood programs, including Head Start and child care, can break the cycle of poverty and disadvantage. Not all programs that serve young children are equally effective. Programs that manage to break the cycle have particular characteristics: They are small, flexible, and interdisciplinary. They often provide more than just early childhood education and child care; they also deliver comprehensive services to meet the child's needs in the family, and the family's needs in the community.

It is taking a long time for this society to make children a national priority. The federal child care bill passed at the beginning of the 1990s, the continued funding of Head Start, and the federal and state dollars increasing child care capacities during the welfare reform period were all steps in the right direction.

This chapter took a look at child care as a child-rearing setting, dealing with a broad range of child care/early childhood education issues. The next chapter looks at one specific aspect of child rearing that occurs in both homes and child care: discipline.

FOR DISCUSSION

1. Do you agree that children are actually "reared" in child care? Can you give the view of someone who agrees? Can you give the view of someone who disagrees?

2. Do you know a parent who works outside the home but found an alternative to having someone else take care of his or her child? What alternative was it? How do you feel about it?

3. What do you think makes up quality care and why?

4. What do you think about trying to match teachers to children's cultural and language background?

5. What did you think of the scene on page 153, in which both the provider and the parent felt resentment? What solution do you see to this problem? How can the provider and parent communicate better and cope with their feelings?

REFERENCES

Aronson, S., & Spahr, P. M. (2002). *Healthy young children: A manual for programs*. Washington, DC: National Association for the Education of Young Children.

Brazelton, T. B., Zigler, E., Sherman, L., Bratton, W., & Sanders, J. (1999). *Quality child care and after school programs: Powerful weapons against crime*. Available on the Fight Crime: Invest in Kids Web site (www.fightcrime.org).

Breaking the link: National forum on child care compensation. (1994, April). National Center for the Early Childhood Workforce.

Bredekamp, S. (Ed.). (1984). *The accreditation criteria and procedures of the National Academy of Early Childhood Programs*. Washington, DC: National Association for the Education of Young Children.

Bredekamp, S., & Copple, C. (Eds.). (1997). *Developmentally appropriate practice in early childhood programs serving children from birth through age 8*. Washington, DC: National Association for the Education of Young Children.

Butterfield, P. M.(2002, February-March). Child care is rich in routines. *Zero to Three, 22*(4), 29–32.

Campbell, F. A., Pungello, E. P., Miller-Johnson, S., Burchinal, M., & Ramey, C. T. (2000). *Early learning, later success: The Abecedarian study early childhood educational intervention for poor children, executive summary*. Chapel Hill: University of North Carolina, Frank Porter Graham Child Development Center.

Children's Defense Fund. (2000). *The state of America's children yearbook, 2000*. Washington, DC: Children's Defense Fund.

Children's Defense Fund. (2004). *Children with disabilities and other special needs: Opportunities to participate in quality programs must be expanded* (From *Key facts: essential information about child care, early education, and school-age care*, 2003 edition). Retrieved August 19, 2004, from the Children's Defense Fund Web site

(www.childrensdefense.org/earlychildhood/childcare/keyfacts2003_childcare.pdf).

Cook, R. E., Tessier, A., & Klein, M. D. (2000). *Adapting early childhood curricula for children in inclusive settings* (5th ed.). Columbus, OH: Merrill.

Cost, quality, and outcomes in child care centers: Technical report. (1995). Denver: Center for Research in Economic and Social Policy, University of Colorado.

Curtis, D., & Carter, M. (2000). *The art of awareness*. St. Paul: Redleaf.

Division of Research to Practice, Office of Special Education Programs. (2001). *Synthesis on the use of assistive technology with infants and toddlers*. Washington, DC: U.S. Department of Education.

Edmiaston, R., Dolezal, V., Doolittle, S., Erickson, C., & Merritt, S. (2000). Developing individualized education programs for children in inclusive settings: A developmental framework. *Young Children, 55*(4), 36–41.

Erikson, E. H. (1963). *Childhood and society*. New York: Norton.

Gandini, L., & Edwards, C. P. (Eds.). (2000). *Bambini: The Italian approach to infant-toddler care*. New York: Teachers College Press.

Goldstein, L. (2002). *Reclaiming caring in teaching and teacher education*. New York: Lang.

Gonzalez-Mena, J. (2000, July). In the spirit of partnership: High maintenance parent or cultural difference? *Exchange, 134*, 40–42.

Gonzalez-Mena, J. (2002). *Infant/toddler caregiving: A guide to routines* (2nd ed.). Sacramento: California Department of Education, with WestEd.

Gonzalez-Mena, J., & Stonehouse, A. (2000, January). Responding in the spirit of partnership: High maintenance parents. *Child Care Information Exchange, 131*, 10–12.

Greenman, J. (2003). Places for childhood include parents, too. In B. & R. Neugebauer, (Eds.),

The art of leadership. Redmond, WA: Child Care Information Exchange.

Greenough, W., Emde, R. N., Gunnar, M., Massinga, R., & Shonkoff, J. P. (2001, April-May). The impact of the caregiving environment on young children's development: Different ways of knowing. *Zero to Three*, 21(5), 16–24.

Greenspan, S. I. (1999). *Building healthy minds*. Cambridge, MA: Perseus.

Greenspan, S. I., & Wieder, S. (1998). *The child with special needs: Encouraging intellectual and emotional growth*. Reading, MA: Perseus.

Illig, D. C. (1998). *Birth to kindergarten: The importance of the early years*. Sacramento: California Research Bureau.

Jamblon, J. R., Dombro, A. L., & Dichtelmiller, M. L. (1999). *The power of observation*. Washington, DC: Teaching Strategies.

Karoly, A. (1998). *Investing in our children*. Santa Monica, CA: Rand.

Kids count data book. (2003). Baltimore: Annie E. Casey Foundation.

Kontos, S., & Wilcox-Herzog, A. (1997, January). Teachers' interactions with children: Why are they so important? *Young Children* 52(2), 4–12.

Kostelnik, M., Onaga, E., Rohde, B., & Whiren, A. (2002). *Children with special needs: Lessons for early childhood professionals*. New York: Teachers College Press.

Kranowitz, C. S. (1998). *The out of sync child: Recognizing and coping with sensory integration dysfunction*. New York: Paragee.

Lee, L. (2002). *Serving families: A handbook on the principles and strategies of the parent services project approach*. San Rafael, CA: Parent Services Project.

Lombardi, J. (2003). *Time to care: Redesigning child care to promote education, support families and build communities*. Philadelphia: Temple University Press.

Noddings, N. (2002a). *Educating moral people: A caring alternative to character education*. New York: Teachers College Press.

Noddings, N. (2002b). *Starting at home: Care and social policy*. Berkeley: University of California Press.

O'Brien, M. (1997). *Inclusive child care for infants and toddlers: Meeting individual and special needs*. Baltimore: Brookes.

Phipps, P. A. (2003). Working with angry parents—Taking a customer service approach.

In B. & R. Neugebauer (Eds.), *The art of leadership*. Redmond, WA: Child Care Information Exchange.

Pinto, C. (2001, Spring). Supporting competence in a child with special needs: One child's story. *Educaring*, 22(2), 1–6.

Ramey, C. T., & Campbell, F. (1991). Poverty, early childhood education, and academic competence: The Abecedarian experiment. In A. Huston (Ed.), *Children in poverty: Child development and public policy*. New York: Cambridge University Press.

Raver, S. A. (1999). *Intervention strategies for infants and toddlers with special needs* (2nd ed.). Upper Saddle River, NJ: Merrill/Prentice Hall.

Ruopp, R., Travers, J., Glantz, F., & Coelen, C. (1979). *Children at the center: Final results of the National Day Care Study*. Boston: ABT Associates.

Schweinhart, L., Barnes, H., & Weikart, D. (1993). *Significant benefits: The High/Scope Perry preschool study through age 27*. Ypsilanti, MI: High/Scope Press.

Segal, M., Masi, W., & Leiderman, R. (2001). *In time and with love: Caring for infants and toddlers with special needs*. New York: New Market Press.

Shonkoff, J. P., & Phillips, D. (2001, April-May). From neurons to neighborhoods: The science of early childhood development—An introduction. *Zero to Three*, 21(5), 4–7.

Starting points: Meeting the needs of our youngest children. (1994). Carnegie Corporation of New York.

Stonehouse, A., & Gonzalez-Mena, J. (2004). *Making links: A collaborative approach to planning and practice in early childhood*. Sydney, Australia: Pademelon Press.

Szanton, E. S. (2001, January). For America's infants and toddlers, are important values threatened by our zeal to "teach"? *Young Children*, 56(1), 15–21.

Tobin, J. J., Wu, D. Y. H., & Davidson, D. H. (1989). *Preschool in three cultures: Japan, China, and the United States*. New Haven, CT: Yale University Press.

U.S. Department of Health and Human Services. (2003). *Making a difference in the lives of infants and toddlers and their families: The impacts of early Head Start*. Washington, DC: U.S. Department of Health and Human Services.

U.S. Department of Labor, Bureau of Labor Statistics. (1999, December). Table 48, Marital and Family Characteristics of the Labor Force from March 1999. In *Current population survey, December*

1999 (p. 293). Washington, DC: U.S. Government Printing Office.

Vinson, B. M. (2001, January). Fishing and Vygotsky's concept of effective education. *Young Children, 56*(1), 88–89.

Whitebook, M., Howes, C., & Phillips, D. (1993) *The National Child Care Staffing study revisited.* Oakland, CA: Child Care Employee Project.

Whitebook, M., & Sakai, L. (2004). *By a thread: How child care centers hold onto teachers, how teachers build lasting careers.* Kalamazoo, MI: Upjohn Institute for Employment Research.

Whitehead, L. C., & Ginsberg, S. I. (1999). Creating a family-like atmosphere in child care settings: All the more difficult in large child care centers. *Young Children, 54*(2), 4–10.

Zigler, E. F., Finn-Stevenson, M., & Hall, N. W. (2003). *The first three years and beyond: Brain development and social policy.* New Haven, CT: Yale University Press.

Zill, N. (2003, May). *Head Start FACES 2000: A whole-child perspective on program performance, fourth progress report.* Washington, DC: U.S. Department of Health and Human Services.

FURTHER READING

Bernhard, J. K., & Gonzalez-Mena, J. (2000). The cultural context of infant-toddler care. In D. Cryer & T. Harms (Eds.), *Infants and toddlers in out-of-home care* (pp. 237–267). Baltimore: Brookes.

Bernhard, J. K., Lefebvre, M. L., Chud, G., & Lange, R. (1995). *Paths to equity: Cultural, linguistic, and racial diversity in Canadian early childhood education.* Toronto: York Lanes.

Butterfield, P. M.(2002, February-March). Child care is rich in routines. *Zero to Three, 22*(4), 29–32.

Chang, H. N. L., Muckelroy, A., & Pulido-Tobiassen, D. (1996). *Looking in, looking out: Redefining child and early education in a diverse society.* San Francisco: California Tomorrow.

Cleveland, G., & Krashinsky, M. (2003). *Fact and fantasy: Eight myths about early childhood education and care.* Toronto, Canada: Childcare Resource and Research Unit, University of Toronto.

Edmiaston, R., Dolezal, V., Doolittle, S., Erickson, C., & Merritt, S. (2000). Developing individualized education programs for children in inclusive settings: A developmental framework. *Young Children, 55*(4), 36–41.

Gonzalez-Mena, J., (2000, July). In the spirit of partnership: High maintenance parent or cultural difference? *Exchange, 134,* 40–42.

Gonzalez-Mena, J. (2002). *Infant/toddler caregiving: A guide to routines.* (2nd ed.) Sacramento: California Department of Education with WestEd.

Gonzalez-Mena, J. (2005). *Diversity in early care and education: Honoring differences* (4th ed.). New York: McGraw-Hill.

Gonzalez-Mena, J., & Stonehouse, A. (2000, January). Responding in the spirit of partnership: The high maintenance parent. *Child Care Information Exchange, 131,* 10–12.

Greenman, J. (2003). Places for childhood include parents, too. In B. & R. Neugebauer, (Eds.), *The art of leadership.* Redmond, WA: Child Care Information Exchange.

Greenough, W., Emde, R. N., Gunnar, M., Massinga, R., & Shonkoff, J. P. (2001, April-May). The impact of the caregiving environment on young children's development: Different ways of knowing. *Zero to Three, 21*(5), 16–24.

Kontos, S. (1992). *Family day care: Out of the shadows and into the limelight.* Washington, DC: National Association for the Education of Young Children.

Kostelnik, M., Onaga, E., Rohde, B., & Whiren, A. (2002). *Children with special needs: Lessons for early childhood professionals.* New York: Teachers College Press.

Lee, L. (2002). *Serving families: A handbook on the principles and strategies of the parent services project approach.* San Rafael, CA: Parent Services Project.

Lombardi, J. (2003). *Time to care: Redesigning child care to promote education, support families and build communities.* Philadelphia: Temple University Press.

Moore, E. K. (1995, May). Mediocre care: Double jeopardy for black children. *Young Children, 50*(4), 47.

Noddings, N. (2002). *Educating moral people: A caring alternative to character education.* New York: Teachers College Press.

Phipps, P. A. (2003). Working with angry parents—Taking a customer service approach. In B. & R. Neugebauer (Eds.), *The art of leadership*. Redmond, WA: Child Care Information Exchange.

Schweinhart, L. (1995, May). The United States needs better child care. *Young Children, 50*(4), 48.

Segal, M., Masi, W., & Leiderman, R. (2001). *In time and with love: Caring for infants and toddlers with special needs*. New York: New Market Press.

Shonkoff, J. P., & Phillips, D. (2001 April-May). From neurons to neighborhoods: The science of early childhood development—An introduction. *Zero to Three, 21*(5), 4–7.

Stonehouse, A., & Gonzalez-Mena, J. (2004). *Making links: A collaborative approach to planning and practice in early childhood*. Sydney, Australia: Pademelon Press.

Szanton, E. S. (2001, January). For America's infants and toddlers, are important values threatened by our zeal to "teach"? *Young Children, 56*(1), 15–21.

Tobiassen, D. P., & Gonzalez-Mena, J. (1998). *A place to begin: Working with parents on issues of diversity*. Oakland: California Tomorrow.

Whitebook, M., & Sakai, L. (2004). *By a thread: How child care centers hold onto teachers, how teachers build lasting careers*. Kalamazoo, MI: Upjohn Institute for Employment Research.

Wong-Fillmore, L. (1991). When learning a second language means losing the first. *Early Childhood Research Quarterly, 6*, 323–346.

Zigler, E. F., Finn-Stevenson, M., & Hall, N. W. (2003). *The first three years and beyond: Brain development and social policy*. New Haven, CT: Yale University Press.

CHAPTER 7

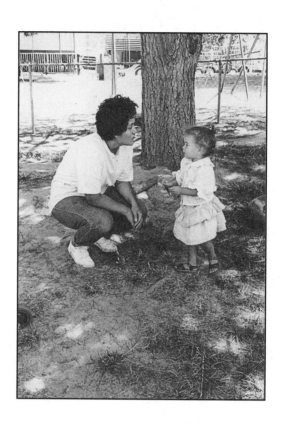

Disciplining for High Self-Esteem

In *this chapter you'll discover* . . .

- Guidelines for disciplining young children
- Ways to prevent misbehavior
- The common themes that underlie child abuse
- How to respond positively to negative behavior
- The difference between punishment and consequences
- When time-out is useful and when it's not
- Why you might want to ignore unacceptable behavior

DEFINING THE WORD *DISCIPLINE*

D*iscipline* is a loaded word. For years, early childhood experts tried to remove it from the vocabulary of teachers, caregivers, and parents, substituting the word *guidance* instead. But too many parents and educators were uncomfortable with what they considered the lack of discipline being advocated by the experts (*guidance* just didn't do it); so the word has refused to die.

Why did the experts want to change the word *discipline* to *guidance*? It has to do with the associations connected with the word. Whenever I've asked college students to draw symbols that show what the word *discipline* means to them, I often get pictures of jails, whips, gallows, electric chairs, and slapping hands. The least painful (in a physical sense) are the corners and stools with dunce caps on them. No wonder educators try to substitute the word *guidance*!

Obviously, to many people, *discipline* means punishment, and punishment means pain or at least humiliation. It doesn't have to be that way!

My own symbol of discipline is a path with two people, a big one and a little one, walking along together—a master and a disciple. (D*iscipline* and *disciple* come from the same root word.) In my book, discipline means guiding and managing behavior, not through punishment, but by being attached to a more experienced partner. This partner is a man or a woman who is wiser, knows more, and has lived longer than the child. Eventually children internalize the master or the older partner and take charge of themselves. This development of *inner controls*, or self-discipline, is the goal of disciplining children.

That is one way of looking at what children need in the way of guidance. I and many others in the field of early childhood education come from a culture that emphasizes independence and individuality, so it is important to internalize the control. There are other cultural views. For example, in some cultures, as mentioned in previous chapters, the emphasis is not on individuality but on being part of the group. Although the partner image may still work, it works in a different way. The idea of "inner controls" at an early age may not be a priority, according to Janice Hale (1986), a longtime advocate for cultural sensitivity to African American children. Hale says that discipline in many African American families depends on what she calls an "external locus of control." She describes how adults in the black community play a social-control role by creating a network of people who firmly correct behavior and report misbehavior to the parent. Therefore, parents are at the center of this social-control network. For the child, this means that he or she is always under the surveillance of adults. The significant feature of the control system is that it seems to operate externally to the child. Therefore, the child seems to develop an external locus of control.

Hale sees a conflict for children when teachers give children responsibility for their own behavior. She says that in schools where adults often behave as if they expect children to monitor themselves without outside help, the children's behavior may be labeled as problematic. The adults aren't functioning in the ways children expect, so the system the children are used to is not present to guide their behavior.

In addition, Snowden (1984) writes about cultural differences between African American and European American child rearing, saying something similar to Hale. Snowden also explains how the responsibility for the control of children's behavior is in the hands of an extensive network of adults. Snowden sees this approach as one of extended parenting, which ensures that children's behavior receives closer monitoring and results in more immediate sanctions than is the norm in the dominant culture. Children feel free to actively explore and take on assertive styles, because they know someone will be there to stop them when they go too far. Adults in charge of programs for children, including school, don't have the same direct and straightforward control over children's behavior. And they expect children to be passive and immobile, which many African American children are not. According to Snowden, the cultural conflict is clearly drawn.

Ballenger (1992, 1999) describes her work with Haitian preschool teachers and Haitian children. She sees a system of guidance that does stress inner controls, but not the way this chapter uses them. Children are not encouraged to reason out behavior choices. They aren't expected to learn from consequences of those choices. In the system Ballenger describes, children are taught to be good through appealing to their emotional connections to family and teachers.

Sandoval and De La Roza (1986) discuss the way extended family and interdependent network orientation work to provide external controls in the Hispanic community. They describe how the mother constantly gives directives to young children, even when they are not misbehaving. It is a way of letting them know that they are constantly being watched and that her "protective eyes" are on them. These constant directives given in public are ways to let others engage in the social control of the children. Anyone who sees children getting into trouble is expected to stop them and treat them as if they were their own.

We can learn from each other, but only if we become aware of what we are doing and begin to discuss it with people who are different from ourselves. One of the advantages for children in early childhood education programs is that parents can learn from each other and from the teachers, caregivers, or family child care providers.

One approach to guidance that some learn when they become early childhood educators or when they enter early childhood programs as parents is called a *consequences approach*. Often used in early childhood programs, the approach is considered an empowering one. Children are allowed to make *choices* about their behavior, within limits. Sometimes those choices lead to uncomfortable or undesirable *consequences*. The choices and the consequences are controlled by the adult so that they don't involve any real risk or harm for the child. But some consequences can still be emotionally painful. It may seem as if using a consequences approach is the same as using punishment, but it is not. Suffering the consequences of your own choices feels different from being punished because someone bigger or more powerful than you decides to do it. Punishment, the time-honored approach to teaching children acceptable behavior, has some side effects that parents, teachers, caregivers, and family child care providers should be aware of.

PROBLEMS WITH USING PUNISHMENT TO TEACH YOUNG CHILDREN

One problem with punishment is the negativity that accompanies it. Often the adult uses punishment to get even, which triggers a spirit of retaliation on the part of the child. This starts a vicious circle that ends only when one or the other triumphs, sometimes leaving quite a path of destruction in the wake of the conflict. Children who are frequently punished become more devious, not more cooperative. They respond to the hurt, loss, or penalty (the punishment) with anger, resentment, and defiance. Thus, punishment prevents the building of good relationships that are the basis of effective discipline and causes resentment and the urge to strike back.

Children who are punished for trying things out and making mistakes in the process can become inhibited in their development of autonomy and initiative. The urge to explore and experiment is squelched when punishment hangs over a child's head. Learning is reduced. Of course, childhood urges are strong, and many survive in spite of what adults may do to discourage them. However, it is important to understand how punishing young children can affect their later development. Children can come to see new situations as potentially "troublemaking" rather than as opportunities to use their initiative to find out more about the world around them. The adults those children become may be afraid to try anything new because they were punished for mistakes as children.

When punishments hurt, the teachable moment is lost. Children are most open to learning right after they've done something wrong or made a mistake. That's the time for helping them see what went wrong. If they are wrapped up in pain (physical or psychological), they can't concentrate on the "lesson" the adult has in mind and may instead learn some other lesson that wasn't even intended.

Physical punishment is not an option in an educational setting, but for those adults who still use it at home, it can be especially problematic because it models aggression. Parents who are trying to keep their children from hurting others or using violence to solve problems work against their own goals when they use physical punishment. The message the children get is that it is OK to hurt people if you are bigger and have a good reason.

Worst of all, physical punishment can lead to child abuse when adults go further than they intend to. When a parent first starts using physical punishment, the result of even a little is often resentment. Just as modern germs build up resistance to medicine, so does the resentful child become resistant to punishment. The parent finds it takes more and more punishment to get the same effect. Some children are willing to take a lot, so the parent continues to escalate. It's a vicious cycle. Some parents end up abusing their children when they get caught up in this ugly pattern.

The discipline I'm advocating is not punishment, but it's not a bed of roses, either. Adults who use the approaches to discipline that I advocate do not allow their children to do whatever they want regardless of anyone else's needs. That's permissiveness. Permissiveness is not good for either children or the adults who are in charge of them.

The discipline I'm advocating is far from permissiveness. It also *isn't* a simplistic, manipulative reward system. It *is* a complex approach that involves meeting needs, understanding developmental issues, expressing feelings, and, above all, preventing problems and using a *problem-solving process* when you can't prevent them. I first learned about this approach from the work of Dr. Thomas Gordon clear back in the 1970s (e.g., Gordon, 1970) and it's as useful now as it was then.

When examining any discipline approach, it's vital to look at your goals. One important goal is to find ways to guide and control behavior without lowering children's self-esteem. They need a positive perspective of themselves if discipline is going to have beneficial long-term effects (Nelsen, 2001). Consider the difference between teaching blind obedience and producing thoughtful children who are both cooperative and responsible.

Ask yourself this: When you are faced with misbehavior, are you more interested in changing the behavior than you are in winning, controlling, and coming out ahead or in making the child suffer? It's important to understand your own motives before you begin to discipline.

GUIDELINES FOR DISCIPLINING YOUNG CHILDREN

Here are some general guidelines for disciplining young children:

- *Communicate what you are doing and why.* Don't reason at length, but provide reasons. If you do this, children will eventually do their own reasoning.
- *Check communication to see whether it is clear.* If it is not, you may have ambiguous feelings—in which case you have to do something about them. An example of ambiguous feelings shows in the parent who wants her children to go to bed but feels guilty about being away from them all day, so she puts them to bed and tells them to go to sleep, but she doesn't insist or follow through and then gets mad when they keep bouncing out of bed or calling her. They pick up on and respond to her ambiguity. Bedtime is a big problem in many homes where there are toddlers or preschoolers.
- *Trust children.* They have a drive toward health, wholeness, and goodness. Misbehavior often comes as a result of their being thwarted in having their needs met. Look closely at any pattern of misbehavior, and take the attitude that this behavior is trying to communicate something. Trust the child to know what he or she needs even though on the surface the behavior may look just plain troublesome or contrary. Just because he seems to be "out to get you" doesn't mean that there aren't needs behind the behaviors.
- *Trust yourself.* You also have needs. You can only make good choices about disciplining children when your own needs are met. When your needs clash with children's needs, strive to find a balance, so that no one's needs are neglected. Convey the message to children that everyone's needs are important—theirs and yours, too.
- *Build good relationships.* Whatever approach you take to discipline will be more effective if it comes from a loving place. Remember in Chapter 5 how Nel Noddings's (2002) approach to creating moral people is to focus on the caring relationship. Her ethic of care involves close, positive, caring relationships. When adults come from a place of genuine caring, discipine measures work much better than when they are used as mere techniques without any relationship with the child.

What follows are 14 concrete examples of ways to discipline that lead to high self-esteem in healthy families.

*Build good relationships.
Discipline is more effective if it
comes from a loving place.*

Discipline as Preventing Unacceptable Behavior

Start with prevention. The following sections present seven things to do *before* the unacceptable behavior occurs. Though they may not seem like discipline techniques, they are because they are a means of guiding and controlling behavior. The first two have to do with the environment, the third with modeling, the fourth and fifth with redirection and control, the sixth with feelings, and the seventh with needs.

Child Abuse: A Story

Carla is dealing with the consequences of abusing her child. Right now she is in a group session with other abusing parents, listening to their stories. She's surprised that some of the themes are the same as hers, though the details are different.

As she listens to the others, she involuntarily goes back to the moment before she threw Cody against the wall, fracturing his skull. She gets a sick feeling in her stomach as the memory floods her.

She had reached the end of her rope that evening—she knew it then and she knows it now. "How much do you think I can take?" she had screamed at Cody, who was standing over a broken plate he had just thrown down from the counter in anger. She remembered the series of incidents that had led up to this confrontation better than she remembered what happened afterward. It had been a bad day!

The problem was that she was so alone. Since her husband had left her, she found herself with fewer and fewer social contacts. She knew she needed friends, but it was so hard to make them with two children to support and raise. They took up all her time. And they drove her crazy sometimes. Like that awful rainy Saturday when Cody ended up breaking the plate.

As the other parents in the circle continued talking, it became obvious that being isolated was a theme for most of them. Another problem for Carla was that Cody was so immature. She had told him time and again that now that his father was gone he was the man of the house. But he just didn't live up to any of her expectations. Sure, he was only 4, but still . . .

Carla didn't know it yet, but this was another common characteristic of parents who abuse their children. They don't understand developmental stages and often have unrealistic expectations for their children. Carla will learn about this subject from the class she is enrolled in.

She will also learn some techniques for guiding and controlling her children's behavior in positive ways. She knows she needs those techniques. Discipline has always left her feeling helpless. She only knows what she learned from her own parents, who used belittling, sarcasm, and, above all, beating on Carla when she was little.

Carla never thought of herself as an abused child. She figured that all children were punished in the same way she was. She knew that she had more scars than some of her childhood friends, but she accepted that as a fact. She never considered that she could question her parents' methods, and indeed she couldn't—she just would have been beaten harder for talking back.

It's not that her parents didn't love her—Carla knows that they did. In her mind they showed their love by hitting her; in fact, they even told her that. In Carla's experience, love and hurt were linked together.

Carla knows now that she *must stop* abusing Cody. No matter what problems she has, there's no excuse for not controlling herself—she knows that now. She also knows that she's not alone anymore. She's getting help, in the form of education, therapy, and, above all, support. Things will be different now, and eventually Cody and his sister Candace will be back home again.

Carla breathes a sigh of relief as she sits back in her chair, ready to talk. It's her turn now. The group looks at her expectantly.

"I have lots of feelings," she starts out.

Set Up an Appropriate Environment.   The younger the child the more he or she needs freedom to move, things to explore, and something to do. For example, you can predict unacceptable behavior when you have a toddler for any length of time in a fancy restaurant, an elegant living room, or a department store. You are more likely to find acceptable behavior when children are in an environment that is age-appropriate as well as suited to their needs and interests.

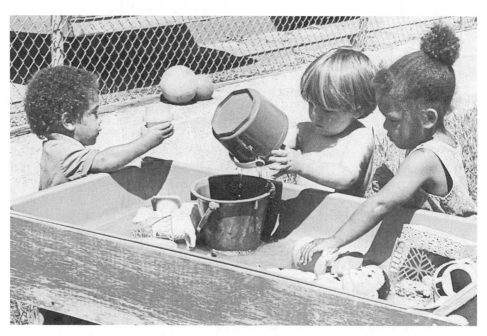

Set up an appropriate environment. The younger the child, the more he or she needs freedom to move, things to explore, and something to do.

Let the Environment Provide the Limits.   Fence off dangerous areas from young children. Most communities have laws about swimming pools, but they don't expect rules alone to prevent drownings. The same approach could be used in the home or child care center. Put breakables out of reach. Lock doors to rooms that are off limits to children.

This principle works beyond childhood. Freeways and throughways are good examples of how the environment provides the limits. Most are designed so you *can't* go off the on-ramp. Center dividers make it impossible to cross into oncoming traffic. The safety principles used by highway designers are a good model to keep in mind as you design appropriate environments for children.

Model Appropriate Behavior.   Model gentleness in the face of aggression. Model courtesy, kindness, sensitivity, sharing, and caring. It works! You may be surprised how much children pick up. If you yell at children to stop yelling, or if you're aggressive in response to aggression, they'll follow your actions instead of your words. Modeling is powerful. It works, either for you or against you.

Redirect Energy.   Much unacceptable behavior is just exuberance. It doesn't need to be curtailed; it just needs to be redirected. Find ways to turn potentially unacceptable actions into acceptable ones. Provide time outdoors for a child who wants to run, for example. If exuberance becomes overstimulation, try some calming activities—water play is a good one for the younger child. Playing with "goop" (a mixture of cornstarch and water) will calm almost anyone. Baths are a time-honored calming device.

Provide Physical Control When Needed.   For the very young child, physical guidance may prevent problems. Stop the hitting hand by gently but firmly taking hold of it, unless you're sure words alone will trigger the control that the child needs to stop his or her own hand. Words may work fine, but don't depend on them by themselves, especially with toddlers. Back up words by providing the physical control that the child may lack. Eventually you can use words alone; perhaps just a look will do it. But they need to know you really mean it—which you show by consistently providing gentle physical control when needed.

To provide this physical kind of guidance, you need to be nearby when trouble threatens. It also helps to know the rule of thumb of interaction distance that early childhood teachers have been using for years. Speak to a child from the distance of 1 foot for each year. When you ask a 2-year-old at 2 feet to control his hitting hand, you're close enough to reach out and control it for him if necessary. Children can hear you shout from across the room, but most won't listen. It takes your close physical presence to be sure that any words they might not want to hear will register.

Teach Appropriate Expression of Feelings.   Feelings are important and should be not only allowed and accepted but also appreciated—by yourself and by children. Children need to learn how to express their feelings in ways that don't harm themselves, anyone else, or the things around them. Teach them to say, "I'm angry!" Teach them to accept the feelings even if they don't show them or act on them. Again, it is important to acknowledge that this acceptance of individual feelings comes from a culture that focuses on individuals. People from cultures that do not focus on individuality might not feel comfortable following this advice. In some cultures, group harmony is more important than individual expression of feelings. Jerome Kagan, a researcher concerned with cultural differences, says about the cultures of Java, Japan, and China that respect for the feelings of elders and of authority "demands that each person not only suppress anger but, in addition, be ready to withhold complete honesty about personal feelings in order to avoid hurting another. This pragmatic view of honesty is regarded as a quality characteristic of the most mature adult and is not given the derogatory labels of insincerity or hypocrisy" (1984, pp. 244–245). When two people with different views about expressing feelings are responsible for the same child (as parents or as early childhood professional coworkers, or professional and parent), they need to talk about their differences and decide how to work together for the good of the child.

Redirection is one way to handle children's feelings as you guide a child from hitting another child to hitting a pillow or pounding clay. Art, music, dance, and physical exercise are classic ways of expressing feelings that should be available to children. You don't have to provide anything elaborate. Some children can get rid of a lot of anger simply through tearing paper into very small bits and throwing them into the wastebasket.

Meet Needs.   A good deal of undesirable behavior can be prevented when children (and adults, too) are feeling satisfied because their needs are met. Basic needs such as food, rest, and exercise come first; but beyond the basics lie higher needs such as security, protection, love, and closeness. Abraham Maslow, a psychologist, emphasized the importance of recognizing needs in his book *Motivation and Personality* (1970). When any needs are unmet, discipline problems can result.

Discipline as Responding to Unacceptable Behavior

When unacceptable behavior occurs in spite of your efforts to prevent it, an appropriate and effective response is in order. The response should not include name-calling, belittling, or global judgments of worth, because such responses lower self-esteem. It's not effective to make children feel bad about themselves in order to motivate them to behave better. In fact, that approach usually works at cross-purposes. Jane Nelsen (2001), famous for her books on discipline, is clear about the effectiveness of using positive approaches rather than negative ones. Children who feel bad about themselves are less likely to behave in acceptable ways unless they are dominated by fear. If you rule by fear, you damage relationships, which does not lead to healthy families or high self-esteem.

The following sections offer seven effective and healthy ways to respond to unacceptable behavior. They include giving feedback, allowing consequences, using time-out, rewarding some behaviors and ignoring others, teaching desired behaviors, and meeting needs.

Give Feedback.   If the problem belongs to the children involved and you can keep your feelings out of it, the best kind of feedback is "sports announcing." For example, when children are fighting over a toy, you can step in and narrate what you see, express the feelings you pick up, and get the children to talk to one another. This kind of sports announcing leads to problem-solving on the part of the children.

If, on the other hand, you have strong feelings because your needs are being trampled on, state them in a sentence that starts with I and contains a feeling word. These are called "I-messages" by Thomas Gordon (1970), a doctor who had great influence on parents and early childhood educators and parents with his book *Parent Effectiveness Training* (called PET for short). He also went on to write *Teacher Effectiveness Training* (TET). When using an I-message, the sentence should also encapsulate the behavior in question. For example, if children are screaming their lungs out and it bothers you, say, "I feel nervous [upset, tired] when I hear you scream." Feedback is different from judgmental criticism or blame, which diminishes self-esteem. Of course, if you are from a culture that does not value individual expression of feelings, an approach such as the one suggested here may feel uncomfortable.

Allow Children to Experience the Consequences of Their Actions.   *Natural* consequences don't have to be arranged, according to Rudolf Dreikurs, who coauthored a classic book some years ago called *Children: The Challenge* (Dreikurs & Soltz, 1964). Variations of that book and its offspring have now been read by several generations of parents. Using natural consequences is a matter of stepping back and not rescuing a child from a decision he or she has made. When a child chooses not to wear a sweater when going out to play, the natural consequence is to feel cold. Next time the child will consider the consequences of going outside without a sweater if he is allowed to feel the cold.

Logical consequences (Dreikurs & Loren, 1990) are set up by adults and reflect the reality of the social world. Logical consequences are a direct result of the child's own actions. When children leave their clothes on the floor instead of in the hamper, the clothes don't get washed. If the child can't be trusted not to go into the street, he or she is taken into the house. Children talk during story time and the adult stops reading. The child who spills the milk sponges it up. These are all logical consequences.

As stated earlier, consequences are different from punishment, even though they may cause anguish, because they are related to the child's own actions. They are reasonable, not arbitrary. Adults must be respectful when allowing or applying consequences. If adults are angry or harsh, consequences become punishment. Using consequences to teach may feel cold and uncaring to people from cultures where the adult role is warm protection and constant close connections are valued. It may be hard to stand back knowing that a child will not like living with a choice he or she is about to make. Some adults feel compelled to protect children from making decisions when the consequence will be unpleasant.

Using Consequences to Guide and Control Behavior

Jean is a mother who decided not to use punishment on her 5-year-old, Trevor, anymore. She had learned about using consequences as a discipline method and was ready to try it. She had the perfect opportunity the day she got tired of trying to get Trevor to put his dishes in the dishwasher after eating.

Trevor was very lazy about this—lazy to the point of stubbornness. Up to now Jean would remind him, time after time, but he'd "forget." She began to feel like a nag. She finally got so frustrated that she resorted to threatening him, but that didn't work either. Nothing worked!

Of course, nothing worked because Trevor knew that if he waited long enough, his mother would put the dishes away for him. Besides, it didn't really matter to him if a few dirty dishes were left lying around. His next meal always arrived right on schedule. The only consequence for leaving dishes on the table was that they magically disappeared eventually anyway. Finally, Jean decided she needed to get more creative about how to handle this problem, which she recognized as *her* problem. She decided that using a "consequences approach" would make it Trevor's problem as well.

She started by asking herself what the ultimate consequence of not putting dirty dishes in the dishwasher would be. She visualized a house full of molding dishes—it looked terrible. Would he mind that? She wasn't sure. Then she visualized an empty cupboard—no dishes for the next meal. That's the ultimate consequence. Even if the dirty house didn't affect him, the empty cupboard would if he didn't find his next meal, all hot and delicious, waiting for him on a clean plate.

So Jean explained to Trevor that she wouldn't remind or nag him anymore about dirty dishes, but she wouldn't put them away, either. She didn't. He didn't, either. By bedtime the first day the place was a dump, but Trevor didn't seem to mind.

Jean was discouraged. She thought she'd see results quicker. How long was this going to take, anyway, she asked herself, looking at the smeared glasses, sticky plates, and crusted forks lying here and there around the kitchen and the family room.

She had a brainstorm. "I'll hurry up the process by adding to the problem," she told her sister, whom she called for moral support. "I'll just quit putting my dishes away, too."

"Do you think it will work?" her sister asked.

"Yes," replied Jean enthusiastically.

That night Jean left a plate on the coffee table, with a dirty glass beside it. The next morning she left her coffee cup on the newspaper by her rocking chair, her cereal bowl and juice glass on the table, and an empty water glass on the television—next to the two empty glasses Trevor had left there the previous day.

It didn't take long. They never got to the point of the bare cupboard. Trevor didn't like the mess once it got really ugly. He picked up his dishes, Jean picked up hers, and that was the end of it.

So how was this different from punishment? For one thing, Jean didn't inflict it on Trevor. She merely quit doing what hadn't worked before and let his own actions show him what the problem was. He learned a lesson about the benefits of household order without being punished. Jean was a bystander—not a moralizer, judge, or jury. She even managed to refrain from saying, "I hope you learned your lesson."

Use Time-Out.   Time-out (sitting apart, being sent to another room or to a certain place in the same room) can be punishing if done in a punishing way (as can any of the approaches listed here). Used properly, time-out is a chance for children to gain control of themselves. This only works when the child is truly "out of control." Those are the times when the adult can become an ally, a helper to the child. The attitude is "I see that you can't control yourself in this situation, so I am going to help you by taking you out of it and getting you into a peaceful, less stimulating situation." This is very different from a punishing attitude, in which the adult is viewed as an adversary rather than as a partner. Time-out should be followed up with a problem-solving session between the child and the caregiver.

Unfortunately, time-out is overused by some adults, who respond to every misbehavior by sending the child off to sit in a chair. It is also abused. Instead of being a positive means of discipline, time-out often takes the place of the old-fashioned stool and dunce cap, which was an old-fashioned shaming device.

Here again cultural differences come into play. If an adult is from a culture where interconnections are stressed more than individuality, time-out may seem like an extreme punishment. Being cut off from the group is called "shunning" by some and is regarded as a very serious sanction. In some groups, time-out as a way of managing children's misbehavior is avoided because even when done kindly and in the child's best interests it feels excessive. Children should not be shunned through time-out or any other device.

Pay special attention to children who are not misbehaving

Reward Desired Behavior.   Notice when children are "being good." Pay special attention when children are being kind, courteous, sensitive, and helpful. Unfortunately, these are the times when we are tempted to ignore children because they aren't causing any problems. This is the behavior we expect, so why should we go out of our way to make a fuss over it?

However, behaviorist learning theory points out the power of the reward—even if it's only adult attention. Behavior that's rewarded tends to continue. Behavior that's ignored tends to disappear. Be careful about going overboard, however. Constant gushing praise doesn't work. In his book *Punished by Rewards*, Kohn (1993) writes about how, when we try to manipulate children's behavior through using incentives, side effects arise and our good intentions backfire. In a subsequent book, called *Unconditional Parenting: Moving From Rewards and Punishments to Love and Reasoning* (2004), Kohn shows parents what he showed teachers back in 1993. Citing hundreds of studies, he makes it clear that the more we use rewards to get children to do what we want, the more they lose interest in doing it. Children don't perform as well and they aren't as creative when we entice them to do something by dangling a reward in front of their noses.

It's not manipulative to be honest and sincere. Use your powers of observation to notice behavior that deserves noticing. For example, if you view a child treating her younger sibling in a gentle manner, you could say, "I see that you're being very careful when you touch your little brother." Just regular manners work, too: "I appreciate it when you help me set the table." "Thanks for feeding the dog." (See Chapter 10 for more on this subject.)

Ignore Misbehavior That Is Designed to Attract Attention.   Everyone needs attention—it's like a life-giving substance. When children don't get the attention they need through positive behaviors, they develop negative ones that are hard to ignore. If the message behind these behaviors is "I'm here, notice me," the only way to change the behaviors is to ignore them, and then give the needed attention at times when the child is acting acceptably. Turn your back on arguing that is designed to get your attention (much arguing among children is for that very purpose). Walk out of the room when a child is trying to annoy you.

Teach Prosocial Behavior.   Don't just teach what *not to do* through the aforementioned approaches. Take a proactive stance and teach what *to do* as well. Indirect teaching comes about through the already mentioned devices of modeling and rewarding. Direct teaching comes about through talking. Avoid lectures. Instead, use stories and role-plays, and even actually practice prosocial behavior by trying it out in little dramas or puppet shows. (See Chapter 5 for more about teaching prosocial behavior.)

Meet Needs.   Children often behave in unacceptable ways because they are needy. Respond to behaviors from that source by meeting the needs. Don't yell at a boy who

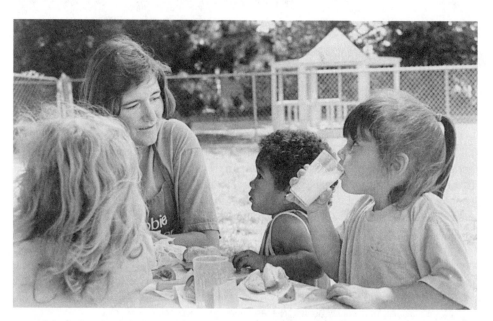

A *good deal of undesirable behavior can be prevented when children are feeling satisfied because their needs are met.*

is fussing because he's hungry; feed him. Don't give feedback to a tired girl who is out of control; put her to bed. Don't prevent restless children from wiggling; take them someplace where they can get the wiggles out. Of course you can't always meet each child's needs immediately, and it doesn't hurt them to learn to wait a bit—but not too long! Do what you can to control the truly unacceptable behavior, and put up with behavior that is only expressing feelings about having to wait.

What One Town Did About Child Abuse

Awhile back, in a medium-sized town in a northern California valley, a baby died as the result of abuse. A group of citizens, led by one individual, decided to do something about child abuse. This was about the time that national awareness was beginning to grow, as emergency room doctors questioned where all those mysterious bruises and broken bones were coming from. It was the same time that psychotherapists were hearing adult stories of early beatings. Each person who dredged up these memories was convinced that he or she was a unique case. No one realized that child abuse was so widespread.

Now, of course, we have one glaring statistic after another showing that for many children, growing up is very dangerous business. As a nation we decided to change the statistics, and we passed laws prohibiting child abuse.

The laws were not enough for this particular group of citizens, who wanted to *prevent* abuse in their community, not just punish it. This motivation on their part coincided with some funding set aside for prevention, intervention, and treatment of child abuse. The group went to work.

First they established a hotline for parents to call, just to talk, when they felt as though they might not be able to control themselves. Then they began to educate the community about child abuse and about using the hotline. What they and the community were surprised to discover was that child abuse crosses all economic, cultural, and racial lines. No one is immune. We're all at risk for "losing it" and hurting our children.

These citizens and others soon discovered that what parents needed was a variety of support services. Some needed parenting information and skills, some needed relief child care, some needed a job, some needed a place to live, and some just needed relief from the many stresses in their lives that led them to take out their frustrations on their children. The picture was much bigger than anyone had ever suspected.

Today many of these services are in place, but many more are needed. The original citizen group went on to establish relief child care, an after-school "phone friend" for children who come home to an empty house, parent support and education groups, an emergency aid fund, and support services for children in foster care. They also provide part-time temporary home service, where parent aides go into the home to help with household and child management through support and role modeling.

A good deal of energy has gone into changing things for children and their parents in this community. The group continues to provide community education by making speakers available and through a regular newsletter. Through its 25-year history, this organization has remained overwhelmingly a volunteer group, with a ratio of more than four volunteers to each paid staff member. Volunteer training is an ongoing focus as new recruits become involved and old volunteers change from one program to another within the organization. The funding now comes from a variety of federal, state, and local sources.

SUMMARY

This chapter discussed how to discipline so the effects are positive and enhance self-esteem, rather than tearing it down (as punishment is apt to do). A final word of advice: When you use any of these 14 approaches, communicate what you are doing and why. Don't reason on and on, but give reasons. Children will internalize your reasons and will eventually do their own reasoning, which leads to self-discipline. Punishment and the resulting possible fear do not lead to self-discipline in the same way.

Because feelings and problem-solving play such a prominent part in matters of discipline, the next two chapters focus specifically on those subjects.

FOR DISCUSSION

1. What do you think the word *discipline* means? What is the dictionary definition? What is the text's definition? What is your definition? How do they compare? How do they differ?

2. Discuss how the environment can be used to curb behavior and restrict a child from doing something dangerous or unacceptable. What is an example of learning from experiencing a consequence? Is your example a logical or a natural consequence?

3. Can you explain the difference between a consequence and punishment? What are some problems with using punishment to teach? Have you ever experienced any of these problems yourself?

4. What was your reaction to Carla's story of fracturing her son's skull on a rainy Saturday, the day she was "at the end of her rope"? If you had been Carla, what would you have done before that rainy day to prevent what happened?

5. Give examples of three prosocial behaviors you would want to teach young children. Have you ever taught these behaviors? If yes, how?

REFERENCES

Avoiding "me against you" discipline. (1988, November). *Young Children, 44*(1), 24–29.

Ballenger, C. (1992, Summer). Because you like us: The language of control. *Harvard Educational Review, 62*(2), 199–208.

Ballenger, C. (1999). *Teaching other people's children.* New York: Teachers College Press.

Berk, L. E., & Winsler, A. (1995). *Scaffolding children's learning: Vygotsky and early childhood education.* Washington, DC: National Association for the Education of Young Children.

Brehm, S. S. (1981). Oppositional behavior in children: A reactancy theory approach. In S. S. Brehm, S. M. Kassin, & F. X. Gibbons (Eds.), *Developmental social psychology theory* (pp. 96–121). New York: Oxford University Press.

Bronson, M., (2000). Research in review: Recognizing and supporting the development of self-regulation in young children. *Young Children, 55(2),* pp 32–36.

Campbell, S. B., Pierce, E. W., March, C. L., Ewing, L. J., & Szumowski, E. K. (1994). Hard to manage preschool boys: Symptomatic behavior across contexts and time. *Child Development 65,* 836–851.

Diaz, R. M., Neal, C. J., & Amaya-Williams, M. (1996). *The social origins of self-regulation: Vygotsky and Education.* Cambridge: Cambridge University Press.

Dreikurs, R., & Loren, G. (1990). *Logical consequences: A new approach to discipline.* New York: Dutton.

Dreikurs, R., & Soltz, V. (1964). *Children: The challenge.* New York: Duell, Sloan, & Pearce.

Drifte, C. (2004). *Encouraging positive behavior in the early years: A practical guide.* London: Paul Chapman Publishing.

Gil, D. G. (1970). *Violence against children: Physical child abuse in the United States.* Cambridge, MA: Harvard University Press.

Goodman, J. F., & Balamore, U. (2003). *Teaching goodness: Engaging the moral and academic promise of young children.* Boston: Allyn & Bacon.

Gordon, T. (1970). PET: *Parent effectiveness training.* New York: Wyden.

Hale, J. E. (1986). *Black children: Their roots, culture, and learning styles.* Baltimore: Johns Hopkins University Press.

Howes, C., & Ritchie, S. (2002). *A matter of trust.* New York: Teachers College Press.

Hyson, M. (2004). *The emotional development of young children* (2nd ed.). New York: Teachers College Press.

Kagan, J. (1984). *The nature of the child.* New York: Basic Books.

Kaiser, B., & Rasminsky, J. (2003). *Challenging behavior in young children: Understanding, preventing and responding effectively.* Boston: Allyn & Bacon.

Kohn, A. (1993). *Punished by rewards: The trouble with gold stars, incentive plans, A's, praise, and other bribes.* Boston: Houghton Mifflin.

Kohn, A. (2004). *Unconditional parenting: Moving from rewards and punishment to love and reasoning.* New York: Atria.

Kranowitz, C. S. (1998). *The out of sync child: Recognizing and coping with sensory integration dysfunction.* New York: Paragee.

Marion, M. (1999). *Guidance of young children* (5th ed.). Upper Saddle River, NJ: Merrill/Prentice Hall.

Maslow, A. H. (1968). *Toward a psychology of being.* New York: Van Nostrand.

Maslow, A. H. (1970). *Motivation and personality.* New York: Harper & Row.

Nelsen, J., (Ed.). (2001). *Positive discipline: A teacher's a–z guide* (2nd ed.). Rocklin, CA: Prima.

Nelsen, J., & Glenn, H. S. (1996). *Positive discipline.* New York: Ballantine.

Noddings, N. (2002). *Educating moral people: A caring alternative to character education.* New York: Teachers College Press.

Ostrosky, M., & Sandall, S. (2001). *Teaching strategies: What to do to support young children's development.* Denver: Division for Early Childhood of the Council for Exceptional Children.

Rand, M. K. (2000). *Giving it some thought: Cases for early childhood practice.* Washington, DC: National Association for the Education of Young Children.

Sandall, S., McLean, M. E., & Smith, B. (2000). *DEC recommended practices in early intervention/early childhood special education.* Longmouth, CO: Sopris West.

Sandall, S., & Ostrosky, M. (1999). *Young exceptional children: Practical ideas for addressing challenging behaviors.* Denver: Division for Early Childhood of the Council for Exceptional Children.

Sandoval, M., & De La Roza, M. (1986). A cultural perspective for serving the Hispanic client. In H. Lefley & P. Pedersen (Eds.), *Cross-cultural training for mental health professionals.* Springfield, IL: Thomas.

Segal, M., Masi, W., & Leiderman, R. (2001). *In time and with love: Caring for infants and toddlers with special needs.* New York: New Market Press.

Siccone, F., & Lopez, L. (2000). *Educating the heart: Lessons to build respect and responsibility.* Boston: Allyn & Bacon.

Snowden, L. R. (1984). Toward evaluation of black psycho-social competence. In S. Sue & T. Moore (Eds.), *The pluralistic society.* New York: Human Sciences Press.

Trickett, P. K., & Kuczynski, L. (1986). Children's misbehavior and parental discipline strategies in abusive and nonabusive families. *Developmental Psychology, 8,* 240–260.

FURTHER READING

Ballenger, C. (1999). *Teaching other people's children.* New York: Teachers College Press.

Baumrind, D. (1996). Parenting: The discipline controversy revisited. *Family Relations*, 45(4), 405–414.

Bell, S. H., Carr, V. W., Denno, D., Johnson, L. J., & Phillips, L. R. (2004). *Challenging behaviors in early childhood settings: Creating a place for all children.* Baltimore: Brookes.

Bronson, M. B. (2000, March). Research in review: Recognizing and supporting the development of self-regulation in young children. *Young Children*, 55(2), 32–36.

Charney, R. S. (2002). *Teaching children to care: Classroom management for ethical and academic growth.* Greenfield, MA: Northeast Foundation for Children.

Diaz, R. M., Neal, C. J., & Amaya-Williams, M. (1996). *The social origins of self-regulation: Vygotsky and Education.* Cambridge: Cambridge University Press.

Drifte, C. (2004). *Encouraging positive behavior in the early years: A practical guide.* London: Paul Chapman Publishing.

Duncan, T., Temple, K. M., & Smith, T. M. (2000, Summer). Reinforcement in developmentally appropriate early childhood classrooms. *Childhood Education*, 76(4), 194–203.

Elicker, J., & Fortner-Wood, C. (1995, November). Adult-child relationships in early childhood programs. *Young Children*, 51(1), 69–78.

Fox, L., Dunlap, G. Hemmeter, M. L., Joseph, G. E., & Strain, P. S. (2003 July). The teaching pyramid: A model for supporting social competence and preventing challenging behavior in young children. *Young Children*, 58(4), 48–52.

Fox, L., & Little, N. (2001). "Starting early: School-wide behavior support in a community preschool. *Journal of Positive Behavior Intervention*, 3, 251–254.

Gartrell, D. (2002). Replacing time-out: Part two—Using guidance to maintain an encouraging classroom. *Young Children*, 57(2), 36–43.

Goodman, J. F., & Balamore, U. (2003). *Teaching goodness: Engaging the moral and academic promise of young children.* Boston: Allyn & Bacon.

Howes, C., & Ritchie, S. (2002). *A matter of trust.* New York: Teachers College Press.

Hyson, M. (2004). *The emotional development of young children* (2nd ed.). New York: Teachers College Press.

Kaiser, B., & Rasminsky, J. (2003). *Challenging behavior in young children: Understanding, preventing and responding effectively.* Boston: Allyn & Bacon.

Kohn, A. (2004). *Unconditional parenting: Moving from rewards and punishment to love and reasoning.* New York: Atria.

Kranowitz, C. S. (1998). *The out of sync child: Recognizing and coping with sensory integration dysfunction.* New York: Paragee.

Lillard, A., & Curenton, S. (1999, September). Research in review: Do young children understand what others feel, want, and know? *Young Children*, 54(5), 52–57.

Marion, M. (1999). *Guidance of young children* (5th ed.). Upper Saddle River, NJ: Merrill/Prentice Hall.

Nelsen, J. (Ed.). (2001). *Positive discipline: A teacher's a–z guide* (2nd ed.). Rocklin, CA: Prima.

Reynolds, E. (2000). *Guiding young children: A child-centered approach.* Mountain View, CA: Mayfield.

Rightmyer, E. C. (2003, July). Democratic discipline: Children creating solutions. *Young Children*, 58(4), 38–44.

Sandall, S., & Ostrosky, M. (1999). *Young exceptional children: Practical ideas for addressing challenging behaviors.* Denver: Division for Early Childhood of the Council for Exceptional Children.

Schreiber, M. E. (1999, July). Time-outs for toddlers: Is our goal punishment or education? *Young Children*, 54(4), 22–25.

Segal, M., Masi, W., & Leiderman, R. (2001). *In time and with love: Caring for infants and toddlers with special needs.* New York: New Market Press.

Siccone, F., & Lopez, L. (2000). *Educating the heart: Lessons to build respect and responsibility.* Boston: Allyn & Bacon.

Wien, C. A. (2004, January). "From policing to participation: Overturning the rules and creating amiable classrooms. *Young Children*, 59(1), 34–40.

Wolfson-Steinberg, L. (2000, May). "Teacher! He hit me!" "She pushed me!" Where does it start? How can it stop? *Young Children*, 55(3), 38–42.

CHAPTER 8

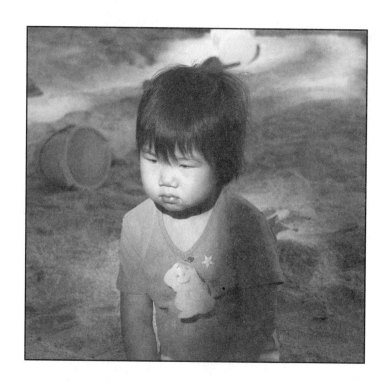

Accepting Feelings

In *this chapter you'll discover* . . .

- How children can be helped to cope with fear and anger
- The difference between expressing and acting on feelings
- How adults give children clues about what to feel in certain situations
- Why some adults react so strongly to children's sorrow
- What's good about anger
- Why there are no negative feelings

An important aspect of socialization is helping children recognize, accept, sort out, identify, label, integrate, express, and cope with their emotions. Perhaps the greatest task of all is helping children become socialized while fully experiencing their feelings. Part of the socialization process involves learning to know in each instance whether to express feelings or how to express them appropriately. Finally, the socialized person must decide whether to act on those feelings or how to act appropriately. This is an enormous lesson to learn.

Not all children grow up with adults who help them with the emotional aspects of development. Many adults promote lopsided emotional development in children. We all know adults who reached maturity skilled in some areas of feelings but unpracticed and unskilled in others. A person may be good at expressing anger and self-assertion and dealing with power relationships but lack the abilities that lead to intimacy and closeness; this individual is unable to be sensitive, nurturing, loving, tender, vulnerable. Another person may be skilled in the nurturing mode but lacking in self-assertion and fearful of his or her own power. These people may hold in their anger, fearing it as they would an untamed animal. They keep it all inside by tying it down, locking it in, because, in their minds, if this vicious animal gets loose it will commit unspeakably violent acts as it rages out of control. This perception of anger as a wild, vicious animal hides deep within many tender, nurturing people.

Then there are the adults who see themselves as a mind walking around in a body; they avoid feelings altogether whenever possible. Many of these adults are so afraid of their feelings that they spend years denying them and teach children to do likewise.

The point of starting this chapter by looking at adult feelings is that children learn about feelings from the adults in their lives. When adults set effective examples and provide modeling of what to do with feelings, children grow up with much more awareness and coping skills than when adults provide restricted models.

This chapter is about parents, as is appropriate, because it is in Part 2 of this book—the section called "The Family." Furthermore, it has pertinent information for early childhood professionals such as teachers, caregivers, and family child care providers, as it looks at emotional development and expression of feelings. It focuses on encouraging children to feel their feelings, to decide whether and how to express and act on them, and, above all, to decide how to cope with them.

Using Anger

Marcie is a 35-year-old stepmother who has recently discovered how to use anger. As a child, she was taught to hide her feelings. She learned early that strong emotion bothered the adults in her life. "Mad is bad" was a motto of her family. She still hears her own mother's voice inside her head telling her "Don't be angry!" and "Oh, just don't think about it!"

And that's just what she learned to do—forget about what was bothering her. But just willing to forget isn't enough. She had to learn some distraction techniques. Those techniques worked well, and she learned to stuff her feelings deep down inside, hiding them even from herself. One technique she used was getting out of her feelings into her head. She intellectualized when she stuffed.

But stuffing caused stewing. Grown-up Marcie is a master stewer. When she's upset, the simmering is practically audible.

Take the other day when her stepdaughter, Serena, screamed at her, "You can't tell me what to do! You're not my mother!" Marcie felt a surge of anger rising, but as was her practice, she stuffed it down inside herself and calmly responded to the 5-year-old in a reasonable voice.

The same thing happened during dinner when Serena complained about the food, only picked at her plate, got up from the table, and 15 minutes later asked for a snack. Marcie handled the situation well, but she was silent and sullen the rest of the evening. When her husband asked her what was wrong, she said, "Oh, nothing. Just tired."

But the problem with stewing is that the stuffed anger builds up until it eventually boils over. Then the rage comes pouring out unexpectedly.

That happened on the weekend. Marcie was still stewing when she emptied out Serena's dirty clothes basket and at the bottom, all wrinkled and smelling of dirty socks, was the little 100% cotton outfit that Marcie had hand-washed and ironed for Serena the week before. Furious that Serena had put it in the dirty clothes without once wearing it, Marcie stomped into the living room where Serena was lying on the floor watching TV. "What's this doing in the dirty clothes?" she screamed at her startled stepdaughter.

"You told me to pick up everything on the floor. And that was on the floor," sassed Serena.

Marcie's reason left her. She began to rage. When she finally finished, she was exhausted and heartsick with guilt. She was extra nice to Serena to make up for her own lack of control. This pattern was familiar to both Marcie and Serena: to stuff anger, stew for a long period, suddenly rage, then feel guilty and try to make it up to Serena.

Marcie needs to learn to break that pattern. She needs to discover that she can recognize anger when it arises and that she can turn off the voices of her parents that tell her to ignore what she's feeling. She can stay with the feeling and fully experience it instead of distracting herself by becoming "intellectual" about it. She needs to know that she can still *think* while she's *feeling*, but she must be careful to accept and acknowledge the feelings.

If Marcie could focus on her anger, she would get a clarity that doesn't come when she's busy distracting and stuffing. Unfelt feelings can be damaging—physically and psychologically. Felt feelings, and the emotional energy they bring, could be used constructively to improve her relationship with Serena. Marcie's tension could be released periodically instead of being buried and then exploding. The tension from the anger could be turned into positive energy that would be useful for solving problems.

Let's suppose that Marcie has learned all that, and today she operates out of new patterns. She's learned to feel her anger and use its energy. The bystander might not notice the difference. Marcie still often decides *not* to express her anger directly to Serena. But now she acknowledges the feelings to herself and experiences them fully. She's replaced the models in her life who were so busy avoiding emotions with ones who make good decisions about feeling, expressing, and acting on their feelings.

Marcie does look happier and more relaxed now that she has learned that anger brings important energy that can be used for problem-solving. Serena looks more relaxed too, since Marcie has left the stuffing, stewing, and boiling-over pattern behind.

WHAT ARE FEELINGS?

Let's look at the word *emotion*, which is what is meant by *feelings*. *Emotion* comes from the Latin word *emovere*, which means "to move out from, stir up, excite." So feelings indicate a stirred-up state of the individual. It is important to remember that the experience of this stirred-up state is subjective. The only way one can know about another's feelings is through communication (verbal and nonverbal), but the communication is not the feeling.

Feelings are complex subjective experiences that are different from but involve the physical and mental aspects of the self. That is a definition derived from Greenspan and Greenspan (1985) in their book, *First Feelings: Milestones in the Emotional Development of Your Baby and Child.* Feelings can be felt, expressed, acted on, and thought about, but each of those experiences of feelings is different.

Actions, thoughts, and feelings may be integrated, but they are not the same. Sometimes we mix them up. We say, "I feel that you aren't being as careful as you should be when you use my computer." That sentence is not about feelings; it's about thought. To discuss feelings one must use an emotion word such as *fear, anger,* or *sadness.* In the prior example sentence, substitute "I think" for "I feel," and the sentence is correct. To put feelings into that sentence, you have to add an emotion word. "I feel *upset* when I see that you aren't being careful when you use my computer."

All Feelings Are Positive

If you made a long list of all the feelings you have ever experienced, it would be tempting to divide them into positive and negative feelings. However, all feelings have value and are useful, even the ones we wish would go away. They serve a purpose. Feelings are a reaction to experience; they help us define and organize experience. They give us direction for action. They give us cause for expression. Some of the greatest works of art, music, and dance have come from feelings—and not always pleasant ones.

LEARNING FEELINGS

Feelings come naturally. From the beginning, in some cultures, adults teach the labels for those feelings. Children come to understand concepts of emotional states; eventually they can think about feeling.

This labeling starts in infancy, when the adult begins to label the child's emotional state: "That loud noise scared you!" or "I see how unhappy you are that your mommy isn't here to feed you yet." Labeling feelings is part of the socialization process.

The socialization process is also involved in feeding children cultural information about feelings and their expression. There is a fine line between the kind of cultural explaining, shaping, and molding of feelings that adults do to socialize children and manipulating them with value judgments that cut them off from their true experience.

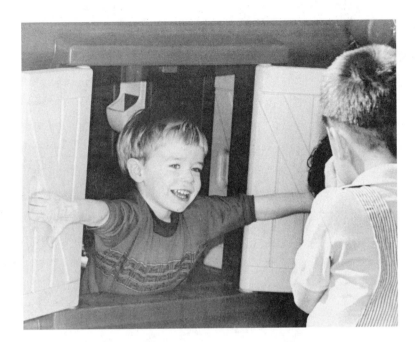

Surprise! Children play with feelings.

Placing values on feelings—teaching children *what* to feel and *what not* to feel—can do great harm. Rogers (1980) wrote about this subject long ago in his book, *A Way of Being*. He wrote about how infants trust their experience. When they are hungry they want food. They are in touch with their deepest needs. But if as they grow their parents begin to tell them what to feel or not feel, they come to distrust their own experience. It's even worse if the parents connect love to the issue of feelings, saying things such as "If you feel that way I won't love you." Doing so can cut children off from their feelings. Adults have a tremendous responsibility for children's emotional development.

How do adults teach children what to feel? One way is through something quite innocent called *social referencing*.

Social Referencing

Have you ever noticed how a young child who is faced with an uncertain situation will turn to parent, caregiver, teacher, or family child care provider for clues about how to react? This is very helpful; the adult can calm fears, for example. The child is approached by Uncle Mario, a large man with a big beard and glasses. This child never saw a human who looked like this before. He turns to the trusted adult for cues. The adult smiles, puts an arm around him and walks confidently toward Uncle Mario, talking to the man as if she trusts him implicitly. Every child won't take the adult's cues, but some will, and what had been a scary situation becomes an ordinary one—the meeting of a new relative. That's social referencing.

Children "try on" feelings like they try on dress-up clothes.

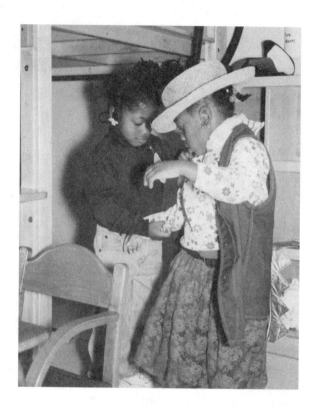

Anyone who has been around young children very much knows that when a young child falls down, she will often look to her parent or other adult to see how she is supposed to feel. That's social referencing.

Adults use social referencing to calm children's fears, warn them of danger, help them like a new food, even infect them with joy. Children constantly receive unspoken messages about how to react to situations through adult facial expressions, body language, posture, and even muscle tone. They eventually build up what can be thought of as *cultural scripts* about how to respond to specific situations.

However, a problem can occur when adults discover their power to influence children's feelings—to mold and shape their attitudes. Some adults overdo it.

Imagine a mother who has an overwhelming desire to make her child into her idea of the good, right, or perfect child, or a father who wants to make his child into a smaller version of himself—a person with the same interests, talents, personality traits. These parents may overuse social referencing. Teachers, caregivers, and family child care providers can also overuse social referencing in the same fashion. They make a fuss over what the child likes and dislikes when these leanings conform to the image of what they want the child to feel; otherwise, they ignore the child's expressions of preferences.

Of course, some children resist this molding of their feelings mightily; they become their own person no matter what their parents, teachers, caregivers, or family child care providers desire for them. But others, anxious to please, take all the spoken and unspoken messages to heart and incorporate them into their personality. They feel what the important adult(s) in their life feel(s). They like what the adult has indicated is worth liking. They're interested only in what interests the adult. They fear what the adult fears. They're angry when the adult is angry.

Most children have some tendency toward being influenced in their feelings by important people in their lives. That means adults must be very careful about wielding this influence, or they'll put children out of touch with their real feelings. They'll cut them off from their true experience.

Recognize the power of social referencing and use it wisely. When a child looks to you for your reaction to something, decide whether it is beneficial to give it to him in that situation. Know that you can remain neutral and let the child decide for himself how to react. *After* he decides, a supportive verbal or nonverbal response from you is appropriate.

Remaining neutral eliminates the possibility of a mistaken response. Consider these two examples of an adult mistake in influencing children's feelings: A toddler falls down. The adult acts as if everything is all right, but the child is hurt. The adult response discounts the child's feeling and makes him question his own reality. Or, conversely, if the adult makes a big fuss over what was only a little hurt, the child learns to ignore reality and exaggerate feelings to get attention.

Social referencing naturally starts in infancy, when babies look to adults to help them understand and interpret the world. The toddler also uses social referencing, but this approach should begin to fade in the preschool years. If it doesn't, its continuing presence may indicate a problem.

The outcome of the overuse of social referencing shows in the joke about the henpecked husband who asks his wife, "Dear, do I like custard?" But it involves more than simple likes and dislikes; it's a matter of a power differential. Take the example of the

Adults influence children's feelings through something called **social referencing.**

slave who when asked, "How's the weather?" looks at the master's face rather than out the window to answer. No one wants children to grow up with a slave mentality, unable to express their own feelings and relate to their own perceptions in the face of powerful others.

Cultural Scripts

All these warnings aside, it is important to recognize that feelings are influenced by cultural scripts that dictate the proper feelings for each occasion. Scripts can be specific to individual families or cultures, telling their members what they are supposed to feel and how to convey it. These scripts are useful in telling us what someone is likely to feel under certain circumstances. We know what emotion is "called for," for example, when someone close dies. Part of the socialization process is to learn these cultural scripts that dictate the correct emotional response to a situation. Even if we don't feel the way the script dictates, it is important to recognize that, in the eyes of others, the definition of *sane* or *normal* depends to some extent on knowing the cultural script.

One advantage of cultural scripts is that we get clues about how another person of our culture feels, even if they don't tell us. But a disadvantage, of course, is that though the unwritten script tells us how someone is *supposed to feel*, there is no guarantee that a person *will feel* as expected. And, of course, our own script may not help us understand a person from another culture unless we know the script of that person's culture as well as our own.

Scripts differ greatly from culture to culture. For example, there is an enormous difference about when it is OK to get angry and express oneself. In cultures such as the European American culture, which stresses individuality, everyone is encouraged to express feelings. The idea is that a person will function better as a group member if he or she enjoys the mental health that comes from expressing feelings. Good early childhood practice requires that adults accept all feelings as valid and convey that message to children, as well as teaching them appropriate expression of those feelings. The adult's job is to teach the child to recognize and express all feelings, especially anger.

Anger gets a lot of attention in European American culture. Some therapists, parents, and early childhood practitioners see the importance of allowing a child to express anger thoroughly, even to the point of raging. The idea is for the child to experience the feeling fully, to "work it through." These people see raging as a process that should not be interrupted until it is finished; otherwise, the unexpressed feelings may remain unfelt and go underground, popping up again and again as a "leftover" instead of arising as a feeling that is clearly connected to the immediate situation and not to the past. These adults may also assure the child that it is all right to feel whatever it is that he or she is feeling. They seek to prove to the child that expression of strong feelings won't result in abandonment. Of course, not all European Americans deal with anger in the same way. There is great variety in the European American culture.

Some European Americans and also people of other cultures don't have the same view of feelings and their expressions as described in the prior paragraph. They are more concerned about group harmony than about individual expression of feelings, particularly anger. They don't see unexpressed feelings as dangerous to either individual mental health or the group.

Lee (1959) says of the Hopi, "It is his duty to be happy, for the sake of the group, and a mind in conflict and full of anxiety brings disruption, ill-being, to the social unit" (p. 21). And Trinh Ngoc Dung (1984) says that in Vietnamese families, "children are taught at an early age to control their emotions" (p. 12).

It sounds as though the mandate is to repress feelings, a situation that is regarded as unhealthy in white, North European-derived American culture. But there are other views, like that of Hsu (1970), who in his book *Americans and Chinese* compares the

> prominence of emotions in the American way of life . . . with the tendency of the Chinese to underplay all matters of the heart. . . . Being individual-centered, the American moves toward social and psychological isolation. His happiness tends to be unqualified ecstasy just as his sorrow is likely to mean unbearable misery. A strong emotionality is inevitable since the emotions are concentrated in one individual.
>
> Being more situation-centered, the Chinese is inclined to be socially or psychologically dependent on others, for this situation-centered individual is tied closer to his world and his fellow men. His happiness and his sorrow tend to be mild since they are shared. (p. 10)

The Importance of Accepting Feelings

In spite of cultural differences in how you teach children to express feelings, it is important that children be allowed to *feel* them. The first 2 years are important in socializing a child to feel or not feel. Children suffer when adults refuse to accept their feelings. Feelings are important to spontaneity, to being in touch with one's experience, and to mental health. We *need* our feelings to develop in healthy ways.

Letting Go of Responsibility

Julie, mother of 4-year-old Alexa, felt shattered when she learned that a friend's teenage son had committed suicide. "I can't believe it," she lamented to another friend, Laura. "She's such a good mother!" All Julie's own hopes and fears about how her parenting skills would ensure her daughter's happiness had come tumbling down around her ears.

"Being a good mother is no guarantee of anything," Laura spouted without thinking. She wanted to comfort Julie, but her words only made matters worse.

A tear rolled down Julie's cheek as she said, "I've always thought if you tried hard and were a good parent, you'd have control over how your children turned out. But this tragedy ruined that theory." She was weeping openly now—tears for her friend and tears for herself.

As the conversation continued, Julie realized she was feeling fiercely protective of her own Alexa. She kept trying to figure out how to keep her happy so that she'd never lose her. What good were parenting skills if they didn't guarantee the happiness and well-being of your child?

Laura wasn't able to comfort her because Julie had learned a cruel lesson about life: Even good parents suffer tragic disappointments and losses because of their children's decisions.

Parents can control (or at least try to control) what *they* do, but they can't control how their children receive, perceive, or react to what they do. They can love their children, but they can't ensure that they feel loved. They can't control their children's personal perspective on things. They can't control the decisions they make about how to act based on those perspectives.

A major task of most parents is to let go. Though the first obvious letting go comes at birth when the cord is cut, letting go continues throughout life, a snip at a time. The most important letting go, and perhaps the hardest, is relinquishing the responsibility for the child's happiness.

Of course a parent's job is to meet children's needs, and that job logically *should* lead to happiness. It sometimes happens that way, but not always, because life isn't logical and because cause and effect are never simple or clear-cut in human development.

As the child gets older, the parent's ability and responsibility for meeting needs diminish, and the child takes over the job. The parent no longer has the same degree of control of creating well-being or bringing about happiness (assuming he or she was able to do it in the first place). This is a hard realization for parents to swallow. Of course all parents want their children to be happy, but they can't *make* them happy!

Parents can only do the best they can—improve their parenting skills and take care of themselves and their children. They'll have their expectations and hopes, of course, but they must realize that too many factors are involved for them to take direct responsibility for their children's feelings and the decisions (even life-and-death ones) that result from those feelings.

Even if it were possible to control the feelings and decisions of others, would that be good? Think what loss of freedom that outside control would mean. Imagine feeling the way your parents wanted you to or turning out exactly as they intended!

Teaching Children Healthy Expressions of Feelings

Acceptable expression of feelings is culturally determined. Since I know middle-class European American culture best, I will deal only with the range of ways approved by that culture. The rest of this chapter is written from that European American perspective. Some of the information may apply beyond this one cultural perspective, but perhaps not all.

I will start by stressing the difference between feelings themselves, the expression of those feelings, and actions based on those feelings. It is never inappropriate to *feel* whatever one feels. That message should be given to children loud and clear. However, it is sometimes inappropriate to express those feelings, and part of the socialization process is to understand when it is appropriate and when it is not. Maturity is in part determined by being able to make good decisions in this area. Deciding when to act on feelings also takes some maturity. Because of all the energy feelings bring forth, the urge is to act each time. However, the young child learns soon enough that getting mad and slugging someone is not a socially acceptable action around most adults. Grabbing what you want has side effects, and taking a bite out of someone because you love them does not get a loving response.

It takes some children awhile to learn these lessons. It is wise to be both kind and patient while the child is learning to control the actions brought forth by feelings and to find appropriate ways to express them. Susan Isaacs, a pioneer in early childhood education, gave advice in 1930 to a parent, and that advice is still valid today (Smith, 1985). She assured the parent that determination, obstinacy, and outbursts of temper are very normal and that it takes patience to socialize children. Often adults respond to these behaviors by getting upset. Isaacs explains that it is better to ignore these difficult behaviors than to display adult emotion, because that can make things worse. When adults get upset, the power that gives the child makes it likely that it will happen again. Or the adult getting upset may cause the child to be afraid. It helps to realize that the child has to learn to accept adult ways and desires and has to also learn to control his own behavior. We can't expect perfection, but we can help the child work toward more and more control, reasonableness, and friendly agreement. Isaacs is clear that teaching by spanking doesn't work because the child can't see the difference between the adult behavior and his own violence. Ruling by fear only increases obstinacy. Adults should avoid unnecessary demands and pick only a few issues, making sure they are ones they can follow through on. When the adult gives lots of choices on smaller matters, it is easier to be friendly and understanding.

It may be hard to follow Isaacs's advice in the heat of the moment, but it is worth having patience as a goal. While being patient, you can be teaching words to express the feelings and help the child move to more acceptable behaviors. When children begin to label feelings, you know they have now conceptualized them, bringing intellectual processes in to help with the emotional ones. Once the mind comes into play, it isn't long until you see the child using "pretend" to help him further understand and cope with feelings. Now the child's mind and body are working in concert with feelings, thus helping the child integrate.

What are some appropriate ways for young children to express their feelings? Many adults encourage direct verbalization and teach children to say, "I'm mad because you took my toy" or "I'm unhappy because my mommy had to go to work." They also teach children to say to each other, "I don't want you to do that" or "I don't like it when you hit me. It hurts."

Many adults agree in this approach—teaching one child to talk to another in a direct way. However, not everyone is comfortable with teaching children to talk so directly to adults. Some feel it is disrespectful for children to tell an adult they are mad at him or her. They are even more uncomfortable if the child translates "I'm mad at you" into "I hate you!" Other adults accept this form of expression, perhaps disregarding the actual words and responding to the feeling behind them. It is common for

Adults have different ideas about how to express feelings appropriately. They may not all agree that what this child is doing is OK.

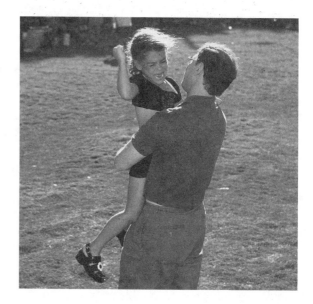

an adult trained in early childhood education to reflect back the angry feeling by saying something such as "You're really mad at me right now."

Whatever ways of expressing feelings are acceptable to the adults in the child's life, those are the ways that should be taught to the child. Imagine how a parent who is very concerned that his child show a certain kind of respect to adults would feel if he walked into the center just in time to hear his child scream "I hate you" at the teacher. Although the teacher may find nothing wrong with this way of expressing anger, it is important to take the parents' perspective into consideration and find some way to accept the feeling and teach another mode of expression.

Examples of ways of expressing feelings that are acceptable to some adults and not to others are as follows:

- ◆ Yelling and screaming
- ◆ Stating negative wishes or imagining violent happenings (e.g., "I hope your new toy breaks" "Maybe you'll break your leg" or "I wish my baby brother would die")
- ◆ Taking out anger symbolically on toys or other objects (e.g., spanking dolls or pounding pillows)

Most adults agree that name-calling and using obscenities are not appropriate ways for young children to express feelings. It's important, though, to realize that to a young child "bad words" have little meaning except that children know certain words hold power for adults. However, if you listen to young children trying to wield power over *each other*, they don't use adult words. They call each other "baby" or say, "I won't like you anymore." Those expressions have more meaning and carry more weight than all the four-letter words they may have ever learned.

TEACHING CHILDREN TO COPE WITH FEELINGS

Developing Self-Calming Skills

One of the greatest skills an adult working or living with young children can have is the ability to calm an upset child. Of course, the optimum is for children to learn to calm themselves, and for that reason adults should respect their attempts to do so. For example, when the crying infant finds a soothing thumb and pops it in, the adult should rejoice and not try to distract or substitute something else. The thumb is an example of a very effective self-soothing device.

If infants are to learn self-calming techniques, the adult must not jump up and respond to each little whimper or tiny demand. Timing is important; it takes skill to create a response gap that is just long enough to allow children to discover ways to meet their own needs. If the adult waits too long, children feel neglected; they may go beyond the place where they can calm themselves. Once the child gets overly excited and chaos sets in, the adult needs to be on hand to stop the momentum and help the child get reorganized. Sometimes this is merely a matter of being present and allowing the child to pick up your calm rhythms. Some adults have the natural instinct of tuning into the child's rhythms, flowing with them until the two are in tune, then slowing the combined rhythm until the child is once more relaxed and calm. Thoman and Browder (1987) give specifics about how this can be done with a baby. They start by advising the adult to find a quiet, softly lit room and relax completely while holding the baby:

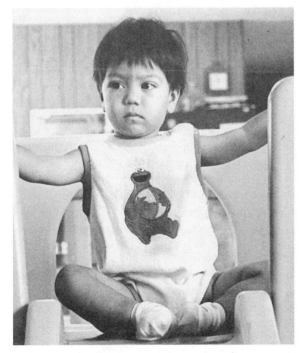

It is never inappropriate to feel what one feels.

"Breathe deeply. Feel all your muscles unwind. . . . Now tune in to your baby. Listen to his breathing. Feel his breathing against your chest. At first, try to match your breathing to your baby's breathing, so you're inhaling and exhaling in unison. Then slowly make your breathing deeper" (pp. 181–182). They say that as the adult changes his or her breathing, the baby's breathing will change to match it.

This approach can be used with some children who are no longer babies. Some children are able to use the adult closeness to bring down their energy level and become calm. Something similar can even be used with a group of children. Some parents, teachers, family child care providers, and caregivers know how to go with the flow of energy and then bring it down to a less chaotic level. There's usually an ideal time to intervene. Determining this ideal time is a skill adults who live and work with young children can acquire through experience.

Coping by Playing Pretend

Playing pretend is a way that children experience feelings in a way that they can control. In a sense, they *practice* emotions through playing. They're in charge of the environment and of themselves, which puts them in a very powerful position—often the opposite of their position when they are overcome by a feeling in real life.

Adults who understand how important pretend play is to emotional development encourage children to engage in it. They give them props to get them started. (That's what the "housekeeping corner" and all the "dress-up clothes" are about in a child care center.) When children don't automatically show interest in playing pretend, adults can get them started by playing with them. Adults who see the value of time spent pretending provide opportunities, space, and stuff to stimulate imagination. They also provide encouragement.

Two early childhood experts, Susan Isaacs and Vivian Paley, working 50 years apart, have important ideas about the use of what is called *dramatic play.* Isaacs (Smith, 1985) says that through what she calls "imaginative play, children symbolize and externalize their inner drama and conflicts and work through them to gain relief from pressures." She explains that through creating make-believe situations, they practice predicting or hypothesizing what might happen and play it out. Children free themselves from the here and now of the concrete world by acting as if something were true. They not only revisit the past but project into the future through playing pretend.

Paley (1988) talks about the kind of pretend play she sees daily in her classroom of preschoolers. She says, "Whatever else is going on in this network of melodrama, the themes are vast and wondrous. Images of good and evil, birth and death, parent and child, move in and out of the real and the pretend. There is no small talk. The listener is submerged in philosophical position papers, a virtual recapitulation of life's enigmas" (p. 6).

As children create their own worlds through pretend play, they gain a sense of power. They transform reality and practice mastery over it. No wonder pretend play is appealing. In addition to personal power, children also gain communication skills. Through play with, for example, small figures, they deal with several levels of communication as the figures themselves interact, and the players who control them also interact. Children engaged in this type of play practice negotiation and cooperation in real life and on a pretend level. They can get very sophisticated at expressing feelings through this medium.

Coping with Simultaneous Feelings

It would be easier to teach children to accept, express, and cope with their feelings if all feelings came singly. However, almost no feelings come as a single pure and simple unit of emotion. Often, two feelings come simultaneously. For example, I feel sad that my dog has died, but I'm greatly relieved that his suffering is over; or I'm delighted about my contract to write a new book, but I'm worried about my ability to do it. Adults recognize those as mixed feelings. Having simultaneous feelings can be an advantage because we can focus on one to help us cope with the other.

However, it is a different story for young children, who can only focus on one feeling at a time; they aren't aware of mixed feelings (Harter & Buddin, 1987). We adults can help them begin to experience more than one feeling by verbalizing for them when we perceive they might have mixed feelings (e.g., "You're happy to stay overnight with your friend, but you're scared about being away from home"). Experiencing simultaneous feelings may take some time, since it only comes as the result of increasing maturity.

Coping with Anger

Sometimes anger carries good, clean, strong energy. Children can learn to use that energy to express themselves, to protect themselves, and, when needs or wants conflict, to work toward problem-solving solutions. The ultimate in problem solving is when the child is able to satisfy the need, thereby eliminating the source of the anger without tearing down or intentionally hurting other people. Anger can give extra strength or insight on how to get needs met and to aid this problem-solving process.

Teaching young children to express angry feelings without hurting anyone or anything is a goal for adults who live or work with them. Adults help children learn these skills by doing the following:

- *Accepting and labeling the feeling.*   "I see how angry you are." "It really makes you mad when she grabs your doll!"
- *Redirecting the energy and helping the child get it out.*   "I know you feel like biting your sister, but bite this washcloth instead." "Why don't you go out and run around the play yard three times and see if you still feel so mad."
- *Calming the energy; soothing the chaos.*   "I see how upset you are right now. Do you want to sit on my lap and rock a little?" (for the younger child). Or for the older child, a neck massage might help or a suggestion to "try messing around with this goop and see if it makes you feel better." (Time-honored substances for "messing around" are mud and its substitutes—wet clay, cornstarch and water, play dough. Water alone is a great soother in a water-play table, a tub, a sink, or a bathtub.)

Adults can help children experience, express, think about, and cope with feelings.

- ◆ *Avoiding a reward for anger.* Some adults respond to a child's display of anger with so much attention that the behavior is reinforced. If a powerless child can achieve a powerful feeling by displaying anger, he is bound to continue to use the same approach unless someone helps him experience power in a different way.
- ◆ *Teaching problem solving.* When children learn to solve problems by communicating in a give-and-take negotiating kind of way, they feel less frustrated and have less need to try to get their way by using anger.

Coping with Fear

Uncomfortable as they may make us feel, fears are useful. They protect us from dangers. The problem is that sometimes fears get in our way of fully experiencing the world. They can limit our explorations and discourage healthy risk taking, the things that give us a fuller life and help us expand our knowledge.

Adults can help children deal with fears by doing the following:

- ◆ *Taking them seriously.* What may not seem significant to an adult may be terrifying to a young child. It is important for the adult to be reassuring without discounting the feeling. Children need their feelings validated, even when the adult is convinced that there is no danger present.
- ◆ *Modeling.* Children can learn fears from other people. They can also learn to not be afraid by watching others interact with the object of their fear. The child who is

Adults can help children deal with fear by taking them seriously and not discounting their feelings.

afraid of dogs may be reassured when both an adult and another child pet the dog in a friendly, trusting way.

◆ *Playing out fears.*   Sometimes an adult can find ways for the child to experience something in a safe environment that he or she is afraid of. Sometimes children will do this on their own through pretend play, either in a dramatic play setting or with small figures. Another example of playing out fears is when an adult encourages a toddler to play with a small amount of water in a dishpan or sink to help cope with bathtub fears:

Dowrick (1986), in his book *Social Survival for Children*, describes how he trains children in relaxation and helps them visualize themselves feeling brave in situations that scare them. He also talks about alleviating fear in children through helping them perform in graduated small steps following a carefully established hierarchy.

Dowrick gives an example of such a hierarchy: A 5-year-old greatly feared doctors yet needed to go to the dentist. The first step was to help him pretend to be a doctor with another child as patient. That was followed by getting him to play patient with another child as doctor. When he was comfortable with that, he was talked into allowing an adult "doctor" to pretend to inspect the inside of his throat. When he was finally able to allow a "pretend" adult doctor to put dental instruments in his mouth, he was ready for his visit to the real dentist. Each step of the play was recorded on videotape and then edited and reviewed by the child. Watching himself in repeated experiences in a benign environment strengthened his coping responses—a kind of self-modeling. In addition, the child was taught relaxation techniques, using positive imagery.

Many early childhood practitioners also use a technique of children helping children cope with fears. The child care teacher sends a gentle, outgoing child over to interact with the fearful child who is hanging back from participating in activities. Some child care and preschool teachers have a real talent for linking up one child with another for the good of both. Some early childhood educators go so far as to suggest to parents that so-and-so might be a good friend to invite over. The friendships that result from these linkages sometimes last for years.

Adults "Being Put Up Against Themselves"

It is hard for adults who grew up without fully experiencing their feelings to be around children who are able and willing to do so. A crying child can touch sore spots deep within adults who then react from their own pain as much as from the child's. Marjory Keenan (1996), an infant-toddler caregiver, calls this phenomenon "putting one up against oneself" as she tells her story of trying to contend with the lengthy separation agonies of three little girls in her care.

Marjory was professional—warm, caring, and supportive of these girls in their grief. She helped them write daily letters to their mommies telling them they were missed. But nothing worked for long to relieve them of the need to chant pitifully, "I want my mama." It took Marjory 2 months to finally face her own deep pain of her mother's death when she was just a little younger than these children. She realized what was happening one day in her classroom when the chanting started again. Marjory found herself thinking, "Shut up! You have a mommy, and your mommy always comes and gets you." Marjory's mommy never came back again, and the 2-year-old inside of her was reacting. Marjory's feelings finally resurfaced when the three little girls "put her up against herself" with their nearly nonstop lamenting.

"The girls in my class were not consciously trying to upset me," Marjory says. "They were only expressing their true feelings of loss, and these were mirroring my deep pain. The more I listened to the child within me, the less my lamenters irritated me. I began to realize that they were speaking the words that I could only feel internally." (Keenan, 1996, p. 75)

SUMMARY

Helping a child recognize, express, and cope with feelings is not an easy job, especially for adults who may have themselves been emotionally stunted as children.

The child's feeling triggers a response in these adults that brings anger or fear and pain. For example, a child sobbing over her mother's departure from the child care center may make her teacher so uncomfortable that the teacher will do whatever she can to distract the child from her feelings. Distraction works, but it doesn't allow the child to experience the full range of emotions and learn to cope with them in creative ways.

Some children seem to live life only on the surface. They are shut off from a full range of experience and emotions. Others show one set of emotions but not another. One child is assertive and powerful and shows a full range of the feelings that accompany those traits, but she is unable to enjoy being close to people. Another child is good at intimacy and love but shies away from any conflict because he is unable to be assertive or protect himself from those who are aggressive. Neither of these children possesses the ability to feel and use the whole range of human emotions.

The goal is for all children to gain feelings of independence and the security of belonging. But they must not do so by sacrificing all the deep and varied human emotions so vital to living life to its fullest and coming out a well rounded person who embraces experience of all sorts.

This chapter explored feelings and some of the ways adults can help children experience, express, think about, and cope with them. Once children can separate feelings and thoughts, they can learn to be good problem-solvers. This learning process starts early and is the subject of the next chapter, in which problem-solving is related to feelings, discipline, and empowerment.

FOR DISCUSSION

1. How does social referencing work? Can you give an example? When is social referencing useful and when is it not? Why would you not want to use social referencing when responding to a toddler who has just taken a spill?

2. Can you give an example of a cultural script? Do you have any cultural scripts? What are they?

3. What are some cultural differences when it comes to expressing anger? How about to expressing fear?

4. What does it mean to "use the energy" that anger brings? What would be some ways to do this yourself? What are some ways to help children do it? Is there something from your own experience that you can apply to working with a child's anger?

REFERENCES

Butterfield, P. M., Martin, C. A., & Prairie, A. P. (2004). *Emotional connections: How relationships guide early learning*. Washington, DC: Zero to Three.

Dowrick, P. W. (1986). *Social survival for children: A trainer's resource book*. New York: Brunner/Mazel.

Dung, T. N. (1984, March-April). Understanding Asian families: A Vietnamese perspective. *Children Today, 13*(2), 10–12.

Goleman, D. (2000). *Working with emotional intelligence*. New York: Bantam.

Greenspan, S. I. (1999). *Building healthy minds*. Cambridge, MA: Perseus.

Greenspan, S. I., & Greenspan, N. T. (1985). *First feelings: Milestones in the emotional development of your baby and child*. New York: Viking.

Greenspan, S. I., & Wieder, S. (1998). *The child with special needs: Encouraging intellectual and emotional growth*. Reading, MA: Perseus.

Harter, S. (1998). The development of self-representations. In N. Eisenberg (Ed.), *Handbook of child psychology*: Vol. 3. *Social, emotional, and personality development* (5th ed., pp. 553–618). New York: Wiley.

Harter, S., & Buddin, B. J. (1987). Children's understanding of the simultaneity of two emotions:

A five-stage developmental acquisition sequence. *Developmental Psychology, 22*(3), 388–399.

Hsu, F. L. K. (1970). *Americans and Chinese: Purpose and fulfillment in great civilizations.* Garden City, NY: Natural History Press.

Hyson, M. (2004). *The emotional development of young children* (2nd ed.). New York: Teachers College Press.

Keenan, M. (1996, September). They pushed my buttons: Being put up against myself. *Young Children, 51*(6), 74–75.

Klein, M. D., & Chen, D. (2001). *Working with children from culturally diverse backgrounds.* Albany, NY: Delmar.

Lee, D. (1959). *Freedom and culture.* Upper Saddle River, NJ: Prentice Hall.

Paley, V. G. (1988). *Bad guys don't have birthdays: Fantasy play at four.* Chicago: University of Chicago Press.

Petersen, S., Bair, K., & Sullivan, A. (2004). Emotional well-being and mental health services: Lessons learned by early Head Start Region VIII programs. *Zero to Three, 24*(6), 47–53.

Rogers, C. R. (1980). *A way of being.* Boston: Houghton Mifflin.

Smith, L. A. H. (1985). *To understand and to help: The life and work of Susan Isaacs.* Cranbury, NJ: Associated University Presses.

Thoman, E. B., & Browder, S. (1987). *Born dancing: How intuitive parents understand the baby's unspoken language and natural rhythms.* New York: Harper & Row.

Van Hoorn, J., Nourot, P., Scales, B., & Alward, K. (2003). *Play at the center of the curriculum* (3rd ed.). Upper Saddle River, NJ: Merrill/Prentice Hall.

FURTHER READING

Barkley, R. A. (1997). *ADHD and the nature of self-control.* New York: Guilford.

Berk, L. E. (1994, November). Vygotsky's theory: The importance of make-believe play. *Young Children, 50*(1), 30–39.

Bronson, M. B. (2000, March). Research in review: Recognizing and supporting the development of self-regulation in young children. *Young Children, 55*(2), 32–36.

Butterfield, P. M., Martin, C. A., & Prairie, A. P. (2004). *Emotional connections: How relationships guide early learning.* Washington, DC: Zero to Three.

Clyman, R. B., Emde, R. N., Kempe, J. E., & Harmon, R. J. (1986). Social referencing and social looking among 12-month-old infants. In T. B. Brazelton & M. W. Yogman (Eds.), *Affective development in infancy* (pp. 75–94). Norwood, NJ: Ablex.

Eisenberg, N. (Ed.). (1998). *Handbook of child psychology: Vol. 3. Social, emotional, and personality development* (5th ed.). New York: Wiley.

Fraiberg, S. (1959). *The magic years: Understanding and handling the problems of early childhood.* New York: Scribner's.

Furman, R. A. (1995, January). Helping children cope with stress and deal with feelings. *Young Children, 50*(2), 33–51.

Goleman, D. (2000). *Working with emotional intelligence.* New York: Bantam.

Greenspan, S. I. (1999). *Building healthy minds.* Cambridge, MA: Perseus.

Greenspan, S. I., & Wieder, S. (1998). *The child with special needs: Encouraging intellectual and emotional growth.* Reading, MA: Perseus.

Hyson, M. (2004). *The emotional development of young children* (2nd ed.). New York: Teachers College Press.

Kitayama, S., Markus, H. R., & Matsumoto, H. (1995). Culture, self, and emotion: A cultural perspective on "self-conscious" emotions. In J. Tangney & K. Fisher (Eds.), *Self-conscious emotions: The psychology of shame, guilt, embarrassment and pride* (pp. 439–463). New York: Guilford.

Klein, M. D., & Chen, D. (2001). *Working with children from culturally diverse backgrounds.* Albany, NY: Delmar.

Kuebli, J. (1994). Research in review: Young children's understanding of everyday emotions. *Young Children, 49*(3), 36–47.

Lieberman, A. F. (1993). *The emotional life of the toddler.* New York: Free Press.

Lillard, A., & Curenton, S. (1999, September). Research in review: Do young children understand what others feel, want, and know? *Young Children, 54*(4), 52–57.

Marion, M. (1997, November). Research in review: Understanding and managing anger. *Young Children*, 52(7), 62–67.

Okagaki, L., & Diamond, K. E. (2000, May). Responding to cultural and linguistic differences in the beliefs and practices of families with young children. *Young Children*, 55(3), 74–80.

Petersen, S., Bair, K., & Sullivan, A. (2004). Emotional well-being and mental health services: Lessons learned by Early Head Start Region VIII programs. *Zero to Three*, 24(6), 47–53.

Simons, B. (2000, January). A more tender separation. *Young Children*, 55(1), 30.

Vance, E., & Weaver, P. J. (2003, July). Words to describe feelings. *Young Children*, 58(4), 45.

Van Hoorn, J., Nourot, P., Scales, B., & Alward, K. (2003). *Play at the center of the curriculum* (3rd ed.). Upper Saddle River, NJ: Merrill/Prentice Hall.

CHAPTER 9

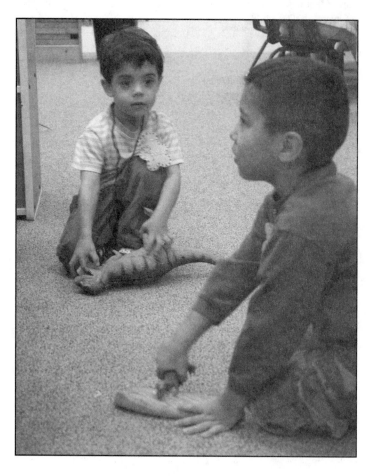

Problem Solving

In *this chapter you'll discover* . . .

- What's positive about having problems
- What parents can do when their needs conflict with those of their child
- What kind of parent is neither permissive nor authoritarian
- How to open up communication in the face of a problem
- Why sometimes you behave just like your parents even when you don't want to
- How problem solving relates to intellectual development

Problems are an important part of life. They are the way we learn. They provide the challenges to keep life interesting. Problems grow out of interactions, and they create situations in which we interact. They are inherent in family life, and they occur in child care programs on a regular basis too. According to Galinsky (1989), a researcher in early childhood education, a number of studies show the importance of the ability to solve problems. In her own research and in the studies she examined, it was clear that those individuals, young and old alike, who could face problems and figure out how to solve them were better off than others.

PROBLEM SOLVING WHEN NEEDS CONFLICT

Problems occur when needs clash. Let's say a parent has the need for peace and quiet; she is overtired and has a headache. Her young children have the need for exercise and interaction. They are joyfully wrestling in the living room at the foot of the couch where she is trying to meet her need. How does she solve the problem?

The Direct Order and Its Disadvantages

One way is with heavy-handed authority: "Stop that right now. Go to your room and color or do something else quiet." What do you think the chances are that her children will listen to her and will obediently leave the room to go do something less active, especially if they are all wound up? My experience is that the chances are slim.

That approach—the direct order—depends on the power of authority and the awe or fear the children have of the parent. Some parents can pull it off, but they sometimes do so at the expense of the relationship. Many parents can't get children to consistently obey a direct order.

Many children are not in awe of their parents. Living with children day in and day out makes for a familiarity that reduces awe. (Have you ever heard a child refer to a parent as "awesome"?) Awe usually comes with distance. If the parent's goal is closeness, awe won't be part of family life.

The Fear-Inducing Approach and Its Disadvantages

Fear is another story. If parents have been punishing or angry in the past, their children may have learned to fear them. After all, they are bigger and more powerful than the children are, so they have the means to make their children fear them. If they establish that fear strongly enough, the children will continue to fear their authority, their wrath, their ability to punish even after they grow to an equal size or larger.

Because of fear, children may have learned to obey a direct order. If the parent were running an army during wartime, this fear would be useful. However, the parent in our scenario, lying on the couch, is living in a family where she is trying to build relationships, meet needs (including her own), and teach her children to meet their own needs. A better goal for her is to teach cooperation rather than obedience. If cooperation is her goal, ruling by fear will defeat her purpose.

Issues Around Obedience

Another problem arises when teaching children to obey direct orders from authority. Although it may make family living comfortable (if the parent is always a benign authority), parents have to consider whether they really want their children to obey someone else's orders all their lives. I don't. I want my children to think for themselves; I can't be sure that all the authorities they will encounter in their lives will be benevolent.

So let's go back again to the parent on the couch with her headache and see what else she can do to solve the problem of her needs clashing with her children's needs.

Suffering Silently

She can suffer in silence and say nothing. Some parents have in them an overdeveloped martyr. Because parenting calls for a good deal of sacrifice just in the normal course of things, some parents learn to deny their own needs and keep their mouths shut. Their children never even know that the parent has needs.

Suffering Openly

The parent can suffer more openly: "Oh, you kids, I have such a headache and feel so awful, and you just keep on and on." (A big sigh goes with this statement.) The parent can try the guilt and blame approach and then go back to suffering in silence when that doesn't work: "You just don't care about anybody but yourselves. You're selfish and insensitive."

Yes, children *are* selfish and insensitive when it comes to getting their needs met, even at the expense of their parents. That is because young children are egocentric. They don't have the intellectual or emotional ability to put themselves into the place of another, look at the world through a perspective different from their own, or feel what someone else is feeling. If a young child is happy, it can be hard for him to understand that someone else is unhappy. There are exceptions to this egocentrism, however. Children, even as young as toddlers, may respond to another's unhappiness by offering comfort with a pat or bringing a special blanket. It is quite possible for them to have sensitivity to the feelings of another. However, it's best not to count on it. In general, assume that young children don't understand another's feelings, unless they voluntarily show you that they do.

Instilling guilt and placing blame don't work right away—it takes years for the lessons to sink in enough to actually control the behavior. And when they do, they create side effects that harm self-esteem and get in the way of meeting needs.

PARENTING APPROACHES

The three parenting approaches named by Diana Baumrind (1971, 1986) and described in the following sections are called the *authoritarian approach*, the *permissive approach*, and the *authoritative approach*.

The Authoritarian Approach

The authoritarian approach is the "do-as-I-say" way of relating to children. Authoritarians see their power as inherent in their position. In conflicts, they see win-lose solutions—and it's important that they win. That's the way they keep their authority.

The strict authoritarian parent demands uncompromising obedience. Rules are established and infractions punished. Parental needs and desires come before child needs and desires. Authoritarian parents may have a good deal of self-respect but often lack respect for the child.

Children from strict authoritarian parents are sometimes withdrawn, discontented, and distrustful of others.

The Permissive Approach

By contrast, permissive parents seek to have little control over their children. These parents may take the role of guides and friends—being warm and involved with their children—or they may be less interested and involved and more lackadaisical. In an extreme permissive approach, parents just lay back, and, if they so desire, their children walk all over them. Parental needs take a backseat to child needs. In a win-lose conflict, the children win because the adult doesn't take any power into his own hands. He grants all the power to the children. Since extremely permissive parents fail to display self-respect, their children win conflicts with them but emerge dissatisfied. It's uncomfortable to be out of control and find few or no limits. It doesn't feel good to treat people like doormats, even when they invite you to do so.

Children of permissive parents sometimes put a lot of energy into controlling their parents and trying to get their parents to control them. As a result, they tend to be lacking in creativity, self-control, and self-reliance.

The Authoritative Approach

The authoritative approach differs from the authoritarian approach. Authoritative parents listen to children's justifications and requests and make decisions that take into consideration the needs of the child. They provide limits and control when necessary. They believe in mutual respect.

Authoritative parents derive their authority from the fact of their experience, size, and ability. They know that they have lived in the world longer than their children and have expertise their children don't have. They see their role as using reason to guide, protect, and facilitate development.

Authoritative parents have firm standards but employ a flexible approach. They are apt to use what's been called a win-win approach to parenting. They are concerned about their children's needs and also about their own needs. When the two clash, they don't sacrifice one for the other but look for solutions in which both their needs and their children's are met. Resolution leaves both parties satisfied. Children of authoritative parents are likely to be self-reliant, independent, socially responsible, and explorative.

An important device for the win-win parenting used by authoritative parents is the problem-solving process.

A Cultural Difference in Parenting Styles

The research on the three types of parenting styles was done on European Americans and applies to European Americans. However, Ruth Chao (1994) at UCLA questions the validity for Chinese parenting. She raises a paradox. Authoritarian styles of child rearing predict low achievement in school, yet Chinese children who are raised by authoritarian parents do well in school. Chao proposes that the concept of authority is ethnocentric and does not explain important facets of Chinese child rearing.

Authoritarian child rearing in the United States was handed down from puritanical beginnings, which advocated harsh treatment of children. This view of authoritarianism in child rearing lasted two centuries. It wasn't until World War II that Americans became more permissive. The history of authority in China is very different. Authority in China is not harsh but gentle, coming as it does from a Confucian tradition related not to predestination but to social harmony.

Though authoritarian-style child rearing is equated with distance and harshness in European American tradition, in China it is equated with closeness, both physical and emotional. (The child sleeps with the mother, for example.) The mother is greatly involved in promoting success in the child and is the main caretaker. That situation contrasts with a European American view of independence and individuality.

Training is another concept that differs culturally. To some European American parents, training involves something militaristic, rigid, and strict. The word has negative connotations. Chinese parents regard training as positive—an act of love.

THE PROBLEM-SOLVING PROCESS

Let's go back again to the parent on the couch with her headache. She has a need— peace and quiet. Her children have a need—exercise and interaction. Here's how she uses a problem-solving process in this situation:

1. *Putting the problem into words.* She starts by stating her need and describing the situation as she sees it in as nonjudgmental a way as she can. She defines the problem as related to, but not the same as, the people involved. She avoids labels, accusations, and blame. She doesn't say, "You're being brats." She doesn't even say, "You're inconsiderate." She *does* say, "We have a problem here. I need some peace and quiet, and you two are making a lot of noise right now."

She doesn't expect this statement to change the behavior, though she may be surprised to find that words alone will do it. However, if her children don't go immediately to the backyard, she goes a step further and states their need: "It looks as if you need to run around and play loudly right now."

They may not be paying attention to her at this point, though it is possible that they will have heard her, since she is being sensitive to them, rather than insensitive. It's amazing how selective our hearing is. Most of us are more apt to pay attention to someone who understands us than to someone who does not.

2. *Get them to focus on the problem.* If the problem continues, she'll have to gather up whatever energy she can, sit up, and find a way to get the children to focus on the problem of their needs conflicting. Just her full attention will probably get them to settle down a bit and talk to her. She'll draw them to her physically, hold them if necessary, and establish eye contact.

"We have a problem here," she'll say. "You want to play loudly and I want to rest quietly. What can we do about that?" she asks. This is not a rhetorical question, nor is it one she already knows the answer to. She is genuinely interested in finding a mutually satisfying solution rather than imposing one she's already decided on. Her tone of voice and facial expression reflect her attitude.

3. *Brainstorm solutions.* "You can go in your room" is one response to her. "You can go outside" is her first reaction—but then she thinks about it and decides that she should respond to the first suggestion rather than coming back with one of her own as a counter. "It's too hot in my room," she responds. That's true. (Otherwise, she should consider moving.) "Why don't you go outside?" she asks.

"Too hot outside" comes the response.

"How about if we watch TV?" is another suggestion. The mother sees immediately that that would solve the problem. However, it isn't a satisfying solution in her mind because she perceives that the need her children have is for moving and interacting (active play), and TV is more like covering up the true need with a drug than it is responding to the physical and social urges the children have at the moment.

"Can we run through the sprinklers?" This suggestion makes sense to all of them. It's hot outside—too hot to roughhouse. But adding water changes the whole complexion of the situation.

"Good idea," she agrees. "Keep the hose on the lawn. The cement gets too slippery—and, besides, you'll be watering the grass so the water won't be wasted." She's setting some limits now and giving reasons for them.

Problem solved. She rolls over and closes her eyes as the children leave the room to change into their bathing suits.

Of course, parents don't always take a problem-solving approach, and it doesn't always work out so well. Parents are human—less than perfect. Most parents, even those dedicated to a problem-solving approach, have certainly taken the authoritarian approach before. Some have made threats, even ones they never intended to carry out. ("Stop that right now, or I'll really give you something to scream about!") Most parents have had their moments of permissiveness too, suffering in silence or whining, fussing, and blaming without doing anything about their own needs.

Problem Solving When the Child Has a Problem

Sometimes the child has the problem, and it has nothing to do with the parent: "I hate my teacher," says Kyle, slamming his backpack down on the couch as he roars into the family room.

Opening Up Communication.   The parent can respond with orders, admonitions, and/or criticisms, which may solve the parent's problem of feelings in response to the child's actions and statement. But those responses won't solve the child's problem, which hasn't even been clearly stated yet. And those responses tend to close down communication instead of opening it up. It's better to listen carefully and reflect the feelings perceived.

Finding Out What the Problem Is.   If the parent is willing to help the child with his problem, he or she first has to find out what it is. Here's how this parent, Kyle's father, did that:

"You're really mad at your teacher," he remarked, reflecting the feeling behind the words and ignoring the vocabulary of the statement.

"I sure am. He's mean!"

Here is another chance for the parent to block the communication by pointing out how nice the teacher has been to the child in the past. However, instead of criticizing the child or sharing his own feelings about the lack of respect for the teacher, Kyle's father continues to listen. Without expecting a response, Kyle plunges on.

"He tells things that are none of his business!"

"You didn't like what he said."

"I sure didn't! What gives him the right to tell anybody I'm adopted?"

"You didn't want him to tell."

"That's my business and I'll tell whoever I want. But he better stick to his own business."

"I wonder how you could let him know that you feel that way." Kyle's father's voice has a speculative tone to it.

"I don't know." Apparently Kyle hasn't thought about that aspect of the situation. "It would be kind of hard to just come up to him and tell him."

"I see what you mean."

"Maybe I could talk to him when the other kids aren't around."

"That might work."

"Or you could talk to him."

"That's another idea."

"Ah, heck, I'll just forget it."

"You could do that, too."

"I think he already knew I didn't like it because I saw him looking at me, and I bet I looked real mad."

"I wonder if he got the message."

"I bet he did! In fact, I'm almost sure that won't happen again. I did look real mad."

"You look like you feel better now."
"Yeah. Want to go play catch?"
"Sure. Go get the ball."
End of problem.

Reflecting Feelings and Exploring Solutions.   Notice that the parent did nothing but restate what Kyle said and put the feelings into words. He didn't suggest a solution but helped Kyle explore several of his own. When Kyle got the whole thing out of his system, he was ready to go on to something else, and his father was still available to help him do that.

When a Problem-Solving Approach Is Culturally Inappropriate

Cynthia Ballenger (1992, 1999), has been observing the differences between European American culture and Haitian culture for many years. She points out some major differences in child-handling techniques between Haitian and North American preschool teachers. North American teachers focus on the individual child, the feelings, the situation, and the problem. They like to help the child look at consequences and make choices. The teacher remains rather emotionally unattached during the process of problem solving. Good or bad behavior is not usually mentioned during a problem-solving process conducted by a skilled North American teacher.

Haitian teachers, on the other hand, clearly distinguish bad behavior. They emphasize group values and the responsibility of the child to the group. Children's feelings are not a focus during this discussion; the discussion is about emotional ties and adult expectation. There's no feeling of detachment as there is when North American teachers are helping a child problem solve a situation. Haitian teachers don't talk about consequences but rather good and bad behaviors, which relate to respect and obedience. Haitian teachers do not use a detached and individualistic problem-solving technique, like North American teachers, but put emphasis on shared values in a moral community.

In spite of the fact that this chapter is about problem solving, it's important to realize there are other cultural perspectives on how to handle problems. You may feel more comfortable with the North American way that Ballenger describes. Or the Haitian way may resonate with you even if you aren't Haitian. Don't think of "right" and "wrong" when you compare these two approaches with managing young children's behavior; think of "different."

Problem Solving When the Adult Has the Problem

Sometimes the adults are the ones with the problem. Say, for instance, that Lynn, a mother, and Shawna, a child care teacher, can't get 5-year-old Jessica to hang up her jacket when she comes into the child care center every day.

The child has no problem at all. She arrives joyfully each morning, running through the door, throwing her jacket on the floor, and heads for the blocks.

Explaining Isn't Enough.   On Jessica's first day, Shawna had explained the procedure of hanging up jackets, and Jessica had complied, with Lynn's help. But the second day, Shawna was busy when Jessica arrived, and Lynn was making an appointment with the director, and nobody saw what Jessica did until Shawna found Jessica's jacket on the floor. She couldn't stand seeing it there, so she hung it up, and when Jessica came in from the other room, she mentioned it to her. Jessica didn't seem to care.

The third day Lynn was in a hurry. When Jessica threw her jacket on the floor and ran off, Lynn made an attempt to get her back to hang it up, but Jessica balked. Lynn, in a panic about being late to work at a new job, gave up, said good-bye, and left. From then on it was a losing battle. Jessica just wouldn't hang up her jacket, even with reminders, which eventually turned into nagging. She did all right sometimes when Lynn was there and had time to insist that she hang up the jacket. But when Jessica came in the car pool, Shawna had a big ordeal on her hands. When the situation didn't change, she got madder and madder. She even started threatening vague punishments, but Jessica still didn't care.

A jacket on the floor doesn't bother the child who put it there. This is an adult's problem.

Finally Shawna appealed to Lynn. What can we do to change Jessica's jacket-tossing behavior? Just by stating the problem in clear terms, they took the first step toward problem solving it. Sometimes it is not so easy to determine what the problem is. In this case both Lynn and Shawna knew exactly what behavior needed changing. So they put their heads together and came up with a plan that involved what each of them would do and, further, how they were going to include Jessica in the problem-solving process.

Taking a Problem-Solving Approach.   First Lynn talked to Jessica about how she had to take responsibility for her jacket herself because her mother wasn't always there to remind her to hang it up: "I'll help remind you when I'm there. When I am not there, you need to do it yourself." That wasn't enough to change what had now become a habit. The next morning was a carpool day, and Jessica ran into the center, ripped off her jacket, and headed away from the coat hooks toward the art table. She was ready to toss the jacket on the floor, but Shawna was right there. "Look here, Jessica," she said, catching her arm. "I have a problem. I get upset when I see you throw your jacket on the floor instead of hanging it up." Jessica was straining at the bit, anxious to get her hands in the finger paint that was enticing her, just out of her reach.

Shawna squatted down and turned her around so they were eye to eye and no finger paint was visible to Jessica. "What are we going to do?"

"Do?" Jessica squirmed.

"Yes, how can I get you to hang your jacket up?"

"There's no room," Jessica pointed out. And indeed when Shawna looked at the hooks, they were all full to overflowing.

"That's true," she admitted, easing Jessica over to the wall where the hooks were. "I'll make room for your jacket," she added, which she did, without letting go of Jessica. Jessica quickly stuck her jacket on a now empty hook and ran off to gooey up her hands in the finger paint.

Trying Solutions.   The next time Jessica arrived, Lynn came in with her and Shawna was right there waiting. "Look, Jessica," she said. "I put a new hook in and it has your name on it. Now you have a special place for your jacket." Jessica hung up her jacket carelessly, without paying attention, and ran off to play. Shawna called after her, "Good job, Jessica." And when Lynn said good-bye, she nodded toward the hanging jacket and gave her a thumbs-up sign.

The next day was another carpool day, and Shawna was busy when Jessica arrived. A few minutes later she turned around, there was the jacket on the floor again! Shawna walked determinedly over to where Jessica was washing dolls in a plastic tub on a table. Touching her on the shoulder, she said, "This is a jacket reminder, Jessica."

"In a minute," said Jessica, turning to leave in the opposite direction from the waiting hook.

"Now," said Shawna firmly, taking her by one soapy hand. "How can I get you to remember when you first come in? Think about it."

Later, when Jessica was painting, Shawna came up to her. "I have an idea," she said. "Make yourself a sign so you'll remember to hang up your jacket."

Jessica's face brightened at the suggestion. She took a clean paper and busily painted great orange blobs and blue swirls across the paper. "Here," she said when she finished. "Here's the sign. It says, 'Jessica, remember your jacket.' And that's me by the hook," she added.

Shawna and Jessica went together to hang up the "sign" in a prominent place by the door so Jessica would see it the next day when she arrived.

When she arrived the next day, hand in hand with Lynn, Shawna was standing by the sign. Jessica noticed both Shawna and the sign, and she smiled and went to the hook to hang up her jacket. Lynn didn't have to do anything. For several days, Shawna helped the sign work. When it wore off, Shawna was still there to remind and direct if necessary. Lynn also did her part when she was there. Eventually jacket hanging became a habit with Jessica, and she no longer needed the sign, Shawna, or Lynn to remind her. Problem solved!

The Process.   Shawna and Lynn were clear about what the problem was and who owned it. The adults were the ones with the problem, and Shawna had the most feelings. Lynn, of course, wanted her daughter to cooperate, but she wasn't the one getting upset about the jacket problem. Shawna had the biggest stake in finding a solution. She stated her feelings to Jessica. Sometimes stating feelings is enough, and the child will change the behavior just to keep the adult happy. In this case, feelings weren't enough. Shawna had to work at solving the problem, and she did, with Lynn's and Jessica's help. Shawna was committed to finding a solution that worked, so she continued to pursue it until it was solved.

Sometimes in this situation a child care teacher will skip the problem-solving process and simply turn to the parent and indicate that it is his or her responsibility to change the behavior. When this happens, the parents may feel pressured to punish children at home for something that happens at school. Problems with punishment have already been discussed in Chapter 7, but in addition to those, there's another issue sometimes called the "wait-until-your-father-gets-home" effect. Punishment that occurs hours after the behavior is over is confusing to children. They have a hard time making a connection between what they did and what they are being punished for. The problem-solving story here shows a far more effective way to change behavior than using punishment. It also shows a parent and teacher cooperating with each other in a way that benefits everybody!

Using the RERUN Process: An Example

Here's an example of a RERUN sequence (explained in Chapter 5), a way to give structure to a problem-solving approach. When you encounter a problem to solve, start by checking your own position. Are you clear about the problem? Do you know for sure what you want? Ambiguity on your part will change the whole situation.

I'll use an example from my own life of something I'm very clear about—young children running into the street. Since I have five children, I've been through this situation many times. I never take chances. I know there's a problem if my child is close to a street and can't be trusted to stay out of it. Let's say my 3-year-old has been playing in the front yard with a toy truck. I have been watching him, because he is on the verge of understanding street safety. But just now he rolled the truck down the driveway and has started down after it. I'm not going to take a chance. I move fast and grab him before he goes into the street. Then I go through the RERUN sequence. Here's how it works:

- *Reflect.* As my child squirms and protests, I let him know that his feelings are received and accepted. I reflect them back with such words as, "I see how unhappy you are about being stopped."
- *Explain.* I help my child understand the situation: "I can't let you run in the street."
- *Reason.* I give the reason for my prohibition: "You might get hurt."
- *Understand.* I tune in to feelings—both mine and my child's. I try to understand the situation from both points of view. I don't have to say anything out loud at this point, I just need to be sure I have clarity. I may have to talk to myself to get it.
- *Negotiate.* Since a 3-year-old can talk, I can discuss the problem, and together we can look for a mutually satisfying solution. If he had been 2, I would have just given two alternatives: "You can stay up here on the porch, or you can play in the backyard." I might do that with a 3-year-old too, if the talk turned into game playing and we weren't working toward a solution.

I try hard not to talk every situation to death. Notice the few words used in this RERUN sequence. The negotiations are the only part that need more than a brief phrase.

With an older child and a less drastic problem, the negotiations can get quite lengthy, but I try to recognize when I'm getting involved in a game. When negotiations are breaking down, I return to the beginning and go through the parts again. I may have to RERUN several times before the problem is solved.

This chapter so far has contrasted three general approaches to parenting and has examined at length one aspect of one approach, problem solving. This approach, the authoritative approach, is likely to lead to independence, respect, cooperation, and high self-esteem. However, everything said here is culturally bound and is based on white European, middle-class American values and may not work for everyone.

PROBLEM SOLVING AND COGNITIVE DEVELOPMENT

Let's look now at a different view of problem solving—one that is not tied to parenting, needs, or discipline. Instead, this view of problem-solving looks at cooperative problem solving in homes and in early childhood classrooms as a way to enhance cognitive development.

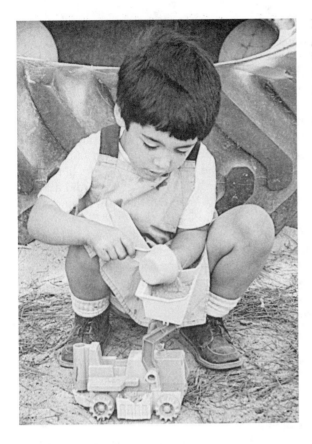

How do children encounter problems to solve? They come upon problems by accident, think up problems while they are playing, or the teachers think them up and present them to the children.

How do children encounter problems at home or in the classroom (other than having needs; finding themselves in conflicts with parents, other adults, siblings, or other children; or misbehaving)? They come upon problems by accident, or they think up problems while they are playing, or the adults think them up and present them to the children.

Child-Initiated Problems

For example, a brother, sister, and a neighbor child want to put on a puppet show. They spend a long time at the kitchen table making puppets out of old socks by drawing faces on them with felt pens. During the process, they talk about which characters they are creating and what the story will be about. As they draw, they try on the roles of the characters. When they have enough puppets for the show, they turn their attention to the stage. What will they use for the stage? One child suggests turning the coffee table in the living room on its side, but the others nix that idea. They know that will get them in trouble. "Let's get a cardboard box out of the storage room" is the next suggestion. A quick trip to the storage room reveals not a scrap of cardboard. It all went to recycling. They keep talking about what to do. The neighbor runs home to get an old bedspread that his mother has let him play with in the past. The other two walk around the apartment to see what they can find to drape the bedspread over. Then they remember the card table that was in the storage room. They ask permission to use the card table. They need help to get it out from the storage room because there are some suitcases piled in front of it. When they get it out and decide on a place to put it, the neighbor child has returned with the bedspread. The three of them cover the card table with the bedspread and then go get their puppets and store them underneath. With the three of them crouched down behind the covered table, they call the rest of the family and put on their puppet show for them. These children did a lot of problem solving to make their idea work, and it turned out that was an important part of the fun.

An example in a preschool involves an old wooden boat in the play yard, which is full of water from the last rain. That doesn't bother some children; they're happy to climb in anyway. But the rule is no water play outside when the weather is cold. So they go to the teacher, who says, "I wonder what you can do." Each child has a different idea, ranging from feasible to unfeasible.

"Turn the boat over," says Angie.

"Too heavy!" says Amber.

"Get a crane," says Charles.

A discussion ensues about how to get a crane or how to make one. The problem is still unresolved when 3-year-old Stefan arrives with margarine cartons, ready to bail. Then they discover no one can reach into the boat far enough to bail.

"We need string," says Amber. Off she goes to the teacher who usually provides what is needed when children think of projects.

She returns a short time later with a ball of string, scissors, and a hole punch. The children set to work cutting lengths of string and trying to tie them onto the margarine cartons.

Suddenly Angie has an idea. "This will work!" she says, running off toward the carpentry bench set up in another part of the play yard.

She comes back with a teacher in tow. In her hand is a child's drill. "Let's make holes and let the water out!"

And so they do. Problem solved.

Adult-Initiated Problems

Perhaps the adult sets up the problem. After talking about a camping trip they are planning for summer, a father suggests they play camping in the backyard. They can get some practice before their trip. They haven't yet bought a tent, so Dad asks how they might make one. The children brainstorm some ideas, and the father supplies them with all kinds of materials for "building tents." He makes available tarps, an old sheet, string, and rope and suggests that they figure out how to make tents. They need no further invitation. The parent acts as a facilitator instead of directing the action, and the children brainstorm solutions about how to support the cloth and keep it spread out. The father, tempted as he is to give them ideas, lets the children do the problem-solving rather than doing it for them.

SUMMARY OF STEPS OF PROBLEM SOLVING

Here are four steps to problem solving adapted from an article on problem solving by Galinsky (1989):

1. *Naming the problem.* Defining the problem or putting it into words is the first step, as has been shown in each of the examples above.

2. *Generating solutions.* It's important to bring forth multiple solutions. Too often children (or adults) get stuck with just one idea and can't move beyond it. Brainstorming as a method implies that all solutions and ideas are encouraged even if they don't seem immediately workable. As a facilitating adult, it is important that you accept all ideas without criticism.

3. *Evaluating solutions.* At this step you start looking at what might work and why. Usually this is an informal process, but it is also possible to write down on a piece of paper the pluses and minuses of each strategy.

4. *Choosing a solution to try and evaluating it.* Sometimes the first choice works, sometimes it doesn't. It's important not to give up, but to go back through the problem-solving process when a solution fails.

Stopping the Cycle of Emotional Abuse

Brian is a stepfather. He and Jennifer got married a year ago, and he made a vow to be the best father possible. But it's been a hard year! Amanda, who is 4, and her 2-year-old brother, Tyler, seem to hate Brian, no matter how hard he tries to love them. Brian's pictures of having a happy family life have slowly faded.

The worst part about this year for Brian has been his struggle with his own behavior. Whenever he gets mad at the children, he finds words rising to his lips that he never dreamed he would say to these sweet, innocent children. Take the other day, for example. The family was getting ready to go out to dinner to celebrate Brian and Jennifer's first anniversary. Tyler was all dressed up in a white sailor suit—he looked so sweet. Brian took Tyler with him to get the car, but turned his back while he was opening the garage door. That was just enough time for Tyler to find a mud puddle. Brian grabbed him, but too late. Tyler stamped in the puddle and both of them were instantly splattered with mud.

The words that came to Brian's throat were choked back. He started to yell "You brat! You filthy pig!" at little Tyler when he realized that those were the very words his father had always used with him. He remembered the number of times he had been in this same situation—but on the other end. It seemed as though his father really wanted to convince him that he was a no-good, filthy pig, a real brat who wallowed in dirt just to make everyone unhappy. In fact, his father had convinced him of that, and it wasn't until he had gone into the Coast Guard as a young adult that he had discovered that down deep he loved neatness.

Brian shut his mouth tight, took Tyler by the hand, and led him back into the house to clean him up. Fifteen minutes later the family was assembled by the waiting car. Tyler was in a blue sailor suit this time, and Brian was in another pair of slacks.

Brian helped Amanda in and was buckling her into her car seat when she announced in a loud voice, "I want pizza." Jennifer explained calmly that they were going to a nice restaurant on the lake because it was a special dinner and that they would go out for pizza another time.

Amanda began kicking and screaming, making it impossible for Brian to buckle her into the belt. "I want pizza!" she repeated over and over.

Brian's inclination was to tell her exactly what he thought of her. The words that came to his mind were, "You selfish little brat. You always want your own way. You don't ever consider anyone else." Then, to add a little more sting, he thought about threatening to leave her home alone if she didn't shut up right away. That's what he thought—not what he said. What he said was, "I'm really upset, and I'm going to go back into the house for a few minutes until I calm down."

While he was in the house, he remembered the number of times his mother had used that same label—*selfish brat*—on him. He had never meant to repeat those words, and there they were trying to come out. She had always called him selfish whenever he wanted something different from what she wanted. When she got mad enough, she even went so far as to remind him that he had been a "mistake." They hadn't wanted another child, but they got stuck with him. How that had hurt. It still hurt to think about it.

Brian left his self-imposed time-out much calmer. By the time he got to the car, he had thought of what to say and was ready to say it: "I see how much you want pizza, but tonight we're going to a different restaurant." But as he slid into the seat beside Amanda, he saw that the storm had passed. She was busy telling her doll how pretty the restaurant by the lake would be. Jennifer winked at Brian, who gratefully squeezed her hand as he put the car in gear and backed out of the driveway.

SUMMARY

When people take a problem-solving attitude, they are empowered. Empowerment makes a difference as adults, and children alike gain in social, emotional, physical, and cognitive skills. Empowered people are more likely to see themselves as capable, feel good about themselves, and have high self-esteem.

The next chapter is also about empowerment. It deals with helping children grow to fulfill their potential by examining the messages we give them about their place in the world, who they are, and what they can do.

FOR DISCUSSION

1. Which of the three parenting approaches mentioned in the chapter do you prefer and why? How were you raised? How do you think the way you were raised affects you now?

2. Give an example of a situation when a child has a problem, and compare it with a situation where an adult has a problem. What is different about taking steps to solve the problems in the two different situations?

3. Make up a scene involving the RERUN process of problem solving.

4. Give an example of how a parent might use problem solving as a way of facilitating cognitive development. Give an example of how a preschool teacher might use problem solving as a way of facilitating cognitive development.

REFERENCES

Ballenger, C. (1992, Summer). Because you like us: The language of control. *Harvard Educational Review,* 62(2), 199–208.

Ballenger, C. (1999). *Teaching other people's children.* New York: Teachers College Press.

Baumrind, D. (1971). Current patterns of parental authority. *Developmental Psychology Monographs,* 4, 99–103.

Baumrind, D. (1986). Socialization and instrumental competence in young children. In W. W. Hartup (Ed.), *The young child: Reviews of research* (Vol. 2, pp. 202–224). Washington, DC: National Association for the Education of Young Children.

Chao, R. K. (1994). Beyond parental control and authoritarian parenting style: Understanding Chinese parenting through the cultural notion of training. *Child Development,* 65, 1111–1119.

David, M., & Appell, G. (2001 [1973, 1996]). *Loczy: An unusual approach to mothering.* Translated from *Loczy ou le maternage insolite,* by Jean Marie Clark; revised translation by Judit Falk. Budapest: Association Pikler-Loczy for Young Children.

Galinsky, E. (1989, May). Problem solving. *Young Children,* 44(4), 2–3.

Noddings, N. (2002). *Educating moral people: A caring alternative to character education.* New York: Teachers College Press.

Parke, R. D., & O'Neil, R. (2000). The influence of significant others on learning about relationships: From family to friends. In R. S. L. Mills & S. Duck (Eds.), *The developmental psychology of personal relationships* (pp. 15–47). New York: Wiley.

Quintero, E. P. (2004, May). Will I lose a tooth? Will I learn to read? Problem posing with multicultural children's literature. *Young Children,* 59(3), 56–62.

FURTHER READING

Ballenger, C. (1999). *Teaching other people's children.* New York: Teachers College Press.

Clark, K. E., & Ladd, G. W. (2000). Connectedness and autonomy support in parent-child relationships: Links to children's socio-emotional orientation and peer relationships. *Developmental Psychology,* 36, 485–498.

Crary, E. (1990). *Kids can cooperate: A practical guide to teaching problem solving.* Seattle: Parenting Press.

Crockenberg, S. (1992, April). How children learn to resolve conflicts in families. *Zero to Three,* 12(5), 11–13.

David, M., & Appell, G. (2001 [1973, 1996]). *Loczy: An unusual approach to mothering.* Translated from *Loczy ou le maternage insolite,* by Jean Marie

Clark; revised translation by Judit Falk. Budapest: Association Pikler-Loczy for Young Children.

Dreikurs, R., & Grey, L. (1990). *Logical consequences: A new approach to discipline.* New York: Dutton.

Eaton, M. (1997, September). Positive discipline: Fostering the self-esteem of young children. *Young Children,* 52(6), 43–46.

Ginott, H. (1956). *Between parent and child.* New York: Macmillan.

Gordon, T. (1970). PET: *Parent Effectiveness Training.* New York: Wyden.

Koralek, D. (2003, September). Encouraging young children to develop and enhance their thinking skills. *Young Children,* 58(5), 10–11.

Noddings, N. (2002). *Educating moral people*: A *caring alternative to character education*. New York: Teachers College Press.

Parke, R. D., & O'Neil, R. (2000). The influence of significant others on learning about relationships: From family to friends. In R. S. L. Mills & S. Duck (Eds.), *The developmental psychology of personal relationships* (pp. 15–47). New York: Wiley.

Quintero, E. P. (2004, May). Will I lose a tooth? Will I learn to read? Problem posing with multicultural children's literature. *Young Children, 59*(3), 56–62.

Reynolds, E. (1995). *Guiding young children*: A *child-centered approach*. Mountain View, CA: Mayfield.

Shure, M. (1994). *Raising a thinking child*: Help your *young child to resolve everyday conflicts and get along with others*. New York: Holt.

Shure, M. B., & Spivack, G. (1978). *Problem solving techniques in childrearing*. San Francisco: Jossey-Bass.

Tudge, J., & Caruso, D. (1988, November). Cooperative problem solving in the classroom: Enhancing young children's cognitive development. *Young Children, 44*(1), 46–52.

CHAPTER 10

Strokes and Affirmations

A Path to Self-Esteem

In this chapter you'll discover . . .

- Why various means of recognition by one person of another are called *strokes* and *affirmations*
- What can be wrong with calling a child "shy"
- How a self-fulfilling prophecy works
- Why a child might reject positive strokes
- The difficulties of trying to change the behavior and attitudes of a child who thinks he is "bad"
- How adult self-esteem relates to child self-esteem
- What is meant by *resilient children*

WHAT ARE STROKES?

New babies need to be touched. The natural course of events right after birth is to stroke the newborn—just as a cat licks each of her kittens. This very human gesture is both physical and symbolic. Whether or not it is absolutely necessary at first, it heralds a lifelong need each of us has: the need to be stroked.

Babies need physical stroking. Besides the loving touch that is given for no other reason than the desire of the adult, the handling and manipulating involved in washing, dressing, and changing convey an important message: "I care for you." Some traditions even go beyond the loving and caregiving touching and perform infant massage in which each movement has a specific purpose. For example, Ellen White, a medicine woman from Vancouver Island in British Columbia, gives workshops about the benefits of infant massage to early childhood educators and interventionists.

But strokes aren't only physical. Many parents and caregivers naturally talk to their babies when they touch them. Experts who work with parents and train early child professionals and interventionists teach adults to talk to babies. Thus, *words* become linked with a pleasurable physical feeling. Although none of us ever outgrows the need to be physically stroked, we eventually learn to take words alone as strokes.

So strokes can be touch, words, or any other means of recognition. Eye contact and facial expressions count as strokes, too.

Words become linked with pleasurable feelings.

Giving strokes is more than just using a positive technique. Offhand stroking with no caring attached may be technically sound, yet ineffective. Real stroking involves a special form of receptive attentiveness on the part of the stroker, which Nel Noddings (2002) calls *engrossment*. Stroking then relates to relationship building, as the stroker both puts out and takes in, aiming energy at the one being cared for. Children can tell the difference between true caring strokes and those designed to merely manipulate behavior.

Many adults were raised without receiving many positive strokes, verbal or nonverbal. Because it's not a part of their experience, they tend not to give positive strokes to children. Parent and teacher educators emphasize the importance of strokes and teach how to give them. For example, when a child does something right, many adults ignore the event; attention comes only when the child misbehaves. However, when adults learn that paying attention to certain behaviors tends to make them reoccur, they see that it's worthwhile to change their approach.

Babies Need Stroking

Susan and her mother, Mary, are having an argument. It started when Susan's new baby, Jake, was crying and Susan went into the other room and picked him up. She brought him out, holding him gently, saying to him, "What's wrong, Jakey? What do you need?"

"You're going to spoil that child!" complained Mary. "He just ate, so he can't be hungry. There's no reason to pick him up. You're just getting him used to being picked up every time he cries. He'll cry more and more if you keep doing that. You're *teaching* him to cry."

"No, I'm not!" responded Susan. "There is a reason to pick him up. He's crying—he needs something!"

"What does he need? He just needs to show you who's boss."

"You're wrong!" says Susan. Turning to Jake she says, "What can I do for you, Sweetheart—you're so upset. How about a burp?"

She jiggles him on her shoulder and then pats his back, and Jake rewards her with a loud belch.

"See?" she turns to her mother. "He did need something. But even if he hadn't needed to be burped, he still needed some attention."

Susan is convinced of the importance of giving her son all the attention and affection he needs, starting right from the beginning. That doesn't mean she spends hours holding him, but she does try to be sensitive to when he really needs to be held and cuddled. Susan's mother grew up in a different era and doesn't see things the same way her daughter does. Mary thinks that if you reward crying in young babies by responding, the crying increases. Susan doesn't buy it.

The next time Susan arrived at her mother's house, she had some new information. "It's about spoiling, Mom," she started out. "Do you know that responding to crying in the early months actually reduces it?"

"That doesn't make sense to me!" answered Mary.

"It does to me," said Susan. "Crying is communication. In fact, it's the major way that babies communicate. Ignoring what they are trying to tell you doesn't make the crying go away; it just means that they have to keep trying. If they learn that you pick up their signals, they cry less, because they've been 'heard.' "

"Mmmmmm," said Mary, not yet convinced.

The conversation stopped when a wail from Jake filled the room. The two women looked at each other. Mary was silent as her daughter walked over to check her son. She stood for a moment looking down at him. His eyes were closed and his breathing steady.

"Well, aren't you going to pick him up?" asked Mary.

"I don't think he needs picking up right now. I don't know what the cry was about, but he's asleep. I think he needs to sleep more than he needs holding."

"Well, you do have some sense," said Mary. "I thought you were going to go overboard on this holding thing."

"Oh, Mom, I'm not the kind who goes overboard. You know that." Susan smiled affectionately at her mother. "I just want to make sure Jake knows I'm here to meet his needs and that he can communicate them. I don't want his crying to go away. It's the way he talks to me."

"Well, I guess you know what you're doing." Mary smiled at her daughter, then gave her a big hug. "I guess I'm just not used to you being a mom, too!"

It is important to look at strokes and affirmations in a cultural context. This chapter focuses mainly on cultures that stress independence and individuality. The idea is to help children feel good about themselves. In some cultures the focus is on downplaying individuality, keeping the child firmly embedded in the group, teaching humility instead of pride, and putting others before self. Strokes and affirmations may seem strange and opposed to the goals of such a family. Also, in some families direct communication is not valued. Subjects may be talked around instead of directly addressed. Indirect communication, in the form of behavior (including body language), is more valued than what is put into words. In fact, in these families, the kinds of statements used in this chapter to illustrate strokes and affirmations may be regarded as uncomfortable or manipulative. When parents want their children to do something, they just tell them to do it, and the children have respect for their parents, so they do it. Those parents don't need to make their children feel good about themselves. The children feel good just being part of the family and fulfilling their role as son or daughter.

These are two very different approaches to child rearing that seem to be oppositional in some ways. The fact that they are different doesn't mean that one way is right and the other is wrong. It means that there are differences, and differences must be acknowledged, accepted, and honored. When people who have diverse perspectives come together, they have opportunities to learn from each other. That is a strong message in this book. We share what we know and believe with others and remain open to what others have to share with us. So with all that in mind, let's look further at strokes.

USING POSITIVE STROKES TO CHANGE BEHAVIOR

Ana's two children have a good deal of trouble getting along with each other. Ugly squabbles constantly break out when they are together. Ana's usual method is to respond to them when they are arguing. She has taught them not to hit each other, but she can't seem to keep them from yelling at each other. She spends a good deal of her time settling their disputes. When Ana talks to her child care provider, Irene, who is taking a class on managing children's behavior, she learns about the principle that when you pay attention to behavior, it tends to continue; when you ignore the same behavior, it tends to disappear. "What you stroke is what you get," says Irene, quoting from the book she is reading for her class, written by Jean Illsley Clarke (1978), who is an expert on strokes and affirmations. She suggests that Ana start ignoring the arguing. She does. It gets worse.

Ana complains to Irene that the suggestion didn't work. "I ignored them and ignored them and they kept right on fighting."

"Maybe," says Irene, "you took away their strokes without replacing them."

"What do you mean?" asks Ana.

"You have to pay attention to them when they *aren't* arguing."

"Oh," says Ana.

She tries that approach. Whenever the two are playing nicely together she remarks about how well they are getting along. It isn't easy to do this, because she's used to doing her housework when there's peace in the family. But she makes a conscious effort. When a squabble breaks out, she leaves the room and starts washing dishes. Sometimes the squabble follows her, but she makes a point of ignoring the angry voices.

Ana doesn't feel entirely comfortable about this approach. It seems dishonest and unnatural to her. Her children ought to be good without her making this special effort. After all, cooperative behavior is what's expected. It shouldn't get special notice. It should be the norm. When she was growing up, her mother didn't have to put up with this kind of annoyance. All she had to do was look at her children and the squabbles stopped. She wishes that would work for her, but it doesn't.

She begins to notice that the squabbles aren't true disagreements, anyway, but are bids for her attention. She continues to use the approach of stroking positive behavior and ignoring the rest.

It works! Of course, her children still have their disagreements, but not so constantly anymore. Furthermore, Ana has grown closer to both of them since she's not so angry at the continual bickering. Ana has learned about the use of positive strokes.

WHAT ARE AFFIRMATIONS?

Ana also learned about affirmations from Irene. Related to strokes, *affirmations* give messages that validate the person as an individual who has needs and rights. Affirmations are positive messages about expectations. They encourage the child to be who he or she is.

Ana learned to use affirmations to help her children feel good about themselves so they wouldn't have such a need to squabble with each other. She had spontaneously been giving certain affirmations since they were born. For example, telling each child regularly that she appreciates them confirms the fact that she's glad they were born and that she has positive feelings about their existence. Expressing appreciation is a form of affirmation.

Ana had a little trouble with the idea that with affirmations she was validating her children as *individuals*. Of course, she recognized that each was a separate person, but what she wanted to emphasize in her family was their *connections* rather than their separateness. She wanted them to learn to put the family's needs before their own needs.

Ana brought up her concern to Irene one day when she picked up her children after work, and the two had a discussion about this issue. "I don't want them to think about their own needs. That makes them selfish. They should put other people first," said Ana.

"But until your own needs are met, how can you think of other people?" asked Irene. "Think of this example," she went on. "When you fly, the flight attendant instructs you that in case of a loss of cabin pressure, you must put your own oxygen mask on before you help other people."

"I think that's an extreme example," Ana responded.

"Maybe, but I think it applies. And it points out that your own needs are important *in order for you to help other people*. Isn't that what your goal is—that your children not be selfish?"

"I see what you mean," said Ana.

The two didn't resolve this issue because Irene tended to *always focus on individuals* when she thought about young children and families, and Ana tended to *avoid focusing on the individual*. Irene seemed to emphasize separateness. Ana liked to emphasize relatedness, embeddedness. But they understood that they disagreed on this issue and were friendly about it.

Affirmations can also be used to let children (or adults) know how they *can be* while accepting how they are at the present moment. Irene, who understood how this principle worked, avoided labeling a rather cautious child as "shy." She didn't use that word to explain his behavior to other people, either. Instead, she helped him learn to determine when it was important to be cautious and when he could trust the situation. She also let him know that it was OK to feel his feelings. If he was slower to accept a new person or situation than other children were, she let him know that that was all right, too. She affirmed his need to feel safe and the individuality of his pace of warming up. She also encouraged him to take a few risks, recognizing his potential as a person who can eventually come out of his protective shell and become more able to explore freely.

Affirmations Can Create Self-Fulfilling Prophecies

The messages that adults give to children can have a great effect on them. What's at work here is something called *self-fulfilling prophecy*, a term that received wide attention back in the 1960s when a study by Rosenthal and Jacobson (1968) showed the power of adult expectations on children. In this study, teachers were shown a list of children who were expected to have a "growth spurt" within the school year. In reality the students were randomly selected. But guess what! Those selected students did show remarkable

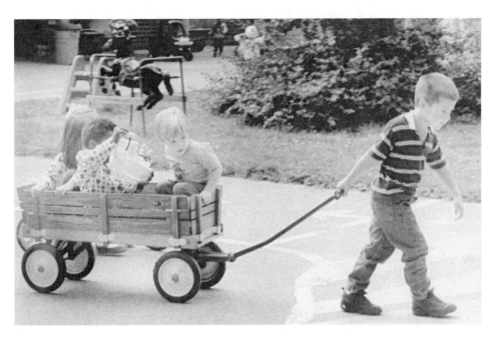

"Look how strong you are!" Affirmations can create self-fulfilling prophecies.

improvement, while the others didn't. What adults believe about children and what they *expect* from them tends to come true, as they send children messages, both verbal and nonverbal. Those messages, even the ones sent unconsciously, influence children's behavior and performance. For that reason it is important to give children *positive* messages in *many* forms, including affirmations and strokes.

All these positive messages can lead to a feeling of self-worth—and greater self-esteem. Parents and early childhood educators who understand what a strong influence early messages have on later behavior can learn to pay attention to what messages they're giving out. They can strive to give positive ones. The idea behind self-esteem is not that the child should feel superior to others. Superiority gets in the way of making connections and relating to others. The goal is connections. After all, this book is about socialization. We socialize children by increasing their ability to relate to others. Obviously children need to operate in a social world. Working on self-esteem is based on the premise that when children feel good about themselves, they have a greater ability to esteem and respect others. When children care *about* and *for* themselves, they are, at the same time, more likely to care for and about others as well.

It is important to note that although it's beginning to sound as though you can control whether a child has high self-esteem, the idea of actually *programming* a child for self-esteem is a simplistic one. A child is not a computer. You can control input to some extent, but you can't control output. You can send messages, but you have no guarantee as to how they will be received.

Take the simple act of telling a child you love her. You may love this child deeply, but what counts is not how much you love but how much the child *feels* loved. There is no way to guarantee that even with many hugs and kisses and "I-love-yous," the child will perceive the messages in the way that they are intended. Taking good care of the child, always being there, fulfilling the role of a good parent or caregiver/teacher does not ensure that the child will feel loved. Feeling loved is a perception, and no one can control the perceptions of another.

So it is with self-esteem. No one can assure that a child's self-esteem will be high. In fact, it's much easier to understand how to tear down self-esteem than it is to build it up. Children who live with constant criticism, who feel uncared for, and who have their needs neglected tend to have lower self-esteem. Still there is no guarantee. Even children raised in abusive and neglectful situations can still feel good about themselves. Remember input doesn't equal output in a one-to-one fashion. It is hard to accept that if you meet a child's needs, guide him or her without constant criticism, and love this child a great deal, you still can't *give* high self-esteem. It's more complicated than that. But even with the complications, it's easy to see that a preponderance of positive input is more *likely* to give positive results.

Children's Response to Affirmations and Strokes

How children respond to positive affirmations and strokes depends on their previous experience, which relates to their opinions of themselves and their reality about how the world is. Some children feel validated by affirmations; others don't. Some children accept the positive strokes they are given; others ignore or reject them.

Why would that be? These patterns have their roots in early experience. Imagine a baby who is ignored most of the time. He knows at some deep level that he needs strokes or he'll die. As an infant, he can't get them except by crying, and even then his cries are often ignored. He does get fed and changed often enough to keep him alive, but he doesn't receive his full quota of strokes. So when he gets old enough to create a ruckus, he does that. He soon learns that some behaviors bring adults to him. If the behavior is unacceptable enough, they even lavish attention on him. But it's not positive attention that he receives. He is yelled at, scolded, even punished. But because he is so desperate for strokes—so needing attention of any kind—he accepts these negative responses. He comes to expect them, and when he's old enough to think about such things, he even may regard negative strokes as his due—somehow convincing himself, consciously or unconsciously, that he deserves them.

That attitude, that concept of reality, is what makes it so hard to get through to a child who is used to getting negative strokes. Positive strokes are ignored. Positive affirmations go in one ear and out the other. They don't relate to the child's reality.

Imagine a child, Michael, who comes from this situation and who arrives in child care at the age of 4. The teachers are kind and loving to him; he spits in their faces. They tell him what a good job he is doing on his carpentry project; he throws it to the ground and stomps on it. He accepts the meals they serve him and accepts their loving back rubs at nap time. But other than those two times, he refuses to accept positive strokes. He seems to *need* the negative ones. And he is an expert at getting them. He hurts other children. He destroys their things and laughs about it. He constantly butts heads with the teachers. He acts like a general all-round menace.

It is tempting to label this child for his behavior. He has a knack for making adults very angry. The staff begins to resent all the time they spend discussing him and his behavior at their regular meetings. No one feels like giving him positive strokes anymore. "That just doesn't work," they all agree.

Michael is a tough nut to crack. He is getting his strokes in the only way he knows how. His reality is that he is "bad," and therefore he believes deep down that he deserves the negative attention he gets. The positive strokes he gets from the staff are brushed off. They are not part of his reality. They don't belong to him.

Besides, the child care program frustrates him because he can't get the same intense reaction to his behavior that he gets at home. The teachers don't show their anger as passionately as the people he lives with. They don't hurt him the way he's used to being hurt. He doesn't understand this reality of the environment he spends his days in.

What to do about Michael? Of course, the first thing to do is to report any suspected abuse. It is illegal to do otherwise. However, the abuse in Michael's case lies in the past. The authorities have already been involved, and the child care staff has been told that the home situation is now under control. Their problem is Michael's behavior at school. Specifically, their problem is helping Michael control his unacceptable behavior, learn some prosocial behaviors, and come to feel better about himself.

Here's how they do it. In spite of the failure of their past efforts, they continue to focus on the positive aspects of Michael's personality. They search for tiny bits of acceptable behavior. Sometimes they joke that they need a microscope to do this searching, but they discover that when they look hard enough they can find positive behaviors—brief though they may be. Every scrap of positive behavior from Michael brings immediate teacher attention—hugs, smiles, words.

They also begin to see Michael in a new light. Instead of a difficult child, they see the behavior for what it is, patterns that he has learned in response to his environment. The patterns are working against him now, rather than for him, but they can be understood as adaptive behaviors. The staff is not so tempted to use judgmental labels now. They also discuss how he could be if he overcame his problems and learned to feel good about himself. Once they even took some time in a staff meeting to visualize this new Michael. They closed their eyes and "saw" the potential that lies beneath the difficult behavior.

When the teachers are with Michael, they control his behavior without rejecting him. It isn't easy. In fact, they really need an extra staff person to do this job properly. But after they realized how much time they were giving to Michael anyway, they agreed to do what was necessary to focus more fully on him.

Little by little they are managing to disconfirm Michael's perception of himself as a "bad person." They're changing his attitude by changing his behavior. They take a prevention approach—physically stopping him before he performs a malicious act.

When they first started this approach, they called in a substitute so they had plenty of staff, thus releasing a staff member to "track" Michael—to keep a constant eye on him. That meant even when the tracking teacher went on a break, he assigned someone else to take over, so that Michael was never unobserved during any part of the first few days of the new approach. His behavior began to improve—so much so that they were able to reduce the "tracking" to difficult parts of the day. This way they could dispense with the substitute and use the director's help for augmenting staffing. Eventually they needed to track only during transition periods, such as after lunch and before nap, which was always a bad time for Michael.

Of course, prevention doesn't always work. Sometimes the staff slips and accidentally lets Michael do something unacceptable. The other day, for example, while his teacher was tying another child's shoelace, Michael grabbed a shovel from a boy who was digging in the sandbox. When the child protested and tried to get the shovel back, Michael kicked him, and he was continuing to kick when the teacher grabbed him.

The teacher's response was to separate Michael from the other children. He took him inside. The teacher stayed with him—not to scold him and tell him how badly he'd behaved (Michael already knew that) but to let him know that someone will provide the control that he still lacks and that he is supported and cared about.

The staff's idea is to not allow Michael to make others reject him, which is what used to happen regularly. He still hasn't made friends among the children, but he's beginning to form an attachment to his teacher—and that's helping build trust and give him a sense of the pleasures of closeness with another person. The Michael who's been locked away inside is starting to emerge.

With Michael, remediation must be done. He must be "reprogrammed." (As already mentioned, it isn't as simple as reprogramming a computer, but the concept is useful here if you don't take it too far.)

Children usually don't need to be reprogrammed when parents and caregivers pay attention from the beginning to what messages they're giving and strive to emphasize positive ones. Messages, of course, don't come just from words. They come from actions as well—even little actions such as facial expressions and gestures of body language.

Not all children who come from an unfortunate background like Michael's have his same needs. Take Jay, for example, another 4-year-old in the same center.

Jay is what's called a "resilient child," a term discussed in Chapter 12. Remember Emmy Werner (1984, 1985, 2000), the developmental psychologist mentioned in Chapter 1, who did a long-term study on resilience? Jay is like the children Werner described, those who tend to have the ability from infancy on to elicit positive responses from people; who have established a close bond with at least one caregiver during the 1st year of life; who have a perspective that allows them to use their experiences constructively; who take an active approach toward solving problems; and who have a view of life as meaningful.

Jay was shuffled from relative to relative after his mother left him in the arms of his grandmother the day he was born. His grandmother was able to keep him until he was 15 months old, but then she had a stroke and Jay went to live with his aunt. He's only seen his mother twice in his young life, once last Christmas when she came to visit and once when he was $2\frac{1}{2}$ and he went to visit her—in prison.

When Jay arrived in this child care center at the age of 3, he had lived in four different homes and had been removed from the last one because of an abusive situation. You'd never know all this to look at Jay. He's a sunshiny kind of child who beams at anyone who notices him, and he's very good at getting people to notice him. There's something about Jay that attracts people to him, children as well as adults. His special friend in the center is the cook, and Jay can often be found hanging around the entry of the kitchen, where she leans over the Dutch door and talks to him. His favorite time of day is when the cook brings the food into the classroom to get the children to help prepare the snack. There he sits, peeling carrots or cutting cheese into chunks with the other children, chatting happily with the cook.

In spite of his difficult home life, Jay seems to have managed to get enough positive strokes when he most needed them—during the 1st year or so of his life. That period with his grandmother seems to have helped him develop an attitude that he's a person worthy of positive attention. As a 4-year-old, he seeks it—*and* he knows how to get it and use it. (See Chapter 12 for more on the subject of resilient children.)

RELATION OF ADULT SELF-ESTEEM TO BUILDING SELF-ESTEEM IN CHILDREN

It has been said that you can't give something that you don't have. Self-esteem falls into that category. There is a direct relationship between the amount of self-esteem adults have and their ability to enhance the self-esteem of the children in their lives.

It's worth noting that the messages we give as adults are strongly influenced by the ones we've been given as children. Often we are unaware of the connection. We don't even know that messages we carry with us are left over from our childhood. One way to get in touch with those messages is to become aware of the voices floating around in your head—the ones that praise, criticize, and tell you how you should act. These voices create what's been called a *life script*. They have influenced you to be who you are. Once you understand the concept of the influence of early messages, you can use this concept to guide you in responding to children in positive ways rather than haphazardly giving out messages that may be negative.

Changing Negative Messages to Positive Ones

If you're walking around with mostly negative messages coming through the voices in your head, it will be hard for you to give out the number of positive ones that children need. So I have a suggestion: Get rid of those negative messages you're carrying around with you.

One way to do that is to become aware of the voices and start writing down their messages—all of them, the negative ones and the positive ones. If you write each one on a separate slip of paper, eventually you'll have an array. Once you have collected at least 10, sit down and sort them out. Put the negative ones in one pile, the positive ones in another, and any that are a mixture in a third pile. Then take the mixture pile and rewrite those messages so they have a positive effect in your life. Put them in the positive pile. Now take the negative messages and see whether you can rewrite some of those as well. Perhaps you can't. Set aside those you can't rewrite and put the rewritten ones in the positive pile.

Now it's time to deal with the negative messages you're stuck with. Start by spreading them out in front of you. Take fresh slips of paper and write down some

There is a direct relationship between the amount of self-esteem adults have and their ability to enhance the self-esteem of the children in their lives.

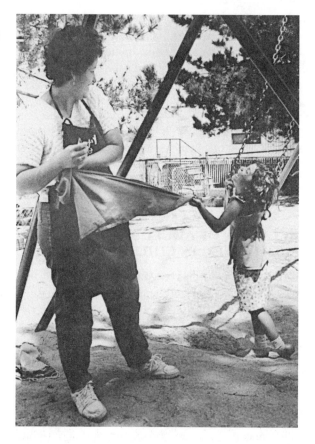

positive messages—ones you'd like to hear. Write one for each of the negative messages in front of you.

Once you have replaced those negative messages with some positive ones, pick up each negative piece of paper, tear it up, and throw it away! Make a big deal out of this act of discarding. As you tear up the paper, think about the conscious choice you have made not to listen to that message anymore. Although we can't program other people, we *can* reprogram ourselves!

Imagine yourself as you can be without those negative messages telling you how you are, directing your actions, and creating your personality. Put a picture in your mind of the *new you* acting in accordance with the stack of positive messages you have at your fingertips. Carry that picture with you. Accept it as true. Review the positive messages regularly. Take charge of your life! You can make choices about who you are and how you act. (This exercise was inspired by Clarke in her book *Self Esteem: A Family Affair* [1978].)

Children also make choices. They make choices about which messages to take in and listen to. (Just as you did as a child.) All the messages that are sent don't necessarily make the same impression. Some stick; others roll off children's backs like water off a duck. It may be that a message they hear over and over isn't one that sticks. But something they just heard once or a few times made such an impression that they took it in and believed it.

Children have choices, but not the same degree of choice that you have about consciously discarding the messages that hurt. They also have very little choice about from whom to get their messages. Children don't decide who they will spend their time with, at least for the first few years. Children don't determine with whom they live or where they spend their time. They have very little control over where they get their strokes. You, on the other hand, can choose to get your strokes from people who really care about you—people who are good for you, who support you, who grant you your needs, and who don't tear you down.

Children may have limited access to stroking people; they usually aren't able to expand the numbers of people who stroke them. Sometimes they get all their strokes from just one person. You, on the other hand, can expand beyond just one person for your strokes. In fact, it is vital that you do so. Think of the total number of strokes you get as a pie. Divide up that pie in your mind (or you can do this on paper). Are your stroke sources evenly distributed, or do you get most of your strokes from one person? If you get more than 25% from just one person, you are at risk for stroke deprivation when that person leaves even temporarily or is for some reason unable to stroke you.

SELF-STROKING

By the way, be sure that your own name is on a piece of your stroke pie. You should be a source of your own strokes. If you don't know how to stroke yourself, learn! Start by noticing whenever you do something well. Congratulate yourself. Pay attention to your needs, and when you meet them in a timely manner, praise yourself. Practice saying, "I did a good job on that!" and "Good for me—I took care of myself."

You should also teach children to be the source of strokes for themselves. You do this by examining your use of praise. Sometimes, in the name of being positive, we overdo praise or use it ineffectively. We teach children to look to us for their rewards instead of looking inside themselves. It's easy to see when this has happened. Observe in a preschool or toddler program and watch children turn to adults for praise after every little accomplishment. "Look at me, Teacher," they say, either verbally or nonverbally. For example, 2-year-old Timmy stacks three blocks carefully and then with great concentration adds a fourth to the stack; then he turns to look at his teacher.

Several different responses are possible. One response might be "Good boy, Timmy!" This is the kind of response someone might give who was just learning about *behavior modification*, which is a particular approach for changing behavior based on behaviorist theory. The idea is that a verbal reward, called *reinforcement* (praise), will increase the behavior. Timmy will be encouraged to try something like this again.

But let's look more closely at that kind of reward. Calling a child a "good boy" when he performs can backfire. What if he tries and tries and doesn't accomplish the feat? Is he a "bad boy"? Or what if he doesn't try at all? Anyone who believes strongly in a positive approach wouldn't tell him that he's a bad boy, but the absence of the label of "good" can easily be interpreted by a child as its opposite. When adults do use both "bad boy" and

*Does this child need a reward for
this accomplishment?*

"good boy" (or "good girl"/"bad girl") to give feedback on behavior, there is a real danger that the children will label themselves in those same terms. As children try to live up to their labels, they limit their options and potential. It's best to avoid global judgments that reflect on the child's worth as a person when using praise to motivate.

The teacher might say "Good job!"—making a nonspecific reference to the behavior (rather than a global judgment of the child). Even better, the teacher might say "Good stacking!"—specifically labeling the skill and the outcome. Or the teacher might focus instead on the process—the effort put in: "You worked hard to get that block to stay on top."

Instead of words, the teacher might give a passing smile or a little pat (nonverbal stroke). All the things mentioned so far are examples of *external stroking*—they come from someone else. However, children need to also learn *internal stroking*. They need to experience intrinsic rewards, to get a feeling of satisfaction.

One way to do that for Timmy, who stacked the four blocks, is to say, "You must feel good that you got that block to stay on top." This statement helps the child tune in on the good feelings of accomplishment. He learns eventually to stroke himself by bringing this good feeling to his conscious awareness. This approach takes the focus off the outside reward and puts it inside, where it does the most good of all.

Watch a group of children playing, with adults nearby supervising. Notice that some accomplish great feats and never look to an adult. Others must get attention for each little success, no matter how small. Adults are that way too, but it doesn't show the way it shows in children.

LEARNING NEW SKILLS

You may be saying to yourself that all of this sounds very artificial and highly manipulative. Why can't we just be natural around children?

The question is: What is natural? *Natural* means something different for each of us because of our individual backgrounds and experiences.

We aren't born knowing how to parent or work with children. We all must learn. What we learn from our own childhood experience seems natural to us, but nevertheless it is learned. Sometimes it is important to *relearn* because the skills we acquired from the way we were raised aren't in accordance with the goals we have for the children we live with or teach. Learning new skills isn't easy. Each new skill requires practice to perfect. Imagine expecting to play the violin beautifully the first time you pick up the bow. The same principle applies to parenting and teaching skills. Unless you are very good at picking up skills from models who were themselves practiced, you'll be less than perfect at first. You won't sound as bad as a beginning violinist; instead of being squeaky, you'll sound fake. When you hear someone talking to a child in an artificial way, it's a sign that he or she is using a new skill. I remember when I was a beginning preschool teacher and my young son visited my class. His question to me afterward was, "Mommy, why were you talking so funny to those kids?"

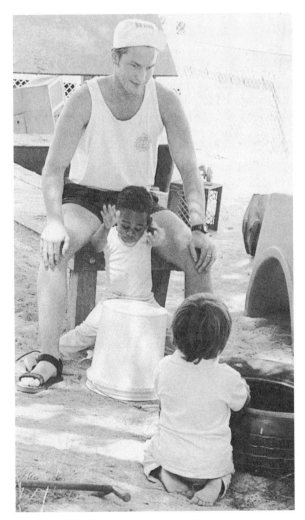

We are not born knowing how to parent or teach children. We all must learn.

Other factors come into play when learning new skills in relating to young children. Cultural and individual differences may create discomfort as the new ways conflict with certain values or what have been called *stroke rules*.

Clarke (1978, pp. 76–77) gives examples of stroke rules that she collected. It's easy to see from the following examples how the rules can limit the strokes the person accepts:

- Strokes must be earned.
- Strokes asked for are not as good as those not asked for.
- Negative strokes are more true than positive strokes are.
- A stroke has to be justified before I'll give or accept it.
- People are supposed to know when you need strokes.

Tips for Getting Yourself Nurtured

Here are some tips for setting yourself up to receive nurturing. One way to get it is to give it and then leave room for reciprocation. (I'll scratch your back if you scratch mine.) If reciprocation isn't forthcoming, one must then ask for nurturing. This is risky business, because when one asks, one might be turned down. However, asking is still a good approach.

Unless we tell others our needs, they'll never know about them. When my last son was born 13 weeks early and was hovering between life and death in intensive care, friends said, "What can we do for you?" My first response was, "Oh, nothing." But then I thought about it and said, "Feed us." And they did. Every day when we came home from our lengthy and frustrating visits at the hospital, there was a cardboard box on our doorstep with a full meal inside it. What a blessing! Without our friends we would have lived on fast food and snacks. Not only the nourishment was important to us, but also the message that we were cared about—cared for. We needed that during that period!

We all need strokes and affirmations all the time, not just during crisis periods. Let's learn to get them so we can give them and give them so we can get them. Think of it this way: The children we are raising and teaching now are the ones who will take care of us in our old age. The positive approaches we take now will pay off in the future!

Sexism in Stroking

Jennifer is a single parent, mother of a 4-year-old boy, Zach, and a daughter Jade, who is 2 $\frac{1}{2}$. She knows about the importance of strokes and affirmations, and she gives them regularly. Here are some examples:

She regularly tells her daughter how nice she looks. She is pleased to note that her little girl is already beginning to take an interest in her own appearance. She notices when her daughter plays nicely with her baby doll, when she pets the cat gently. Lately she's been amazed to see that her daughter is trying to help her do things around the house. Small as she is, she works to make the bed, tries to unload the dish drainer, and wants to fold clothes. Jennifer is very happy about these behaviors and, naturally, wants them to continue, so she praises her daughter when she shows a willingness to help. Once when Jennifer was feeling very down about losing her job, Jade caught her with a tear rolling down her cheek. She left the room and came back dragging her own precious "blankey," which she tenderly gave her mother to help her feel better. Jennifer was really touched by this gesture and she told Jade that.

Zach is his mom's "big boy." He feels that he is the "man of the house" and that he needs to be responsible. Of course he slips now and then, but his mother still loves him greatly—accepting his need to play instead of being grown-up. She thinks his loud manner and his rough play are appropriate, even when they bother her a little. She's proud of the way he figures things out. "You have a good head on your shoulders!" she tells him regularly. She's pleased that he spends so much time playing with the construction toys she's bought him. He creates truly amazing structures and machines. She talks to him about what he'll be when he grows up and how happy she'll be if they can figure out a way to get him into a good college. She has great hopes and aspirations for her son.

When Jade does something well, Jennifer says, "You angel!" When Zach does something well, Jennifer points out what was so good about how he did it. She's more specific with Zach than with Jade.

Anything wrong with this picture? Jennifer is using strokes and affirmations effectively, but she is selective. She is stroking her daughter for some qualities and her son for others. Her children respond accordingly. Her daughter is becoming more and more interested in her appearance and in nurturing others, and her son is coming to see himself as a "doer" and as a capable problem-solver who can use his head. Imagine the messages they are receiving about their futures. Will Jade come to see herself as someone beyond an angel who pleases others and makes them happy both by her appearance and by her nurturing actions? Will Zach learn to be a nurturer? How will Zach, the doer, relate to his family when he is grown? Will he go beyond providing the financial support that will come from the brilliant career he's being programmed for?

What Jennifer needs to do is to help her daughter also see herself as a "doer," not just a helper. She needs to catch Jade "thinking." Girls need to know that they are "smart" and capable just as much as boys do. It wouldn't hurt to talk to Jade about college, too, even though the event is far in the future. She could also encourage her to play with a wide range of toys, not just those advertised for girls.

Zach needs to see himself as a nurturer as well as a problem solver. His heart should be as big and strong as his head and body. Jennifer can help him do this by finding nurturing men to expose him to, by making it clear that nurturing is appropriate for boys, and by stroking him for any nurturing he might do.

This little family provides a lead-in to the next chapter, which deals with the issues of sexism and sex roles.

SUMMARY

This chapter explored a particular type of nurturing (strokes and affirmations) that children need for their socialization process. It focused on adults as much as on children, because they are the ones who give children this kind of nurturing. However, adults can only give nurturing if they get it, and many adults learn early that you can't just sit back and wait for people to nurture you. You're as likely to be walked all over as nurtured if you're just sitting there waiting. Most people need to put some effort into discovering how to get nurturing for themselves.

Throughout this section so far, no distinction has been made between the socialization process for boys and for girls. The next chapter examines that subject at length, including why it is important to be aware of differentiation in stroking patterns.

FOR DISCUSSION

1. How might you use positive strokes or affirmations to change behavior? Give some examples.

2. How do labels relate to self-fulfilling prophecy? Can you give examples from your own experience?

3. What is an example of three messages you carry around left over from your childhood, and how might those affect the way you relate to children? Do you have some ideas of how to change negative messages about yourself left over from your childhood that may be affecting you today?

4. What are some ways that a parent could encourage self-stroking in his or her children? How could an early childhood teacher, caregiver, or family child care provider encourage the parent to teach self-stroking to his or her child?

REFERENCES

Clarke, J. I. (1978). *Self-esteem: A family affair.* Minneapolis: Winston.

Goldstein, L. (2002). *Reclaiming caring in teaching and teacher education.* New York: Lang.

Noddings, N. (2002). *Educating moral people: A caring alternative to character education.* New York: Teachers College Press.

Rosenthal, R. (1987). Pygmalion effects: Existence, magnitude, and social importance. *Educational Researcher, 16*(9), 37–41.

Rosenthal R., & Jacobson, L. (1968). *Pygmalion in the classroom: Teacher expectations and pupils' intellectual development.* New York: Holt, Rinehart & Winston.

Shirilla, J., & Weatherston, D. J. (Eds.). (2002). *Case studies in infant mental health: Risk, resiliency, and relationships.* Washington, DC: Zero to Three.

Werner, E. E. (1984, November). Resilient children. *Young Children, 40*(1), 68–72.

Werner, E. E. (1995, June). Resilience in development. *Current Directions in Psychological Science, 4*(3), 81–85.

Werner, E. E. (2000, February-March). The power of protective factors in the early years. *Zero to Three, 20*(4), 3–5.

FURTHER READING

Barnard, K., & Brazelton, T. B. (Eds.). (1990). *Touch: The foundation of experience*. New York: Bantam.

Berne, E. (1964). *Games people play*. New York: Grove.

Busch-Rossnagel, N. A., Knauf-Jensen, D. E., & DesRosiers, F. S. (1995). Mothers and others: The role of the socializing environment in the development of mastery motivation. In R. H. MacTurk & G. A. Morgan (Eds.), *Mastery motivation: Origins, conceptualizations, and applications* (pp. 117–145). Norwood, NJ: Ablex.

Clark, K. E., & Ladd, G. W. (2000). Connectedness and autonomy support in parent-child relationships: Links to children's socio-emotional orientation and peer relationships. *Developmental Psychology, 36*, 485–498.

Goldstein, L. (2002). *Reclaiming caring in teaching and teacher education*. New York: Lang.

Greenberg, P. (1991). *Character development: Encouraging self-esteem and self-discipline in infants, toddlers, and two-year-olds*. Washington, DC: National Association for the Education of Young Children.

Hitz, R., & Driscoll, A. (1988, July). Praise or encouragement? New insights into praise: Implications for early childhood teachers. *Young Children, 43*(5), 6–13.

Hauser-Cram, P. (1996). Mastery motivation in toddlers with developmental disabilities. *Child Development, 67*, 236–248.

Hauser-Cram, P. (1998, July). I think I can, I think I can: Understanding and encouraging mastery motivation in young children. *Young Children, 53*(4), 67–71.

Klaus, M. H., & Kennell, J. H. (1982). *Parent-infant bonding* (2nd ed.). St. Louis: Mosby.

Noddings, N. (2002). *Educating moral people: A caring alternative to character education*. New York: Teachers College Press.

Shirilla, J., & Weatherston, D. J. (Eds.). (2002). *Case studies in infant mental health: Risk, resiliency, and relationships*. Washington, DC: Zero to Three.

Weinreb, M. L. (1997, January). Be a resiliency mentor: You may be a lifesaver for a high-risk child. *Young Children, 52*(2), 14–20.

Werner, E. E., & Smith, R. S. (1992). *Overcoming the odds: High risk children from birth to adulthood*. Ithaca, NY: Cornell University Press.

CHAPTER 11

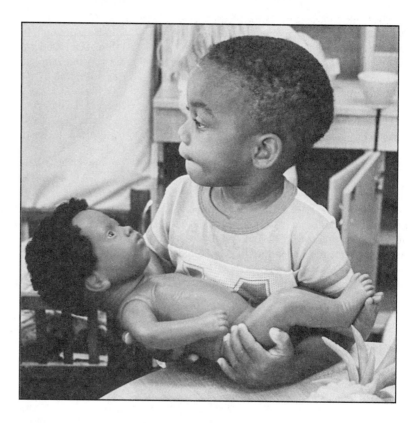

Modeling and Teaching Gender Roles

In this chapter you'll discover . . .

- How toys help define gender roles
- What girls may miss out on if they never play with blocks
- How to make boys feel comfortable expanding their "dramatic play"
- Another term for *fireman*
- The connection between language and power
- How children learn gender roles by imitating adults
- What's wrong with a lot of children's books

WHY THINK ABOUT TEACHING GENDER ROLES?

We live with many misconceptions concerning gender roles.[1] It may seem as though gender roles come automatically when children are born—and to some extent that is true. Shaping the gender role may even start prenatally now because many parents know the sex of their baby *before* birth. What many people don't think about when they accept traditional gender roles as a given is how narrow and confining they can be to children who grow into adults molded into a role they may not fit at all. Many don't consider how unfair, to both men and women, traditional gender roles can be. The unfairness shows up when we look backward at history to a time when women were clearly considered inferior to men and therefore had few rights as citizens. It's hard to believe that people are still alive today who remember the time when women in the United States couldn't vote. It may be startling to realize that the women's rights movement started in 1838, but it wasn't until 82 years later that women gained the right to vote. And the right was won only for some women. Others, because of the color of their skin or their lack of education, faced literacy and education taxes, intimidation, and violence at the polls. These women were kept from voting for almost half a century longer, until the passage of the 1964 Voting Rights Act and its 1974 amendments.

Imagine having no say in your government just because you happened to be born female instead of male, dark-skinned instead of light-skinned, or poor and uneducated instead of comfortable and educated. Also, imagine, if you can, a woman being considered her husband's property along with his children and cattle. We think those times are long gone, but remember, each generation is socialized into gender roles, and all the steps toward equity between the sexes could disappear if we don't continue to think carefully about how we socialize boys and girls. We must continue to guard against children's lives being shaped by restrictive gender roles, myths about their capabilities, and laws both written and unwritten that work against them.

THE WOMEN OF TODAY

Every citizen can vote now, but life's still no bed of roses. Many African American, Hispanic American, Native American, Asian American, and immigrant women are still undereducated and work in hard jobs for low wages while trying to care for their families (as do growing numbers of European American women who are single parents). Women still earn less for equal work than men do. Barriers still exist for women who are exploring nontraditional jobs and who are struggling to reach higher in the business world. In many arenas the "glass ceiling" that keeps women at a lower level than men is still in place. Although women have worked their way into most professions, it is still surprising when flying to hear a woman's voice from the cockpit say, "This is your captain speaking."

---

[1]Sometimes a differentiation is made between *sex* and *gender*—*sex* meaning the biological fact of being male or female, and *gender* referring to the person's identification as male or female through a socialization process. Usually sex and gender roles coincide, but in some cases a child of one sex may be socialized to be the opposite gender (Money & Ehrhardt, 1973).

Women who manage to work their way into jobs that have traditionally been men's have to be "superwomen." It's not easy for them to succeed with so many expectations put on them. It used to be that success came only if women acted like men when they competed in the traditional masculine arena. Now women are exploring new ways to do their jobs, using their feminine perspective, styles, systems, and skills. But sometimes they are punished for their femininity.

Yes, times have changed. The old riddle doesn't work anymore—you know the one about the father and son who were in an accident and the father was killed? When they brought the injured boy in for surgery, the brain surgeon took one look, paled, and turned away, saying, "I can't operate on him—that's my son!" It used to be that people wondered how the father could be the brain surgeon if he was dead. (You knew the answer is that the brain surgeon was the boy's *mother*, didn't you?)

Broader roles mean that mothers of young children are less likely to be criticized when they take jobs outside the home. Broader roles mean that some men feel freer to participate more fully in parenting their children; more and more men even choose to be full-time, stay-at-home parents. Men can now enter more traditional women's fields such as nursing. However, when the average citizen meets a man and a woman dressed in green scrubs in a hospital corridor, the assumption still is that the man is the doctor and the woman the nurse.

Whether we will continue to move forward in eliminating institutionalized oppression of women, broadening gender roles, and creating an increasing range of opportunities for all individuals is an unanswered question. Whether women and men are fully able to be who they are and do what they choose depends on how the next generations of children are raised. We can't just sit back and assume that men and women already are or will one day be freed from confining gender roles. Gender roles are learned by every generation. A danger of complacency exists as the younger generations accept as normal what feminists have worked so hard for. How easy it would be to lose the gains isn't clear, but it should be a worry.

GENDER EQUITY AND CHILD REARING

Many forces work to confine children in narrow gender roles, prune back their potential, and limit their opportunities. It may seem like steady progress was made in the last half of the 20th century toward broadening gender roles, but when comparing a 1975 study of children's bedrooms (Rheingold & Cook) with one done in 1990 (Pomerleau, Bolduc, Malcuit, & Cossette), little difference showed. Researchers looked at bedrooms of children from 1 month to 6 years of age. They carefully recorded the toys, decorations, and furniture. They found many more action-oriented toys—machines and vehicles, war-related, and sports equipment—in boys' rooms as compared to dolls and more family-focused toys in girls' rooms. Even the curtains and bedspreads were a contrast. Fifteen years didn't make any difference.

In 1999 (Parke & Brott) parents were still dressing their children in ways that clearly distinguished the boys from the girls. Is this a way to make sure that everyone knows what gender the child is? Do clothes shape gender roles? Certainly baby girls in dresses can't crawl the way boys in pants can. Is that a gender socialization message about being more or less active?

Consider how television pounds out the message that some clothes and toys are for girls and others are for boys. This advertising works against what some nonsexist parents work for. The Family Lifestyles Project starting in the 1970s studied the socialization of children in families that emphasized gender role equality (Eiduson, Kornfein, Zimmerman, & Weisner, 1988). Weisner and Wilson-Mitchell (1990) assessed the children over a 3-year period and found them broader in their selection of activities and interests than a comparison group. Without a strong plan beyond just buying trucks for their girls and dolls for their boys, parents run up against their children's opinions once they learn from TV which toys are for whom.

Toys and Gender Roles

Toys play an important part in defining gender roles. If parents buy girls dolls, dollhouses, high-heeled shoes, and makeup, they give one set of messages. If they buy boys chemistry sets, tool kits, doctor's bags, building blocks, and wheel toys, they give another set of messages. Children learn roles and skills from playing; the toys they have to some extent determine which roles and skills they learn.

Visit a child care program and examine the environment, specifically the block area and the dramatic play corner. Vivian Paley (1984) deals with this subject at length in her informative, easy-to-read book *Boys and Girls: Superheroes in the Doll Corner*. Though the book is not new, the superhero play hasn't changed. Only the names of the heroes and few heroines change regularly. No more He-Man or Teenage Super Ninja Turtles. Superman is still around, and Spiderman is big. While you are looking into the dramatic play area, notice whether more girls are there or boys. Check out the block area. Is that where you find the boys? If this is the case, examine the factors that might contribute to this situation. Sometimes the adults in the program subtly encourage this kind of gender differentiation. Notice the way the environment is set up. If the dramatic play area is a traditional "housekeeping" corner with frilly girls' clothes, shoes, and purses, most boys won't be attracted. If a variety of male or non-gender-specific hats, shoes, ties, and accessories are added, that can help. What helps most of all is adding a little water to the play sink, and maybe some soap suds and sponges.

Because boys tend to dominate block play in many programs, some teachers have tried a variety of approaches to encourage girls to go into the area also. One technique is to arrange the environment so that the blocks are close to the dolls or to put a dollhouse in with the blocks. Another idea is to put up "girls only" signs occasionally to give the message that this is valuable play for both sexes.

Why does it matter if boys never play house and girls never play blocks? It doesn't, if in other areas of their lives they are getting the skills they miss out on by avoiding these two activities. Dramatic play gives boys a chance to be nurturers, to experience domestic relations, to feel comfortable trying on a variety of emotions. Blocks give girls experience in spatial relations. They learn mathematical concepts as they build things. Ordinary wooden "kindergarten" blocks, called by some *unit blocks*, represent multiples of the basic square that is found in the set. Block play contributes a good deal to the concrete experience behind math knowledge, as well as giving the player experiences with principles of physics. Frank Lloyd Wright attributed his success as an architect to the set of blocks his mother brought home from a kindergarten conference in Europe back before anyone in the United States had heard of giving children blocks to play with.

It isn't just where children play or what they play with. It's also with whom they play. Young children tend to separate themselves by gender. One kindergarten teacher, Stacey Zeitlin (1997), describes how she purposely matched up boys and girls for a science activity. She made a conscious decision not to let the children select their own partners, as she usually did, but assigned them each a partner of the opposite sex. She was worried how it would work, because the children liked to team up with their same-gender best friends during an activity like this one. Surprisingly, it worked very well, and she saw how it broke down gender barriers. Children who had never spent time together before spent the rest of the day together. Some continued to seek out their partners as playmates the rest of the year. Zeitlin is now committed to reducing the self- and peer-imposed gender segregation that she sees children practicing.

Parents can take note of some of the practices early childhood professionals are using and support those practices while adding to them at home. At home, parents can also take note about arranging play dates, buying toys, setting up a nonsexist environment, and encouraging broader gender roles.

The Power of Language

Language has an influence on gender role development. Language shapes perceptions. If you talk about firemen, policemen, and chairmen, you set an expectation that these jobs are filled by men and that it's an exception when there's a "woman policeman." Better to make these titles non-gender-specific. That can be accomplished by using the terms *firefighter, police officer,* and *chair* or *chairperson.* Children will get the message that either gender may fill these roles.

Some titles are already non-gender-specific—for example, *teacher, doctor,* and *president.* However, children may consider them as gender-specific because of their own experience. There's the story of the English girl who asked her mother, "What are they going to call the new prime minister now that Mrs. Thatcher's gone?"

"By his name, of course," answered the mother.

"But what's his *title*?" persisted the child.

"Prime minister," answered the mother.

"But that's a woman's title!" said the child.

Interruption as an Indicator of Power and Importance.   Studies of "conversational politics" have found that people use language to show their power, as one person exerts control over another. For example, men tend to interrupt women more than the reverse. Interruption is an important indicator of relative power and importance. Children learn these interruption patterns early from their parents. Parents, teachers, and other early childhood professionals need to be aware of these patterns, so when they see them occurring they can put a stop to them. That's not easy to do when you're an involved party, but it's possible. It's easier to look for the patterns when they occur between boys and girls and then intervene, insisting that the girls get their say. Empowerment of girls is important if there is to be gender equity.

Using Language That Is Direct and Informative.   Female parents and teachers can also help empower girls by teaching them to use assertive language. To do this, they need to model such language themselves. Women who live or work with girls can pay attention to how often they end a sentence with a question that dilutes the message. For example, "I want you to sit down in your car seat, OK?" or "It's time for lunch—will you come in now?"

Females can model assertive language by cutting down the number of times they hedge with phrases such as *sort of* and I *guess*. They can also quit being ultrapolite. For example, "Your shoes are sort of muddy. It'd be really nice if you took them off before you walk on the rug. I'd sure appreciate it." That way of talking is very courteous, but it depends on the goodwill of the listener to be effective. When being polite gives the message that the speaker is powerless, it's a good idea to find more assertive ways to speak. It's more powerful for a person to say what she means—to be direct and informative. That's what a lot of men do, and that's why they are more likely to be listened to than women. For example, a direct way to deal with the muddy shoes is this: "Please take off your muddy shoes. They'll dirty the rug." Or: "Muddy shoes belong on the mat by the door." Or if necessary: "If you walk on the rug with muddy shoes, you're going to have to clean it."

USING MODELING TO TEACH

As the preceding section indicated, modeling is an important method of teaching gender roles. Children imitate the important people in their lives, so when girls see their mothers act helpless in the face of a flat tire or their female preschool teachers wait for a man to appear on the scene to unclog toilets or fix the broken handle on the cupboard, they pick up silent messages about women's capabilities. When a boy sees his father hand his mother a needle and thread and a shirt with a missing button, he gets a silent message about men's capabilities.

When children see their father reading the newspaper while their mother fixes dinner, then watching the news on TV while she cleans up after dinner, they get silent messages about gender roles. They come to see some activities as for women only and some for men only. They see a sexually determined power differential. In a household where tasks are shared, children get a broader idea of capabilities as well as appropriateness.

A good deal of modeling comes from television. *Power Rangers*, a children's television program widely criticized for its violence, at least has both boy and girl rangers. However, the "bad guy" is an evil old woman. Powerful elderly females as evil is a stereotype that has been with us for centuries. The witch hunts of the past show how such a negative stereotype can be used to oppress, even kill. Some older feminists facing the negative stereotype of being feminine and old have decided to redefine themselves as "crones"—the old woman as powerful, knowledgeable, and wise, but not evil.

Books can leave strong stereotypical images. In early readers, Dick was always busy fixing something, while Mother, Jane, and Sally stood helplessly looking on. Dick and Father were active in a variety of ways. Mother, Jane, and Sally were passive except in the kitchen. It seems as though times should have changed by now, but as late as 1986, when books read to kindergartners were analyzed, the main character was male more than 70% of the time. In 1996 females in books were more passive and dependent than their more active and assertive male counterparts. They were shown engaged in a narrower range of occupations than men (Turner-Bowker, 1996). Still today it is easy to see that children's books are more often about boys than girls, male animals instead of female ones. You can also easily find females being dependent more often than independent and poor damsels needing help.

DIFFERENTIAL SOCIALIZATION

Adults socialize girls and boys differently, which results in females ending up in subservient roles. How does this happen? Besides modeling, how else do children learn gender roles and develop a gender identity? Why do many boys gain confidence, competence, mastery, and assertiveness and many girls come to see themselves as lacking those qualities? Why do many girls fail to identify themselves as strong, responsible, and powerful?

Gender Roles and Cultural Differences

Two parents meet outside the door of the child care center where they have just arrived to pick up their children at the end of the day. They know each other slightly and feel a connection because they are of the same culture, although one was born in the United States and the other in the "old country." Both speak English, but they are more comfortable talking to each other in their own language, which is what they are doing now:

"How did you like the last parent meeting?" inquires Parent A, making conversation.

"Well, to tell the truth, it upset me," answers Parent B.

"Oh?" responds Parent A.

"All that talk about letting boys act like girls and encouraging girls to be powerful bothered me a lot. I just don't think that's appropriate!"

"Yes, I know what you mean . . . ," says Parent A.

"I can't stand the thought of my son playing house and wearing dresses. That makes me sick to my stomach. And they let him do that if he wants to."

"Does he want to?"

"How do I know? I'm not there!"

"It does seem kind of strange to me, too, but I don't think it hurts anything." Parent A leans casually against the stair rail.

Parent B stands, nervously rubbing her arms as if she is cold. She looks distressed.

"But the worst thing of all is that the teacher told me to send my daughter in pants and sneakers. She says that she's afraid to get dirty and that it's hard for her to run and climb with a dress and good shoes on. I guess she thinks I want her to look ugly, get dirty, and run around like a wild person!"

Parent A touches her friend's arm. "That really bothers you."

"Yes! That's not proper behavior for a girl! Do you think it is?"

"Well," says Parent A slowly, brushing her hair back from her face, while carefully considering her words, "I don't really like my daughter to get dirty, but I have to admit that what the teacher said is convincing."

"What's convincing? All that garbage about sexism?"

The two parents stop talking in their own language and switch to English as another parent arrives at the bottom of the steps. They greet her and move over to let her go up the steps and into the child care center.

"Yes, sexism and oppression!" continues Parent A, as if there had been no interruption.

Parent B replies passionately, "I don't see that my daughter is restricted in her development. She's going to grow into a woman. She has to know how women act in our culture. She has to fit in. She'll never get a decent husband if she starts acting like the other girls in this country. I don't want her to be like them. I don't want her to lose her culture."

"I know what you mean," says Parent A slowly. "But I've been thinking about whether women's inferior status is something we should just accept because that's the way it's always been."

"Oh, you're as bad as they are!" snorts Parent B angrily, stepping backward on the stair. "I thought you would understand."

"I *do* understand," comes the answer, "but at the same time I'm confused. I just don't know what I think."

"Well, I do. And I warn you, if you listen to them, you'll end up like them. You'll be melted right into the melting pot! How would you like that?"

"I don't know," answers Parent A, looking doubtful as she slowly turns and walks to the door of the center. "But I think," she says, pausing and turning around to watch Parent B climb up the rest of the steps, "that ensuring that my daughter grows up with a sense of her self-worth as a person is a good idea. I don't think oppression has to be part of our culture."

"I disagree that women who dress and act the way they are supposed to are oppressed. That's ridiculous. Look at me. Am I oppressed?" Parent B is at the door now, too.

"I'm beginning to understand what you mean about losing our culture. I don't want that to happen. I can be American and still be part of my culture. That's important to me. Let's talk more later," says Parent A, opening the door and stepping back to let her friend walk through first.

Differential Treatment from Parents

Differential treatment starts at birth, when parents perceive their daughters to be more fragile than their sons (Weitzman, 1979). Fathers play rough and tumble more with their sons and talk to them in ways that indicate toughness, like "Hi, Tiger!" (Parke, 2002). From early on, many parents encourage their sons to be active, assertive, and strong, and they protect their girls. They do more touching and talking to girls; they stress independence, self-reliance, and achievement-related skills to their boys. Although some parents make an effort to support egalitarian roles, they tend to start when their children are older, and not at the beginning (Ruble & Martin, 1998). When children leave babyhood, if the differential treatment continues into toddlerhood and beyond, eventually, lo and behold, the boys have a tendency to be active, clever, assertive, and aggressive doers, and the girls often turn out to be sweet, dependent, verbal, and social. Whatever natural inclinations that fit with what the children might have been born with can be diminished or magnified by the socialization process.

Differential Treatment in Preschool

This same differential treatment continues when the children leave home for child care or preschool. In 1973, Serbin, O'Leary, Kent, and Tolnick looked at how preschool teachers treated girls and boys. They found that teachers paid attention to boys' disruptive behavior, which reinforced it; the attention acted as a reward and encouraged the behavior to continue. Girls, on the other hand, received attention only when they stood or played near the teacher. Direct reinforcement, even when it is unintended, is a powerful way to influence behavior.

Things haven't changed much from the early 1970s. Observe for yourself how adults in group care spend a lot of time looking over the heads of the girls who hang around them (being dependent and getting attention for it) to notice the boys, who are throwing blocks,

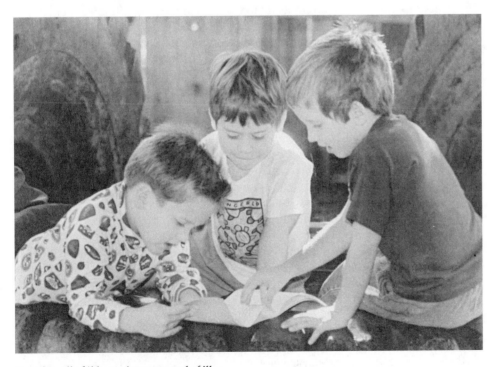

Broaden all children's interests and skills.

hitting each other, or climbing the fence of the play yard. The untrained adult will yell at the boys. The trained one will leave the cluster of girls and go over and handle the problem with the boys in some professional way—often touching them, getting down to their level, and making eye contact while he or she describes the unacceptable behavior and explains why it must stop. Both the yelling and the more professional intervention strategies are rewarding. They say to the boys, "I'm paying attention to you." The attention and the behavior that preceded it become solidly linked. Many boys never learn any other ways of getting the teacher to notice them. And many of the girls never break out of the "be-dependent-to-get-noticed" pattern.

While you are observing, notice how adults make conversation with young children. I'm sure you'll discover that girls are often noticed for their appearance. Child care staff and visitors regularly make remarks such as "Oh, you got your hair cut—it looks very pretty" and "I see you got new shoes!" and "What a nice design on your shirt." Those same adults are more likely to notice boys' abilities. They say things like "How strong you are to lift that heavy piece of wood" and "I saw you climb all the way up to the top of the jungle gym!" and "How clever you are. You figured out how to make that work!"

Differential Treatment in Elementary School

Some patterns similar to those that Serbin and her colleagues found in preschool-age children were reported by Thorne (1993), who looked at children in elementary school. Thorne reports that boys control much more space on the playground than girls do— up to 10 times more. The girls play closer to the building and remain near adult aides who watch over them and protect them. Boys invade girls' space more often than the reverse. And boys are more likely to define girls as "polluting" or contaminated in the old game of "cooties." Thorne also noticed that though boys and girls segregate them- selves, when they are mixed together by adults, boys and girls interact in more relaxed ways. When adults are the ones who organized the mix, it legitimizes the togetherness and removes the risk of teasing.

While all this is going on in early childhood programs, at home parents tend to give help to their daughters more than to their sons (and the girls ask for help more often, which is not surprising, because they are rewarded for doing so). Girls are also more likely to be criticized for touching, handling, and manipulating objects, and for active play. In other words, girls are taught to be dependent and quiet, even passive, at home and at school, and boys are encouraged to figure things out for themselves and to be active in their play.

Socialization of girls has been of interest to feminists for years because of what happens when no thought is given to equity. But what about the boys? Who worries about their socialization? Those are questions that many people are asking. Two popu- lar books published in the late 1990s do what they can to answer those questions. One is called *Real Boys*, by William Pollack (1998), and the other is *The Wonder of Boys*, by Michael Gurian (1997). Both address the issues around what makes boys act the way they do. They also look at how adults can shape boys into men and move beyond myths and stereotypes about masculinity.

THE ROLE OF BIOLOGY IN CREATING DIFFERENCES BETWEEN BOYS AND GIRLS

When we look at socialization of boys and girls, it seems as if they learn their roles and that's all there is to it. It's important to recognize that while learning is taking place, physiology is also contributing to male-female differences. Exposure to hormones during pregnancy, genetic influences, and other biological factors can influence the development of sexual identity and roles. There is a dispute about to what degree differences are learned and to what degree physiology influences how children see themselves and what skills they develop. Research in the 1960s and 1970s seemed to end the dispute. Money and Ehrhardt (1973), who did some rather startling research then, were convinced that they proved that babies are born gender-neutral and can be assigned one gender or the other without harmful effect. These assignments were done to children with ambiguous external genitalia and sometimes the assignments were wrong. Hormonal corrections were made at puberty when the mistake was discovered, so that the child could continue in the previously assigned gender role to which he or she had been socialized. Other times the assignments were made when something went wrong with a circumcision and a boy would then be castrated and raised as a girl. The research seemed to show that gender roles are more learned than they are natural. In other words, in spite of the fact that genetically the child was a boy, being socialized as a girl made him exhibit typically female behavior.

The case of a person named "Joan" disputed this research. In an article called "A Boy Without a Penis," Gorman (1997) tells the story of Joan, named by researchers Milton Diamond and Keith Sigmundson in a follow-up study looking at the long-term effects of assigning gender. The baby, a male, was surgically made into a female after a botched circumcision destroyed the penis. The article is about the agonies Joan went through rebelling against the gender assignment she was given. She knew she was a boy, but no one would confirm that. In 1977 at the age of 14, Joan decided she had only two options, to commit suicide or live life as a male. When she confronted her father with her decision, he finally told her the truth and a sex change operation eventually gave her a body to go with her identity. To what extent are gender roles learned and to what extent are they natural? No one has the final answer to that question yet.

How does growing up in a family with same-sex parents affect gender roles and sexual orienation of the children? Studies suggest that what children learn about gender roles in heterosexual families isn't significantly different from what children learn in gay and lesbian families. Further, there is no evidence to suggest that children reared in same-sex families are likely to develop a gay or lesbian sexual orientation. Their gender-role behavior and sexual orientation are similar to children reared in heterosexual households.

No matter what is discovered about gender roles and sexual orientation, we still have equity issues to consider. We know that the adults in young children's lives have a great influence over their gender role socialization and their attitudes about same-sex families. What are some ways that these adults can help children accept each other and honor the family that each comes from? How can adults empower both boys and girls? How can they promote equality of development for both sexes? With stereotypes still such a part of all our lives, how can adults counteract their influence and help boys learn that they can express feelings and be nurturing, and help girls learn to be independent, assertive, and capable problem-solvers? What can adults do to enable each child to fulfill his or her own potential rather than grow up bound by restrictive gender roles?

GUIDELINES FOR PARENTS AND EARLY CHILDHOOD EDUCATORS

Here are some guidelines for teaching young children about gender equity:

♦ *Help children develop awareness of sexist stereotypes.*   Point out such stereotypes in pictures, in books, and on TV. Look for stereotypes in commercials as well as in regular programs and movies.

♦ *Create a nonsexist environment.*   Find books and pictures that show all kinds of families, including single-parent families (not just single mothers), gay and lesbian families, and extended families, for starters. These books and pictures should show men and women doing similar activities and pictures of women and men in nontraditional occupations. Invite visitors who are in nontraditional jobs to the home, child care, or preschool to talk about their work. (Or visit these workers at their workplaces.) Expand children's awareness beyond narrow views and stereotypical gender roles.

♦ *Watch your own behavior.*   Do you treat girls differently from boys? What do you notice about them? What do you remark about? Do you give both sexes equal physical freedom? Do you allow both to express feelings? Do you encourage both to seek help at times and to be independent as well? Be observant of yourself and catch the ways you may be promoting narrow gender roles. When children ask about the difference between boys and girls, stick to anatomical differences and avoid mentioning dress, behavior, or personality traits.

♦ *Teach an antibias attitude to young children and give them the skills they need to challenge sexism.*   Teach them to recognize injustice and to speak out against it. When Brandon says to Lindsay, "You can't come in our fort. Only boys are allowed," help her speak up and say, "That's not fair!" If he tries to exclude her on the basis of her behavior, the situation is different. For example, if he says, "You can't come in because last time you grabbed all the toys," she's getting feedback about something she can change. She can't, however, change the fact of being a girl, so for him to exclude her for that reason is unfair discrimination. Children need to learn to speak up for their own rights. Teach them to do that.

♦ *Help all children develop empathy.*   Notice when they are sensitive to the feelings of another. Pay attention to behaviors that show caring for another person. Model empathy yourself.

♦ *Help all children become problem-solvers, in both the physical and the social worlds.*   Teach them to troubleshoot. Help them extend their perspective to include many possibilities. Help them learn to negotiate.

Teach an antibias attitude to young children and give them the skills they need to challenge sexism.

◆ Broaden *children's views of themselves and their capabilities.*   Entice them to develop skills they've been avoiding. Find ways to get the girls that need to be out in the yard more into activities that increase their strength, courage, and dexterity. Figure out a way to get the boys who never sit down at tables, given the choice, involved in activities that take eye-hand coordination and require careful manual skills. Some boys who avoid traditional preschool art projects will glue wood scrap sculptures or take apart an old radio.

◆ *Notice how clothes get in the way, especially girls' clothes, and determine activities accordingly.* The crawling baby is hampered if she's in a dress or has lots of ruffles and flounces on her clothes. The slippery shoes of the preschooler keep her from running or climbing. Light-colored pants get stained knees if a girl crawls around on the grass or in the dirt. Will this situation cause problems for her, and serve to restrict her activities?

◆ *Last, but definitely not least, check out your own attitudes.*   If you see the male of the species as more important, more deserving of power, worthy of a higher status, you need an attitude adjustment. Until you deal with that attitude problem, you'd better watch yourself carefully when you are around young children. You can't promote equity if down deep you don't believe in it! That's a strong statement, and one that may get me in trouble for including it in a book that claims to be sensitive to cultural differences. In some cultures gender roles are strictly defined. That may fit the culture and the people in it just fine. The problem for me is when one sex is in power and the other is in a powerless position. I have been told that because I'm judging from outside the culture, I don't really understand the power relationships between the sexes. I have to admit that is a possibility. Still when oppression exists and I'm told it's cultural, that fact puts me in a double bind, because I feel it is important to accept and honor differences; *however*, I must also stand up against oppression.

SUMMARY

This chapter examined the role socialization plays in creating differences between boys and girls. It came out strongly for equality of the sexes. In the next chapter the theme is continued, as we look at stresses in families and find that some of those stresses have to do with the feminization of poverty and the inferior status of women.

FOR DISCUSSION

1. What part does TV play in limiting children's concept of gender roles? Give specific examples. What can be done about any limitations that you perceive?

2. What part does language play in carrying out inequities? How does language influence children's ideas of their capabilities. What can be done to broaden children's views?

3. What if children are exposed to limited models of men's and women's roles? How can children learn about gender equity?

4. Brainstorm some ideas about how to empower both boys and girls.

5. What are some cultural views that are different from the gender equity goals promoted in this chapter?

REFERENCES

Bailey, J., Bobrow, D., Wolfe, M., & Mikach, S. (1995). Sexual orientation of adult sons of gay fathers. Special issue: Sexual orientation and human development. *Developmental Psychology*, 31, 124–129.

Eiduson, B. T., Kornfein, M., Zimmerman, I. L., & Weisner, T. S. (1988). Comparative socialization practices in traditional and alternative families. In G. Handel (Ed.), *Childhood socialization*. (pp. 73–101). Hawthorne, NY: Aldine.

Fagot, B. I. (1978). The influence of sex of child on parental reactions to toddler children. *Child Development*, 49, 459–465.

Gorman, C. (1997, March 24). A boy without a penis. *Time*.

Gurian, M. (1997). *The wonder of boys*. New York: Putnam.

Money, J., & Ehrhardt, A. A. (1973). *Man and woman, boy and girl*. Baltimore: Johns Hopkins University Press.

Paley, V. (1984). *Boys and girls: Superheroes in the doll corner*. Chicago: University of Chicago Press.

Parke, R. D. (2002). Fatherhood. In M. Bornstein (Ed.), *Handbook of parenting* (2nd ed.). Mahwah, NJ: Erlbaum.

Parke, R. D., & Brott, A. (1999). *Throwaway dads*. Boston: Houghton Mifflin.

Patterson, C. J. (2002). Lesbian and gay parenthood. In M. H. Bornstein (Ed.), *Handbook of parenting* (2nd ed.). Mahwah, NJ: Erlbaum.

Pollack, W. (1998). *Real boys*. New York: Random House.

Pomerleau, A., Bolduc, D., Malcuit, G., & Cossette, L. (1990). Pink or blue: Environmental gender stereotypes in the first two years of life. *Sex Roles*, 22, 359–367.

Rheingold, H. L., & Cook, K. V. (1975). The content of boys' and girls' rooms as an index of parent behavior. *Child Development*, 46, 459–463.

Ruble, D. N., & Martin, C. L. (1998). Gender development. In W. Damon (Gen. Ed.) & N. Eisenberg (Vol. Ed.), *Handbook of child psychology* (Vol. 3, pp. 933–1016). New York: Wiley.

Serbin, L. A., O'Leary, F., Kent, R. N., & Tolnick, I. J. (1973, December). A comparison of teacher response to the preacademic and problem behavior of boys and girls. *Child Development*, 44(4), 776–804.

Thorne, B. (1993). *Gender play: Girls and boys in school*. New Brunswick, NJ: Rutgers University Press.

Turner-Bowker, D. M. (1996). Gender stereotyped description in children's picture books: Does "Curious Jane" exist in literature? *Sex Roles*, 35, 461–488.

Weisner, T. S., & Wilson-Mitchell, J. E. (1990). Nonconventional family lifestyles and multischematic sex typing in six-year-olds. *Child Development*, 61, 1915–1933.

Weitzman, L. J. (1979). *Sex role socialization*: A focus on women. Mountain View, CA: Mayfield.

Zeitlin, S. A. (1997, September). Finding fascinating projects that can promote boy/girl partnerships. *Young Children*, 52(6), 29–30.

FURTHER READING

Chow, E. N., Wilkinson, D., & Zinn, B. (1996). *Common bonds, different voices*. Newbury Park, CA: Sage.

Collins, P. H. (1990). *Black feminist thought: Knowledge, consciousness, and the politics of empowerment*. Boston: Unwin Hyman.

Derman-Sparks, L., & the ABC Task Force. (1989). *Antibias curriculum: Tools for empowering young children*. Washington, DC: National Association for the Education of Young Children.

Faludi, S. (1991). *Backlash: The undeclared war against American women*. New York: Crown.

French, M. (1992). *The war against women*. New York: Summit.

Gallas, K. (1998). *Sometimes I can be anything: Power, gender, and identity in a primary classroom*. New York: Teachers College Press.

Kenway, J., Willis, S., Backmore, J., & Rennie, L. (1998). *Answering back*. St. Leonards, Australia: Allen & Unwin.

MacNaughton, G. (2000). *Rethinking gender in early childhood education*. St. Leonards, Australia: Allen & Unwin.

Neighbors, H. W., & Jackson, J. S. (Eds.). (1996). *Mental health in black America*. Newbury Park, CA: Sage.

Parke, R. D. (2002). Fatherhood. In M. Bornstein (Ed.), *Handbook of parenting* (2nd ed.). Mahwah, NJ: Erlbaum.

Patterson, C. J. (2002). Lesbian and gay parenthood. In M. H. Bornstein (Ed.), *Handbook of parenting* (2nd ed.). Mahwah, NJ: Erlbaum.

Powlishta, K. K. (1995, July). Gender segregation among children: Understanding the "cootie" phenomenon. *Young Children*, 50(4), 61–69.

Ruble, D. N., & Martin, C. L. (1998). Gender development. In W. Damon (Gen. Ed.) & N. Eisenberg (Vol. Ed.), *Handbook of child psychology* (Vol. 3, pp. 933–1016). New York: Wiley.

Sheldon, A. (1990, January). Kings are royaler than queens: Language and socialization. *Young Children*, 45(2), 4–9.

Turner-Bowker, D. M. (1996). Gender stereotyped description in children's picture books: Does "Curious Jane" exist in literature? *Sex Roles*, 35, 461–488.

CHAPTER 12

Stress and Success in Family Life

In *this chapter you'll discover* . . .

- The characteristics of a successful family
- The stories of six families and the stresses they face
- Why stress is sometimes good for us
- Some factors that are common to resilient children
- How "protective factors" can counteract the effects of stress

All families experience stress and always have. Stress is nothing new to family life, though it may seem now with the times changing so rapidly that we are under more stress than in the past. Certainly family structure is changing, and that alone can create stress in those who think back with longing to what they consider the good old days. This chapter looks at the kinds of stresses that affect families today. It also looks at what makes for successful families.

It's important to take into account the strengths of families in stress who manage to socialize their children successfully. What enables these families to function effectively under difficult or demanding circumstances? Why do some families remain organized and supportive of each other under extreme pressures? Early childhood educators need to learn how to promote that same kind of togetherness in families that lack it. They need to understand more about how the effects of classism, racism, and sexism, as well as cultural and ethnic biases.

You can't take families out of their cultural context. The early childhood profession needs to focus less on universals and more on understanding a variety of cultural patterns of child rearing as they relate to socialization. It's important to recognize that the cultural imperatives of families determine which competencies it is appropriate to foster in children. It is important to understand how socialization techniques and child-rearing practices work to promote the survival of any given culture, even though to a critical eye outside the culture they may look undesirable. Early childhood professionals must avoid equating cultural survival with what may seem to be harmful practices and family breakdown.

Remember that in the introduction to Part 2, families were defined in a broad way so that there is room for all kinds of families in the definition. There's a lot of talk today about the family breaking down. When a family is not functioning well, raising children is difficult and there's cause to be concerned. However, the definition of *functional family* varies from culture to culture. It's tempting to see a family as dysfunctional when its patterns or structure are different from your image of what they should be, but family structure alone doesn't tell you how well the family functions. It only tells you that it's different from what has been regarded as a traditional family.

For too long society, the researchers, and the media have been thinking of the two-parent, white, middle-class family and their birth children as the standard by which all other families are to be judged. For too long those families that differed were thought not to measure up and were labeled as lacking or deprived. It's time to give legitimacy to cultural differences and alternative lifestyles.

A good start is to get rid of the term *broken family*, which sounds as if something is wrong, when in reality the so-called broken family may be quite functional. You can't tell by family structure whether a family functions in healthy ways. The single-parent family in apartment A may be quite functional compared with the two-parent, *intact*, but highly dysfunctional family in apartment B next door.

You have to be very careful about making generalizations about family structures. For example, some African American family structures have been portrayed as deficient. Stereotypes of domineering mothers, absent fathers, disorganized families plagued with abuse and neglect sometimes overshadow the reality of families that don't fit what is sometimes thought of as the ideal structure.

It's time to quit looking at differences as deficits, rather than as legitimate forms in themselves. Families of all types and sizes are fully capable of producing healthy children and providing a support system for all of the people who comprise the family. You can't judge a family's degree of functionality by its structure, patterns, or makeup.

Instead of automatically labeling some family structures as deficient and looking at them as social problems, it's time that we started to see their strengths. We should be supporting diversity in family structure. When we, as a society, come from a point of view that the family is breaking down, rather than changing in form, we put all of our resources into looking at causes of the breakdown. We already know something about what causes stress in families. We know that you can't separate the way families function from the social, economic, and political realities that influence their lives.

SUCCESSFUL FAMILIES

A successful family is one that functions in healthy ways; it supports and nurtures its members so that everyone's needs are met. Although happiness and satisfaction may come periodically to members of successful families, those aren't the only emotions they experience; they feel a wide range of emotions and are free and able to express them when appropriate. A successful family isn't a perennial sunshine family. It has its ups and downs, just as its individual members do.

There is much talk about dysfunctional families these days. Many people have begun to discover that some of the ways they were reared weren't good for them—their families were abusive, created codependencies, and taught family members to ignore their own needs. The statistics vary, but it has been said that up to 98% of us grew up in dysfunctional families. If 98% of us are raised in a particular way, that way must be *normal*—a word often equated with *right* and *good*. So where does that leave us as far as dysfunctional families are concerned?

Because the family prepares its members for society, we'd better look beyond the family to see what this high rate of dysfunction is about. A quick look will show that the so-called dysfunctional family is not so out of tune with the present society, which nurtures a system in which some have power over others and not everyone gets needs met. Power, both in the society and in the family, is often wielded like a sword rather than radiated like light. Privilege and hierarchy, sanctioned by the societal system, often squelch our ability to be who we really are; they take our personal power from us. The dysfunctional family reflects the dysfunctional parts of society.

The theme of the strong dominating the weak is pervasive both in the family and in the society. If we take that theme to extreme, we see that world peace in the past has depended on the strongest nations stockpiling enough weapons to stop each other from making war. That's the ultimate in the power approach to getting along with others. No wonder families have been hard-pressed to help their members grow in healthy, sane ways to become who they really are as unique people—each able to radiate the power inside.

We're beginning to change our approach—but change doesn't happen in an easy, linear way. It is often accompanied by periods of uncomfortable chaos, when things seem to get worse instead of better.

Many who desire this change are beginning to create their own scripts instead of living by the old myths of power in which the strong overcome the weak, one race dominates another, and men control the lives of women. They are altering the themes that have been handed down for generations.

Families are starting to rear their children for the emerging society—one in which it will be possible to raise children without abusing them and to be both connected and autonomous, one in which the dominator model gives way to a true equity model. Parents are learning how to use their power *for* or *with* their children instead of overpowering and dominating them. They are learning to *empower* their children—that is, to allow them to experience personal power, which gives them the feeling of being able to be themselves and of having some effect on the world or the people in it. People who are empowered don't need to overpower or manipulate others. They are free to experience being who they really are—to fulfill their unique potential; they will resist being cast into some preset mold.

No matter how much things change, all family systems will continue to have some degree of dysfunction, or they wouldn't be of human origin. We'll never live in a perfect world, but we can improve it by focusing on what kinds of traits make for successful families—the traits that will allow each member to function effectively within the family and in the society beyond. What are these traits?

TRAITS OF SUCCESSFUL FAMILIES

Healthy involvement with each other is one trait of a successful family. Its members feel attachment to each other. They care. They don't just fulfill a social role; they have a deep sense of commitment. They give time and attention to the family. They don't get overinvolved in activities that exclude the family.

People in successful families recognize the signs of unhealthy *codependence*, in which one person encourages and enables another to lean too heavily on him or her, creating bonds that trap both of them. People in successful families understand the importance of independence and healthy *interdependence*. They know how to get their needs met in a relationship that allows the other person to get his or her needs met as well. They know how to take care of others without making them overly dependent on that care. They understand mutual nurturing.

Successful families tend to build and maintain self-esteem in their members instead of continually tearing it down. They know how to discipline children and to guide and control behavior in ways that leave self-esteem intact.

They know how to communicate effectively. They can both give and receive feedback. They have some skill at resolving conflicts in ways that do not neglect anyone's needs. They use problem-solving methods to deal with even small problems when they arise. They know how to cope with problems that can't be solved. They know how to express feelings in healthy ways. They know how to give and get strokes.

Successful families know how to protect their members, providing a secure environment within the home. Though a safe home is a haven from the outside world, it is also important that family members connect to the greater society. Therefore, two important family functions—protection and connection—seem to be opposites, but in reality they balance one another.

Parents and elders in successful families know how to pass on values to the next generation, through modeling, discussion, teaching, and problem-solving. They also know how to accept differences when value conflicts arise.

So what does a successful family look like? Do they all have fulfilling jobs, live in nice houses, drive "newish" cars, and live stress-free lives? Of course not. Successful families come in all sizes, shapes, configurations, and financial conditions. Circumstances contribute to success, of course, but they aren't the sole determiners. If they were, rich people in good physical health would automatically be better at creating successful families than sick poor people, but that just isn't the way it works, is it?

No family is 100% successful, but some work at it. All families are in process. Think of success as a path—a path where no one gets to the final destination (just as no one reaches human perfection). Some start out on this path farther behind than others.

Compare two families. The first is made up of a couple who both came from stable families where their needs were fairly well met. When they had children, they tended to create the kind of home life they both experienced as children. They have their problems, of course, but they seem to take things in stride. They work at their marriage, at their individual development, and at their parenting. They had good models in their parents for this work. They are on the path of success.

The second family is composed of a couple who came from less stable homes. They are also working at their marriage, at their individual development, and at their parenting, but they have to work harder because they haven't had the firsthand experience that the first couple had. They've had to come to the realization that their own upbringing was lacking—which means that they've had to *learn* healthy ways of dealing with their children. It didn't just come to them naturally. They are also on the path to success, but it's a rockier road for them, with numerous barricades to climb over and potholes to fall into.

What the two families have in common is that they have a vision of success. They are both on the path, moving toward their vision—and they are determined to make progress.

Let's take a look now at six families who, in spite of a number of pressures in their lives, are also struggling along the path to become successful families. Some are much farther along than others. Stress is a theme in all of their lives. Let's see what kind of stresses they are coping with. One thing that these six families have in common is that all enrolled in a government-subsidized child care program that takes both low-income and full-cost families. The program runs a center and satellite family child care homes.

Sara's Family

Meet Sara. She was a teen parent when she had Ty 4 years ago; now she is 20. Ty and his 2-year-old brother, Kyle, are both in the center because Sara is in nursing school at the local community college.

Sara has had a hard time of it since she became a mother at 16. She lived with her mother for the first couple of years, but they argued over how she was raising Ty, and she left to join the homeless population of her city. She and Ty lived for awhile in her car until the poor old thing quit running, sat in one place too long, and got towed. Then she lived under a bridge between the highway and the river. Pregnant again (as the result of being raped), hungry, and desperate, she finally found a social worker in an agency that hooked her up to some of the services available in her community (more about this in the next chapter).

Now Sara is in nursing school, and life is better, but it still isn't easy. She has financial aid and a place to live, but she's going crazy trying to go to school all day, study all night, and raise her boys at the same time. They reflect her stress and they have stresses of their own. Ty seems to have an attention deficit problem; although the teachers in the center are working with him, he moves from one activity to another so fast that it's hard to keep track of him. He never seems to settle on any one thing and becomes frustrated very easily when he tries to do something. The result is that he throws regular tantrums.

Then there's Kyle. He appears to be a very sweet child, cuddling up to the teachers whenever he gets a chance. But his brother beats on him, which is starting to make him aggressive toward other children. He has to be watched all the time because he bites. The staff is thinking of putting him in one of the satellite family child care homes available to the center because the stimulation of the center seems to be too much for him to handle.

Sara is learning about communication, discipline, and family relations from a parenting class and from her therapist. She doesn't feel very successful as a family head, but she is moving in the right direction. When she looks at her past, she sees that she has come a long way. She has hopes for the future.

Roberto's Family

The second family is Roberto's. His 4-year-old daughter, Lupe, is in the local Head Start program in the morning, and she comes to the center in the afternoon. Roberto transports her from one program to the other when his old pickup is running and he's not working. Otherwise, his wife, Maria Elena, who takes classes in English as a second language at the adult school, uses the bus to pick up Lupe and deliver her to the center. Maria Elena takes their baby, Paco, with her in the morning to class, where they have child care, but she brings Paco to the center in the afternoon while she cleans houses to support the family. Roberto does odd jobs when he can get them and has been looking for steady work for some time.

Lupe has a hearing loss, and the teachers in the center keep telling Maria Elena and Roberto that they must take her to see a specialist. But they went once and there were so many papers to fill out, none of which they understood, and no one was there to translate for them—so they walked out and haven't gone back. The center staff is working to find them a translator so they can get the help that Lupe needs, but so far they haven't found one. Maria Elena is very worried about Lupe, and so is Roberto, but he is hesitant to put his name on any kind of papers that might bring him to the attention of the government. He just doesn't trust what might happen once the government becomes aware of him and his family. It was bad enough signing up for Head Start and for child care, but at least those papers were in Spanish and he knew what he was signing. He didn't have to depend on someone with limited Spanish trying to explain them to him. His neighbor tells him he's being paranoid about this, but Roberto's family has had some bad experiences with government officials, and he doesn't want to repeat them. Roberto is wary!

Roberto has never even thought of whether his is a "successful" family or not. He's too involved in the daily struggle for survival.

He is anxious that his family live according to the traditions he grew up with, but he sees all of them being changed by rubbing up against other cultures. He resists that change, but at the same time he appreciates what he and Maria Elena are learning about child rearing from their involvement with Head Start and the child care center. They are beginning to examine some of the "givens" of their own upbringing and thinking about whether they contribute to the goals they have for their children. They are most anxious to retain their culture and be the best parents they can be!

Junior's Family

The most vocal member of the third family is 12-month-old Junior. He cries all the time. The staff at the child care center tries hard to comfort him, but what works with other children doesn't work with Junior. The whole family—refugees from their homeland—are obviously suffering from having had to flee, but the loudest sufferer is Junior. The center staff has never had a baby in the program who has been so unhappy for so long. He cries all day, every day, except for the periods when he sleeps.

The staff doesn't know too much about Junior's family, except that they live with a number of relatives in a small house that they're pooling their money to buy. Although the house is crowded in the evenings and on weekends, there's no one home during the day to care for little Junior. Everyone's out working. Great-Grandma used to take care of him, but she's sick now and can barely care for herself. Perhaps he misses her, and that's why he cries so much.

Language must be a problem for Junior, too. No one in the center knows more than a word or two of his language, and that must be very scary for him. And he doesn't stop crying long enough to listen to English.

The staff has tried to find out about Junior's diet, but his mother is very vague. She doesn't speak English too well, so she leaves things like food decisions up to them. The center provides the food for the children, but the staff is anxious to respond to any special cultural or family food preferences. They just can't find out from Junior's family what those might be.

Like Roberto's family, Junior's family is also rubbing up against other cultures, but they are so busy surviving in the new country, with its different cultures and different languages, that they are in culture shock. They are still reacting to what is new and strange to them, and they are not yet able to take in any benefits from the broadened experience.

Michael's Family

The fourth family has one child enrolled in the child care center. Three-year-old Michael is a quiet boy with long dark eyelashes that sweep down on his cheeks when he lowers his eyes, which he does a good deal of the time. He is cautious and slow to warm up to people, but his slightly withdrawn manner has captured the hearts of the staff.

Michael's parents, Margaret and Beth, are a lesbian couple. Although the child comes every day, the staff has barely talked to his parents. They seem to move in and out of the center like shadows. Margaret usually brings Michael. She is friendly to staff but always in a hurry. Because the staff members have mixed feelings about this couple, several are rather glad the two women are so unobtrusive and seemingly unwilling to engage in conversation. However, one staff member has strong feelings about the bias this family may be experiencing in the center. She wants to change the atmosphere and be sure that the parents and the child feel comfortable and accepted. She has begun to introduce the subject of antibias regularly at staff meetings, and this has brought forth some discomfort among the staff. At the last meeting she pointed out that although the program is committed to "celebrating diversity," there is no physical evidence in the center that lesbian and gay couples are considered normal families. Pictures abound (on the walls and in books) that show all kinds of family configurations, except same-sex parents. No books in the center show gay or lesbian families.

"What can we do to make school more comfortable for and accepting of Michael and his family?" was the teacher's question to the rest of the staff.

"Good question," responded one teacher. "This is something we should talk about. I'm concerned about Michael," she added emphatically.

"I*'m* concerned about his parents as well!" said the first teacher, equally emphatically. "What can we do to raise their comfort level?"

The staff is still working on this question, because they are in conflict with each other about what should be done. They can't even agree about the idea of bringing in books and pictures of families like Michael's. Some feel strongly that it's an equity issue they are discussing; others are taking a moral or religious stance. In the meantime, it's easy to see the discomfort level rise in Michael and his parents as they pick up unspoken messages from various staff members.

Although Michael's parents have many traits of the successful family, they are unable to benefit from what the staff might have to offer them to increase their knowledge of child development and family relations because of limited communication.

Courtney's Family

Family 5 commands a good deal of staff attention for all sorts of reasons. Courtney, the mother, has been married before, and two of her four children are in the program. Roland, her 4-year-old, was abused by his father, and the family lives in fear that one day he'll arrive at school, claim his son, and take off with him. The staff has been warned of the situation and is aware of the restraining order that gives them the authority to refuse to let the father take Roland. Roland, after all his bad experiences, is fearful of men—and he doesn't get along with the other children, either.

Courtney, Roland's mother, is married to Richard, who is Native American. They have their own child, a 2 $\frac{1}{2}$-year-old named Soleil. Roland's half-sister looks more like her father than her mother, and her beauty is remarkable—literally. Adults passing through the center stop to discuss what a lovely child she is.

Soleil is remarkable in other ways too. She is intellectually mature far beyond her years, but socially she's still a baby. She confuses adults, who don't know what to think of her. They marvel at the way she is teaching herself to read but become distressed by the fact that she kicks, screams, and even bites when a child refuses to give her a toy that she wants to play with.

Courtney is in a drug recovery program and has just decided to continue her education. She wants to become a lawyer. Richard works in construction and he's going to college part-time to become a history teacher. He has very strong feelings about his heritage, which the teachers found out about last Thanksgiving when they put up pictures of Pilgrims and Indians on the walls.

One of the teachers was just stapling the last picture up when Richard arrived with Roland and Soleil. He stopped, stared intensely at the picture, then turned abruptly to the teacher and said, "I'm sorry, but it's offensive to me that you're using caricatures of my people as decorations. It feels as if you're making fun of my culture."

The teacher stopped, stapler in hand, shocked by his words. "I don't understand. Thanksgiving stands for friendship and love. That's what these pictures are about—brotherhood—people helping people."

"Maybe that's the way you see it," explained Richard, "but what I see is that you're celebrating a day that marks the beginning of the genocide of my people. I don't want my children to have any part of such a celebration." He left the room abruptly, taking the children with him.

Later, during nap time, the other teachers were shocked to hear such a different version of the happy holiday they had always celebrated. But they took the pictures down and agreed to stress the harvest aspects of Thanksgiving rather than give it a "historical slant."

Richard heard about this through Courtney, who brought the children back later in the day. When he arrived the next morning, children in hand, he remarked about the missing pictures to Roland's teacher and expressed his gratitude about the staff's willingness to see his point of view and make some changes in their celebration. As a cross-cultural family, Courtney and Richard are exploring where their concepts of a successful family coincide and where they collide.

The Jackson Family

Holidays are a big issue for the sixth family—the Jacksons—as well. They have three children in the program and are pleased with everything but the celebration of what they consider Christian holidays. At a recent parent meeting, they got caught in the middle of an argument between two groups of parents. It started when Mrs. Jackson asked the staff to downplay religious celebrations. "I don't want my children to learn someone else's religion," she remarked. "We'll teach our religion at home, so please leave religious observances out of the program."

One parent answered her by insisting that Christmas had nothing to do with religion. Two other parents rose to their feet, arguing loudly that it was a terrible shame that Christ had been removed from Christmas and that there ought to be more religion in the center rather than less.

When the director finally got the parents calmed down, Mrs. Jackson spoke up once again, this time about dietary differences. She was concerned that her children were being fed food that violated the dietary restrictions of her religion.

She spoke politely and with great concern. The director asked her to make an appointment for another time to discuss the problem.

Mrs. Jackson arrived the next day at the agreed-on time and found the director in her office waiting for her. The two had met here earlier: Before the family came into the program, they had several discussions about whether the oldest Jackson child, who has spina bifida, could be accommodated in his wheelchair. Several modifications to the environment were required, which Mr. Jackson worked on with the help of Sara and Richard, who both have carpentry skills.

Mrs. Jackson and the director expected to have a good talk this time, because they had gotten along well in the past. Mrs. Jackson expressed her feelings that the teachers were not watching what her children ate, and the director promised to do all she could to make sure that the Jackson children were carefully monitored at meal and snack times. She also asked Mrs. Jackson if she would be willing to do a cooking activity with the 4-year-old group and teach them how to make one of the special dishes of her culture. She agreed, and that was the beginning of her involvement in the program.

At present Mrs. Jackson is working night and day on a big fund-raiser for a climbing structure for the play yard. She's finding it very satisfying to use her talent, skills, and connections in the community to benefit the program and the children, some of whom, she realizes, are severely financially deprived. She has involved a number of other parents, and they are getting to know and appreciate each other in ways that only come from working together toward a common cause—something they could never have done by just attending parent meetings.

The Jacksons have a lot going for them as a successful family. But, like the rest of the families, they still have a way to go.

Comparing the Six Families

These six families have varying concepts, images, and dreams of what a successful family is. They all have many stresses in their lives. Their successes include varying degrees of the following:

+ Commitment
+ Attachment to each other
+ Individual independence and group interdependence

- Ability to give and receive nurturing
- Ability to get needs met
- Coping skills
- Methods of building self-esteem
- Effective communication
- Ability to pass on culture, goals, and values

Their stresses include the following:

- Poverty
- Special needs of their children
- Problems with substance abuse
- Divorce and custody issues
- Stepfamilies and blended families
- Lack of support
- Communication difficulties
- Inaccessible resources
- Bias issues

Besides being in the process of building toward success and experiencing stress, what else do all of these families have in common? They're in the same child care program. They love their children and want the best for them, although they have different ways of showing their love and different ideas about what "the best" is and how to achieve it.

How are they different? They represent different cultures and traditions, different family structures (with different degrees of outside acceptance of those family structures), and different degrees of match to the mainstream culture of the center. They also differ in their ability to handle the stress in their lives.

Real-Life Families: Some Statistics

According to the Children's Defense Fund (2004), the teen birth rates are going down. In 1990, 59.9 out of 1,000 females aged 15 to 19 gave birth to babies, while in 2002 the rate was 43.0. That's good news; however, the number of children raised in poverty is growing. In 2002, one in six children lived in a poverty-level family, as defined by an annual income below the government poverty level (Children's Defense Fund, 2004). That's 12.1 million children. Poverty makes meeting needs difficult, if not impossible. The Children's Defense Fund keeps track of the statistics affecting children. Here are some more:

- There were more poor children in 2002 than in the 1970s.
- The proportion of families leaving welfare without work increased from 50% to 58% between 1999 and 2002. Two-thirds of these families report running out of money to buy food.
- There were 1.8 million poor children living in female-headed families with no income from either work or welfare.

- A child from France, Canada, Germany, Britain, or Spain is less likely to be poor than an American child.
- An American child is 5 to 8 times as likely to be poor as a child in Sweden, Norway, or Finland.
- Many members of poor families work but don't receive enough payment to rise above poverty level.
- Many families above the poverty level don't make enough to afford food and rent.
- Poverty affects children's health, which affects education.
- The United States ranks 23rd in infant mortality rates among industrialized nations.

It is interesting that President Lyndon B. Johnson's War on Poverty was 40 years ago, yet children are still the largest group of poor people in the United States. We are the richest nation on earth—first in GDP (gross domestic product) among industrialized nations. We have the greatest number of millionaires and billionaires and are way out ahead in health technology, yet rank 18th in the percentage of children in poverty.

It's not that we don't know what to do to keep poverty factors from affecting child outcomes. We have found antipoverty policies that work. Two different projects provide examples of ways to make a difference in outcomes for children. An antipoverty experiment called the New Hope Project in Milwaukee, Wisconsin, showed that child outcomes can be affected by society support. The project provided an above-poverty income, health insurance, and child care. As a result children's literacy test scores improved and children showed more positive social behavior 5 years later. Another study, the Minnesota Family Investment Program, also found that supplementing income of poverty families results in a measurable difference in outcomes for their children. The results included improvements in children's behavior and school performance(Children's Defense Fund 2004).

Now think about the six families under stress in this chapter. Although poverty was a big factor in the majority of the six families, they had other stresses as well. All families have stress. Stress is part of life. When stress eats on people and overwhelms them, it has harmful effects, but stress doesn't have to be bad.

STRESS AS A POSITIVE FORCE

When the six families and the child care staff at the center to which they are all connected think about what to do to help their children, they can start by recognizing that stress isn't necessarily bad. We all need some stress in our lives. Stress can be a growth factor. A physical example of how stress is useful can be seen in the way a baby's bones form to enable the child to walk. The leg bones that connect to the hip socket have a different shape in the newborn than in the child about to walk. What makes the shape change to accommodate walking? Stress—the stress of weight being put on them. A similar example relates to old age. The older woman at risk for osteoporosis babies her bones by never exercising and creates the very condition she's trying to avoid—her bones grow weak and brittle. Her bones need some stress to help keep them strong.

Stress isn't necessarily bad—we all need some stress in our lives. Stress can be a growth factor.

Of course, too much stress isn't any better than too little. Again an example from physiology: Look at the sports injuries of children who overuse their pitching arms, for example. Irreparable damage occurs from too much stress.

What is too much stress for one family, or for one person, may be optimum stress for another. Some people are knocked down by seemingly minor setbacks; others manage much harder situations. Still others seem to take on adversity as a challenge and grow from it.

When I was first learning about child development, I took a trip to the high country above the California desert. There I observed a natural phenomenon that I have never forgotten: the bristlecone pine. I saw this gnarled, ancient tree, bowed by the wind and stunted by lack of water and the thin air and soil of its habitat, as the perfect symbol for the benefits of stress. Instead of weakening under adverse conditions, these trees grow stronger than other plant life in less stressful situations. Using their adversity to the maximum, they survive longer than any other living thing on earth. Somehow they take the hardships life has to offer and use them to their own advantage. Some children do that too.

We know that poverty, abuse, neglect, being shuffled around, lack of attachment, and not getting needs met can adversely affect children's lives. Obviously it is better for children to get what they need, be raised by people who care for them, have a stable home life, and meet loving acceptance inside and outside the home rather than having to live with abuse, neglect, bias, and discrimination. Yet we all know about "resilient children"—those children who, in spite of much hardship, manage to turn out with healthy personalities and find success and happiness in life.

WHAT WE CAN LEARN FROM STUDIES OF RESILIENT CHILDREN

Studies by Werner (1984, 1995; Werner & Smith, 1992) and others (Luthar, Cicchetti, & Becker, 2000) show that there are some protective factors and personality traits that are common to *resilient children*—children who have the psychological strength to recover from misfortune or who emerge intact from a history of severe distress. One vital factor that the children had in common was a sense of connectedness to someone in the early years. These children found attachment, usually in the 1st year (not necessarily to a parent). Many of the children whose parents were not able to meet their needs found or recruited surrogate parents, inside or outside the home. Werner uses the term *recruited* to indicate that attachment wasn't just by chance, that the children had more than a passive role. From this recruited attachment, the resilient children received enough attention and nurturing early on to gain a sense of trust. Their lives may have been marked by abandonment, either physical or emotional or both, but at some period they found someone to believe in them and care about them. Even if they were shuffled from family to family, never belonging anywhere, they found sources of support. They made connections, and those connections seem to have provided enough to keep them going in positive directions.

Resilient children have experienced a sense of connectedness at some point in their lives.

One reason these resilient children were able to make connections was that they had the ability to elicit positive responses from others. Even at a very young age, they were somehow able to gain other people's positive attention.

These children were problem-solvers, taking an active approach toward negotiating, communicating, and grappling with the obstacles that life presented to them. They had not only the willingness but also the skills to take an active rather than a passive role.

Another important commonality these resilient children had was that at some point during their lives they found themselves needed by someone else. They had responsibility thrust on them. They were required to help another person—a younger sibling, for example. Relating to someone else's helplessness gave them a sense of their own power.

Most important of all, perhaps, these children had a tendency to perceive their experiences constructively and each held a positive vision of a meaningful life. In spite of their hardships, life made sense. In other words, their attitude made all the difference in the world.

Interestingly enough, it wasn't just the resilient children identified by the study who were able to get over their unfortunate beginnings and move on to lead healthy, fulfilling lives. The other participants in the study—the ones who didn't have the above factors going for them—also were able to work beyond their early childhood problems. It took them longer, but by their 30s and 40s, most were living meaningful lives.

What can adults who live or work with children and have responsibility for their socialization learn from this research? How can children from families in stress be helped to be less vulnerable and, indeed, resilient? How can children grow up in stressful conditions such as poverty, family strife, instability, disabilities, bias, abuse, and neglect and not be harmed in their development? How can we help them grow in positive ways?

The key is to balance the stressful life events with protective factors. The stress must be decreased or the number of protective factors increased or, when possible, both. The protective factors are those just mentioned—a sense of connection, sources of support, skills for solving problems and for eliciting positive responses from others, and, above all, a positive attitude toward life and a feeling that it will all work out somehow.

HELPING ALL CHILDREN BECOME RESILIENT CHILDREN

How does that information translate into adult behavior? What are some guidelines for parents, teachers, caregivers, family child care providers, and others who work with children and families in stress?

1. *Provide support for the child and for the family.* Encourage connections; help build networks. Children and families need all the support they can get—both formal and informal. The Parent Services Project (PSP), started in California by Ethel Seiderman and now nationwide, specifically addresses this need for support for families by child care programs (Lee & Seiderman, 1998; Links, Beggs, & Seiderman, 1997). The idea behind PSP is that by supporting the family you make the family more able to support the child. One of PSP's

guiding principles is that support is important to all families and that social support networks reduce isolation and promote the well-being of the child, the family, and the community.

2. *Teach the skills necessary for making connections and gaining support.* Teach children social skills. Teach them ways to initiate contact and maintain it. This means being there with them while they are playing with peers to guide them toward effective ways to enter play and resolve the issues that come up while playing. Reinforce contacts with peers and adults. They'll learn better if they start early (even in infancy) and have a chance to practice with small numbers of people. Encourage families to focus on positive discipline techniques (see Chapter 7). Model prosocial behaviors, then pay attention to and reward such behaviors.

3. *Teach problem solving* (see Chapter 9). Crockenberg (1992) observed 95 mothers using negotiation with their 2-year-olds to get them to pick up toys. Crockenberg came up with some interesting conclusions. The effective strategies combined a directive with an explanation, persuasion, or accommodation. That way the mothers gave the message that their wishes were important but also the child's wishes were important. By using this approach, the mothers conveyed information to their children about the way conflicts with others can be resolved. When parents adopt negotiation as an approach to resolving conflicts, they teach their children long-term relationship skills that they can apply to peers.

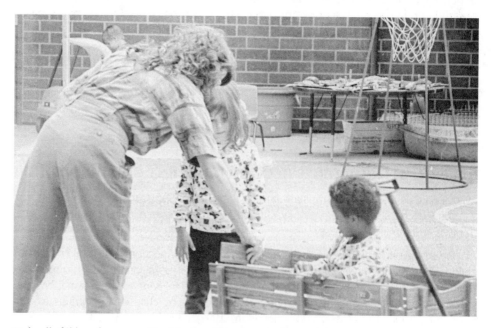

Help all children become resilient by teaching them problem solving.

4. *Give children responsibilities.* Require them to help out. Hook them up to someone who is less capable than they are and needs them. When chores at home or in child care are shared, children gain a sense of being important and belonging. In China, real work is brought into child care centers to be done by the children and then sent back to the factory where it originated. Making real contributions is important. In families with several children, older children can help care for younger ones. In child care centers where children are separated into groups by age, caring for each other can take the place of caring for someone younger. Also plants and animals require care, which can be done by children. In family child care and in other settings where there are mixed age groups, adults can give older children responsibilities for children younger than themselves.

5. *Most of all, provide role models.* Children and families need to see people they can identify with doing all the things just mentioned—finding support, demonstrating social skills and the ability to make connections, using problem-solving skills, and taking responsibility. For early childhood institutions, finding positive role models for children becomes part of the recruitment and hiring process. Training helps, too. In addition, children need role models who have faith that things will work out and that life has meaning. If adults don't have it, they must be seeking it. No one can tell another person just how to do that seeking. Certainly spiritual traditions and religious institutions are a possible path. Therapy can help, too.

I don't mean to downplay the effect that stressful conditions have on children's socialization by painting too positive a picture. Neither do I mean to overemphasize resiliency. Some obvious changes could make a difference in some families' lives so that unnecessary stress would be eliminated and children wouldn't need to be superresilient.

To end on a cheery note, here's what Galinsky (1989) says: "Things can be hard, but they don't have to do us in. It isn't whether good or bad things happen to you; it's how you handle them that matters" (pp. 2–3). She talks about how important it is to teach parents and their children to face problems, practice generating multiple solutions, figure out how to change what can be changed, and learn to cope with what can't. It's a matter of taking a can-do attitude and engaging in continuous problem-solving. It's also a matter of getting together as a society to face the conditions that create ever growing poverty and changing them.

School Success Linked to What Goes on at Home

It's not social class, family structure, parent's marital status, ethnic background, or the amount of money a family has that makes a difference in how well children eventually will do in school. What counts most is what goes on at home.

Parents can be poor, unmarried, and uneducated and still manage to groom their young children for a successful school career. It may be harder if one is poor, unmarried, and uneducated, but it is possible.

How do families manage to create early childhood experiences that result in future school success? They do it in a number of ways—including the way they relate to the children, the kind of home life they provide for them, and what they teach them.

First, children must be protected. Families who groom their children for future success in school know how to protect them, keeping them from physical and psychological harm. They set limits. They monitor whereabouts and behavior.

These families see their children as capable and hold a vision of the future that includes the child as an able student. They encourage learning of all sorts by the ways they relate to their children, how they talk to them, and the activities they provide.

They teach their children social skills, defining appropriate behavior for them. They give them feedback to increase their sensitivity to others. They do this in a warm and nurturing way, creating an emotionally supportive environment that emphasizes decision making.

They help them learn to express themselves. They give them chances to develop a sense of responsibility and learn both leadership and follower skills. They encourage them to concentrate, focus, be attentive, and follow through. Most of all, they respect their children and themselves.

SUMMARY

This chapter started by examining traits of successful families and went on to look at a lot of problems. It may seem that the situations of some of the families portrayed are fairly bad. Yet, they are not hopeless, and each is working on acquiring more and more of the traits of successful families outlined at the beginning. Some arrived at the center already knowing about these traits; others are learning them from each other and from the center staff. In addition, each of the families is connected to some of the many community resources that address the variety of difficulties they are having. The next chapter looks at the community resources available to help families meet challenges, to alleviate some of their stress, and to support them in their coping.

FOR DISCUSSION

1. Give examples of three of the traits of successful families that are present in a family that you know.

2. Have you ever known a family like one of the families in this chapter? How was the family the same as the one in the chapter? How was it different?

3. Have you ever known a resilient child? What do you think made this child resilient? Did this child share the common protective factors and personality traits described in the chapter?

4. Give examples of some things you could do to help all children become resilient.

5. Think of an example of how the following sentence plays out in someone's life: "It isn't whether good or bad things happen to you; it's how you handle them that matters."

REFERENCES

Akbar, N. (2003). *Akbar papers in African psychology*. Tallahassee, FL: Mind Productions.

Blimes, J. (2004). *Beyond behavior management: The six life skills children need to thrive in today's world*. St. Paul, MN: Redleaf Press.

Carnegie Task Force on Meeting the Needs of Young Children. (1994, July). Starting points: Executive summary of the report of the Carnegie Corporation of New York Task Force on Meeting the Needs of Young Children. *Young Children, 47*(5), 58–60.

Casper, V. (2003, January). Very young children in lesbian- and gay-headed families: Moving beyond acceptance. *Zero to Three, 23*(3), 18–26.

Children's Defense Fund. (2004). *The state of America's children 2004*. Washington, DC: Children's Defense Fund.

Crockenberg, S. (1992, April). How children learn to resolve conflicts in families. *Zero to Three, 12*(5), 11–13.

DeJong, L. (2003, March). Using Erikson to work more effectively with teenage parents. *Young Children, 58*(2), 87–95.

Galinsky, E. (1989, May). Problem solving. *Young Children, 44*(4), 2–3.

Korfmacher, J., & Marchi, I. (2002, November). The helping relationship in a teen parenting program. *Zero to Three, 21*(2), 21–26.

Lee, L., & Seiderman, E. (1998). *Families matter: The Parent Services Project*. Cambridge, MA: Harvard Family Research Project.

Links, G., Beggs, M., & Seiderman, E. (1997). *Serving families*. Fairfax, CA: Parent Services Project.

Luthar, S. S., Cicchetti, D., & Becker, B. (2000). The construct of resilience: A critical evaluation and guidelines for future work. *Child Development, 71*, 543–562.

Morrison, J. W. (2001, Spring). Supporting biracial children's identity development. *Childhood Education, 77*(3), 134–138.

Odom, S. L., Teferra, T., & Kaul, S. (2004, September). An overview of international approaches to early intervention for young children with special needs and their families. *Young Children, 59*(5), 38–43.

Okagaki, L., & Diamond, K. (2000, May). Responding to cultural and linguistic differences in the beliefs and practices of families with young children. *Young Children, 55*(3), 74–80.

Parke, R. D., & O'Neil, R. (2000). The influence of significant others on learning about relationships: From family to friends. In R. S. L. Mills & S. Duck (Eds.), *The developmental psychology of personal relationships* (pp. 15–47). New York: Wiley.

Payne, R. K. (2003). *A framework for understanding poverty*. Highlands, TX: Aha Process.

Seploch, H. (2004, September). Family ties: Partnerships for learning: Conferencing with families. *Young Children, 59*(5), 96–100.

Stonehouse, A., & Gonzalez-Mena, J. (2004). *Making links: A collaborative approach to planning and practice in early childhood services*. Castle Hills, NSW, Australia: Pademelon Press.

Swick, K. (2004). *Empowering parents, families, schools, and communities during the early childhood years*. Champaign, IL: Stipes.

Werner, E. E. (1984, November). Research in review: Resilient children. *Young Children, 40*(1), 68–72.

Werner, E. E. (1995, June). Resilience in development. *Current Directions in Psychological Science, 4*(3), 81–85.

Werner, E. E., & Smith, R. S. (1992). *Overcoming the odds: High risk children from birth to adulthood*. Ithaca, NY: Cornell University Press.

FURTHER READING

Akbar, N. (2003). *Akbar papers in African psychology*. Tallahassee, FL: Mind Productions.

Alderete-Baker, E. (1998). *Internalized achievement-related motives of Native American women*. Unpublished doctoral dissertation.

Allen, P. G. (1998). *Off the reservation*. Boston: Beacon.

Beaglehole, R. (1983). Validating all families. *Interracial Books for Children Bulletin, 14*(7, 8), 24–26.

Bell, D. (1992). *Faces at the bottom of the well: The permanence of racism*. New York: Basic Books.

Bernhard, J. K., Freire, M., Torres, F., & Nirdosh, S. (1998, Spring–Summer). Latin Americans in a Canadian primary school: Perspectives of parents, teachers, and children on cultural identity and academic achievement. *Canadian Journal of Regional Science*, 19(3), 217–237.

Blimes, J. (2004). *Beyond behavior management: The six life skills children need to thrive in today's world*. St. Paul, MN: Redleaf Press.

Brown, J. L., & Pollitt, E. (1996, February). Malnutrition, poverty, and intellectual development. *Scientific American*, 274(2), 38–43.

Casper, V. (2003, January). Very young children in lesbian- and gay-headed families: Moving beyond acceptance. *Zero to Three*, 23(3), 18–26.

Children's Defense Fund. (2004). *The state of America's children 2004*. Washington, DC: Children's Defense Fund.

Chow, E. N., Wilkinson, D., & Zinn, B. (1996). *Common bonds, different voices*. Newbury Park, CA: Sage.

Clark, K. E., & Ladd, G. W. (2000). Connectedness and autonomy support in parent-child relationships: Links to children's socio-emotional orientation and peer relationships. *Developmental Psychology*, 36, 485–498.

Clay, J. W. (1990). Working with lesbian and gay parents and their children. *Young Children*, 45(3), 31–35.

Coll, C. G., Lamberty, G., Jenkins, R., McAdoo, H. P., Crnic, K., Wasik, B., Hanna, G., & Vazquez, H. (1996). An integrative model for the study of developmental competencies in minority children. *Child Development*, 67, 1891–1914.

Comer, J. P., & Poussaint, A. E. (1992). *Raising black children*. New York: Plume.

Cummins, J. (1996). *Negotiating identities: Education for empowerment in a diverse society*. Ontario, CA: California Association for Bilingual Education.

DeJong, L. (2003, March). Using Erikson to work more effectively with teenage parents. *Young Children*, 58(2), 87–95.

Delpit, L. (1995). *Other people's children: Cultural conflict in the classroom*. New York: New Press.

Dorris, M. (1978). Why I'm *not* thankful for Thanksgiving. *Interracial Books for Children Bulletin*, 9(7), 6–9.

Fadiman, A. (1997). *The spirit catches you and you fall down: A Hmong child, her American doctors, and the collision of two cultures*. New York: Noonday.

Fernea, E. W. (1995). *Children in the Muslim Middle East*. Austin: University of Texas Press.

Gonzalez-Mena, J. (1997, July). Cross-cultural conferences. *Exchange*, 116, 55–57.

Harkness, S., & Super, C. M. (Eds.). (1996). *Parents' cultural belief systems*. New York: Guilford.

Harwood, R. L., Miller, J. G., & Irizarry, N. L. (1995). *Culture and attachment: Perceptions of the child in context*. New York: Guilford.

Hildebrand, V., Phenice, L. A., Gray, M. M., & Hines, R. P. (1996). *Knowing and serving diverse families*. Upper Saddle River, NJ: Merrill/Prentice Hall.

Huntsinger, C. S., Huntsinger, P. R., Ching, W.-D., & Lee, C.-B. (2000, November). Understanding cultural contexts fosters sensitive caregiving of Chinese American children. *Young Children*, 55(6), 7–15.

Kagiticibasi, C. (1996). *Family and human development across cultures*. Mahwah, NJ: Erlbaum.

Korfmacher, J., & Marchi, I. (2002, November). The helping relationship in a teen parenting program. *Zero to Three*, 21(2), 21–26.

Landau, S., & McAninch, C. (1993, May). Young children with attention deficits. *Young Children*, 48(4), 49–58.

Lee, L. (1997, July). Working with non-English-speaking families. *Exchange*, 116, 57–58.

Luthar, S. S., Cichetti, D., & Becker, B. (2000). The construct of resilience: A critical evaluation and guidelines for future work. *Child Development*, 71, 543–562.

McLoyd, V. (1990). The impact of economic hardship on black families and children: Psychological distress, parenting, and socioemotional development. *Child Development*, 61, 311–346.

Moore, E. K., & McKinley, M. K. (1972). Parent involvement/control in child development programs. In D. N. McFadden (Ed.), *Early childhood development programs and services: Planning for action* (pp. 77–82). Washington, DC: National Association for the Education of Young Children.

Morrison, J. W. (2001, Spring). Supporting biracial children's identity development. *Childhood Education*, 77(3), 134–138.

Neighbors, H. W., & Jackson, J. S. (Eds.). (1996). *Mental health in black America*. Newbury Park, CA: Sage.

Odom, S. L., Teferra, T., & Kaul, S. (2004, September). An overview of international approaches to early intervention for young children with special needs and their families. *Young Children* 59(5), 38–43.

Okagaki, L., & Diamond, K. (2000, May). Responding to cultural and linguistic differences in the beliefs and practices of families with young children. *Young Children*, 55(3), 74–80.

Payne, R. K. (2003). *A framework for understanding poverty*. Highlands, TX: Aha Process.

Randolph, S. M., & Koblinsky, S. A. (2001, August/September). The sociocultural context of infant mental health in African American families. *Zero to Three, 22*(1), 29–37.

Rogoff, B. (1990). *Apprenticeship in thinking*. New York: Oxford University Press.

Rogoff, B., Stott, F., & Bowman, B. (1996). Child development knowledge: A slippery base for practice. *Early Childhood Research Quarterly, 11*(2), 169–184.

Seploch, H. (2004, September). Family ties: Partnerships for learning: Conferencing with families. *Young Children, 58*(5), 96–100.

Soto, L. D. (1991, January). Understanding bilingual/bicultural young children. *Young Children, 46*(2), 30–35.

Swick, K. (2004). *Empowering parents, families, schools, and communities during the early childhood years*. Champaign, IL: Stipes.

Tobaissen, D. P., & Gonzalez-Mena, J. (1998). *A place to begin: Working with parents on issues of diversity*. Oakland: California Tomorrow.

Valdes, G. (1996). *Con respeto: Bridging the distances between culturally diverse families and schools*. New York: Teachers College Press.

PART 3

The Community
Socialization in the Community Context

Part 3 looks at the broader issues of socialization. We examined the child's developmental issues (Part 1) unfolding within a family context, which also included child care as a child-rearing environment and a sort of extended family context (Part 2). Now we view the child's socialization in a community context. This socialization occurs in the family's immediate community—the group they identify with and/or the people who live in proximity to them—and also in the greater society and its institutions. We look at how television can influence the child and give messages that conflict with the goals and values of the family and the society. We examine how racism and classism enter into the socialization process.

We also look at child abuse. Everyday 2,455 children in the United States are confirmed as abused or neglected—that's 12.3 out of every 1,000 children (Children's Defense Fund, 2004). What are some of the factors contributing to child abuse? What puts families at risk for damaging their children in the socialization process? Families in which abuse is present tend to be isolated from the community. That's an issue that Part 3 addresses—families and social networks. Many families don't know how to get the support they need. They are alone with their child rearing.

Parents who abuse their children often were themselves abused as children. The model they grew up with was that love hurts. Affection was coupled with pain. Because they are often isolated, they have no healthy models. They know no other ways to approach child rearing.

Isolation also creates the possibility that parents will hold unrealistic expectations of their children. They don't have basic child development information that spells out needs and capabilities at each stage. They expect far more from children than their developing abilities allow. For example, an abusive parent may expect her baby to understand her needs and take care of them. Perhaps she expects her baby to know that his crying is getting on her nerves. She tells him to stop, expecting that he can control himself. He can't. When the baby doesn't perform as expected, the parent may try to beat him into submission, seeing it as a matter of his will against hers. This child may learn early to read his mother's signals, stretching every capability he has to prevent himself from being abused. Abused children become very wary, and many learn early to care for their parents in surprisingly mature ways. Those children are robbed of their childhoods.

Abuse occurs because the parents didn't get their own needs met in their family of origin and don't know how to get them met now. The needy little child in the parent competes with the needy little child the parent is raising. But there is no competition; the parent's needs win out because he or she is bigger and stronger. Abusive parents don't see that they are the ones who should be parenting the child and not the reverse.

But it's important to realize that although children who grew up in abusive families may be more likely to become abusive parents, it's not inevitable. Only one-third of abused children grow up to be abusive parents (Cicchetti & Toth, 1998).

Abuse occurs in all kinds of families, not just the ones who are economically challenged and lack education, though that particular group of families is more likely to abuse their children (Duncan & Brooks-Gunn, 2000). The difference is the ratio of risk factors to protective factors. Protective factors include a positive marital relationship and a supportive social network plus availability of community resources. Couple those with education, above average intelligence, and good health—and you have a family less likely to abuse its children than a family that lacks those protective factors. Children who are abused are usually in families with multiple problems, including financial issues, lack of education, little support, isolation, unemployment, substance abuse, and dysfunctional behavior such as a parent who is overly self-involved and lacks the ability to be sensitive to the child and his or her needs (Cicchetti & Toth, 1998).

It's more likely to be the mother who abuses the child, probably because she spends more time with him or her than anyone else. Some mothers are also isolated, which contributes to the risk of abuse. Child abuse is more likely to occur in large families and to children under age 3. If a number of risk factors are present in a family, the personal characteristics of a particular child may be contributing factors resulting in that child becoming the abused child.

A serious problem lies in the neighborhoods many children grow up in. Some children live in high-risk neighborhoods and others in low-risk ones. The high-risk neighborhoods lack social resources including informal ones such as friends, neighbors, and relatives. People in high-risk neighborhoods are more likely to be exploited than supported (Leventhal & Brooks-Gunn, 2000), which relates to the isolation factor. Social isolation has long been associated with higher rates of abuse (Golden, 2000).

Obviously child abuse is not just an individual concern; it is also a community concern. It needs the help of the community to stop. Many steps are being taken in that direction. Programs that work on parents' self-esteem, educate them about child development and child-rearing practices, and provide support networks have been found to lower rates of abuse (Golden, 2000).

An important part of addressing the child abuse problem is mandated reporting. Those who work with children or their families are required to report suspected abuse to the authorities. The purpose of this legal and moral mandate is to save children and help families. The focus is on family support and prevention rather than just on detection and punishment. Isolated families must be drawn into the community, and that's just what is happening all over the country.

Though illegal in this country at present, child abuse as a way of socializing children worked toward a special societal need in the past. Cultures through history have used abusive child-rearing approaches in the family to create the tough, warrior-type men and submissive women that the society valued and needed for protection and survival. It makes sense to teach children to withstand pain, to conquer feelings of fear, and to armor themselves in a society in which war is a constant reality. Those most able to fight (men) must be ready to kill and be killed to protect the group. Women, who, in general, are not as capable on the front lines, are needed to serve behind the lines to take care of the warrior men. It's easy to see where gender inequity arose when one acknowledges this model. Abusing children can prepare them for this kind of future, in which basic needs and feelings must be put last and the survival of the group is what counts.

But it is time now for us, as a society, as a world community, to put aside the dominator model. We can no longer look to war as a means of group survival. A war that gets out of hand can easily kill us all—and the rest of life on earth. We must look beyond war to other means of solving problems. The survival of the planet depends on finding peaceful solutions. Outlawing child abuse and teaching healthy ways of raising children is a good start.

We must go further. We, as a society, must make some changes in the conditions that work against family health and functionality and the ability to socialize children in positive ways. We must take a good, long look at the equality principle on which this country was founded and take further steps to eradicate racism, classism, and sexism, as well as educational, social, economic, and political inequities. Change takes individual effort. It also takes individuals working together. The book ends on this note—giving a view of how we can use advocacy to bring about the healthy changes that are needed for the future of America.

To become an advocate and make changes, all of us need to see that it is in our own best interests that our country be made up of healthy families living in healthy communities. Those who live on the other side of town can't ignore the poverty that lies just across the tracks because it isn't part of their lives. Perhaps we don't see the connection right now, but we must become aware of the connection of our country's present condition and how the future will unfold. The success of the country lies in the success of its families and its communities. It's all related, affecting each and every one of us.

In spite of the notion of equality on which America was founded, we've been handed a picture of society as a hierarchy—with some on the bottom, some in the middle, and some at the top. We unconsciously operate out of the model. I'd like to suggest that it is more realistic to imagine society as a net. Have you ever climbed on a cargo net—one of those rope affairs stretched on a wooden climbing structure in the park or playground? When you are on it alone, your every movement affects the entire net. Then, when you are sitting oh so still and someone else climbs on it, you are greatly affected. No matter how hard you try to stay still, the net moves this way and that.

Society is like that. What happens way over in another part may be out of the range of your senses, but it affects you—it affects us all. We need to acknowledge our interconnectedness. We aren't just individuals in families—we are all part of the community of Americans and of the world beyond!

REFERENCES

Children's Defense Fund. (2004). *The state of America's children* 2004. Washington, DC: Children's Defense Fund.

Cicchetti, D., & Toth, S. L. (1998). Perspectives on research and practice in developmental psychopathology. In W. Damon (Gen. Ed.), I. E. Sigel, & K. A. Renninger (Vol. Eds.), *Handbook of child psychology*: Vol. 4. *Child psychology in practice* (pp. 479–583). New York: Wiley.

Duncan, G. O., & Brooks-Gunn, J. (2000). Family parenting, welfare reform, and child development. *Child Development*, 71, 188–195.

Golden, O. (2000). The federal response to child abuse and neglect. *American Psychologist*, 55, 1050–1053.

Leventhail, T., & Brooks-Gunn, J. (2000). The neighborhoods they live in: The effects of neighborhood residence upon child and adolescent outcomes. *Psychological Bulletin*, 126(2), 309–337.

CHAPTER 13

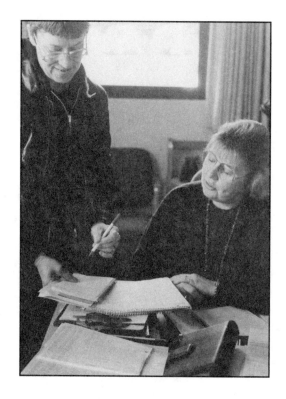

Community Resources

In *this chapter you'll discover* . . .

- ◆ What isolation can do to a family
- ◆ Social networks and community resources
- ◆ Why families need more support than ever before
- ◆ How six families use and contribute to community resources
- ◆ How to go about looking for a community resource

The preceding chapter examined what makes a successful family—the traits that allow the system and its members to function effectively. It also looked at six families under stress who are struggling along the path to becoming successful. This chapter looks at the community's contribution to helping families in their struggles. We'll examine how the community and the institutions and people in it support the family and help it function.

Remember, this book is about the socialization of children. You may wonder what "community resources" have to do with that subject. For families to socialize their children in healthy ways, many have needs that exceed their resources. Few families are entirely self-sufficient. All depend on their community and the resources in it. Some families are more able to seek out those resources than others. That's why it is important for those who work with children and families—such as teachers and child care providers—to understand what the resources are and how to access them, so they can advise families.

SOCIAL NETWORKS

Some families already see themselves as part of a larger social network, and they know both how to contribute to and make use of this network. They do not isolate themselves from the outside community if they can help it. They have a broad perspective that includes the world beyond the family, and they use feedback from that world. They are able to give and receive help from the outside social network.

Some families don't seek help or support from the larger community. They prefer to see themselves as self-sufficient and regard outside support as a sign of weakness. Others see themselves as part of family or kinship networks but hesitate to use the formal institutions that have been set up to help them. They may also regard needing outside help as a sign of weakness, or perhaps they have just never considered it. Many families have no idea what is available in their communities. Some of these families get along fine; others experience a feeling of isolation.

Isolation has a number of negative effects on families. It limits role models for children. It can lead to a sense of hopelessness. And it can even lead to child abuse. (See the introduction to Part 3 for more information about child abuse.)

Developing a Broad Base of Support

In healthy families each member has a broad base of support and knows how to get strokes from people outside the immediate family. Without such a broad base of support, undue pressure falls on those within the family; if those who usually give strokes are unable to do so, the individual is left depleted.

How does one know that his or her support base is broad enough? An exercise called "stroke pie" was discussed in Chapter 10 as a means to help you examine your own stroke sources. The idea is to use pie wedges to represent the people who give you strokes. If you have just a limited number in your pie, you may be overly dependent on a few people.

In healthy families, each member has a broad base of support and knows how to get strokes from people outside the immediate family.

Here are sample stroke pies of two people, Kim and Jennifer:

Kim assigned three-quarters of the pie to her boyfriend and the remaining quarter-slice to her mother. Then came the day that her mother discovered she had cancer, which was about the time the boyfriend found someone else. Kim's strokes disappeared all at once, and she had no one to turn to for support.

Jennifer used to be in that position, too: She was dependent on her husband for most of her strokes, with a few coming from her sister. But when she became a parent and discovered that she needed to give out more strokes than she got back, she knew she'd better broaden her base of support. She purposely developed a close relationship with two mothers she had met in her Lamaze class and another mother she met in the park. She not only started swapping child care with these women but also used them for information and for nurturing too.

Four years after Jennifer's son was born, her stroke pie looked very different from the way it had looked when she first became a mother. Her pie was now divided into 19 pieces, with friends, relatives, neighbors, son, office mates, parenting support group, and two jogging buddies all represented by slices. Her husband's huge slice was cut down to less than a quarter of the pie, and their relationship was blossoming since she had quit depending on him and her sister so heavily to meet all her emotional needs.

Jennifer created a social network for herself. Each individual and each family has a stroke pie that comprises their social network. Each looks slightly different.

Forms Social Networks May Take

In some families, individual members have their own social networks. In others, the family shares a network that consists of individuals and groups that comprise what can be thought of as a greater family, or an extended family. Some families are attached to a number of people beyond their own relatives in formal and informal ways. In a Mexican family, for example, this attachment may include, besides relatives, *compadres*—the children's godparents. *Compadres* are more than friends; they have a special kind of family relationship even though they may not have blood ties. Other families have special friends who are "aunts and uncles" to the younger generation. They are like family but are not blood relatives.

For some families, the neighborhood where they live may be the most important part of the social network. Neighbors can become a close-knit group that serves as a mutual aid society—sharing resources, providing guidance for children, and contributing to the social life of its members through periodic gatherings and celebrations of all sorts. These kinds of neighborhoods are becoming more scarce as the American population increases in mobility and at the same time isolates itself from those who live nearby, but they still exist in some places.

For some families, a religious institution or spiritual practice group serves the same functions as the close-knit neighborhood described earlier. It provides friendship, a social life, mutual aid, social services, support, counseling, and education, along with worship services, celebrations, and/or spiritual guidance.

Community Institutions That Serve Families

Other formal and informal groups and institutions with specialized functions make up a part of the social network of the community. Some of them have been around since the country began, such as police and fire departments; others are just now in the process of developing in response to changing needs.

Four ongoing trends illustrate needs for formal and informal support for families. Those trends are increasing numbers of mothers of infants and young children in the workforce, the growing challenge for low-income families to attain economic self-sufficiency, the feminization of poverty, and teenage parenting.

◆ *Employed mothers.*   More mothers than ever before are working. Adding to the trend are the changes in the welfare system, which means that mothers of children of infants are a fast-growing group in the labor force. Many of these women are single heads of families who are the only source of financial support of their families. One out of three families with young children earns less than $25,000 a year, while their annual child care costs can reach $4,000 to $10,000. Others—mothers in two-parent households—are working to make ends meet because one salary isn't enough. Two parents working full-time, earning minimum wage, only bring in $21,400 a year together (Children's Defense Fund, 2000, p. 46). The response to this current trend by the greater society has been to provide outside child care in a number of forms. Government, schools, employers, churches, corporations, and individuals are getting involved in the child care scene.

◆ *Economic challenges.*   Growing numbers of families today find themselves in acute economic distress. Because parents are unable to work for a variety of reasons or are working for wages that keep the family mired down in the bog of poverty, children are greatly influenced by lack of money, food, and even shelter. The community response to this problem is lagging far behind the need, as witnessed by the numbers of homeless in many communities.

◆ *The feminization of poverty.*   Someone once said that most women are just one husband away from poverty. Look around you. Who is most needing financial help? Women. One in five children are in poverty; of those children, 9 out of 10 live in female-headed households. A generation ago most poor people were old. That has changed now as a result of a local, state, and national response to conditions and problems of the elderly. The poverty rate today for the elderly is 10.5% and has never been lower (Children's Defense Fund, 2000, pp. 5–6). The composition of the new poverty group is different, and community response has been slow, unfortunately.

◆ *Teenage parenting.*   With a good deal of attention to the issue of teenagers giving birth, there has been progress in slowing the rate since 1991. In l998, the teen birthrate fell by 2%. The overall birthrate for 15- to 17-year-olds reached a record low of 30.4 per 1,000. The drop is due to federal, state, and local efforts to support teen pregnancy prevention (Children's Defense Fund, 2000, p. 34). However, the rates are still high compared to other countries. There is still a need to devote significant resources to reducing the rate further. Because 83% of teen parents are from low-income families (Alan Guttmacher Institute, 1999), they are often undereducated and have trouble finding employment. They may also be undersupported and struggle greatly through the early years of their children's lives. The number of teen parents contributes to the feminization of poverty. The children of teen parents often grow up themselves to be teen parents. A mother of a daughter who is now 4 says, "My mother had her first baby at 15; so did I. Now my daughter is 4, and I have about 10 years to figure out how to keep this pattern from continuing." Programs exist across the country to address the needs of teen parents, including infant programs on high school campuses that provide parent education for young mothers and contribute to their skills and self-esteem by allowing them to finish school while their babies are cared for.

FAMILIES USING COMMUNITY RESOURCES

Let's take a look now at how the families introduced in the preceding chapter reflect these trends and how they connect with the social networks outside themselves. Notice how they both use and contribute to the community resources available.

Sara's Family

Remember Sara? She's the 20-year-old with two sons—Ty and Kyle—who is in nursing school at a community college. She went through a very difficult period, being homeless for awhile. But by now she's an expert in the resources her community has to offer. She's tied into the financial aid program at her college, which gives her support. She also receives child care in an on-campus subsidized program for low-income students, which is funded by the state. She gives back to these two community resources by serving on the advisory committee of the financial aid program and by contributing volunteer time to the child care center. She was asked to help with fund-raising for the center but made a decision to take care of herself and her sons by declining. She knows that fund-raising can be very time-consuming, and with her studies and her family, time is at a premium right now.

When Sara was pregnant the first time, she received assistance from WIC (Women, Infants, and Children), a federally funded nutrition program designed to help ensure that children get the nourishment they need through the prenatal period and into the 1st year of life.

Ty was born prematurely, which made life even harder for a time. Going to a support group for preemie parents for awhile helped Sara get through this period. The group, which was hosted by her local hospital, was led by a social worker and funded by a special foundation grant.

By the time of her second pregnancy (which resulted from being raped while she was homeless), the WIC funding had been cut in half, and she could no longer get into the program, which was unfortunate because she and Ty often didn't have food. She worried about her unborn baby a lot during that period. Kyle too was born prematurely, and by then the funding for the preemie support group had also been cut, so she was on her own. But she did finally get into a teen parent program that enabled her to finish high school. Now she has moved on to college with a plan and hope for her future through the vocational program she is in.

When Sara first went on the Temporary Assistance to Needy Families (TANF) program, she lived in terror that someone would decide that she was neglecting her children and take them away from her. She had seen this happen to several women during her homeless period. She couldn't bear the thought of losing Ty and Kyle, so she was very cautious whenever she discussed anything with her social worker. She felt she had to protect herself. It took her a long time to decide that the worker understood her situation, saw her as a good mother, and wasn't about to report her for neglect to Child Protective Services, which is the government agency in her county that handles child abuse cases.

Recently Sara discovered a food co-op where, by paying a small amount to join and volunteering a few hours, she can get a good deal of food at very reasonable rates. She's also discovered that she can get family counseling services, which the child care center recommended because of Ty's attention deficit problem and Kyle's aggressive behavior (you may remember that he bites). The director of the child care program is also talking about referring both boys to a special education preschool program run by the county office of education. Sara is hesitant about taking the next steps for this service because she hates the thought of changing programs. Besides, the hours of the special ed program don't fit her school schedule very well and she'd still need child care. Transportation would be a problem, and she doesn't want her boys shuffled back and forth from one program to another, so she's dragging her feet on following up her investigation of what could be done further for her children. What she doesn't know is that there is a strong movement to include children with special needs in programs with their typically developing peers. It's possible that she can get the special services her boys may need without moving them to another program.

Because of her low-income status, Sara is entitled to health benefits from the government, but she sometimes has a hard time finding a doctor who will see her and the boys.

Sara has been in a lot worse shape in the past than she is now. She remembers eating once a week at a community dinner for the homeless, served in a church by a local women's service group. Sara had very mixed feelings about being there. She couldn't help being grateful, of course, but she felt strangely alienated from everyone there, not only from the other homeless people but also from the good-hearted women who donated their time, energy, and casseroles. She hates being on the receiving end of charity!

Christmas always brought up the same awful feelings; it still does, even now. It's great that the community rallies once a year to provide gifts for her boys and a turkey for her table, but every year she has those same mixed feelings of gratitude, shame, and anger. She'll be glad when she gets through school and can support herself. Then she'll be the one doing the giving for a change. She can hardly wait.

Roberto's Family

Roberto's family, if you remember, is composed of his wife Maria Elena, his 4-year-old daughter Lupe, and baby Paco. Roberto at first resisted signing up for any community resources because he was too proud; besides, he was suspicious of anything connected to any government. But one day he found himself persuaded to send his daughter to Head Start, a federally funded preschool program for low-income children. He discovered early on that with Head Start comes a community aide, who helps the family get connected to other services that they need, many of which are provided right at school for the children, such as vision and hearing screening. The hearing screening proved to be a problem because they discovered that Lupe has a hearing deficit, and now the family is expected to do something about it. Roberto is convinced that it would have gone away on its own if it hadn't been discovered. Roberto and Maria Elena went to the place the school told them to go, but there were many papers to fill out and no one spoke their language, so they left. Now Roberto feels very uncomfortable every time he gets a notice from school urging him to follow up on the referral they gave him.

While he was still getting used to all the changes in his life that came as the result of enrolling Lupe in Head Start, Maria Elena announced that she wanted to take classes in English as a second language at the adult school. "I won't have time to drive you," Roberto told her firmly, convinced that that would end the matter.

"I can take the bus," said Maria Elena.

"And who will take care of Paco?" asked Roberto.

"They have child care at the school," Maria Elena shot back.

Roberto was stunned. This had all been worked out without him. What would happen to him if his family didn't need him any more? He felt shaken.

He needed to talk to somebody, so he went first to his *compadre*, Juan, godfather of Lupe, and told him how he felt. Just talking about it made him feel better. Then he went to his priest and talked some more. The priest suggested counseling, but Roberto thought that would show the world that something was wrong with him, and that was exactly the problem he wished to avoid. He felt that enough was wrong with him because of what was happening in his family; he certainly didn't want to announce to the world that he was weak and needed help. The priest made another suggestion, however, that Roberto followed up on. He told him about a clinic that might help with Lupe's problem. It was a community effort run by bilingual volunteers, so he would at least be able to talk to someone in his own language—someone who knew something about medicine. Roberto felt much better when he came home from talking to the priest. Maria Elena noticed the difference and gave him a big hug when he came in the door.

Junior's Family

The refugee family is so busy working that they haven't had time to find out about any resources in their community except for child care; and that isn't working out too well, because Junior cries all the time he's there. The family has been relocated several times, and Junior seems to be expressing the suffering all of them feel. Being crowded is nothing new to this family; they've always lived in close quarters with the extended family in one residence. Their house is packed most of the time. They have to eat in shifts, but they work in shifts, too, so that comes out all right.

One thing they're glad of is that Junior doesn't cry at home the way he does at the center. It's not that crying babies haven't always been part of their lives, but now Great-Grandma is sick, and they worry about disturbing her. Oh, yes, they do use a community resource—a home health nurse who comes in to look after Great-Grandma. Although they were suspicious at first of medical care that they didn't understand, they decided it wouldn't be such a bad idea to learn about how things work in this country. The only problem is that language creates terrible barriers, and they don't understand as much as they want to. They often wonder what the nurse is doing and what the various medications are for, but they have to wait until the oldest cousin, who understands English, gets home to find out. Even then things don't always make sense because the approach to health care is so different.

There have been some scary misunderstandings about health matters—like the time Great-Grandma had a reaction to some medication and they had to take her to the hospital emergency room. That was a horrible experience because they had no idea what was going on. And when they put her in the hospital for 2 days, it was very frustrating because the medical staff wouldn't let the family take care of her. In fact, they were asked to leave. They didn't understand this at all!

The family is very lonely at times when they think of home, but they are learning to make this country home. They know how to support each other, pooling resources and knowledge, which helps a lot. They aren't used to getting outside help, so that's something new to them. They are learning English rapidly and soon will have an expanded view of the community they live in and what is available to them.

Michael's Family

Michael, a 3-year-old, is the son of a lesbian couple. Michael and his parents are isolated from many of the social networks that support other families. They don't want to be, but they have had bad experiences in the past when they reached out and found themselves rejected. They have their own group of friends, and they find closeness and community there. In some ways they are like Junior's refugee family, who necessarily looks close to home for support.

In other ways they are not like Junior's family, because the institutions that they deal with don't recognize them as a family. This became clear and evident the day that Michael fell and needed stitches. Margaret, his birth mother, was at work in another town and couldn't get to the hospital right away. Beth, his other mother, had to hold the crying Michael in the emergency room—no treatment could be started until Margaret arrived to sign permission papers. Beth had no recognized legal connection to Michael.

Having their relationship disregarded as valid and legal by community agencies was nothing new to them, but this hurt the most because it involved Michael. They had had previous difficulties not experienced by heterosexual married couples—like not being able to get a loan to buy a house and being refused job-related medical benefits. That doesn't even count the difficulties of living in a neighborhood where some neighbors didn't like them even though they had never gotten to know them.

Beth and Margaret aren't without friends. They both have jobs, and each has found personal friends and support systems at work. But these systems don't help the family much, because except for a few, the work friends don't know about the rest of the family.

Margaret especially feels isolated at work, because of the secret she keeps from her friends and associates there. But in her last job she was more open, and she ended up feeling a lot more isolated than she does now. She finally left that job because she couldn't stand it anymore.

Both Margaret and Beth worry about their son and what will happen when he is old enough to understand what outsiders say about the family. They feel very protective of him and of each other and sometimes feel as though they live in a little cocoon separate from the rest of the world. They don't really want to live that way, but they wish they could keep the cocoon for Michael. They know, however, that soon he's going to grow beyond their protection and will be on his own in what feels to them like a cold and cruel outside world.

Margaret is secure about her relationship to Beth, but she suffers from the reaction she gets from so many who find out about it. She felt angry a lot of the time, and she knew she needed help in coping with the anger. She finally found a therapist to talk to. It took a long time, because she looked for someone who really understood her and could help without judging her family composition. She is surprised that being open and honest with a professional therapist can be so helpful. She's urging Beth, who has the same angry feelings about the way she's treated, to talk with someone, too. However, Beth hesitates, feeling that going into therapy means she's admitting that something is wrong with her.

Things are a little better now, because Beth has found a teacher at Michael's center who is accepting and friendly. She feels relieved that at least one outsider isn't cold and cruel.

Courtney's Family

Courtney's family consists of her second husband, Richard; 4-year-old Roland, from Courtney's first marriage; and 2 $\frac{1}{2}$-year-old Soleil, Courtney and Richard's daughter. Roland's two older brothers are also part of this family, but they live with Courtney's parents.

This family has been involved with the legal system for some time, starting with drug abuse and then child abuse during Courtney's first marriage. Now the family lives in fear of the boys' father returning to heap more abuse on previously abused little Roland. There's a restraining order to keep the father from coming near the boys, but Courtney still worries.

Courtney is just about to graduate from a drug rehabilitation program and is very proud of herself for being clean. She has turned her life around and is enrolled in college, the first step toward becoming a lawyer. She has strong feelings about making the legal system work better for everybody.

Richard also has strong feelings about the system. He is a Native American who, though born outside the reservation, has spent periods of his life going back to connect with his roots. He finds the tribal system and the religion of his people appealing, in contrast to impersonal institutions. He knows what real community is—people linked in emotional, social, and spiritual ways that provide mutual help and support. His dream is to become a history teacher and help the next generation see that change is necessary if this country (and, indeed, the planet) is to survive.

Courtney, like Sara, went through a difficult time in the past, which resulted in her being connected with a number of social service institutions. Some of them seemed to be supportive of her; some she regarded as "the enemy."

She remembers a very difficult period when she was told that if she didn't leave her boys' father because of the abuse he poured on them, she would lose her children. She felt extremely helpless at that point, and if it hadn't been for a local women's shelter, she never would have been able to take such a big step. When she finally left the shelter and struck out on her own, she was still threatened with the loss of her children because she couldn't provide decent housing for them. The only place she could afford that would rent to her was very run-down. Luckily, there was a new program in her community that was designed to help families overcome obstacles like that. A social worker from this program, instead of removing her children to foster care, came out with tools to show her how to fix the broken windows, replace the screens, and repair the plumbing, so that she and her children would have a safe place to live. This same social worker gave her some skills for guiding her children's behavior and got her into the rehabilitation program that turned her life around. Courtney is very grateful for the community resources that she sees as saving her life and helping her keep her children.

The Jackson Family

The Jackson family is different from some of the other families because they haven't been through a hard time. They're a stable family, clear about their identity, values, and lifestyle. They're not looking for changes as much as trying to keep things the way they are. Like Margaret and Beth, Michael's parents, the Jacksons' problems arise from being different from and therefore misunderstood by the greater community.

They are not in crisis and so are not looking for the same kind of support as some of the other families examined so far. The community resources they use and enjoy are both those of their own group—the religious and cultural groups they belong to—and those of the greater community, resources such as the library, recreation programs and facilities, museums, and other institutions that enhance the quality of their lives and the lives of the other families described in this chapter as well. The Jacksons appreciate music and plays and support the local groups that provide them. This family has no need for general assistance, food programs, housing support, social services, child abuse programs, or legal agencies, at least at present.

It's not that this is a perfect family; they have their problems, too. Their child born with spina bifida, a debilitating condition caused by a birth defect involving the spine, needs specialized services that they get from the school district. Taking care of him used to take up most of Mrs. Jackson's time, but now that he has enrolled in the child care center, she has more time to herself. Unfortunately, she is feeling isolated at home, and she's thinking of looking for friends outside her religious community. She had hoped to find a friendly group when she moved into the neighborhood she lives in. In her old neighborhood the women got together regularly and talked over coffee. In this one, however, the neighbors don't seem to want to get to know each other. The women are gone during the day and seem to be busy evenings and weekends. Mrs. Jackson invited both next-door neighbors over when she first moved in, but although they were polite and pleasant, they never reciprocated, and now they just talk once in a while across the driveway.

Now, however, Mrs. Jackson has gotten involved with fund-raising at the child care program, and she's beginning to feel connected to a group. She likes the women who are working with her, and she hopes to continue enjoying their company after the fund-raiser is over.

Mrs. Jackson is also involved in a new project. Her father, who has lived by himself since his wife died, is growing more and more feeble, and the Jacksons recently decided that he should move in with them. She is busy investigating what kinds of services are available to help them out. She has discovered the senior center near the library, where her father can enjoy company, take part in various classes and activities, and have a hot lunch on the days she works. She's feeling good about how this move will work out. It will be nice to have her father with her—and good for the children to know their grandfather better.

CONNECTIONS TO THE COMMUNITY

Each of these families has connections to the community beyond their own doors, yet each perceives that community in a slightly different way. Each uses the services of agencies and informal groups. Some give back as much as they receive; others either aren't in a position to reciprocate or don't yet understand the give-and-take aspects of community living. Many of the families we've examined live with multiple stresses in their lives. Some find the support and services they need; others feel the need for more. Some are denied access to available resources.

Let's look at a summary of the kinds of institutions and programs available in varying degrees to most of these families.

A Summary of Community Resources

Though none of these families have needed police or fire protection lately, they all know that they are two community services that are available at the touch of the telephone push-buttons. They also know about the community resources that are available to enhance the quality of their lives—the parks and recreation department, the library, the local museum, and the 2-year community college, all of which have regular programs for adults and children.

Some community resources are available only to eligible families, but many, such as local libraries, are available to all.

Child care programs, Head Start and other early education programs, and schools, both public and private, provide education to all members of the family. Local hospitals and the county health department provide preventive care and health maintenance to varying degrees, including some perinatal services and a variety of health education programs. They also, of course, provide services for the sick.

One big community resource designed to support people with children who can't work made a major change in the 1990s. Welfare in the form of Aid to Families with Dependent Children (AFDC) became Temporary Assistance for Needy Families (TANF) in 1996 and has stricter requirements than the old system. Also, there is a time limitation. Training institutions are full of former welfare recipients getting themselves qualified for the job market. These changes in the system and new challenges to families have created more need for child care than ever before—especially for infant care.

Some other community resources are designed to support families in times of emergency and stress, such as child abuse prevention programs, which offer telephone hotlines, parent education services, and respite child care. Mental health programs that offer therapeutic services and counseling programs are designed as short-term crisis intervention, and some provide long-term help to individuals and families as well. These programs periodically experience reduced funding, which makes them less effective at times. Families who can afford to pay for services continue, of course, to find them available. Substance abuse programs run by both professionals and volunteers also help people get on their feet and live satisfying and productive lives.

Most communities have a variety of support groups. Support groups can be both formal and informal and can respond to any number of needs: general parenting groups, women's and men's support groups, substance abuse, codependency, Overeaters Anonymous—you name it, there's a support group somewhere for it. Mrs Jackson has even found a spina bifida support group that is attended by parents whose children were born with this condition. She found it through a local family resource network designed to offer support, information, referral, advocacy, and training to families in her community who have children with special needs.

Finding Community Resources

How do you find out what resources are available in your community? A simple way is to start with the phone book; some have a special section right in front. Or the library may have a listing. In some communities, a local organization such as Head Start or a child care resource and referral agency puts together and updates lists of resources that are available to families.

Of course, anyone who knows how to use a computer and surf the World Wide Web can find countless resources right on the computer screen. For those without a computer, the local library can provide not only the computer but also some support and technical assistance to use the system.

Word of mouth is the way many families find out about the individuals and institutions that can serve them. If a family is connected to a child care center, the chances are someone on staff knows what's available for specific problems.

Some families enter "the system" because of a crisis or a problem. That's the way they get introduced to the world of accessible resources in their community. In some cities and towns, a crisis center is available 24 hours a day to serve those who are in serious trauma for whatever reason. Some communities also have women's shelters where the abused and their children can find refuge. Public health and mental health systems are usually also able to respond to crisis situations.

If your child seems to have a special need, a place to start asking about it is your doctor's office. If you're not connected to a medical system, public schools have the resources to assess special needs or may be able to refer you to another source.

Clergy often serve as counselors and advisers to individuals and families. They can guide their clients to appropriate community resources for their particular problem.

It's not always easy to find just what you need—in fact, it is sometimes downright difficult. However, with persistence, you'll usually locate whatever there might be. Unfortunately, most communities lack the full range of resources that they need, and many families are left with solving their own problems or looking for help or support from relatives, friends, and neighbors.

Availability of Community Resources

Although the list of community resources may be lengthy, not all are available in all communities. Even those communities that have a variety may not make them available to all families. What are some of the factors that determine availability of community resources?

Funding is one factor—often there's not enough to go around, or it's stretched so thin that no one can do a good job of helping and supporting families. Lack of funding results in declining services and increased competition for limited resources.

Some programs serve a specific population, and families must qualify to be eligible to receive services. Furthermore, some families qualify for services but have no access to them because of lack of transportation or language barriers. (Or perhaps they don't even realize that such services exist.)

When families do connect with services available to them, they may find the services inappropriate to their need—sometimes because of cultural insensitivity on the part of the service providers. Lack of respect may be a factor when there's a mismatch between services and the families they are designed to serve. When clients are looked down on by the people who serve them, it's often because the agency is using a deficit model to define the people who come to them for help. This model may be quite out of tune with the reality of cultural or class differences.

Each of the community resources that families deal with has a spoken or unspoken set of goals and values. When these goals and values are in tune with those of the family, a match is made, and the chances are better that the support or intervention will be effective. Some goals and values are conscious, written into the agency, some are misinterpreted by outsiders, and some are unintended.

For example, one medium-sized town has two agencies serving pregnant women. One is Planned Parenthood, whose purpose is to offer a variety of services as well as counseling that allows women to make decisions that are right for them about family planning. Planned Parenthood is not just for pregnant women; it has a wide range of services for both men and women. It offers abortion as one of several options for pregnant women to consider.

On the other side of town is a group called Birthright, whose goal is to help pregnant women opt against abortion. They provide counseling and support to women who might otherwise find it difficult to have their babies, doing what they can to make it more attractive to continue the pregnancy than to end it. These two agencies, which serve the same population, have contrasting goals and values and are clear about their differences.

Usually an agency's goals are not so clear, and often families don't look beyond the offer of services to understand the agency's goals or value system anyway. Of course, they can find them by examining incorporation papers, mission statements, or patterns of board policies. However, families do not usually set out to investigate the goals and value systems of the agency where they seek help or support. They may become aware of a lack of communication, a mismatch, or a lack of respect, which signals a goal or value conflict, but most of us don't even clarify our own goals or values very often, let alone compare them with those of an agency. However, goals and values do make a difference if we are to serve our community and be served by it. Goals and values are themes in the two chapters that follow.

SUMMARY

This chapter looked at how the community supports families and provides resources through informal and formal social networks, institutions, and agencies. Examples of how several families use the resources made up a good portion of the chapter. It ended with a look at goals and values, which are themes in the two chapters that follow.

FOR DISCUSSION

1. What do you know about the negative effects that isolation can have on families?
2. Name some social networks that you are acquainted with.
3. Give examples of how the families in this chapter might both use and contribute to community resources. Choose examples that haven't been mentioned in the chapter.
4. What would you tell a family about how to find the community resources they might need?
5. Do you know someone who needed a community resource, but it wasn't available to that person? Why wasn't it available? Do you know someone who used an agency that didn't fit their culture or their needs?

REFERENCES

Alan Guttmacher Institute. (1999). *Facts in brief: Teen sex and pregnancy.* Available on the Web site of the Alan Guttmacher Institute (www.agi-usa.org/pubs/fb_teen_sex.html).

Bushman, B. J., & Anderson, C. A. (2001). Media violence and the American public: Scientific facts versus media misinformation. *American Psychologist, 56,* 466–489.

Bushman, D., & Huesmann, L. R. (2001). Effects of televised violence on aggression. In D. Singer & J. Singer (Eds.), *Handbook of children and the media.* Thousand Oaks, CA: Sage.

Children's Defense Fund. (2000). *State of America's children* 2000. Washington, DC: Children's Defense Fund.

Children's Defense Fund. (2004). *The state of America's children* 2004. Washington, DC: Children's Defense Fund.

Clark, K. E., & Ladd, G. W. (2000). Connectedness and autonomy support in parent-child relationships: Links to children's socio-emotional orientation and peer relationships. *Developmental Psychology, 36,* 485–498.

Duncan, G. O., & Brooks-Gunn, J. (2000). Family parenting, welfare reform, and child development. *Child Development, 71,* 188–195.

Golden, O. (2000). The federal response to child abuse and neglect. *American Psychologist, 55,* 1050–1053.

Lally, J. R. (1998, May). Brain research, infant learning, and child care curriculum. *Child Care Information Exchange, 121,* 46–48.

Maccoby, E. E. (1998). *The two sexes.* Cambridge, MA: Harvard University Press.

National Research Council and Institute of Medicine. (2000). *From neurons to neighborhoods: The science of early childhood development.* Board on Children, Youth, and Families, Commission on Behavioral and Social Sciences and Education. Washington, DC: National Academy Press.

Parke, R. D., & O'Neil, R. (2000). The influence of significant others on learning about relationships: From family to friends. In R. S. L. Mills & S. Duck (Eds.), *The developmental psychology of personal relationships* (pp. 15–47). New York: Wiley.

Payne, R. K. (2003). *A framework for understanding poverty.* Highlands, TX: Aha Process.

Schneider, B. H., Atkinson, L., & Tardif, C. (2001). Child-parent attachment and children's peer relations: A quantitative review. *Developmental Psychology, 37,* 86–100.

Shonkoff, J. P., & Phillips, D. (2001, April-May). From neurons to neighborhoods: The science of early childhood development—An introduction. *Zero to Three, 21*(5), 4–7.

Shore, R. (1997). *Rethinking the brain: New insights in early development.* New York: Families and Work Institute.

Signorielli, N., & Morgan, M. (2001). Television and the family: The cultivation perspective. In J. Bryant & J. A. Bryant (Eds.), *Television and the American family* (2nd ed., pp. 333–351). Mahwah, NJ: Erlbaum.

Tan, A. L. (2004). *Chinese American children and families: A guide for educators and service providers.* Onley, MD: Association for Childhood Education International.

Tinsley, B. R. (2002). *How children learn to be healthy.* New York: Cambridge University Press.

White, E. (Qoyawayma, P.). (1992). *No turning back: A Hopi woman's struggle to live in two worlds.* Albuquerque: University of New Mexico Press.

Wright, J. C., Huston, A. C., Murphy, K. C., St. Peters, M., Pinon, M., Scantlin, R., & Kotler, J. (2001). The relations of early television viewing to school readiness and vocabulary of children from low-income families: The early window project. *Child Development, 72,* 1347–1366.

Zigler, E. F., Finn-Stevenson, M., & Hall, N. W. (2003). *The first three years and beyond: Brain development and social policy.* New Haven: Yale University Press.

FURTHER READING

Akbar, N. (2003). *Akbar papers in African psychology.* Tallahassee, FL: Mind Productions.

Bernstein, B. (1991). Since the Moynihan report. In R. Staples (Ed.), *The black family: Essays and studies* (4th ed., p. 24). Belmont, CA: Wadsworth.

Children's Defense Fund. (2004). *The state of America's children* 2004. Washington, DC: Children's Defense Fund.

Clark, K. E., & Ladd, G. W. (2000). Connectedness and autonomy support in parent-child relationships:

Links to children's socio-emotional orientation and peer relationships. *Developmental Psychology, 36*, 485–498.

Duncan, G. O., & Brooks-Gunn, J. (2000). Family parenting, welfare reform, and child development. *Child Development, 71*, 188–195.

Dunst, C., Trivette, C., & Deal, A. (1988). *Enabling and empowering families.* Cambridge, MA: Brookline.

Edwards, P. A., & Jones Young, L. S. (1992, May). Beyond parents: Family, community, and school involvement. *Phi Delta Kappan, 73*(9), 72–80.

Families USA. (1999). *Losing health insurance: The unintended consequences of welfare reform.* Washington, DC: Families USA.

Fernea, E. W. (1995). *Children in the Muslim Middle East.* Austin: University of Texas Press.

Golden, O. (2000). The federal response to child abuse and neglect. *American Psychologist, 55*, 1050–1053.

Hale, J. E. (1992). An African-American early childhood education program: Visions for children. In S. A. Kessler & B. B. Swadener (Eds.), *Reconceptualizing the early childhood curriculum: Beginning the dialogue* (pp. 205–224). New York: Teachers College Press.

Hernandez, D., & Charney, E. (Eds.). (1998). *From generation to generation: The health and well-being of children in immigrant families.* Washington, DC: National Academy Press.

Karoly, L. A., & Greenwood, P. W. (1998). *Investing in our children: What we know and don't know about the costs and benefits of early childhood interventions.* Santa Monica, CA: Rand.

Lyons, J. D., & Russell, S. D. (1998). *Child care subsidy: The costs of waiting.* Chapel Hill, NC: Day Care Services Association.

Neighbors, H. W., & Jackson, J. S. (Eds.). (1996). *Mental health in black America.* Newbury Park, CA: Sage.

Parke, R. D., & O'Neil, R. (2000). The influence of significant others on learning about relationships: From family to friends. In R. S. L. Mills & S. Duck (Eds.), *The developmental psychology of personal relationships* (pp. 15–47). New York: Wiley.

Payne, R. K. (2003). *A framework for understanding poverty.* Highlands, TX: Aha Process.

Porter, K., & Primus, W. (1999). *Recent changes in the impact of the safety net on child poverty.* Washington, DC: Center on Budget and Policy Priorities.

Ross, A. C. (Ehanamani). (1989). *Mitakuye oyasin: We are all related.* Denver: Wichoni Waste.

Tan, A. L. (2004). *Chinese American children and families: A guide for educators and service providers.* Onley, MD: Association for Childhood Education International.

Tedla, E. (1995). *Sankofa: African thought and education.* New York: Lang.

United Nations Children's Fund. (2000). *The state of the world's children 2000.* New York: United Nations Children's Fund.

U.S. Department of Health and Human Services. (1999). *Eliminating racial and ethnic disparities in health: Overview.* Available on the Department of Health and Human Services Web site (http://raceandhealth.hhs.gov/sidebars/sbinitOver.htm).

U.S. Substance Abuse and Mental Health Services Administration. (1999). *Summary findings from the 1998 National Household Survey on drug abuse.* Rockville, MD: U.S. Department of Health and Human Services.

Werner, E. E. (1995, June). Resilience in development. *Current Directions in Psychological Science, 4*(3), 81–85.

Werner, E. E., & Smith, R. S. (1992). *Overcoming the odds: High risk children from birth to adulthood.* Ithaca, NY: Cornell University Press.

Whirlpool Foundation. (1995). *Women: The new providers.* New York: Families and Work Institute.

White, E. (Qoyawayma, P.). (1992). *No turning back: A Hopi woman's struggle to live in two worlds.* Albuquerque: University of New Mexico Press.

CHAPTER 14

Socializing Agents

In *this chapter you'll discover* . . .

- ◆ How bias affects young children
- ◆ That social class isn't as invisible as it seems
- ◆ The effect of school "tracking"
- ◆ Some things about kindergarten readiness that you probably never thought of
- ◆ How to decide by looking at a classroom whether the teacher celebrates diversity
- ◆ The influences of peer groups
- ◆ Some problems with expecting television to socialize children

The family is the first and major socializing agent, and as such it has responsibility for early socialization patterns. As the child grows and moves outside his or her home, other agents in the community come into play. In the past, outside agents were fewer; relatives, neighbors, religious institutions, and informal community networks shared a good deal of responsibility for socialization. Peers also played a part. Today television is usually the first socializing agent outside the family, with child care a close second. Later, school comes into the picture, with after-school activities and perhaps eventually clubs such as Scouts. Peers are important as the child grows and become a strong socializing force. The socialization process today is shared. Other institutions such as hospitals, government agencies, and service industries may also come into the picture. These organizations have taken over many of the activities that were once the function of the family, the extended family or kinship network, and neighbors, all of whom used to make up the informal community.

This chapter looks at four major socializing agents: the family, the school, the peer group, and television.

SOCIALIZATION AND THE FAMILY

Because Part 2 devoted a whole section of this book to the family, you may be wondering why the family is also included here in Part 3, on the community. The family is such an important socializing agent, it appears and reappears throughout the whole book. This chapter deals with the family's place in and interface with society as it examines the influence of the community on the family and therefore on the child.

Each family belongs to subcultures and networks that reflect their social class position, ethnic group membership, and, possibly, their kinship. These subcultures and networks influence the ways in which families socialize their children. The language the parents use, and sometimes insist that their children use, influences to some extent their ties to one group or another. "Speak Spanish," demands a mother who sees her children drifting away from their roots to dissolve into mainstream America. "Speak English," demands another, who sees language as a way to carry out her upward-bound goals. "Don't say *ain't*," admonishes another because she feels that's what uneducated people say, knowing that language helps people fit into the right group. "Gettin' kinda uppity, ain't ya?" asks another mother, who feels alienated by her son's new way of speaking when he comes back from college for the first visit home. She sees language as a divider.

In addition to social class and ethnic group, families are sometimes tied to other families through occupations or interests, which also affect children's socialization. The family that plays music together, for example, influences the socialization of their children differently from, say, a family that plays sports together. The experiences of the children in those two families may be quite different from the children of workaholic parents who are tied to their corporate "family."

Many families have a primary focus of attention; it may be religious activities, or school achievement, or even income opportunities. Some actively mold their children to their own interests by constantly involving them. They also do it by evaluating other people, so the children come to see whom the family prefers them to associate with and who should be avoided. The family whose members devote themselves to nature and to ecology issues may be quite critical of the family next door—a nightclub comedian and his singer wife who spend most of their work and leisure time in bars at night in smoke-filled rooms (depending on the state in which they live), or the family on the hill that owns the manufacturing plant in town that has been suspected of polluting the environment.

Status—that is, the family's position in society—affects socialization and can in turn affect where the child finds herself when she grows up. Children of wealthy families have a different set of experiences and expectations than, for example, children of poverty-level families. Consider the difference between a child born into a Beverly Hills family with two parents, four cars, and a pile of money compared with a child who was born in jail and who is sent to live with her grandmother in a run-down trailer park near the railroad tracks while her mother finishes serving a term for dealing drugs. Which child is most likely to grow up defining her choices as the "sky's the limit"?

The family not only gives the child status but also makes him or her aware of the status of others. Family members teach, whether consciously or not, whom to copy and whom not to copy. The message about the status of outsiders is clear in some families—just who is above and who is below.

The "goodies" that society has to offer are more available to some children than to others. For some, privilege is a major socializing force; for others, privilege's counterparts—bias and discrimination—play that role.

The Issue of Bias

Bias is everywhere, and we've all felt its effects, though some of us are targeted more than others. We feel bias because of our gender, social class, skin color, ethnic background, the way we talk, body type or condition, mental capabilities, age, sexual orientation, the amount of money or education our family has, or our family configuration, to name a few of the factors that make us the targets of bias.

Bias hurts everybody—and especially children. It hurts those who are its targets because they must put energy into struggling against the negative messages that they receive—energy that could be used for development. In addition, it hurts them because they find their opportunities limited; doors are shut to them.

Bias also hurts those who are not targets when they participate in the belief that they and others like them are superior. This belief not only dehumanizes them but also distorts their reality. Bias is bad for everybody!

We need to become aware of our areas of privilege and how bias works. We need to become sensitized to help ourselves and others think critically and to speak up in the face of bias. The key is empowerment. Target groups must be empowered to develop a strong self- and group identity so they can stand up in the face of attack. Nontarget groups must also develop a strong self-identity, but without a feeling of superiority. Each individual must be free to, and indeed encouraged to, develop to his or her full and unique potential.

Classism.   Let's look more closely at one area of bias—social class—by examining children from two families who are targets for classism.

The first child is Max, whose family is working-class and proud of it. His father, Joe, is a truck driver, and his mother, Mary, is an assembly line worker in a factory. Max lives with his parents and his two sisters, Sonia and Sally, in a modest house located in a working-class neighborhood that is at the bottom of the hill from a new upscale housing development. The school district drew new boundaries when they built the school for this area, and they included Max's neighborhood in the attendance area, so every day Max's sisters walk him to kindergarten before they go off to their own classrooms in the new elementary school they now attend.

The family is having some problems with what's happening as a result of the contact between their children and the children on the hill. Clothes are one of the problems. The girls feel they need different clothes from what they have always worn. Designer labels have become important to them. They complain that the kids won't like them if they don't dress right. Designer labels aren't an issue for Max. In fact, the rule is that children have to wear old clothes to preschool so they can experience all the sensory activities that the school offers (which tend to be messy).

The issue for Max is T-shirts. The program is doing fund-raising, and they want the families to buy the school T-shirt, which is then worn on T-shirt Day. All the other kids have them, but they cost a lot. T-shirts aren't the only fund-raising project going on. It seems that papers are always coming home from school announcing something to buy, sell, or donate to. For free public education, there seem to be a lot of expenses, like field trips that require the price of an admission ticket to go to plays or get in the museum. And the parties the children get invited to are expensive, too. Each one requires a present and usually transportation, which presents difficulties. Sometimes specialized equipment is needed, such as roller skates or sleeping bags for slumber parties.

Lately the parties have slowed down. That situation is good for the pocketbook but bad for the children's morale. They have begun feeling that they aren't good enough to associate with their classmates, and that's why they aren't getting invited to parties. At the first open house at school, their parents began to understand their feelings. No one was warm or welcoming to them. Then they started up a conversation with one couple in the preschool group about the building of the school, and the man started complaining about how the school opening had been delayed because of a strike. He made it clear that he thought unions were the root of the economic problems in the United States. Joe told him that he was a union member and that was the end of the conversation. Joe and Mary remembered the old school where everyone was more like them and they felt at home. Here they feel out of place, and they wonder whether the other parents and the teachers are looking down on them.

Is what they are feeling real or just their imagination? It is hard to tell. Maybe some of both. Whether imagination or not, Joe and Mary have vowed to help their children feel good about who they are and do what they can to help them see that money doesn't buy happiness.

The other family we will examine has a different story. Peter, who is 4, was born into a middle-class family. However, soon after Peter's birth, his father left his mother.

Daddy came back just long enough to make a baby brother before departing for good, leaving Peter's mother with two little boys to raise. The family slipped into poverty practically overnight.

Although Peter's mother was raised with the values, expectations, and behaviors of the middle class, she began to change as the effects of poverty molded her. She couldn't keep up her same connections. When she was single and after she was first married, she used to enjoy lunch out with her friends; now her lunch hour was full of errands and appointments, and, anyway, she didn't have the money to squander on a nice lunch. She struggled hard to remain on her former level, but try as she would, she was pulled down. She began to feel strange around people who had so much more money than she did. She also felt strange around the other mothers she met whose children were in Peter's Head Start class. She didn't seem to belong anywhere anymore.

She remembered how she and her friends used to criticize poor people who didn't keep their kids clean. "It doesn't cost anything to keep clean," she used to say. But she discovered that it did. She had to go to the laundromat to wash; that cost plenty—in money, time, and energy. And since her water heater broke, even bathing the boys was harder. She had called the landlord three times already to get it fixed, but she was still without hot water after 4 days.

The last straw came when she popped back into the child care center to leave the diaper bag she'd forgotten to drop off and found Peter's little brother being scrubbed down in the sink. She knew then that she'd crossed the line and had become one of the people she used to frown on. She remembered a conversation with a teacher friend about how some kids arrive at school so dirty and smelly that you just want to give them a good scrubbing. Now her own child had become one of them. She was embarrassed to tears—and angry as well. How dare they bathe her baby without her permission? He wasn't *that* dirty. She'd heated water on the stove and given him a sponge bath that very morning!

We don't know whether this mother was really experiencing a biased attitude. We don't know why the teacher was washing the child or how she felt about it. She perhaps thought she was doing the mother and the child a favor, but the mother perceived the action as an insult, maybe because she had once been on the other side of classism.

Peter's mother being newly poor has experienced both sides of the poverty line. Some families have never been on the upside of it. They come from a long tradition of poverty and have never known anything else. They are used to people looking down on them and perhaps even blaming them for their poverty.

For some Americans, social class is hard to see, because we, as a society, deny the existence of such a thing. For a long period, the middle and upper classes were even able to pretend that social class didn't exist because they didn't see poor people before their very eyes. All that is rapidly changing; poverty shows everywhere. Poor people aren't tucked away on the other side of town anymore. They're apt to be downtown and even in the parking lots of shopping malls, holding up signs that say "Will work for food."

Social classes exist even though they aren't the permanent, set-in-stone phenomena we see in other countries. We still don't commonly call them *social classes*, though

Sociologists speak of "socioeconomic levels." Whatever you call them, there are differences in the experience of the children who are raised at each level.

Social class is one factor in socialization and race is another; however, they are often lumped together. Social class may be ignored entirely, for example, when comparing cultural differences of African Americans and European Americans. Often poverty-level African Americans are compared with middle-class European Americans without acknowledging that there are class differences. It's important to be aware that there are poverty-level people in all cultural groups—and also middle-class people—and you can't just be blind to social class differences.

Let's turn now to racism, which is another important factor in socialization of children.

Racism.   Those who have experienced racism don't have to read about it to understand it. If you haven't experienced it, it's hard to understand to what extent it exists and what it feels like. It's easier for those who aren't a target of racism to understand it in terms of its counterpart, *privilege.*

Privilege can be thought of as an "invisible package of unearned assets," which it's possible to cash in on whenever it pleases the person carrying the privilege. Most of those who have it are quite unaware of their privilege; they regard it as the way things are. Those who don't have privilege are very aware of its lack. Privilege shows more in its absence than in its presence.

Let's look at the privileges that a 4-year-old white, middle-class child, Lindsay, enjoys because of her skin color:

> Lindsay doesn't have to represent "her people," who, in fact, are seldom lumped into one skin color category. If she arrives at preschool dirty, it's an individual family matter or perhaps attributed to her social class, but it doesn't reflect on white people in general. She can wear secondhand clothes. She can pick her nose or even use bad words, and it's her family that's reflected, not the white race. If her family gets her to school late, no one attributes it to either their genes or their culture. If she arrives at school tired, the teachers may blame the parent, but not anyone else. Lindsay's family has the privilege of representing only themselves, not reflecting or living in the reflection of stereotypes of a group of other people with their same skin color.
>
> Lindsay lives in the best neighborhood her family can afford; though money is, of course, a factor, it is not the major factor. They have the privilege of choosing where they want to live within their price range, and they made that choice assuming that their neighbors would display good or at least neutral feelings toward them. If they have alienated their neighbors, it's more likely because of something they've done rather than because of who they are.
>
> Lindsay will come to see herself and her family as "normal," if she hasn't already. She sees herself and her people represented on television and in books, magazines, and newspapers. She easily finds the food her family eats in the local supermarket. Lindsay's mother can take her anyplace she likes to get her hair cut and feel reassured that someone there will know how to cut it. When Lindsay is older and learns about history, she'll be shown that her people (or at least the males) made this country what it is.

Lindsay's mother doesn't worry about educating her children to detect racism. She doesn't even consider teaching them how to operate when racism is present or how to protect themselves from it.

Angelica and her twin brother, Mario, who go to Lindsay's preschool, have a different experience:

Angelica and Mario's mother is well aware of the possibility of racist attitudes toward her children. One of the antiracist strategies her mother uses is to send them to school fashionably dressed. The teachers sent Angelica home with a parent handbook the first day, with the sentence highlighted that said, "Please send your child in old play clothes." After a week, one teacher stopped the three of them as they were leaving and complained that it was hard for the children to participate in all the many and varied messy activities because of their clothing. She asked that they come in old clothes that didn't matter. The mother listened, but the next day Angelica arrived dressed in a new fancy dress and her brother in a starched shirt and a pair of slacks. The teachers never understood why their message didn't get through. If they had been able to have a heart-to-heart talk with this mother they would have discovered that she sees her children's appearances as reflecting on their family. She wants her children to look well cared for. She doesn't want her children to fit into any stereotypes racists may have of her people. Although racists are everywhere, if Angelica and Mario are well dressed and look well cared for, it will be harder for some people to see them as inferior to other children. She is also well aware that clothes and grooming won't matter to a real racist who will only see skin color.

For Janice, the issue is hair:

Janice is the parent education coordinator at a fairly large child care center. One of the parents she has concerns about is Betsy, who is the adoptive mother of Lacy, an African American 5-year-old. Betsy doesn't know how to take care of her daughter's hair, and it bothers Janice a lot. She sends her in the morning looking uncombed. After nap time, she wakes up looking even worse. Janice has taken to combing Lacy's hair twice a day, on arrival and after nap. Lacy loves it! Janice keeps meaning to ask Betsy for a conference to explain to her some of the things she doesn't know about her daughter's hair. She also wants her to understand that an African American child can't afford to look as if nobody cares about her, even if it's not true. People will judge her, and her people!

These three stories show some of the factors that affect socialization. The child's race, family income level, and circumstances influence how others respond to him or her on a personal level.

The stories also provide examples of the problems that can arise when teachers and parents aren't partners. For early childhood programs to be positive socializing agents, the partnership model must be in place. Throughout this book the theme of parent-professional partnerships has been stressed. These stories show the sad effects when the teacher operates out of a one-way model. The teacher is in charge and the parent is the recipient of the teacher's knowledge and expertise. What's lacking in that model is the teacher's awareness and acceptance of the funds of knowledge families already possess when they bring their children to the program.

A child's race, family income level, and circumstances can determine the kind of formal education that the child is likely to receive. We've already examined child care and early education in other chapters. Now we turn our focus to the public school system.

SCHOOLS AS SOCIALIZING AGENTS

This whole book is about the socialization of young children and early childhood programs as socializing agents. This section focuses on subjects that haven't been covered elsewhere, such as public school expectations of behaviors and mismatches that occur when children arrive with behaviors that work elsewhere but not in school. Antibias curriculum is another aspect of school as a socializing agent that is discussed in this section, as well as the effects of testing on socialization. A large part of this section focuses on a huge issue in early childhood education that has an effect on socialization: kindergarten readiness. The readiness approaches become problematic when they are more concerned with the intellect and particularly academic skills without regard to the role that social-emotional development plays in "getting children ready." Socialization is affected when those pushing a narrow aspect of readiness fail to understand the implications of focusing on just one aspect of development and disregarding the others.

Some children arrive in kindergarten already less ready to grapple with the kindergarten curriculum than other children. Sometimes this is merely a matter of developmental differences. However, some children enjoy a variety of early experiences that fit nicely into what they need for kindergarten. Other children's early experiences are different; kindergarten presents an alien world to them. As a result, children are sometimes labeled and separated into groups by their "abilities" (this is called *tracking*). If children are tracked and labeled early, their educational course is set, sometimes for life. That means some are given the message that they're learners—winners in the race called school. They tend to take the ball and run with it; they're successful. Others learn early that they're "slow," which they translate to mean "stupid"; they're losers. Once tracking begins, the educational opportunities become limited for some and expanded for others.

Getting into Kindergarten

Even getting into kindergarten may be an issue facing families who send their 5-year-olds off to public school. Public school administrators and teachers are under a great deal of pressure to provide accountability to government funding sources. Those who pay the bills want to be sure they're getting their money's worth. The way they determine accountability is through test scores, so testing has finally reached clear down to to kindergarten and even beyond into preschool.

As a parent volunteer in my son's elementary school, I have seen the effects of testing on 5-year-olds. The day I helped with the standardized achievement tests in kindergarten stands out in my memory. The children were told not to be nervous and that this was nothing to worry about—a double message because everything about the atmosphere that day said, "This is *very important.*" In addition, the parents had been sent

Schools are socializing agents.

a notice to be sure that the children got a good night's sleep and a hearty breakfast every day during the week of the testing. So in some cases, the atmosphere both at home and in the classroom conveyed the message that tension existed around these events—that they were different from what the children usually experienced in kindergarten. Even though the children were told not to be nervous (which in itself makes one suspicious enough to be nervous), two cried, one threw up, and one had to go home with a headache. These events alone were enough to influence the test scores, not only of the afflicted group but also of the group not showing any symptoms.

Ready to Learn

A narrow and simplistic view of what "ready to learn" means focuses on teaching academics to young children. That view ignores the huge societal changes that need to come about to ensure that all children have an equal chance for academic achievement in school. To truly have an equal chance for school success we need to eradicate poverty, give everybody health care benefits, ensure enough nutrious food, and provide decent housing. Focusing on early academics is a cheaper but far less effective road to school success than what the brain research indicates. Good health and social-emotional stability in the early years of life are the real road to later achievement. Cognitive development is vitally tied to the social-emotional realm of development (Lally, 1998; Shore, 1997; Zigler, Finn-Stevenson, & Hall, 2003). Instead of working toward a decent life for every child, the major societal approach is to use standardized tests to see who is behind in academic skills and then use remediation devices to catch them up. It will take a few years to discover that this band-aid approach won't work to take care of the wounds too many children in this country suffer in their early years.

It may not take years to discover the other problems inherent in basing educational systems solely around standardized tests. Testing works as a stratifying tool through cultural bias. Teachers, in order to raise their class test scores, find themselves "teaching to the test," which means they minimize problem-solving and creativity in their classroom activities. The tests dictate what children need to know regardless of their knowledge, experiences, and cultural differences.

Kindergarten readiness, a hot topic among politicians, is also a hot topic among parents. With that in mind, let's look at how kindergarten readiness goes far beyond the ABC's and starts way back in infancy. Here are some general indicators that early childhood educators agree show that children are prepared to enter kindergarten:

1. *Children who are ready for kindergarten are those who feel good about themselves.* The problem is that much of the discipline used makes children feel bad about themselves. Children don't feel good about themselves by being made to feel bad. Discipline should not only leave self-esteem intact but also actually raise it when adults use modeling, guidance, and feedback. Communication is an important part of discipline when adults discuss feelings and behavior instead of criticizing the child. Adults who understand such things separate the child from the behavior, saying things like "I won't let you hit your sister—it hurts her" instead of "Stop that, you bad boy!"

2. *Children who are ready for kindergarten are those who gain knowledge from mistakes.* Some of the best lessons come from things that don't work. It's easy to take the lesson out of a mistake by rescuing children so they don't learn about consequences of their actions. Or the opposite situation occurs when the adult reacts to a mistake with harsh punishment. When children become fearful of mistakes, they quit risking. Reasonable risks are good learning devices. The child who avoids them misses out on a lot of important lessons.

3. *Children who are ready for kindergarten can communicate.* They have lots of experience in talking and listening. They know how to carry on a conversation. A conversation means not just talking but listening and responding appropriately as well. Adults should start emphasizing communication early. Even infants enjoy conversations and taking turns "talking." They also play with language. As they grow older, keeping a playful attitude toward language helps encourage it.

4. *Children who are ready for kindergarten can weigh alternatives and make sound choices.* Visualizing alternatives and their consequences is an important life skill. Children who arrive in kindergarten with plenty of opportunities to practice this skill come better prepared. When the "prepared child" gets hit by another child, she asks herself, "What are some ways I can react, and what are the consequences of each?" The child without the ability to visualize alternatives just lashes back without thinking. Aggression in the face of aggression is a poor choice. Some

children never learn that, unfortunately. Some children have no ability to imagine any response other than hitting.

5. *Children who are ready for kindergarten can concentrate and focus.* If they can't do that, the problem may be too much television. It might seem as though children develop a long attention span from watching television, because they are willing to sit and stare at it for hours. But turn it off and what happens? They don't know how to entertain themselves. We add to the problem by overscheduling their time. Children don't develop long attention spans when they are never allowed to just play for long periods, never free to follow their inclinations to get involved in something of their own choice, never encouraged to work at length on some project they are interested in. Adults tend to interrupt them, hurry them up, get them going on the next event. Preschool programs can contribute to the problem if they keep children on a tight schedule, move them rapidly from one activity to another, and never give them a chance to work at length or in depth on anything.

The effect of linking accountability to achievement as proved by testing is to make teachers anxious to have only the most teachable children in their classrooms. Say a child enters in September who isn't ready to buckle down and do whatever the teacher, the school, the district, or the state considers kindergarten work (which more and more reflects the test items that will appear during the spring testing period). This child wants to play, and his motivation is so strong that it takes all the teacher's behavioral management techniques and more to get him to settle down to "seat work" for even a few minutes a day. It's easy to say this child isn't ready for kindergarten. And it's even easier to decide to determine readiness *before* the child enters and settles into the class. Therefore, some schools now have screening tests to decide who can come into kindergarten and who can't.

On the surface, that approach may make sense, but dig down just a little. Think about the child who has been at home with an overburdened parent for 5 years—a parent who doesn't have the time or the resources to contribute to his informal education. Is he better off spending another year in the same environment? Not that home can't be a rich and wonderful learning environment—it can, but by age 5 many children are ready to move out from home a little. In another case, the school may kindly advise the parent that the child needs preschool, but there is no money for a private one and no access to any other kind. Why can't he go to the free public kindergarten that's offered conveniently close to home? Why can't the kindergarten *provide what he needs* rather than requiring him to fit a predetermined curriculum?

Think about the child who has been in preschool and has outgrown it. For 3 years he's done the wonderful activities his school offered and taken part in a variety of field trips and many cognitive and socialization experiences. He's done it all, and now he's ready to move on. But he didn't "pass the kindergarten test," as his parents put it, so now they are trying to talk the preschool into enrolling him for a 4th year.

Think about the upwardly mobile family who considers education the key to their child's success and is absolutely devastated to learn, as they put it, that "he flunked kindergarten before he even got in." Their expectations are shattered as they see the child they once considered bright defined, in their own minds, as "dull."

Classroom Behavior

Kindergarten readiness is one issue, closely linked to another—that of classroom behavior. Most public school classroom teachers depend on parents to send their children with ingrained behaviors that allow them to perform according to the rules and enable them to learn in the style the school sees as appropriate to the group size and the ratio of children to teachers. Some parents manage to comply with this expectation. And some children, even in spite of their parents or their home life, are willing and able to conform to what school requires. But other children aren't or can't. Expected school behavior may be quite alien to what's needed by some children at home and in the neighborhood where they live. Social skills taught at home may not work in school.

Consider the streetwise inner-city child who has learned, even by the age of 5, to survive by interpersonal skills that allow him to manipulate people and situations. He gets little chance to use those skills in school—except out of the teacher's sight during recess. Interaction during class time is strictly controlled and certain expectations are enforced according to a set of rules. He comes to school self-reliant and independent, but his manner borders on defiance and that attitude gets him in trouble. He's also aggressive. He knows he can solve problems through physical action, but at school he finds he's expected to use words alone. "Fight back and don't tattle" is the rule at home. School rules are different: "Don't ever touch anybody; tell the teacher if you have a problem." The child who has incorporated the home rule is going to have problems in school, starting right away in kindergarten.

It may seem reasonable to try to give this family a new set of child-rearing practices to help their child do well in school and eventually rise out of the circumstances the family is in—if not immediately, at least by the next generation. But the truth is that it's not easy to change child-rearing practices. And an outsider taking on such a task is taking on a good deal of responsibility unless he or she clearly understands how the child-rearing practices serve the culture, the family, and the child. In addition, it is quite difficult to teach people how to raise their children unless they have a special reason for wanting to change. Changes in child rearing tend to come *after* social and economic changes have been effected.

In the meantime, this little streetwise child has a problem. If he conforms to classroom expectations, learns the rules, and takes them home to apply them, they won't work in the same way they do at school. Some children are flexible enough to learn a new set of skills and apply them where they work while keeping the old set for the times when the new set doesn't work. However, other children never adjust to the school environment.

Not all children who don't fit valued classroom behavior are physical and aggressive. Take the little girl who finds herself in a classroom where self-direction, initiative, independence, and competitiveness are the skills stressed. These skills are the ones seen as functional to the higher-level, higher-paying, middle-class occupations and social positions. But the little girl doesn't see the connection and perhaps has no expectations of growing up to a high-level job anyway. She only knows that while the teacher is urging her to be special, to do well, to stand alone, to stick out, and to be a winner, all she wants is to fit in and be loved. She doesn't want more stars on her star chart than anyone else. She doesn't want to sit isolated and do her own seat work without talking or looking at someone else's paper. She wants hugs and attention from the teacher. She wants to sit on her lap at story time. She wants to socialize with her classmates. She wants the same warm group feelings that she gets at home. She wants to be a part of things, not separate and individual and alone.

This little girl won't get in trouble like the little boy in the first example. She'll be thought of as sweet but probably not too bright (though she may, in fact, be quite intelligent). Eventually she will fade into the background and become invisible like the other children who don't give the teacher problems. Feeling that she doesn't fit in, she may give up on education early and find something else to do with her life. Or, less likely, she'll figure out how to learn even under the alien conditions of the classroom and end up going all the way through college as an invisible person, doing very well, but not drawing attention to herself (McKenna & Ortiz, 1988).

Responding to Diversity

When children arrive at school, they may or may not find a cultural environment that reflects themselves or the diversity of the American population. The environment reflects the attitudes of the people who create it. If the teacher sees only the dominant culture as valuable and therefore worth recognizing, the classroom will show only white faces in the pictures on the walls, will acknowledge only dominant culture heroes and holidays, and will contain only books written for, by, and about dominant culture people.

Sometimes teachers who have this attitude don't realize the limitations of what they offer to children. If they are European Americans, they might not understand any culture but their own, which they naturally see as normal and right—the only way. Such culture-blind teachers may claim to be color-blind. In their attempt not to be bigoted, they ignore differences, thinking that noticing them shows prejudices.

Other teachers regard differences as important and take an ethnic studies approach toward acknowledging them. They accept and promote differences in a attempt to increase understanding and acceptance of them. Taking a "multicultural tourist" approach, these teachers may emphasize ethnic holidays, serve ethnic foods, and teach about customs, history, art, or artifacts of assorted cultures. This approach can make some children feel accepted who wouldn't otherwise feel that way, as well as broaden the view and experience of all the children in the classroom. A difficulty is that studying cultures in bits and pieces tends to trivialize or exoticize them. A multicultural tourist approach may also focus more on foreign cultures than on how those cultures have evolved when transplanted to the United States. This approach represents an add-on to the curriculum, rather than a change in it. The classroom reflects the multicultural tourist curriculum by having pictures displayed and books available that show, for example, African tribespeople, Balinese dancers, and Chinese New Year's celebrations. A typical theme for December in a multicultural tourist curriculum is "Christmas Around the World" or the broader "December Holidays," showing celebrations of Hanukkah, Christmas, Santa Lucia Festival of Lights, and Kwanzaa.

Some teachers approach diversity in the classroom by looking at commonalties in the everyday world rather than just celebrations. "We're all ethnic and cultural beings—same and different at the same time" is the message. This approach may take the theme that we all have needs, but how we meet those needs varies. Teachers may have their children study, for example, ways of carrying babies or kinds of grains eaten by various cultures. Studying breads from around the world as a theme is an example of approaching diversity from the we're-the-same-but-different angle.

Other teachers—more and more since Derman-Sparks's book, *Antibias Curriculum*, came out in 1989—see the importance of changing their whole curriculum to reflect an attitude of respect and dignity toward differences. An antibias approach aims at true integration and equity, regarding empowerment as an issue. Teachers who use this approach teach their children to be sensitive to realities different from their own as well as to think critically about injustice. Antibias is not just a cognitive approach; it includes feelings and actions, too. A full antibias curriculum includes promoting equity for all aspects of human diversity—culture, race, ethnicity, gender, sexual orientation, ability, and age.

Inequity and Schools

How well children are educated and how good their school experience is for them depends on many factors, not the least of which is how many resources are available to the school they attend. Kozol (1991) has written an eye-opening book called *Savage Inequalities* about the discrepancies between the funding of inner-city schools in poor districts and schools in richer districts. In a nutshell, his message is that many children are being cheated out of a decent education—they don't have a chance.

Inner-city children tend to arrive in kindergarten to find an overburdened teacher trying to handle too many children in a decaying classroom that is badly in need of repair. Equipment, if there is any, is run-down; materials and books are minimal. Children who live in the suburbs have a different experience. They arrive in kindergarten to find much better conditions, even though now, in these hard times, few schools enjoy an abundance of economic resources. Even so, some of the wealthier districts have twice the funding per child of poorer districts in the same geographic region. In addition, parents in those wealthier schools get heavily involved in serious fund-raising to augment the tax-based income. Parents who know how to fund-raise and have connections to wealth have moved far beyond little bake sales. We have great discrepancies in our public school system in America today. It's quite likely that the child of wealthy or even middle-class parents will get a much better education than the child of poor parents.

THE PEER GROUP AS AN AGENT OF SOCIALIZATION

Although the peer group is not as important for younger children as for older ones, it is nevertheless an influence. Who makes up the peer group for young children? Kids in the apartment complex, on the block, and in school or child care become friends and playmates. Sometimes the composition of the peer group is controlled by parents as they arrange to get their children together with other children by making play dates. The formal or informal play group is an example of this kind of peer group. Other times children form their own peer group.

Children don't play in groups at first, though they may interact a good deal with whomever is around. If you watch toddlers in a group situation, such as an early education program, you find that they often play side by side—aware of each other but not interacting very often. One might influence the content and actions of the other's play, but each remains headed in his or her own direction, carrying on a private conversation and individually involved with toys or materials. Then you see that more and more often these pairs of children begin to interact. Soon the pairs become threesomes, and the peer group begins to form, eventually becoming a solid group with activities, norms,

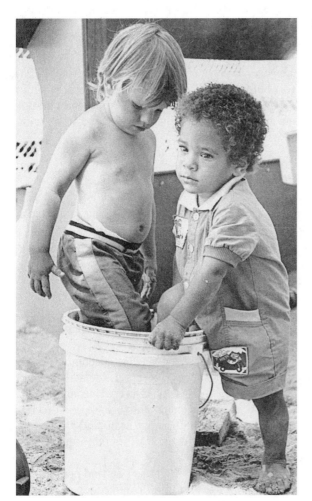

Peers are a socializing force.

interests, rules, traditions, expressions, and gestures of its own. The peer group becomes a subculture.

Children's choices of playmates are sometimes affected by gender. Children under age 7 may be willing to choose playmates of either gender, but most have a tendency to prefer those of their own gender. By elementary school this influence of gender on choice of playmates becomes notable (Maccoby, 1998).

To see the peer group influence, watch how something called *behavior contagion* works in a preschool classroom. One child starts screaming excitedly over something. In a few minutes the whole room is screaming and racing around after the leader who started it. Or one child starts swinging belly down on the swings, and soon all the swinging children have flipped over to prone positions.

Communication among peers can involve a very sophisticated set of signals. Watch a couple of 4-year-olds playing with action figures in a sandbox. Each knows what's pretend and what's not. Adults may not be so sure. When angry noises are heard from a distance, the protective adult may rush over to see what's happening and discover that the children are only pretending. Both children know it's pretend, but the adult isn't sure—it sounded so real!

Usually adults don't teach children how to play pretend. They learn informally from each other how to choose up and sort out roles and characters, how to determine the direction the action will take, and how to signal when something is pretend and not real. They agree on all this as they go along, usually in a manner that's so smooth it's hard to notice, as an observer, how it's coming about.

Functions of the Peer Group

The peer group functions so that children learn to give and take as equals. That's a different lesson from relating to parents or teachers. The peer group has its own system of modifying behavior through rewards and punishments, which mostly come in the form of acceptance and rejection: "If you don't play nice, I won't invite you to my birthday party!"

Learning to get along with others who are your age and status is important. Developing relationships of one's own choosing is also important and different from learning to get along with the people who just happen to be in your life because of the family you were born into.

The peer group also teaches a set of lessons that children don't get from adults; some of these lessons lie in areas that are sensitive and taboo. Much sex education comes from peers—whether parents and teachers like it or not.

The peer group serves as a step in developing independence, as children move out from their parents and family into a new set of circumstances. The group is centered around its own concerns and not necessarily bound by adult norms. It has its own hierarchy.

Another function of the peer group is to place the child in history. We don't recognize ourselves as members of a particular generation until we grow up and look at the generation coming up behind us. It is through the contrast that we identify ourselves as a generation of peers.

Adults can help children get along with their peers. Both teachers and parents can model desirable behavior, reinforce children when they display it, and coach children in social skills. Parents have a big influence on their children's peer relationships (Parke & O'Neil, 2000). A close attachment in infancy helps children develop social competency (Schneider, Atkinson, & Tardif, 2001). When parents interact with their children in ways that promote positive social behavior that takes feelings into account, the children tend to do the same with peers. When parents are negative and controlling in their interactions, such behavior can transfer to their children's interactions with peers and makes them less successful socially (Clark & Ladd, 2000).

THE MEDIA AS AN INFLUENCE ON SOCIALIZATION

Mass media—newspapers, magazines, comic books, radio, movies, and especially television—present a very different form of socialization than any other, because they offer no opportunity for interaction. Television is an influence on children from a very young age and affects their cognitive and social development (Wright et al., 2001).

Television is the medium with the greatest socialization effect, surpassing all the other media by far in its influence on the young child. The very fact that television is not an interactive agent is greatly significant to the development of young children. While watching, children have the feeling that they're interacting, but they're not. That's one of the disadvantages of television as a socializer—it satisfies social needs to some extent, but doesn't give children the social skills (or the real-life practice in those skills) that allow them to function effectively with people. Since the average child watches 3 to 4 hours of television a day, the time left for playing with others and learning social skills is drastically reduced. Even infants average about an hour and a half a day between the time they are born and age 2 (Wright et al., 2001).

Television is a passive form of socialization and replaces real interactions in many young children's lives.

Of course, parents can control the time their children spend watching television, but many don't. They can monitor the selection of programs, but some allow their children to watch whatever happens to be on. Some parents don't consider how they could use television to teach decision making. They don't make children aware that when one program ends they can either weigh the various merits of next offerings or turn the set off. Some children, especially those with a remote control in hand, flick through the channels periodically, randomly stopping at whatever catches their interest at the moment. That's very different from critically examining options and consciously deciding on one.

Children learn through watching television. Some of the things they learn are beneficial; others are not. They learn about the world and the ways of the society. They learn something about occupations, for example, getting an idea about what a nurse does, what a doctor does, and how the two relate to each other. They learn about the institutions of the society—what goes on in court, for example. They learn the language to go with these roles and settings—and they learn some language you'd rather they didn't know!

Children also learn about current themes and issues, both from newscasts and dramas—issues such as kidnapping, the homeless, and the spread of AIDS. Most of these issues and themes are not happy ones, and many are very frightening, especially when children watch programs that are intended for adults.

Children learn more than facts from television; they also get a good daily dose of stereotypes and a lot of misleading information about their world. Most of all, they get a big helping of violence and another of commercial advertising.

Television and Young Children

The following list of television guidelines may seem drastic and unrealistic, but television has a powerful impact on children, so drastic measures to counteract it are called for.

1. *Don't expose infants to television.* Don't use it as entertainment, and don't get in the habit of using it as a babysitter, no matter how tempting it is to do so. Infants are distracted by the disconnected noise and movement of television. They don't need distractions; they need personal interactions with people and objects in the real world.

2. *Examine your own television habits.* If you are addicted to the tube, the chances are any children around you while you are watching will also become addicted. Deal with your own addiction and take precautions so that children don't become TV addicts.

3. *One way to avoid the risk of addiction in children is to avoid exposing them to television altogether.* Children grow up just fine with no TV. If you decide you want children exposed, do it with caution and awareness. Don't turn the TV on and flip channels. Using a TV guide, make a conscious decision about what program to watch, turn the set on to watch it, and then turn it off when it is over.

4. *Sit with children while they watch television.* Then you are there to handle feelings, explain what needs explaining, clarify any confusion, and clear up misconceptions. You are also there to turn off the set when the program is over.
5. *Whatever you do, don't let children fill their time with television.* Active play should be the major pastime of the early years, not uninvolved visual entertainment.

These guidelines have been used by adults with good success. If you grew up with TV in your life and have never been without it, consider trying 2 weeks without TV; you'll find it makes a positive difference in your life, once you get over your withdrawal symptoms. Getting loose from the clutches of the tube will also make a positive difference in young children's lives.

Commercial Advertising

What's wrong with commercials? They're compelling, eye-catching, and even more interesting than a lot of programming. What's wrong is that they create artificial needs in children (and, indeed, in all of us). They are as manipulative as they can be, coaxing us, practically forcing us, in subtle ways, to go out and buy, buy, buy. They teach consumerism very effectively.

If you want to see how effective television commercials are, stand in the cereal aisle of a grocery store for just 10 minutes and watch the interactions between parents and children. None of the child's biological signals related to nutritional needs are in play in the cereal aisle. In fact, even if the shelves were rearranged so the most nutritious cereals with the least additives were at children's eye level, little hands would be reaching and pointing at the familiar sugar-filled cereal boxes they know so well from television. In one study, children indicated that they had successfully influenced their parents' buying decisions (Tinsley, 2002).

Violence

Turn on the television set during prime time, and, unless you select your programs carefully, you're likely to see an act of violence within 5 minutes and several more not too long afterward. Saturday morning is even worse. Eight of 10 programs contain violence, with prime-time programs averaging five violent acts per hour and Saturday morning cartoons averaging about 20 per hour (Gerbner, Gross, & Signorielli, 1986). The average child in the United States has seen 8,000 murders and 100,000 other violent acts during childhood (Bushman & Anderson, 2001), not to mention vulgar language and sex. Violence, sex, and vulgar language are interesting—and interest sells products—so we get exposed to a good deal of it. The question is: What does all this do to children?

For one thing, it eventually desensitizes them. If it didn't, how could people sit and eat a meal while watching people in living color be tortured, mutilated, shot, and even blown sky-high before their very eyes? That's enough to turn one's stomach, yet we get used to it by watching television.

Years of studies show that television watching and aggression go together. Children who watch more television are more aggressive. However, it's hard to tell whether television *causes* the aggression or whether children who are more aggressive just tend to watch more television. However, some experimental studies show that children who are exposed to a violent televised episode are more aggressive when they are put immediately into a real-life anger-provoking situation. These children show more physical aggression than children who watch something nonviolent before being put into the same situation. Bandura and Walters (1963) did the classic study of children modeling the behavior of adults they saw on films punching an inflated "knock-down" figure. Many other studies since have shown similar results.

Television viewing of violence and real-life violence are connected. A long-term study followed 300 boys for 30 years. The boys who watched more TV violence at age 8 turned out to do more espousal violence and more criminal violence by age 32 (Huesmann & Miller, 1994).

One way to discover the effects of television on children is to study a group of children who have not been exposed to television and then observe them after television comes into their lives. Such a study was done in northern Canada in a remote place where television hadn't yet penetrated. Then, when television was introduced, researchers were able to make comparisons. They found that violent behavior increased in both boys and girls (Hirsch, 1997).

If we want to confront violence in our society, we must pay attention to these kinds of studies. We must regard television as the dangerous device it is and bring it under conscious control. We must not let it continue to influence children in negative ways. The children slouched in front of sets today are the ones who grow up to be tomorrow's citizens. What kinds of citizens will they be?

This is not just a concern for families, but also for the community, for the society. Violence affects all of us. There was a time when the society took charge of protecting children from the media. The Federal Communications Commission (FCC) put regulations into effect in the 1930s, which by the 1960s were strengthened enough to protect the first of the television generations. These regulations allowed intervention in cases where children were exposed to commercial exploitation or other forms of abuse by the media. The idea was to ensure that television provided for social good, rather than increasing social ills. When the FCC deregulated television, that protection disappeared and was then left up to families, many of whom are not aware of the problems with unmonitored TV watching by children. It's time now to reinstate those regulations. We allow other regulating bodies to protect our children from unhealthy influences. It's time to allow the FCC to continue to do the good work they started. When children watch TV violence they see it works and some of them begin to use violence themselves as a way to solve problems and deal with conflict (Bushman & Huesmann, 2001). Television is a strong social force. It needs to be used in growth-enhancing ways (Carlsson-Paige & Levin, 1990).

Television is a powerful teaching tool because it is in virtually every home across the nation. Whether you're focusing on the negative or the positive effects, or both, it's easy to see that television viewing influences the knowledge, behavior, and attitudes of children. If the lessons are to be beneficial, the positive aspects of the medium must be emphasized and attention must be paid to the negative, because unmonitored watching can teach racial and gender stereotypes, ideas about sexual relationships, and aggressive sexual behavior (Signorelli & Morgan, 2001), as well as general aggression and violence—all while commercially exploiting young children. When adults concern themselves with what children are watching and for how long, TV can be a teaching tool. The tool works best when adults watch with children, explaining what they don't understand and putting a moral light on what children watch. To be an effective early teacher, television must increase developmentally appropriate and growth-enhancing options for children among its offerings. In addition, parents must become aware of its potential—both good and harmful. A strong campaign of parent education is needed. Imagine the good that could come of a national conference on children's television that could provide opportunities for media representatives to talk with children's advocates, educators, parents, and sponsors about television strategies to work *for* the good of children and society (Boyer, 1991).

To summarize, television influences the socialization of children in a number of ways. It replaces active involvement with the world and the people in it, giving children little chance to learn and practice a variety of social skills. The average young child who watches 4 hours of television a day misses out on his or her full share of early *active* learning. Television also replaces real needs with artificial ones that are created by product manufacturers and distributors to get children to want, want, want. And it affects children's behavior through the sheer quantity of violence that is portrayed.

Television has benefits, too, especially when adults concern themselves with what children are watching and for how long. It can be a teaching tool when adults watch with children, explaining what they don't understand and putting it into a moral context.

Whether you're focusing on the negative or the positive effects, or both, it's easy to see that television viewing influences the knowledge, behavior, and attitudes of children.

SUMMARY

This chapter looked at four major socializing agents: the family, the school, the peer group, and television. Throughout this chapter and the preceding ones, a number of societal issues concerning the socialization of the young child were mentioned. The next chapter wraps up the book by exploring how public policy relates to these issues.

FOR DISCUSSION

1. What other socializing agents can you think of besides the four discussed in the chapter?

2. Give an example of how the status of the family affects the child's socialization. Give an example of how being the target of bias can affect socialization.

3. How can a family's income level affect the way its children are socialized?

4. Do you know someone who was "tracked" in school? How did that experience affect that person?

5. How are children expected to behave in kindergarten? Do you know a child who doesn't behave that way? Why doesn't he or she? How might that behavior affect that child's kindergarten performance?

6. What would you expect to find on the walls of a kindergarten room where the teacher had an antibias curriculum?

7. What are your feelings, ideas, and experiences in relation to television and young children? How do they relate to what the chapter said about television? What do children learn from watching TV?

REFERENCES

Bandura, A., & Walters, R. H. (1963). *Social learning and personality development*. New York: Holt, Rinehart & Winston.

Boyer, E. L. (1991). *Ready to learn: A mandate for the nation*. Princeton, NJ: Carnegie Foundation for the Advancement of Teaching.

Bushman, B. J., & Anderson, C. A. (2001). Media violence and the American public: Scientific facts versus media misinformation. *American Psychologist, 56,* 466–489.

Bushman, D., & Huesmann, L. R. (2001). Effects of televised violence on aggression. In D. Singer & J. Singer (Eds.), *Handbook of children and the media*. Thousand Oaks, CA: Sage.

Carlsson-Paige, N., & Levin, D. E. (1990). *Who's calling the shots: How to respond effectively to children's fascination with war play and war toys*. Philadelphia: New Society.

Clark, K. E., & Ladd, G. W. (2000). Connectedness and autonomy support in parent-child relationships: Links to children's socio-emotional orientation and peer relationships. *Developmental Psychology, 36,* 485–498.

Derman-Sparks, L., & the ABC Task Force. (1989). *Antibias curriculum: Tools for empowering young children*. Washington, DC: National Association for the Education of Young Children.

Gerbner, G., Gross, L., & Signorielli, N. (1986). Living with television: The dynamics of the cultivation process. In J. Bryant & D. Zillman (Eds.), *Perspectives on media effects*. Hillsdale, NJ: Erlbaum.

Hirsch, K. W. (1997). Media violence and audience behavior. In A. Wells & E. Hakanen (Eds.), *Mass media and society* (5th ed., pp. 479–505). Greenwich, CT: Ablex.

Huesmann, L. R., & Miller, L. S. (1994). Long-term effects of repeated exposure to media violence in childhood. In L. R. Huesman (Ed.), *Aggressive behavior: Current perspectives* (pp. 153–186). New York: Plenum.

Kozol, J. (1991). *Savage inequalities: Children in America's schools*. New York: Crown.

Lally, J. R., (1998, May). Brain research, infant learning, and child care curriculum. *Child Care Information Exchange, 121,* 46–48.

Maccoby, E. E. (1998). *The two sexes*. Cambridge, MA: Harvard University Press.

McKenna, T., & Ortiz, F. I. (Eds.). (1988). *The broken web: The educational experience of Hispanic American women*. Encino, CA: Floricanto.

National Research Council and Institute of Medicine. (2000). *From neurons to neighborhoods: The science of early childhood development*. Board on Children, Youth, and Families, Commission on Behavioral and Social Sciences and Education. Washington, DC: National Academy Press.

Parke, R. D., & O'Neil, R. (2000). The influence of significant others on learning about relationships: From family to friends. In R. S. L. Mills & S. Duck (Eds.), *The developmental psychology of personal relationships* (pp. 15–47). New York: Wiley.

Schneider, B. H., Atkinson, L., & Tardif, C. (2001). Child-parent attachment and children's peer relations: A quantitative review. *Developmental Psychology, 37,* 86–100.

Shonkoff, J. P., & Phillips, D. (2001, April-May). From neurons to neighborhoods: The science of early childhood development—An introduction. *Zero to Three, 21*(5), 4–7.

Shore, R. (1997). *Rethinking the brain: New insights in early development*. New York: Families and Work Institute.

Signorielli, N., & Morgan, M. (2001). Television and the family: The cultivation perspective. In J. Bryant & J. A. Bryant (Eds.), *Television and the American family* (2nd ed., pp. 333–351). Mahwah, NJ: Erlbaum.

Tinsley, B. R. (2002). *How children learn to be healthy*. New York: Cambridge University Press.

Wright, J. C., Huston, A. C., Murphy, K. C., St. Peters, M., Pinon, M., Scantlin, R., & Kotler, J. (2001). The relations of early television viewing to school readiness and vocabulary of children from low-income families: The early window project. *Child Development, 72*, 1347–1366.

Zigler, E. F., Finn-Stevenson, M., & Hall, N. W. (2003). *The first three years and beyond: Brain development and social policy*. New Haven: Yale University Press.

FURTHER READING

Boutte, G. S., LaPoint, S., & Davis, B. (1993, November). Racial issues in education: Real or imagined? *Young Children, 49*(1), 19–23.

Bushman, B. J., & Anderson, C. A. (2001). Media violence and the American public: Scientific facts versus media misinformation. *American Psychologist, 56*, 466–489.

Bushman, D., & Huesmann, L. R. (2001). Effects of televised violence on aggression. In D. Singer & J. Singer (Eds.), *Handbook of children and the media*. Thousand Oaks, CA: Sage.

Clark, L., DeWolf, S., & Clark, C. (1992). Teaching teachers to avoid having culturally assaultive classrooms. *Young Children, 47*(5), 4–9.

Lally, J. R. (1998, May). Brain research, infant learning, and child care curriculum. *Child Care Information Exchange, 121*, 46–48.

Maccoby, E. E. (1998). *The two sexes*. Cambridge, MA: Harvard University Press.

National Research Council and Institute of Medicine. (2000). *From neurons to neighborhoods: The science of early childhood development*. Board on Children, Youth, and Families, Commission on Behavioral and Social Sciences and Education. Washington, DC: National Academy Press.

Parke, R. D., & O'Neil, R. (2000). The influence of significant others on learning about relationships: From family to friends. In R. S. L. Mills & S. Duck (Eds.), *The developmental psychology of personal relationships* (pp. 15–47). New York: Wiley.

Schneider, B. H., Atkinson, L., & Tardif, C. (2001). Child-parent attachment and children's peer relations: A quantitative review. *Developmental Psychology, 37*, 86–100.

Shonkoff, J. P., & Phillips, D. (2001, April-May). From neurons to neighborhoods: The science of early childhood development—An introduction. *Zero to Three, 21*(5), 4–7.

Shore, R., (1997). *Rethinking the brain: New insights in early development*. New York: Families and Work Institute.

Signorielli, N., & Morgan, M. (2001). Television and the family: The cultivation perspective. In J. Bryant & J. A. Bryant (Eds.), *Television and the American family* (2nd ed., pp. 333–351). Mahwah, NJ: Erlbaum.

Tinsley, B. R. (2002). *How children learn to be healthy*. New York: Cambridge University Press.

Wright, J. C., Huston, A. C., Murphy, K. C., St. Peters, M., Pinon, M., Scantlin, R., & Kotler, J. (2001). The relations of early television viewing to school readiness and vocabulary of children from low-income families: The early window project. *Child Development, 72*, 1347–1366.

Zigler, E. F., Finn-Stevenson, M., & Hall, N. W. (2003). *The first three years and beyond: Brain development and social policy*. New Haven: Yale University Press.

Zillmann, D., Bryant, J., Huston, A. C. (Eds.). (1994). *Media, children, and the family: Social scientific psychodynamic, and clinical perspectives*. Hillsdale, NJ: Erlbaum.

CHAPTER 15

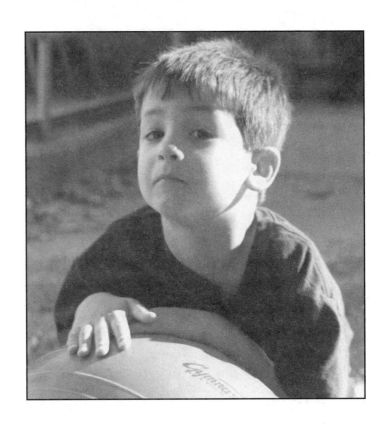

Social Policy Issues

In this chapter you'll discover . . .

- More about the national "ready to learn" goal
- What "ready to learn" means
- What health and nutrition have to do with the "ready to learn" goal
- Head Start
- A proposed "children's movement"
- The directions in which child care policy should move
- How "prevention" is more cost-effective than "remediation"
- The Children's Defense Fund
- How to be an advocate for children

This book has looked at ways families and their early childhood education partners socialize children for high self-esteem as well as how the community contributes to the socialization process. Along the way we examined obstacles in the way of a healthy socialization process, not the least of which are poverty, lack of access to quality education and child care, and the media.

What can we do, as a society, to address these issues? What can the community do to ensure that all children get an equal chance to develop high self-esteem and fulfill themselves in this society? How can we help all children "make it"? This chapter examines social policy issues that relate to these questions.

WHO IS RESPONSIBLE FOR AMERICA'S CHILDREN?

An underlying social policy on which this nation was founded is that families are responsible for their own children. However, it is becoming clearer and clearer that, although families must still take primary responsibility for their children, many

What's keeping us from putting forth a giant effort to meet the needs of our children?

families are not, at present, able to be completely self-sufficient. It's not that these families care any less about their children than more self-sufficient families do; it's just that they find themselves in circumstances that prevent them from being able to meet all their children's needs. The question is: If families can't meet their own children's needs, how much will the society take over the responsibility for those unmet needs?

The future of America depends on *somebody* providing for the needs of America's children—all of them. If we've reached a place in our economic, political, social, and moral history where masses of children are neglected, it's time for us, as individuals and as a society, to change that situation.

What's keeping us from putting forth a giant effort to meet the needs of America's children—of *our* children? One often unspoken theory behind the society's reluctance as a whole to put forth monumental effort to improve the lives of all its citizens is the idea that we each get what we deserve. This perspective justifies leaving things as they are. Those who are society's successes, the top of the heap, are given credit for their ability to work hard and be rewarded; the people who fall to the bottom are seen as not having tried hard enough. The view is that the people who live on the crumbs at the bottom of the barrel were born with the same chances of getting the whole contents of the barrel as everyone else. On the surface that may seem to be true. After all, this is America, land of opportunity, home of the free.

Does Every Child Get an Equal Start?

The Carnegie Report of the Task Force on Meeting the Needs of Young Children (1994) indicates that many children under age 3 are affected by one or more risk factors that make healthy development difficult. Of the children born in this country, 26% are to unmarried mothers. Many of these mothers are teenagers; according to the report, about 1 million adolescents become pregnant each year. According to more recent statistics, 43 of every 1,000 females between the ages of 15 and 19 gave birth to a baby in 2002 (Children's Defense Fund, 2004).

Poverty is a factor in the lives of 16.6% of children under 18 in the United States. Although in a recent 20-year span (between 1971 and 1991) the number of children younger than 6 increased by 10%, the number of *poor children* in that age range increased by more than 60%!

Great numbers of children are now in early care and education programs. In 2002, 64% of mothers with children under 6 were in the labor force, and that number rose to 78% for mothers of children older than 6 (Children's Defense Fund, 2004). With the research on benefits of quality early care and education programs, those numbers can be considered the good news. The bad news is that federal and state funding for the parts of the programs that give them the high quality they enjoy are in jeopardy as the lagging economy makes it essential to cut costs.

Children and Equal Opportunity

Let's look a little closer at who makes it and who doesn't and see whether they were indeed born with the same opportunities. Take three pregnant women who live 20 miles apart from each other: the first, a 16-year-old who lives with her mother and two sisters in a run-down two-room apartment in a gang-ridden neighborhood at the edge of a decaying industrial section of a large city; the second, a 25-year-old who lives with her jobless husband in a small duplex in the older part of a suburban area; and the third, a 28-year-old who lives with her executive husband in a single-family home, surrounded by grass and flowers on a pleasant tree-lined street in a newer development in the sprawling part of the outer suburbs.

The 16-year-old's baby starts out already behind because of her mother's age, physical condition, and situation, which includes lack of prenatal care, poor diet, the stress of living in poverty, and the industrial pollution of the neighborhood. The second woman's baby also starts out behind because when her husband lost his job, they lost their insurance and medical benefits, so she's not getting prenatal care either. In addition, she supports the family by working in a child care center for minimum wage, which barely pays the rent, let alone utilities and food. This family is sometimes hungry. The wife receives no benefits from her job, except for sick leave, which she has used up because of frequent illness from being exposed to the children she works with. She worries constantly about the family's financial condition, about her husband, who is deeply depressed, and most of all about her baby. The third woman's unborn baby gets all she needs before she is born, including good food, plenty of prenatal monitoring, and a relatively healthy and peaceful environment.

Which of these babies will even be alive at the end of the 1st year? The chances are excellent that one will, but the other two face the risk of dying before their first birthday. According to Shames (1991), in *Outside the Dream: Child Poverty in America*, the United States ranked 19th in the industrialized world at keeping its infants alive and 49th (behind Albania and Botswana) in immunizing its nonwhite infants against polio, mostly because of a high level of poverty. By comparison, 9 years later the Children's Defense Fund yearbook, *State of America's Children* 2000, said that the United States ranked 22nd, meaning that other industrialized nations had a lower infant mortality rate than the United States. How could that be, with all our technology and scientific advances including new vaccines, organ transplants, cancer treatments, and improvements in neonatal intensive care?

True, we have technology for sick and premature babies. We save lives, especially in dramatic cases. But the poverty factor enters in. Babies born in many families still die before their 1st birthday. To assess the situation, you have to look closer at the statistics. Throughout the Children's Defense Fund yearbook (2004), statistics are given showing the differences between the lives of children of one group compared to others. For example, on page 180, it says that black infants die at more than twice the rate of white infants. Are all children born with equal opportunities in the United States?

What about when these three babies reach kindergarten? What are their relative chances of entering public school ready to learn? According to a national survey of kindergarten teachers, in California 38% of children enter kindergarten not ready to participate successfully. In Hawaii, it's 47% percent; in Arkansas and Delaware, 42%; in New Mexico, 40%; and in New York, 36% (Boyer, 1991, p. 140). Which of the babies of the three pregnant women is most likely to arrive at kindergarten prepared? Any guesses?

READY TO LEARN: A GOAL FOR ALL OF AMERICA'S CHILDREN

Ready to learn—what does that mean? In the preceding chapter it was pointed out that readiness is far more than teaching 4-year-olds across the nation their ABC's. It means that children must get their basic needs met—food, shelter, health care, security, and peace in the family. They need to know how to make connections with others, cooperate, get along, and feel good about themselves and others. Socialization is an important part of learning and learning is an important part of socialization. All children need a variety of early experiences that enrich their minds, tickle their curiosity, fill their hearts, and enliven their spirit. They need adults in their lives who understand developmentally appropriate practices and cultural sensitivity and encourage them to embrace learning joyfully.

Let's look again at this issue of "ready to learn," which was a goal put forth in the early 1990s by President George H. Bush and agreed on by the governors of all 50 states. The goal was stated: By the year 2000, every child in America should start school ready to learn. Did we reach that goal? Although numerous programs are in full swing across the nation today, indications are that we haven't yet come to the point that all children start kindergarten on an equal footing. Why not?

First, what does "ready to learn" mean, anyway? Anyone who has studied infancy and learning knows that babies are born ready to learn. If we couldn't tell by observation, we now have impressive brain research to back up what a lot of people knew before technology got so advanced (see Shore's 1997 book, *Rethinking the Brain: New Insights into Early Development*). Babies have a lot of learning to do, even in their 1st year, and in most cases, they come fully equipped to do that learning. So it was a bit naive of Bush (the elder), and the governors to think that learning starts in kindergarten.

Rob Reiner, Hollywood producer and entertainer, wasn't thinking kindergarten when he put together a huge campaign to bring the results of the brain research to the parents and early educators in this country in the late 1990s. A television special called "I Am Your Child" showed an array of Hollywood stars telling the nation's parents, early childhood educators, and policy makers that the 1st years last forever. What happens in those early years makes all the difference. Later that same year, Reiner passed out 7,000 free copies of a videotape with the same theme to participants at the National Association for Education of Young Children annual conference in Anaheim, California. The campaign has continued and expanded. For instance, in 1998 it supported an initiative on the ballot in California (called Prop 10) to place a 50-cent tax on cigarettes that would go to promoting development in the early years. The voters passed the tax.

Today Prop 10 councils in every county in the state decide what to do with their share of the tax money designated to help the lives of young children. We don't have to look only to government to make things happen. It's remarkable what a private citizen can do to make a difference.

So the "ready to learn" campaign took avenues beyond what former President Bush and the governors had in mind in the 1990s. And it all started long before anybody was looking at the face of the new millennium and before George H. Bush had the idea. Early childhood educators have been working for 100 years to make things better for children and families. Their work came to public attention in the 1960s when Head Start began its project of trying to enhance the lives and learning of young children.

Head Start

Head Start was originally conceived as a quick catch-up summer school program that would teach low-income children in a few weeks what they needed to know to start kindergarten. But once it was determined that you can't make up for 5 years of poverty with a 6-week preschool program, Head Start expanded far beyond its original beginnings.

Head Start has been successful in its efforts to meet many of the needs of the population it serves. As an early childhood program that goes beyond educating children, Head Start has had a comprehensive approach designed to provide services that address a variety of family needs. These services have made a difference in the lives of young children and their families. Head Start continued to evolve to do an even better job by expanding and modifying its program to meet even more needs. An original weakness was that Head Start didn't have models that responded to teen parents' and working parents' needs. That changed over the years until Head Start was doing a great job—but unfortunately, changes and funding cuts have put Head Start into turmoil. The program served 912,000 children in 2003, but that represents only 3 out of 5 eligible children (Children's Defense Fund, 2004). Originally conceived as a prekindergarten program for 4-year-olds, Head Start has moved downward to serve families of younger-aged children. Early Head Start grants are now being used to provide services to infants and toddlers, pregnant women, expectant fathers, parents, and guardians. The goal is to help families fulfill parental roles and move forward toward economic independence while providing for their children's physical, social, emotional, and intellectual development.

Head Start's purpose has always been to involve low-income families in the solutions to their own problems by empowering them politically and economically, instead of just offering them services. Head Start was not just a preschool, but a comprehensive program. Unfortunately, the trend seems to be to cut it back to a narrow preschool focus. It is imperative that Head Start retain its family focus because the strength of the family directly relates to their children's future. To make a difference, a program like Head Start can't just deal with children; it has to include the whole family.

Head Start is a national effort, aimed to be locally responsive and locally controlled. If the federal government doesn't provide full Head Start services to each community, the model could be adopted by communities who want to start their own Head Start programs.

Child Care

It is time for this society to consider young children as a national priority. We have a peace movement, a civil rights movement, a women's movement, and an ecology movement. We need a children's movement. The Federal Child Care bill, which was passed at the beginning of the 1990s, is a step in the right direction. A demonstration at the nation's capital on June 1, 1996, was another step. The "I Stand for Children" demonstration drew people from across the country to stand in the Capital Mall and show by their presence their concern for the nation's children. The theme has been taken up by local communities since then, and each June 1 different events signal the Stand for Children theme around the country. Clinton's White House Conference on Children in the mid-1990s was a first and helped bring further attention to the nation's responsibility to its children. George W. Bush along with wife Laura held a somewhat similar White House Conference when he first got into office, gathering early childhood leaders from around the country to listen to his ideas about what he had in mind for the field.

Culturally Responsive Care

Changing demographics present a challenge to child care programs: They must now more than ever before discover how to deliver *culturally responsive care.* A report from California Tomorrow (Chang, Muckelroy, & Pulido-Tobiassen, 1996) proposes five core principles for care in a diverse society:

1. Principle 1 involves adults' understanding how racism impacts the development of children's self-identity and their attitudes toward others.
2. Principle 2 advocates building on the culture of the families and promoting cross-cultural understanding among children in child care.
3. Principle 3 relates to preserving children's home language and encouraging all children in child care to learn a second language.
4. Principle 4 has to do with child care staff working with families to nurture the well-being of children.
5. Principle 5 involves child care staff engaging in ongoing dialogue with families as well as self-reflection about diversity.

In addition to the five principles, professional development, recruitment and retention of a diverse workforce, ongoing research, and dissemination of research results to parents are all essential to the kind of care that promotes children's healthy development in a diverse society.

This report relates directly to the National Association for the Education of Young Children's (NAEYC) 1996 position statement "Responding to Linguistic and Cultural Diversity: Recommendations for Effective Early Childhood Education." Both organizations—California

Tomorrow and the NAEYC—have as a goal to build support for equal access to high-quality educational programs that recognize and promote all aspects of children's development and learning, enabling all children to become competent, successful, and socially responsible adults.

In the future, we, as a society, must offer enough choices so that parents can find child care and early education in tune with what they want and need for their children. Stopping the funding cuts and expanding Head Start and providing more child care centers aren't the only answers. The choices must include ways parents can care for their own children and a wide variety of systems that provide for care by others. We already have some models in place besides Head Start and center care. Family child care and shared in-home care are just two examples. Creative alternatives in the workplace that allow working parents a greater role in caring for their own children include flextime, which allows parents to stagger work schedules; part-time work; job sharing; parent subsidies, which allow parents to be at home more with their children; flexible benefits plans; and flexible leave policies.

We need more child care; we haven't come close to meeting the need. Children from low-income families frequently lack the opportunity to enroll in early care and education programs. Only 40.4% of children from low-income families were in early care and education programs, compared to 68.3% of families with income over $75,000. In addition, waiting lists reflect the need for child care assistance. In California 280,000 children are on waiting lists, with 48,000 in Texas and 46,960 in Florida (Children's Defense Fund, 2004). We need more child care, but we can't just have *more*—we need to have *better* child care. Cuts to quality initiatives reflect how states are scaling back efforts to improve quality in early care and education programs, including some cuts that involve basic health and safety. For example, Oklahoma's cuts included reducing provider education funding, grants for quality improvement, and fire code compliance (Children's Defense Fund, 2004).

We have to upgrade the training, status, and salaries of child care teachers, who are grossly underpaid, putting them in the ranks of the poor. Children suffer from burned-out teachers and high turnover rates. Quality child care makes a difference. We can't promote economic independence for families without also promoting good child care. Child care is a means to family preservation and a key component in school readiness. Indeed, child care is often seen as the answer to problems of the economy, a means of addressing the miseries of poverty, and a strong tool for eradicating bias in the next generation, besides providing general early education for young children.

The problem is that poorly funded child care doesn't live up to all the dreams we have for it. Quality is a major issue. Without quality, child care doesn't do its job. It is hard to have quality when no one wants to pay the cost, including the government. A Children's Defense Fund (2000, p. 49) study determined that in 1999 only 13 states' child care assistance programs paid providers at the 75th percentile rate or higher. The rest of the states paid lower rates. In other words, families in the 13 top-paying states who needed quality child care in 1999 had access to only three out of four providers and not the ones who charged the most. Quality doesn't come cheap. Instead of recognizing and acknowledging that fact, consumers and funding sources continue to allow child care policy that keeps child care workers at poverty-level wages.

Early childhood programs, such as Head Start, and quality child care can help break the cycle of poverty and disadvantage by helping the parents and by preparing the next generation to take full advantage of educational and training opportunities. The most effective programs do far more than merely deliver early childhood education and care for children. To meet children's needs, they provide comprehensive services to the whole family. They connect the family to the greater community.

An example of such a program is the Parent Services Project (PSP), mentioned in Chapter 12, which was started by Ethel Seiderman (Lee & Seiderman, 1998; Links, Beggs, & Seiderman, 1997). This project serves as a model of how child care can go far beyond just providing care for children, by also supporting families.

MOVING TOWARD FULL-INCLUSION PROGRAMS

The United State Congress since 1975 has been passing legislation designed to move children with special needs out of isolation and into programs that serve their typically developing peers. The Individuals with Disabilities Education Act (IDEA) of 1990 has supported what's called "inclusion"—that is, integrating cildren with special needs into early care and education programs of all sorts, including center-based care, family child care, and infant-toddler programs. Inclusion programs encourage children with disabilities to reach higher levels of achievement and develop a broader range of social skills. It exposes them earlier to the larger world that they will live in as adults. All children benefit when children with special needs are integrated into classrooms with their typically developing peers. They can't just be thrown together, however. Care must be taken to be sure everyone's needs are met and the children with special needs are helped to feel that they belong. That takes training of teachers, caregivers, and family child care providers.

For example, children with disabilities may need support when it comes to making use of a rich environment. Materials should be selected to fit all children's capabilities, including those with special needs. Accessibility is important too. It doesn't do any good to put a child in a rich environment if he can't get to what he's interested in.

Some children need to be taught how to use an environment set up for learning through play. It helps if a teacher is nearby observing and commenting, modeling, and even making suggestions. Judging how a play environment is working depends on observing how children are using it. All children should be using the toys, materials, and activities creatively and to the best of their abilities. They should be able to make choices and use the materials as independently as they can. The degree of engagement can vary widely, but should be an indication of how the environment is working.

ECONOMIC DEVELOPMENT

You can't just take the child out of the family and provide education and child care without looking at the factors that influence what the child goes home to. Poverty is a big influence on family life and therefore on children's early development, which affects their ability to learn when they reach kindergarten age.

A key to alleviating poverty is jobs—jobs that pay enough to live on. Increased employment can be enhanced by community involvement in identifying available jobs, improving access by reducing discrimination and other barriers, improving training, and developing job search and interview skills in underemployed people.

Who is going to do all that? We all must. No single approach will eliminate poverty in America. It will take a massive effort on the part of government at all levels, educational institutions, corporations, foundations, communities, and individuals.

ADEQUATE HEALTH SERVICES AND NUTRITION FOR ALL

Go back to those pregnant women at the beginning of the chapter. The point of those vignettes is that good health and nutrition are vitally linked to later achievement. To enter kindergarten equally prepared, every child must have a healthy birth,

Good health and nutrition are vitally linked to readiness to learn. To enter kindergarten ready to learn, every child must have a healthy birth, adequate nutrition, and medical protection and care in the early years.

adequate pre- and postnatal care and nutrition, and medical protection and care in the early years.

Adequate nutrition starting before birth is a must for healthy development. WIC (Women, Infants, and Children), a federal nutrition program already in place, can accomplish this goal. Unfortunately, WIC doesn't reach everyone who is eligible for the services.

Health care delivery has been a patchwork system involving federal, state, and private sectors. Unfortunately, this system does not meet the need. For health care to be available to all, each sector of the society must commit to finding ways to make it accessible and affordable to everyone who needs it. After welfare reform occurred and Aid to Families with Dependent Children (AFDC) was replaced by Temporary Assistance to Needy Families (TANF), the numbers of children without health care rose. Attempts to correct that situation are continuing to be made.

Public health insurance should be expanded to all poor families. Additional community and migrant health centers should be established to serve the medically underserved. The National Health Service Corps, which provides scholarships and loan repayments to health professionals, should be adequately funded. The childhood vaccination program should be augmented to serve all infants and preschoolers who now go unprotected. Community health centers should receive adequate financial support for maternal and child health programs. Employers should offer subsidized health insurance with dependent coverage to all employees regardless of pay level. Plans should fully cover cost-effective services such as prenatal care and preventive care for children. In addition, employer wellness policies should support families by providing adequate sick and family leave. Employers can also provide increased on-site health education.

But just providing services is not enough. Families must take responsibility to seek out and use the services that are available. Some may need to be educated about how to use medical care services.

TAKING A PREVENTIVE APPROACH

It sounds as if a lot is being done at this point with all these examples. However, what is being done is a drop in the bucket compared with the need. Unfortunately, a good many of the services mentioned respond to emergency situations rather than preventing them in the first place. Here's a little parable to illustrate the point:

> *Once there was a kindly man walking by a river. He looked out into the strong current and saw a young child struggling in the swirling waters. He threw off his shoes and plunged into the swiftly moving water. It took all the strength he had, but he finally managed to pull the child from the grip of the river, drag him up on the bank, and give him CPR. The child was saved! But lo and behold, the man looked up from the child he had just rescued and saw another child in the water. Again he raced into the river, fought hard, and managed to save this child too. But the same thing happened. He looked up in time to see yet another child struggling in the swift current. Dead tired, he dragged himself once more*

to the river and plunged in. He continued in this manner until he collapsed from exhaustion and was no longer able to save any more children. That was the end of his rescue mission. Sadly enough, he had been so busy saving children that he was never able to leave long enough to walk upstream to stop whoever was throwing the children into the river in the first place!

This parable shows how our society operates in regard to children at this point. Instead of taking adequate prevention measures, we allow children to flounder in dangerous waters, and then we try to rescue them. It would be much more economical and energy-effective to walk upstream and stop them from being thrown in! It's cheaper and better to prevent damage than to repair it.

A common problem of the rescue approach is that children too often must be rescued from their own parents because they don't get adequate care. That kind of rescuing can be disastrous. Children placed in foster care must deal with the emotional effects of separation and are often left with lifelong scars. Many children could remain at home if there were more programs that focused on strengthening families rather than on removing children. The costs of taking children from their families are enormous. Besides the emotional costs, there are financial burdens that taxpayers must shoulder. It costs much more to provide foster care than it would to give families what they need to keep their children home. Happily, there has been a recent trend for keeping families together. This trend is reflected in the proposals of the Children's Defense Fund group, which is continually making recommendations for systemic reforms aimed at keeping families intact.

Here are three recommendations that would prevent the society from having to rescue floundering children:

1. Create in every community a network of comprehensive services to strengthen families and give them the tools they need to support and nurture their children.

2. Make family preservation services and other specialized community-based treatment available to all families in crisis.

3. Improve the quality of out-of-home placements so that special needs are met and children are returned to families or adopted as appropriate.

ADVOCACY

Marian Wright Edelman, the founder of the Children's Defense Fund, gives this advice to her children: "If you see a need, don't ask, 'Why doesn't somebody do something?' Ask, 'Why don't I do something?' " That's good advice for all of us. Anyone who cares about America's future must become an advocate for making the world a better place for children and families. Here are some ways to do that:

1. *Get involved!* Start by informing yourself about the status of children and families in your neighborhood, community, state, and nation. Use your own eyes. Visit local programs that serve low-income children and see the effects of poverty. Read.

Speak out for children. They can't speak out for themselves.

Get a current copy of *The State of America's Children*, published each year by the Children's Defense Fund (122 C Street NW, Washington, DC, 20001; [202] 628–8787).

2. *Speak out for children!* Inform others through speaking to religious groups, at candidate forums, and to community groups. Write a letter to the editor of your local newspaper.

3. *Do something this week to help children.* If you're not already involved, volunteer at a Head Start program, a child care program, or a school. If you are already busy during the day or don't want to work directly with children, offer your services as a fund-raiser. Every program needs more money than it has, and most are involved in varying degrees of fund-raising efforts. If you want to feel good, take a look at a director's face when you arrive in his or her office and offer to help with fund-raising.

4. *Be a role model for your community.* Don't wait around for someone else to take the reins. If you show you care, others are likely to follow your example.

5. *Register and vote.* Elect candidates who keep children and families a priority.

6. *Understand how public policies make a difference.* Public policies, though they may be conceived of on a national, state, or more local level, influence our lives and those of our children. Policies are decisions about goals and objectives, which become plans of action, translating eventually into programs.

The part of the advocate in helping create policy involves the following steps (adapted from Goffin & Lombardi, 1989, which gives a lot more information about how to be an advocate for children and families):

1. Identify a problem that requires action.
2. Convince someone to accept responsibility for helping to solve the problem. This someone may be the government.
3. Develop and propose acceptable solutions to the problem.
4. Monitor the implementation of the solution.
5. Evaluate the program.

It's important to hold your leaders accountable. One way to do this is to keep track of how lawmakers vote on issues of importance to children and their families.

SUMMARY

This chapter examined how we, as a society, can use the social policy we have, as well as instituting new policies, to upgrade the lives of the children of this nation. It examined the issue of who is responsible for America's children, concluding that we all are.

We, as a society, need to make our children a top priority. We need a children's movement in order to ensure that all children have their needs met. We could put an enormous effort into upgrading the quality of children's lives by strengthening their families, providing for their needs, and making available rich early experiences that engage their minds and bring joy, spirit, and curiosity to their lives.

We, as an American community, can work toward making a greater contribution to the socialization processes of our children. We can look for ways to give all children the opportunities necessary to build a healthy sense of self. We can keep the view that all children deserve an equal chance to fulfill themselves in this society. It won't be easy, but what better way to use our energy to prepare for the future of the United States than through caring for its children?

FOR DISCUSSION

1. What are your ideas, feelings, and experiences related to equal opportunity for children? Does Head Start contribute to equality of opportunity? If yes, how? What are your ideas about getting the nation's children "ready to learn"?
2. What are your experiences with the health care system, and how do you think it affects young children?

3. If you were to make recommendations to create or improve on our national child care system, what would those recommendations be? What could child care programs do to support parents that they aren't doing now? What would they need in order to be able to do what you suggest?

4. Have you ever been involved in advocating for children? If yes, what are your experiences? If no, how might you become involved?

REFERENCES

Boyer, E. L. (1991). *Ready to learn*: A *mandate for the nation*. Princeton, NJ: Carnegie Foundation for the Advancement of Teaching.

Carnegie Task Force on Meeting the Needs of Young Children. (1994, July). Starting points: Executive summary of the report of the Carnegie Corporation of New York Task Force on Meeting the Needs of Young Children. *Young Children*, 49(5), 58–60.

Chang, H. N. L., Muckelroy, A., & Pulido-Tobiassen, D. (1996). *Looking in, looking out: Redefining child and early education in a diverse society.* San Francisco: California Tomorrow.

Children's Defense Fund. (2000). *The state of America's children*. Washington, DC: Children's Defense Fund.

Children's Defense Fund. (2004). *The state of America's children* 2004. Washington, DC: Children's Defense Fund.

Cook, R. E., Tessier, A., & Klein, M. D. (2000). *Adapting early childhood curricula for children in inclusive settings* (5th ed.). Columbus, OH: Merrill.

Dahlberg, G., Moss, P., & Pence, A. (1999). *Beyond quality in early childhood education and care*. London: Falmer.

Edmiaston, R., Dolezal, V., Doolittle, S., Erickson, C., & Merritt, S. (2000). Developing individualized education programs for children in inclusive settings: A developmental framework. *Young Children*, 55(4), 36–41.

Goffin, S. G., & Lombardi, J. (1989). *Speaking out: Early childhood advocacy.* Washington, DC: National Association for the Education of Young Children.

Gonzalez-Mena, J. (2001). Cross-cultural infant care and issues of equity and social justice. *Contemporary Issues in Early Childhood*, 2(3). Available online at the Web site of Symposium Journals, a division of wwwords Ltd. (www.wwwords.co.uk/ciec).

Kelly, J. F., & Booth, C. L. (1999). Child care for children with special needs: Issues and applications. *Infants and young Children*, 12(1), 26–33.

Lee, L. (2002). *Serving families: A handbook on the principles and strategies of the Parent Services Project approach.* San Rafael, CA: Parent Services Project.

Lee, L., & Seiderman, E. (1998). *Families matter: The Parent Services Project.* Cambridge, MA: Harvard Family Research Project.

Links, G., Beggs, M., & Seiderman, E. (1997). *Serving families.* Fairfax, CA: Parent Services Project.

Lombardi, J. (2003). *Time to care: Redesigning child care to promote education, support families, and build communities.* Philadelphia: Temple University Press.

Love, J., Raikes, H., Paulsell, D., & Kisker, E. E. (2000). New directions for studying quality in programs for infants and toddlers. In D. Cryer & T. Harms (Eds.), *Infants and toddlers in out of home care* (pp. 117–162). Baltimore: Brookes.

McLoyd, V. (1998). Socioeconomic disadvantage and child development. *American Psycholgist*, 53(2), 185–204.

Moddings, N. (2002). *Starting at home: Care and social policy.* Berkeley: University of California Press.

National Association for the Education of Young Children. (1996, January). Position statement: Responding to linguistic and cultural diversity: Recommendations for effective early childhood education. *Young Children*, 51(2), 4–12.

Nieto, S. (2000). *Affirming diversity: The sociopolitical context of multicultural education* (3rd ed.). New York: Addison Wesley Longman.

O'Brien, M. (1997). *Inclusive child care for infants and toddlers: Meeting individual and special needs.* Baltimore: Brookes.

Odom, S. (Ed.). (2002). *Widening the circle: Including children with disabilities in preschool programs*. New York: Teachers College Press.

Putname, J. W. (Ed.). (1998). *Cooperative learning and strategies for inclusion* (2nd ed.). Baltimore: Brookes.

Shames, S. (1991). *Outside the dream: Child poverty in America*. (Introduction by J. Kozol; afterword by M. W. Edelman.) New York: Aperture.

Shore, R. (1997). *Rethinking the brain: New insights into early development*. New York: Families and Work Institute.

Thaxton, S. M. (2003). Grandparents as parents—Understanding the issues. In B. & R. Neugebauer

(Eds.), *The art of leadership* (323–325). Redmond, WA: Child Care Information Exchange.

Whitebook, M., Phillips, D., & Howes, C. (1993). *National Child Care Staffing Study revisited: Four years in the life of center-based child care*. Oakland, CA: Child Care Employee Project.

Zigler, E. F., Finn-Stevenson, M., & Hall, N. W. (2003). *The first three years and beyond: Brain development and social policy*. New Haven: Yale University Press.

Zigler, E., & Styfoco, S. J. (2004). *The Head Start debates*. Baltimore: Brookes.

FURTHER READING

Campell, F. A., & Ramey, C. T. (1994). Effects of early intervention on intellectual and academic achievement: A follow-up study of children from low-income families. *Child Development,* 65, 684–698.

Children's Defense Fund. (2004). *The state of America's children 2004*. Washington, DC: Children's Defense Fund.

Cook, R. E., Tessier, A., & Klein, M. D. (2000). *Adapting early childhood curricula for children in inclusive settings* (5th ed.). Columbus, OH: Merrill.

Dahlberg, G., Moss, P., & Pence, A. (1999). *Beyond quality in early childhood education and care* London: Falmer.

Dubow, E. F., & Ippolito, M. F. (1994). Effects of poverty and home environment on changes in the academic and behavioral adjustment of elementary school–age children. *Journal of Clinical Child Psychology,* 23, 401–412.

Galinsky, E., & Bond, J. T. (2000). Supporting families as primary caregivers: The role of the workplace. In D. Cryer & T. Harms (Eds.), *Infants and toddlers in out-of-home care*. Baltimore: Brookes.

Gonzalez-Mena, J. (2001). Cross-cultural infant care and issues of equity and social justice. *Contemporary Issues in Early Childhood, 2*(3). Available online at the Web site of Symposium Journals, a division of wwwords Ltd. (www.wwwords.co.uk/ciec).

Liaw, F., Meisels, S. J., & Brooks-Gunn, J. (1995). The effects of experience of early intervention on low birth weight, premature children: The infant health

and development program. *Early Childhood Research Quarterly,* 10, 405–431.

Lombardi, J. (2003). *Time to care: Redesigning child care to promote education, support families, and build communities*. Philadelphia: Temple University Press.

Love, J., Raikes, H., Paulsell, D., & Kisker, E. E. (2000). New directions for studying quality in programs for infants and toddlers. In D. Cryer & T. Harms (Eds.), *Infants and toddlers in out of home care* (pp. 117–162). Baltimore: Brookes.

McLoyd, Vonnie. (1998). Socioeconomic disadvantage and child development. *American Psycholgist,* 53(2), 185–204.

Meisels, S., & Atkins-Burnett, S. (2004, January). Public policy viewpoint: The Head Start national reporting system: A critique. *Young Children,* 59(1), 64–66.

Moddings, N. (2002). *Starting at home: Care and social policy*. Berkeley: University of California Press.

Nieto, S. (2000). *Affirming diversity: The sociopolitical context of multicultural education* (3rd ed.). New York: Addison Wesley Longman.

Odom, S. (Ed.). (2002). *Widening the circle: Including children with disabilities in preschool programs*. New York: Teachers College Press.

Raver, C. C., & Zigler, E. F. (2004, January). "Public policy viewpoint: Another step back? Assessing readiness in Head Start." *Young Children,* 59(1), 58–62.

St. Pierre, R. G., Layzer, J. I., Goodson, B. D., & Bernstein, L. (1997). *National impact evaluation of the comprehensive child development program: Final report*. Cambridge, MA: ABT Associates.

Thaxton, S. M. (2003). Grandparents as parents—Understanding the issues. in B. & R. Neugebauer, eds., *The art of leadership*. (323–325). Redmond, WA: Child Care Information Exchange.

Zigler, E. F., Finn-Stevenson, M., & Hall, N. W. (2003). *The first three years and beyond: Brain development and social policy*. New Haven: Yale University Press.

Zigler, E., & Styfoco, S. J. (2004). The Head Start debates. Baltimore: Brookes.

NAEYC Program Standards for Accreditation

FOCUS AREA: CHILDREN

Program Standard 1: Relationships

The program promotes positive relationships among all children and adults to encourage each child's sense of individual worth and belonging as part of a community, and to foster each child's ability to contribute as a responsible community member.

Rationale: Positive relationships are essential for the development of personal responsibility, capacity for self-regulation, and for constructive interactions with others. Warm, sensitive, and responsive interactions help children develop a secure, positive sense of self and encourage them to respect and cooperate with others. Children who see themselves as highly valued are more likely to feel secure, thrive physically, get along with others, learn well, and feel part of a community.

Program Standard 2: Curriculum

The program implements a curriculum that is consistent with its goals for children and promotes learning and development in each of the following domains: aesthetic, cognitive, emotional, language, physical, and social.

Rationale: Curriculum that is goal-oriented and incorporates concepts and skills based on current research fosters children's learning and development. When informed by teachers' knowledge of individual children, a well-articulated curriculum guides teachers so they can provide children with experiences that foster growth across a broad range of developmental and content areas. It also brings intentionality to planning a daily schedule that incorporates time and materials for play, self-initiated learning, and creative expression, and provides opportunities for children to learn individually and in groups according to their developmental needs and interests.

Program Standard 3: Teaching

The program uses developmentally, culturally, and linguistically appropriate and effective teaching approaches that enhance each child's learning and development in the context of the program's curriculum goals.

Rationale: Teachers who use multiple instructional approaches optimize children's opportunities for learning. These approaches include strategies that range from structured to unstructured and adult-directed to child-directed. Children bring different backgrounds, interests, experiences, learning styles, needs, and capacities to learning environments. Teachers' consideration of these differences when selecting and implementing instructional approaches helps all children to succeed. Instructional approaches also differ in their effectiveness for teaching different elements of curriculum and learning. For a program to address the complexity inherent in any teaching-learning situation, a variety of effective instructional approaches must be employed.

Program Standard 4: Assessment

The program is informed by ongoing systematic, formal, and informal assessment approaches to provide information on children's learning and development. These assessments occur within the context of reciprocal communications with families and with sensitivity to the cultural contexts in which children develop. Assessment results are used to benefit children by informing sound decisions about children, teaching, and program improvement.

Rationale: Teachers' knowledge of each child helps them to plan appropriately challenging curriculum and to tailor instruction that responds to each child's strengths and needs. Further, systematic assessment is essential for identifying children who may benefit from more intensive instruction or intervention or who may need additional developmental evaluation. This information ensures that the program meets its goals for children's learning and developmental progress and also informs program improvement efforts.

Program Standard 5: Health

The program promotes the nutrition and health of all children and staff and protects them from preventable illness and injury.

Rationale: To benefit from education and maintain quality of life, children need to be as healthy as possible. Children depend on adults, who also are as healthy as possible, to make healthful choices for them and to teach them to make such choices for themselves. While some degree of risk taking is desirable for learning, a high-quality program prevents hazardous practices and environments likely to result in adverse consequences for children, staff, families or communities.

FOCUS AREA: TEACHING STAFF

Program Standard 6: Teachers

The program employs and supports a teaching staff that has the educational qualifications, knowledge, and professional commitment necessary to promote children's learning and development and to support families' diverse needs and interests.

Rationale: Children benefit most when their teachers have high levels of formal education and specialized early childhood professional preparation. Teachers who have specific preparation, knowledge and skills in child development and early childhood education are more likely to engage in warm, positive interactions with children, offer richer language experiences, and create more high-quality learning environments. Opportunities for teaching staff to receive supportive supervision and to participate in ongoing professional development ensure that their knowledge and skills reflect the profession's ever-changing knowledge base.

FOCUS AREA: FAMILY AND COMMUNITY PARTNERSHIPS

Program Standard 7: Families

The program establishes and maintains collaborative relationships with each child's family to foster children's development in all settings. These relationships are sensitive to family composition, language, and culture.

Rationale: Young children's learning and development are integrally connected to their families. Consequently, to support and promote children's optimal learning and development, programs need to recognize the primacy of children's families; establish relationships with families based on mutual trust and respect; support and involve families in their children's educational growth; and invite families to fully participate in the program.

Program Standard 8: Communities

The program establishes relationships with and uses the resources of the children's communities to support the achievement of program goals.

Rationale: As part of the fabric of children's communities, an effective program establishes and maintains reciprocal relationships with agencies and institutions that can support it in achieving its goals for curriculum, health promotion, children's transitions, inclusion, and diversity. By helping to connect families with needed resources, the program furthers children's healthy development and learning.

FOCUS AREA: LEADERSHIP AND ADMINISTRATION

Program Standard 9: Physical Environment

The program provides appropriate and well-maintained indoor and outdoor physical environments, including facilities, equipment, and materials, to facilitate child and staff learning and development. To this end, a program structures a safe and a healthful environment.

Rationale: The program's design and maintenance of its physical environment support high-quality program activities and services and allow for optimal use and operation. Well-organized, equipped, and maintained environments support program quality by facilitating the learning, comfort, health, and safety of those who use the program. By also creating a welcoming and accessible setting for children, families, and staff, program quality is enhanced.

Program Standard 10: Leadership and Management

The program effectively implements policies, procedures, and systems in support of stable staff and strong personnel, fiscal, and program management so that all children, families and staff have high-quality experiences.

Rationale: Excellent programming requires effective governance structures, competent and knowledgeable leadership, and comprehensive and well functioning administrative policies, procedures, and systems. Effective leadership and administration create the environment for high-quality care and education by: assuring compliance with relevant regulations and guidelines; promoting fiscal soundness, program accountability, effective communication, helpful consultative services, positive community relations, and provision of a comfortable and supportive workplace; maintaining stable staff; and instituting opportunities for ongoing program planning for staff and career development and for continuous program improvement.

Source: National Association for the Education of Young Children. 1998. NAEYC Program Standards for Accreditation. Washington, DC: Author.

Index